HEALTHCARE KAIZEN

Engaging Front-Line Staff in Sustainable
Continuous Improvements

Advance Praise for *Healthcare Kaizen: Engaging Front-Line Staff in Sustainable Continuous Improvements*

"I hope you will discover, as we have, the incredible creativity that can be derived by engaging and supporting each and every employee in improvements that they themselves lead."

Robert (Bob) J. Brody
CEO, Franciscan St. Francis Health

"In *Healthcare Kaizen*, Mark Graban and Joseph Swartz show us that Kaizen is more than a set of tools. What we have learned through our application of the Virginia Mason Production System is that Kaizen is a management methodology of continuous improvement that must permeate the fabric of the entire organization. Front-line staff must know, understand, embrace, and drive Kaizen and its tools to achieve incremental and continuous improvements. This book will help healthcare organizations around the world begin and advance their journey."

Gary Kaplan, MD, FACP, FACMPE, FACPE
Chairman and CEO, Virginia Mason Medical Center

"Unleashing the energy and creativity of every employee to solve problems everyday should be the sole focus of every healthcare leader. Unfortunately, there are only a handful of examples where this is happening. *Healthcare Kaizen* provides examples of front line staff coming up with solutions to problems on their own and implementing them. Healthcare leaders need to read this book to understand that their management role must radically change to one of supporting daily Kaizen if quality safety and cost are to improve in healthcare."

John Toussaint, MD
CEO, ThedaCare Center for Healthcare Value

"The healthcare industry is in the midst of truly fundamental change, and those organizations that engage their front line staff in developing the strategies for improving care, enhancing satisfaction, and streamlining processes to reduce unnecessary variation and expense will be well positioned to thrive in a post-reform environment. In their book *Healthcare Kaizen,* Graban and Swartz create a roadmap for using incremental, staff driven changes to inculcate performance improvement into the culture of an organization in a sustainable manner. This book represents a wonderful resource for healthcare leaders looking to foster innovation at all levels."

Brett D. Lee, PhD, FACHE
Senior Vice President, Health System Operations
Children's Healthcare of Atlanta

"*Healthcare Kaizen* is a practical guide for healthcare leaders aspiring to engage front-line staff in true continuous improvement. Graban and Swartz skillfully illustrate how to foster and support daily continuous improvement in healthcare settings. Health systems struggle to move beyond improvement work as extra work done in "special projects" facilitated by experts. This book can guide organizational transformation so that continuous improvement becomes part of the daily work of frontline staff."

John E. Billi, MD
Associate Vice President for Medical Affairs
University of Michigan

"At a time when many hospitals and health systems have relegated Lean to the 'Project of the Month Club', Graban and Swartz remind us of the fundamentals that help organizations keep their Lean initiatives alive and thriving. I hope everyone reads this book and recommits to the fundamentals of Lean, particularly the involvement of front-line staff in process redesign."

Fred Slunecka
Chief Operating Officer
Avera Health

"Kaizen has marvelously engaged so many of our staff and enabled them to improve the world around them to the benefit of staff, patients, and community."

Paul Strange, MD
Corporate VP of Quality
Franciscan Alliance

"Successful practitioners recognize Lean as a method for comprehensive and widespread continuous improvement, not just a set of tools for isolated project improvements. Everyone in the organization has an active and intentional role to play in this journey. Through description and example, Mark Graban and Joseph Swartz present a clear pathway for successful Lean practice in *Healthcare Kaizen*. This should be on every healthcare system's reading list."

Dave Munch, MD
Senior Vice President and Chief Clinical Officer
Healthcare Performance Partners

"We are challenged with improving the health of individuals and populations while reducing costs. Mark and Joe provide real-life examples of how those who do the work provide ideas for small changes that add up to BIG results. *Healthcare Kaizen* is a must for leaders whose focus is the patient and how to effectively and efficiently deliver quality and safety with improved outcomes. The methods shared are foundational in changing our healthcare system for the better."

Betty Brown, MBA, MSN, RN, CPHQ, FNAHQ
President, National Association for Healthcare Quality

"The healthcare industry has long struggled to tap one of the biggest sources available to it for ideas to improve outcomes and reduce costs – its front-line staff. *Healthcare Kaizen* lays out a step-by-step approach that any healthcare organization can use to get the dramatic results that come when its workforce is fully engaged in Kaizen activities on a daily basis. This inspirational book is packed with examples and is informed by the authors' years of experience on the 'front-lines' themselves, helping leading healthcare organizations around the world to build successful Kaizen programs."

Alan G. Robinson, PhD
Professor, Isenberg School of Management at the University of Massachusetts
Author, *Ideas Are Free: How the Idea Revolution Is Liberating People and Transforming Organizations*

"At Beth Israel Deaconess Medical Center, everybody improving every day is a critical aspect of our Lean and quality improvement efforts. *Healthcare Kaizen*, is full of relatable examples as well as practical ideas that will inspire staff, clinicians and leaders at all levels."

Alice Lee
Vice President, Business Transformation
Beth Israel Deaconess Medical Center

"For the past 7 years I have been leading a successful lean healthcare transformation at Chugachmiut, the non-profit organization I lead in Alaska. During that time, I have learned that respect for the people who work for you is key to any transformation. Mark Graban and Joseph Swartz do a great job of capturing this truth in their book, *Healthcare Kaizen: Engaging Front-Line Staff in Sustainable Continuous Improvements*. Every employee can learn the tools of lean and improve processes as a result. However, sustaining a lean transformation and resisting entropy requires engaging front-line employees in a long-term vision for serving their customers and in true continuous improvement. Employees who work in a culture that removes blame and shame, operates on facts, and seeks improvement continuously have great leadership and will respond with incredible results. This book is a long needed addition to my growing lean healthcare library."

Patrick Anderson
Executive Director
Chugachmiut, Anchorage, Alaska

"The vision of a world in which our healthcare institutions operate with a universal discipline of relentless, patient-centered improvement remains a vitally important yet distant dream. In *Healthcare Kaizen*, Mark Graban and Joseph Swartz illustrate just how to make that dream a reality.

Matthew E. May
Author of *The Elegant Solution* and *The Laws of Subtraction*

"At last, a crystal clear description of Kaizen as a philosophy and a work culture, not another top-down tool. Graban and Swartz show, in unequivocal detail, that Kaizen need not be viewed as a formal, five-day event, requiring X, Y, and Z participants, components, and steps. The compelling examples from Franciscan Health and others paint a picture of a hospital culture steeped in respect for people and continuous improvement—the very elements of Lean, Kaizen, and scientific inquiry. By busting the myth of the five-day 'event,' the authors show the true, sweeping potential of Kaizen in the healthcare workplace."

Naida Grunden
Author, *The Pittsburgh Way to Efficient Healthcare*
Co-author, *Lean-led Hospital Design: Creating the Efficient Hospital of the Future*

"The term 'Kaizen' has been interpreted in many ways since we learned of the Toyota Production System in healthcare. Mark and Joe demystify the term, help us understand its real meaning, and help us see how using Kaizen can help us improve in healthcare and, frankly, how we can use Kaizen to save lives. The philosophy, tools, and techniques discussed in the book work, and work well, in any environment. We in healthcare must improve—we owe it to our patients and communities—and Mark and Joe are helping to show us the way."

Dean Bliss
Lean Improvement Advisor
Iowa Healthcare Collaborative

"What Mark Graban and Joseph Swartz have done in *Healthcare Kaizen* is to bring hope and light to a part of our society that is facing increasing challenges. Full of examples and illustrations from hospitals and healthcare professionals leading the way in the journey to patient-centered, error-free care delivery, this book makes it easy to connect with this very powerful concept of Kaizen. By putting Kaizen within the broader tradition of quality improvement, shedding light on its historical development and pointing out potential pitfalls in its application in healthcare, the authors provide a great service to the healthcare community. I was especially impressed by the authors' important insights on what a Kaizen culture feels like and how people at all levels can and must engage in daily improvement. *Healthcare Kaizen* will be a reference on the subject for many years to come."

Jon Miller
CEO, Kaizen Institute

"Unfortunately the Lean movement has too often turned into a race to implement as many of the tools of Lean in as many places as possible. This is totally alien to the spirit of Kaizen or the purpose of the Toyota Production System. The purpose is to create a culture of continuous improvement with people at all levels thinking deeply about their idea vision for the people and process, and purposefully taking steps to achieve the vision. The vision should be for the good of the enterprise, not to check the box for the Lean folks who are auditing 5S and visual management.

Mark and Joe have a deep understanding of the purpose of TPS and what is needed in healthcare to raise this from a program to a true culture that can tackle all the difficult challenges that face modern medicine. They have been steeped in the healthcare field for years and have great examples to illustrate Kaizen, both small and big changes. In this book, they take on the challenge of driving Kaizen down to the level of every work group—truly the deepest meaning of Kaizen. This takes exceptional leadership, a second nature understanding of the tools, and always working at the gemba to solve the real problems. Hopefully this book will become a blueprint for healthcare organizations everywhere that truly want to be great!"

Jeffrey Liker
Professor of Industrial and Operations Engineering
University of Michigan
Author of *The Toyota Way*

"Years ago, an elderly Japanese gentleman asked, 'How will you engage team members, Pascal-san?' This engagement is arguably the leader's greatest challenge. Fixing healthcare may be our generation's great test. We'll need to engage all the good people who currently work in broken systems. Mark and Joe have helped to show us how."

Pascal Dennis, Lean Pathways, Inc.
Author, *The Remedy* and *Andy & Me*

"One of the greatest leadership and cultural challenges when embarking on a Lean transformation is the shift that MUST occur where the frontlines have the skills for and are authorized to make daily improvement. This shift not only accelerates results, but it fully engages the workforce, a precondition for achieving organizational excellence. Graban and Swartz present the Kaizen philosophy in the most accessible way I've seen yet. They present a powerful model for preparing managers for their new role as improvement coaches and the frontlines for taking a far more active role in delivering greater value to the healthcare industry's various customers. THIS is the missing link in healthcare reform."

Karen Martin
Author, *The Outstanding Organization* and *The Kaizen Event Planner*

"In the last decade, implementation of the Lean production model in a healthcare setting has produced remarkable outcomes and revolutionized the way we deliver care. Using examples from Franciscan Health and other forward-thinking medical groups, the book contains valuable strategies for organization-wide cultural transformation to create a more efficient, patient-centered healthcare system dedicated to continuous quality improvement."

Donald W. Fisher, PhD
AMGA, President and CEO
Anceta, LLC, Chairman

"Kaizen is an easy, *no-pressure* way for people who do the work to improve the process of the work."

India Owens, RN, MSN, CEN, NE-BC
Director, Emergency Services & EMS Operations
Franciscan St. Francis Health

"I don't know why all of healthcare hasn't gone to this!"

Michael A. Russell, MD, FACEP
Assistant Clinical Professor, Dept. Emergency Medicine, Indiana University School of Medicine
Vice President, Emergency Physicians of Indianapolis

"Filled with practical examples of improvements initiated by employees at all levels, this book vividly demonstrates how to tap into the creativity of all employees to ensure healthcare remains a mission that serves all."

Chuck Dietzen, MD
Founder and President, Timmy Global Health
Chief Medical Officer, iSalus Healthcare`

"Kaizen is exactly what healthcare needs—with ever increasing change coming at us—Kaizen gives all our employees the opportunity to continually reassess and communicate differences to improve our outcomes and improve our ability to change more rapidly."

Robin Eads MSN, RN, ACNS-BC, CEN
Clinical Nurse Specialist—Emergency Department
Franciscan St. Francis Hospital

"When healthcare organizations take initial steps on their Lean journey, they often focus very heavily on tools and grand solutions, and may create new barriers to innovation. In *Healthcare Kaizen*, Mark and Joe remind us of the great power of daily problem-solving. Their examples reinforce that learning is a result of the repeated tests of changes that are often small and simple, and less by hitting the home runs of improvement. The story of Franciscan is compelling, where leaders created the opportunity for great people at the frontline making great improvements for patient care."

Michel Tétreault, MD, President and CEO
Bruce Roe, MD, Chief Medical Officer
St. Boniface Hospital
Winnipeg, Canada

"Kaizen has been a key differentiator for us. Besides contributing many benefits to our staff, customers, and organization, it has vitally contributed to developing our workforce's capacity and capability for continuous improvement and change."

Keith Jewell,
Sr. VP & COO, Franciscan St. Francis Health

"Simple and actionable, *Healthcare Kaizen* is filled with practical information, great examples, and is an inspiring read. Improving quality and decreasing costs can be daunting and seemingly impossible when you look at trying to solve the problem in one stroke. Once you understand that every single person can be a part of the solution, the problem becomes manageable and feasible. Kaizen is a big part of the solution, a very big part, and this book will give you the nuts and bolts of how everyone can be part of the solution."

Gregory Jacobson, MD
CEO, KaiNexus

HEALTHCARE KAIZEN

Engaging Front-Line Staff in Sustainable Continuous Improvements

Mark Graban and Joseph E. Swartz

Foreword by Masaaki Imai,
Author of *KAIZEN, The Key
to Japan's Competitive Success*

Introduction by Norman Bodek,
Author of *How to Do Kaizen*

CRC Press
Taylor & Francis Group
Boca Raton London New York

CRC Press is an imprint of the
Taylor & Francis Group, an **informa** business

A PRODUCTIVITY PRESS BOOK

CRC Press
Taylor & Francis Group
6000 Broken Sound Parkway NW, Suite 300
Boca Raton, FL 33487-2742

© 2012 by Mark Graban and Joseph Swartz
CRC Press is an imprint of Taylor & Francis Group, an Informa business

No claim to original U.S. Government works

Printed in the United States of America on acid-free paper
Version Date: 20120525

International Standard Book Number: 978-1-4398-7296-3 (Paperback)

Library of Congress Cataloging-in-Publication Data

Graban, Mark.
  Healthcare kaizen : engaging front-line staff in sustainable continuous improvements / Mark Graban, Joseph Swartz.
    p. ; cm.
  Includes bibliographical references and index.
  ISBN 978-1-4398-7296-3 (pbk. : alk. paper)
  I. Swartz, Joseph E. II. Title.
  [DNLM: 1. Franciscan St. Francis Health (Indianapolis, Ind.) 2. Franciscan Alliance. 3. Hospital Administration. 4. Quality Improvement. WX 153]

  362.109772'52--dc23

                                                                                              2012010144

Visit the Taylor & Francis Web site at
http://www.taylorandfrancis.com

and the CRC Press Web site at
http://www.crcpress.com

Contents

SECTION 3 KAIZEN LESSONS LEARNED

Preface

While this book has two co-authors, Mark Graban and Joe Swartz, we have done our best to write in a single voice. Any work that we directly participated in is written about in the third person to avoid confusion about who was writing particular sections.

Franciscan St. Francis Health is a three-hospital system in Indianapolis. Throughout this book, we will often refer to individual hospitals in this system in an abbreviated form like "Franciscan." That three-hospital system is part of the Franciscan Alliance, a 14-hospital system located throughout Indiana and Northeastern Illinois. Where we focus on one of their other 11 hospitals, we will call them out uniquely, such as Franciscan St. Elizabeth Health.

How to Read This Book

Kaizen is a very nonlinear subject, so we expect readers will jump around and even skip chapters, depending on their interests and their experience level with Kaizen. The book is structured as follows.

Section 1: What Is Kaizen?

This section covers conceptual frameworks and the history of Kaizen, or continuous improvement, starting with other industries and moving into healthcare. Chapter 1 sets the context, definitions, and core concepts of Kaizen, along with some initial examples. Chapter 2 provides a brief historical overview of continuous improvement and staff engagement efforts, including the last 25 years in healthcare. Chapter 3 includes different types of Kaizen improvements, including some of the frameworks used by hospitals around the world. Chapter 4 describes the cultural aspects of an organization that has fully embraced continuous improvement.

Section 2: Kaizen Methodologies

This portion of the book shares specific methodologies for finding, initiating, completing, documenting, and sharing Kaizen improvements. Chapter 5 covers the Quick and Easy Kaizen methodology, especially as practiced by Franciscan. Chapter 6 details an alternative, but complementary, method called the Visual Idea Board, as practiced by Children's Medical Center (Dallas) and others. Chapter 7 includes many examples of Kaizen improvements from around the world, documented in different formats, further illustrating how Kaizen can benefit patients, staff, and healthcare organizations. Chapter 8 discusses the art of Kaizen, including strategies for mobilizing support and working most effectively with others.

Section 3: Kaizen Lessons Learned

The final section covers lessons learned about the incredibly important role of leadership and about creating broader Kaizen programs. Chapter 9 details key mindsets and actions required by leaders from the charge nurses to the CEO. Chapter 10 discusses key elements of an organization-wide Kaizen program, taking Kaizen from a department to the entire healthcare enterprise, such as a hospital or health system. Chapter 11 shares some of the broader Lean methods that Franciscan has used to support its Kaizen approach and vice versa. Chapter 12 covers Franciscan's encouragement of people to practice Kaizen in their everyday lives.

Tips for Different Types of Readers

We think this book will be useful to readers in different ways, depending on your role in your organization and your needs.

If you are a front-line staff member or supervisor looking to dive into improvement right away, we suggest you read Chapter 1 as a brief introduction and then Chapter 5 on Quick and Easy Kaizen or Chapter 6 on Visual Idea Boards.

Front-line or middle managers looking to create a departmental program may want to also start by reading more about the culture and leadership aspects of Kaizen, including Chapter 4 on culture, Chapter 8 on the art of engaging others in Kaizen, and Chapter 9 on the role of leaders.

Executives looking for a quick overview could read Chapters 1 and 4, along with Chapter 9 and Chapter 10 on organization-wide Kaizen programs.

Internal process improvement groups may also be most interested in Chapters 2 and 3, which give more historical context and depth about the different types of Kaizen, along with Chapter 11, which discusses how core Lean concepts can be incorporated along with Kaizen.

Acknowledgments from Mark Graban

There are many people I need to thank, first of all my coauthor Joe Swartz. This book has been a wonderful partnership since I first raised the idea at the Society for Health Systems annual conference in early 2009. Without Joe's passion and hard work for Kaizen at the Franciscan St. Francis Health System, this book would not have the depth of his years of experience and lessons learned.

I also want to thank my mentors in Kaizen, including Norman Bodek, whose never-ending enthusiasm and his belief in everybody's ability to participate in Kaizen have been inspiring. Thanks also go to Norman for his formal training and certification in "Quick and Easy Kaizen" and to Rick Malik, the worldwide director of ValuMetrix Services, for his support in allowing me to take Norman's workshop. Norman first introduced me to my coauthor, Joe, back in 2005 because Norman knew we were both transitioning from manufacturing into healthcare, so I appreciate his networking and sharing.

Many thanks are also due to my other mentors and role models in my study and practice of Kaizen, including John Shook and Jim Womack of the Lean Enterprise Institute, Pascal Dennis of Lean Pathways, Inc., and John Toussaint, MD, of the ThedaCare Center for Healthcare Value.

Thanks to all who graciously shared examples of Kaizen, either anonymously or with recognition for their organizations. Most of them are quoted or cited in the book. Without their passion for improving patient care and creating a better healthcare workplace, along with their willingness to share with others, this book would not be possible.

Thanks go also to my trusted colleagues and friends who reviewed early drafts and provided valuable feedback and advice, including Brian Buck, Lewis Lefteroff, Ken LePage, Jim Adams, Michael Lombard, Greg Jacobson, Karen Martin, Helen Zak, and Naida Grunden. I also want to thank Jon Miller, of the Kaizen Institute, for helping secure Masaaki Imai's support and foreword. Thanks also go to Cheryl Fenske of Fenske Communications, who provided editing support and feedback, in small batches, as I worked on the manuscript. Thanks to my editor Kris Mednansky for her support on this project and for my first book, *Lean Hospitals*.

Finally, I want to thank my parents, Bob and Marlene, for their love and the educational opportunities they created for me. Thanks go to my wonderful wife, Amy, for her love, support through this project, and for her patience about all of the time I was off in my office writing. Thanks also go to my in-laws, Charlie and Debbie, for their encouragement and support during the writing process, as well as the wonderful fajitas (and margaritas!) and other meals that were offered up so I could spend time writing, instead of cooking.

I would like to dedicate this book to the caring, hardworking healthcare professionals around the world. Thank you for your service to your patients and communities. Thanks especially for your dedication toward process improvement and for working toward providing the best patient care possible.

Acknowledgments from Joe Swartz

I am grateful for the opportunity to have worked with my coauthor, Mark, on this book. Although an extremely accomplished and highly intelligent person, he treated me graciously as a full partner throughout this work. I appreciate his patience, his extensive expertise, and his ability to listen to the many voices in the domain of Kaizen and to discern and continually pull together the vision for this book. He is an inspiration.

I bow to honor Franciscan St. Francis Health. To their leadership, Bob Brody, Keith Jewell, and Paul Strange, MD, for giving me the opportunity to participate in their amazing organization and mission. To the staff for significant and meaningful Kaizen contributions, which enrich each reader's ability to translate Kaizen to their unique workplace.

Many heartfelt thanks to my colleagues and friends—to my team at St. Francis for helping me develop the Kaizen program showcased in this book: Mischelle Frank, Julia Dearing, and Tom Pearson. To Heather Woodward for introducing me to Franciscan. To Marcia Ellett, writer and wonderful friend who encouraged me and held my hand throughout the writing of this book. To Jim Huntzinger, Brian Hudson, and Tim Martin whose deep Lean knowledge helped me keep Kaizen real. To Dan Lafever for calling me sensei when I should be calling him sensei. To Norm Bodek who continually encouraged me to write. To John Feller, MD, and Chuck Dietzen, MD, childhood and best friends who have been by my side coaching me on the high-leverage knowledge of healthcare.

I wish to thank those who carved time out of their busy day to review selected chapters and gave such good feedback: Diana McClure, Laura Louis, Rebecca Branson, Paula Stanfill, Joe Click, Nik Janek, Vicki Wright, Kyle Ellen Brown, and Amy Lynelle.

To my parents, James B. and Kathleen Swartz, who set the pattern for the person I am and who inspired me to write; to my children, Jordan, Paul, and Madison, who are the loves of my life; to my brother Greg and sisters Laura and Julie, who have been such a joy in my life; to my friends for simply being my friends; to God for life and possibilities.

Finally, I am appreciative for the privilege Mark and I had to learn the field of Lean and Kaizen by standing on the shoulders of giants and for having the opportunity to convey some of what we have learned from those giants.

Like Mark, I dedicate this book to the caring, hardworking healthcare professionals around the world. Thank you for continually sharing your life purpose and meaningful reasons why you are called into the field of healthcare. Thank you for your heart of service, care, and compassion. You have touched my family so much more significantly than you know.

Foreword

In my book *KAIZEN: The Key to Japan's Competitive Success* (McGraw-Hill, 1986), I ended with the following words:

> It is my sincere hope that we will be able to overcome our "primitive" state and that the KAIZEN strategy will eventually find application not only in the business community, but also in all institutions and societies all over the world.

Looking back over the last 25 years since its publication, I am profoundly frustrated with the slow pace at which Kaizen strategy has been embraced by the business community. On the other hand, I am encouraged to note that Kaizen is rapidly gaining momentum in the non-manufacturing institutions like healthcare, services, and government.

I believe that Kaizen is essentially a "human business." Management must meet the diversified requirements of its employees, customers, stakeholders, suppliers, and its community. In this sense, the healthcare profession can probably best benefit from Kaizen because its central task is people. I am honored to write a foreword to this book by Mark Graban and Joseph Swartz.

Taking this opportunity, I wish to mention a few reminders for successfully embracing the Kaizen strategy.

1. Embracing Kaizen is a long-term journey. It is not a flavor of the month and requires the cultural change, commitment, and self-discipline that needs to be sustained over many decades until they become routine business practices.
2. Top management commitment is the only way to successfully embrace Kaizen, without which nothing else you do will matter.
3. We need to approach our daily business in two phases. One is to maintain the status quo, in which the standard (the best way to do the job) is established and followed. This process is called maintenance and requires dedicated management effort to sustain it, but it is often overlooked or belittled.

The second phase is Kaizen, which means to find a better way and revise the current standard. Thus, maintaining and improving the standard becomes the main task of management.

4. My definition of Lean is to employ minimum resources for the maximum benefits. Therefore, Kaizen leads to Lean, and Lean leads to green. Kaizen is the most environmentally friendly approach.

5. Welcome problems. The more problems, the better, because we have more Kaizen opportunities. We only need to establish priorities in dealing with problems. When the problem is correctly identified, the project is halfway successful.

6. One of the best ways to identify problems is to observe the flow of operations. In the medical institutions, there are many types of flows, such as information, physical movement of patients and families, medicines, and supplies. Wherever and whenever the flow is disrupted, there is a Kaizen opportunity.

7. A majority of disruptions of the flow can be easily detected and solved with common sense and do not require sophisticated technologies.

8. Remove the barriers between professionals and laymen.

I sincerely hope that you will find your Kaizen journey to be challenging, but most rewarding.

Masaaki Imai
Chairman, Kaizen Institute

Introduction

In healthcare, enormous investments are made in things like buildings, technology, and pharmaceutical development, but little is spent to tap into the creativity of every single healthcare provider and professional. Yes, the new machine or new drug might do wonders, but people like Mark and Joe, the coauthors of this book, are demonstrating there is a much greater opportunity for improvements by enlisting everyone in the healthcare community to identify and solve problems. For example, Baptist Hospital in Pensacola was rated lowest in the state of Florida until they started asking for small improvement ideas from their staff. They became number one in the state and also received, in 2003, the coveted Malcolm Baldrige National Quality Award.

The person doing the job in healthcare, as in any industry, has great knowledge about their work, but they are rarely asked to look around their work area to identify small problems and to implement solutions to those problems. As you go through this book, you will see numerous examples of improvements made by many different people. Each Kaizen might only save a few dollars, but collectively they add up to millions of dollars in savings for an organization, and billions for a state or country. As you will see from this wonderful book, the process is quick to implement and easy to get people involved in. But even more important than the dollars saved are the improvements in communication and coordination that result when everyone is involved in the Kaizen process, leading to fewer errors, improved patient safety, higher quality, and lives saved.

To get started with Kaizen, you should do the following. First, read this book. Second, ask your employees to read the book. Third, ask your employees to begin a Kaizen system. It is just that simple. You just ask, and you will get what you ask for. Just do it and learn from the process. Of course, you might make some mistakes, and since the ideas are normally very small, the mistakes will be very small, and you will all learn from those mistakes.

The United States needs Kaizen, as does the rest of the world. We all need a better healthcare system, and Kaizen will play an important part.

Kaizen is fun, and Kaizen will bring you vast benefits and peace of mind.

Norman Bodek
President, PCS Press.
Author of How to Do Kaizen
bodek@pcspress.com   www.pcspress.com

About the Authors

Mark Graban is an author, consultant, and speaker in the field of lean healthcare. He is the author of *Lean Hospitals: Improving Quality, Patient Safety, and Employee Engagement* (2nd edition). Mark has worked as a consultant and coach to healthcare organizations throughout North America and Europe. He was formerly a senior fellow with the Lean Enterprise Institute and continues to serve as a faculty member. Mark is also the Chief Improvement Officer for KaiNexus, a startup software company that helps healthcare organizations manage continuous improvement efforts. Mark earned a BS in Industrial Engineering from Northwestern University and an MS in Mechanical Engineering and an MBA from the MIT Sloan Leaders for Global Operations Program. Visit his website at www.MarkGraban.com and his blog at www.LeanBlog.org.

Joseph E. Swartz is the Director of Business Transformation for Franciscan St. Francis Health of Indianapolis, IN. He has been leading continuous improvement efforts for 18 years, including 7 years in healthcare, and has led more than 200 Lean and Six Sigma improvement projects. Joseph is the co-author of *Seeing David in the Stone* and was previously an instructor at the University of Wisconsin. Joseph earned an MS in Management from Purdue University as a Krannert Scholar for academic excellence.

1

WHAT IS KAIZEN?

Chapter 1

Kaizen and Continuous Improvement

It is not the strongest of the species that survives, nor the most intelligent, but the one most responsive to change.

—Charles Darwin

Paula Stanfill's husband had open-heart surgery. Paula is the manager of the neo-natal intensive care unit (NICU) at Franciscan St. Francis Health, a three-hospital system in Indianapolis, Indiana. In the recovery room, Paula's husband could not speak because he was intubated with a breathing tube. He was trying to communicate by furrowing his eyebrows and squinting. He knew sign language and was motioning at his arm and trying to use his fingers to tell Paula something, but he could not make his hands do what he wanted them to do. Paula remembers her panic in realizing that something serious might be happening to her husband. He also began to panic, thinking the surgery had caused a serious problem with his arms. They were deeply distressed until the anesthesia wore off and he could speak again.

Paula learned her husband's arms and hands were numb. He was a big man, and when the surgeons performed the procedure, they had leaned over his arms and put pressure on them, reducing the blood supply and causing the numbness. His arms remained numb for several weeks.

After this episode, Jessica Clendenen, a nurse in Franciscan's cardiac operating room, learned that several other patients had experienced similar postoperative numbness. She decided to do something about it. In January of 2011, Jessica found some sled positioners that could be used to help tuck the patients' arms in place in a way that allowed the IV lines to be seen through the clear material, as documented in Figure 1.1.

This small, simple improvement can be described as a "Kaizen." It was an improvement that made a difference to open-heart patients at Franciscan and was

Open Heart Arm Protectors		Franciscan ST. FRANCIS HEALTH
Before		**After**
Patients' arms were tucked with a sheet for open heart procedures. Patients had noticed numbness in the hands.		Found arm sled positioners that could be used to help "tuck" their arms in place without placing too much pressure on the arms. Clear, giving visual to the IV lines.
Effect		
Prevents pressure from leaning of the surgical personnel. Results in less pressure on the patient, improved quality, patient safety and patient outcomes.		
Name	**ID #**	**Dept #**	**Supervisor**	**Date**
Jessica Clendenen		Cardiovascular Operating Room	Victoria Pratt	1/20/2011

Figure 1.1   A simple improvement that can be described as a Kaizen.

one that Paula will never forget. When she started making these improvements, Paula never realized it would touch her so personally. But, after her husband's experience, Paula realized that the heart of Kaizen is the difference it can make in people's lives. Kaizen was no longer just a concept or a program to her; it had become a way of life.

Kaizen = Change for the Better

The word Kaizen is translated from Japanese in a number of ways, most simply as "change for the better."[1] The Japanese characters are shown in Figure 1.2.

Breaking down the word:

- "Kai" means "change."
- "zen" means "good."

A "Kaizen" is a small improvement that is made by those who do the work. It is a small, low-cost, low-risk improvement that can be easily implemented.[2] Kaizen is an ongoing methodology and philosophy for challenging and empowering everyone in the organization to use their creative ideas to improve their daily work.

The word Kaizen, the way it is typically used, is synonymous with the phrase "continuous improvement." An effective Kaizen approach is about making improvements that are connected to measurable results and a deeper purpose. Children's Medical Center (Dallas, Texas), has a process improvement campaign that asks the simple question, "Is there a better way?" Clay York, manager of the

Figure 1.2   "Kaizen" in Japanese kanji characters.

core laboratory, and other leaders help tie the department's local improvement efforts to the organization's mission and purpose by asking team members if proposed changes will help provide "better care for kids."[3]

Beyond the measurable results, Kaizen organizations value the personal and organizational learning that results from the improvement process, as well as the personal pride and satisfaction of all who are involved.

IU Health Goshen Hospital has saved more than $30 million since 1998 with a program called "The Uncommon Leader" as part of its broader improvement program. In 2009, CEO James Dague promised to shave his head if employees generated ideas that saved $3.5 million that year. The hospital more than doubled that savings goal, so Dague shaved his head in front of his colleagues. The culture at Goshen has shifted to one where every person is empowered to make improvements to his or her daily work, making suggestions that can impact cost, quality, and patient care. For example, an emergency nurse educator saved $4,000 by changing the type of napkins used on patient trays and the GI department saved $22,000 by switching from disposable paper gowns to cloth gowns.[4] Goshen has gone 17 years without layoffs, undoubtedly being a key reason its employees are so enthusiastic about improvement.[5] Goshen was also named one of the top ten large employer workplaces in Indiana, in part due to its "workplace culture where employees feel valued."[6]

Bubbles for Babies

Hope Woodard, an ultrasound tech at Franciscan St. Francis Health, noticed that her young patients were often uncomfortable when she pressed the cold hard ultrasound probe to their skin. They had difficulty staying still during the procedures. The parents would get frustrated and often could not find a way to calm their child down.

Hope thought about how she could create a better experience for her little customers. She brought in a small bottle of bubbles from a wedding she had attended and asked the parents to gently blow them over the top of the child to calm and entertain them, as documented in Figure 1.3. The bubbles were a real crowd pleaser, as they kept the babies calm for their procedures. Happy, distracted children allowed Hope and the other techs to capture better images for the radiologist that were obtained more quickly, making it better for the patient, for the parents, and for the ultrasound techs. In the course of making her job easier, Hope was also adding value to the customer experience. Her Kaizen was

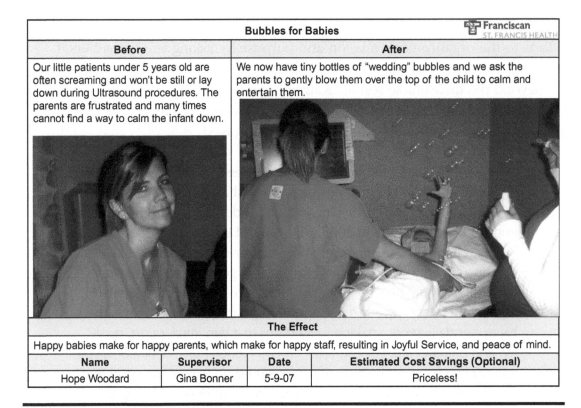

Bubbles for Babies			Franciscan ST. FRANCIS HEALTH
Before		**After**	
Our little patients under 5 years old are often screaming and won't be still or lay down during Ultrasound procedures. The parents are frustrated and many times cannot find a way to calm the infant down.		We now have tiny bottles of "wedding" bubbles and we ask the parents to gently blow them over the top of the child to calm and entertain them.	
The Effect			
Happy babies make for happy parents, which make for happy staff, resulting in Joyful Service, and peace of mind.			
Name	**Supervisor**	**Date**	**Estimated Cost Savings (Optional)**
Hope Woodard	Gina Bonner	5-9-07	Priceless!

Figure 1.3 A simple Kaizen that improved staff and patient satisfaction.

a win for her and a win for everyone involved. It created more joy in her work life every time she used bubbles for babies.

These first examples of Kaizen have several things in common. They increase customer and patient satisfaction while, at the same time, improve the productivity and the quality of healthcare delivery. Small, low-cost improvements can indeed make a difference to patients while increasing the pride and joy felt by healthcare professionals.

Kaizen: A Powerful Word

The largest room in the world is the room for improvement.

—Author unknown

Kaizen. It is a strange-looking word. It might seem a little difficult to pronounce. Said out loud, it sounds a lot like "try–zen," and we can equate it with the idea that we can try to improve and make things more zen-like in the workplace. Yes, Kaizen leads to a calmer, better-organized, more productive workplace that provides better patient care. Kaizen seems like a simple concept, really. But is this Japanese word intimidating to people in healthcare workplaces outside of Japan? Does the broader idea of improvement scare or intimidate people at all levels?

Hang in there, as this little word might be one of the most powerful words and concepts for improving healthcare processes and quality. Hospitals around the world are using this concept, often as part of a broader "Lean management" initiative. The period of "Lean healthcare" adoption that started around 2000 has proven that hospitals and healthcare organizations can improve when we have a highly engaged workforce focused on providing value to patients and minimizing waste in the delivery of care.

> "Lean healthcare" is a set of practices, a management system, and an organizational culture based on "Lean manufacturing" or the Toyota Production System.[7] It might seem strange for healthcare organizations to learn from a manufacturing company like Toyota. The idea is to make our healthcare organizations the best they can be by building upon the proven quality improvement methods and aspects of Lean. Lean healthcare works tirelessly to provide ideal patient care—improving quality, reducing waiting times, and minimizing costs, all while furthering and enhancing the mission and caring nature of healthcare.

Many organizations embrace the idea of Kaizen and practice its specific principles, but they call it Continuous Improvement, Process Excellence, or Plan-Do-Study-Act (PDSA) instead of Kaizen. That is perfectly fine; what we call it does not matter as much as the patient benefits, staff engagement, and organizational improvements that we achieve with these practices.

This is a book about improvement—the sort of improvement that occurs every day in leading hospitals around the world. One of these organizations is Franciscan St. Francis Health. In 2005, after several years of declining margins and a flat-lined quality improvement record, Dr. Paul Strange, the organization's vice president of quality, convinced the leadership team to launch a "Lean Six Sigma" program. Robert J. Brody, president and chief executive officer (CEO) of St. Francis Health, and Keith Jewell, the chief operating officer (COO), brought in a team of people from the outside, including one of this book's coauthors, Joe Swartz, along with professors from Purdue University. Their Lean Six Sigma journey began in 2006, and Franciscan added a formal "Quick and Easy Kaizen" program in April 2007. Throughout this book, we will be sharing stories from Franciscan and other hospitals to demonstrate how they engaged their staff in small improvements and how it made a difference for all of their stakeholders: patients, employees, physicians, and the organization itself.

Everybody knows that healthcare organizations and professionals around the world are under a lot of pressure to improve. The need for improvement includes the dimensions of quality and patient safety, cost, waiting times, and the morale of healthcare providers and employees. Kaizen is proving to be part of the solution to these problems.

Kaizen Is Not Just Change, It Is Improvement

With Kaizen, we want more than a lot of activity and change; we really want improvement and learning. Improvement comes when we can state that things have been made better in one or more dimensions, including safety, quality, productivity, or having a less frustrating workplace. Not all changes are necessarily improvements. For example, a change to a process that makes it harder for nurses to gather the supplies needed to start an IV would likely not be considered an improvement, because it would delay patient care and cause more work for the nurses.

Kaizen involves finding a better way to do your work and changing the method you use to do your work. Kaizen is not about cutting corners. If you cut a step out of your work, you will want to talk to your coworkers to ensure that cutting out that step does not negatively impact the patient or someone else in the process. For example, it would not be a Kaizen if a nurse decided to save time by checking only one patient identifier instead of two when giving a medication, because this would increase the risk of errors and harm to the patient.

A planned improvement should be proposed as a hypothesis to be tested in practice. For example, a materials management team might propose, "If we rearrange the clean utility room to stock items in the order of their computerized order number, then it reduces the amount of time required to restock rooms each day." After testing that change for three days, the materials management team might conclude that they, indeed, saved 30 minutes per day, in addition to the hours spent rearranging the first utility room in which they tested their change. As their test confirmed their expectations, the materials team might decide to share this change with other units.

Large, complex organizations, such as those in healthcare, need to be aware that one area's improvement may cause side effects in other areas. For example, if the change benefitted materials management but made work more difficult for the nurses who take items (often urgently needed) from the supply rooms, then, when looking at the big picture, the change might not be an improvement after all.

We Often Succeed as the Result of Failing More

In organizations that do not practice the philosophies of Kaizen, a change that does not meet improvement goals or targets (or an idea that just flat out does not work as expected) might be considered a *failure*. This might be a source of shame, embarrassment, or punishment for the people who had the idea that was deemed a failure.

Some small changes have a clear, indisputable benefit. For example, a laboratory medical technologist rearranges supplies and equipment on her workbench so that the most frequently used items are at arm's reach instead of being buried in ankle-height drawers. This change saves time and improves ergonomics, leading to faster test results for the patient—this is a change for the better.

Later on, this same technologist might decide, unilaterally, to run a certain low-volume test just one day a week instead of once each day. The technologist's idea is to save the waste of unused reagents in a test pack, as the kit costs the same whether it is used for one test or three. The technologist is trying to save money by making better use of each kit. Unfortunately, a local cost saving like this might not be a change for the better of the overall system if the batching of the tests causes delays in medical decision making or extends a patient's length of stay.

In a culture that embraces Kaizen principles, this sort of "failure" is seen as a learning opportunity for individuals and the organization. These failures are really an opportunity for leaders to coach people so they can understand the broader impact of their improvements. Leaders need to recognize the effort and desire to improve while teaching people how to make better improvements in the future. The Kaizen approach to management requires that leaders' daily actions encourage ongoing improvement rather than stifle it.

Fall seven times. Stand up eight.

—Old Japanese Proverb

Kaizen, PDSA, and the Scientific Method for Improvement

Plan-Do-Study-Act (PDSA), sometimes referred to as Plan-Do-Check-Act (PDCA), is often known as the "Deming Cycle" or the "Shewhart Cycle," after Dr. W. Edwards Deming and his teacher, Walter Shewhart. The word "Act" is sometimes replaced with the word "Adjust." PDSA (or PDCA) is an iterative learning, improvement, and problem-solving model based on the scientific method. Since the term PDSA seems to be the more commonly used in healthcare than PDCA, we will use that term through the rest of the book.

The PDSA steps are:

- **Plan:** Initiating a change by understanding the current situation and root cause of problems; developing a change and stating a hypothesis about what will occur with the change
- **Do:** Carrying out a small-scale test, or pilot, of the change
- **Study:** Testing the change and its hypothesis: gathering data, observing the changes and outcomes
- **Act:** Based on those results, deciding to accept, adopt, and spread the change, or making adjustments (or trying something different)

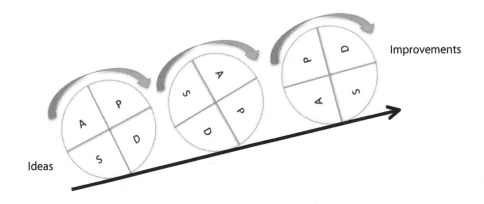

Figure 1.4   Illustration of a sequential or serial PDSA Model.

PDSA is an iterative model, so even a successful change leads us to a new starting point for continued improvement. Our process for spreading a change will include testing it in a larger area or in different conditions, learning from each successive cycle. This sequential or serial PDSA model is illustrated in Figure 1.4.

If the Study phase shows that a change was not really an improvement, we need an environment where people are not punished for their attempts at Kaizen. If we have fear and punishment, people will be afraid to suggest changes or they will become incredibly cautious, only proposing those things that are certain to work. Quoting Mike Rother's book *Toyota Kata*, "The idea is to not stigmatize failures, but to learn from them."[8]

Failure is only the opportunity to begin again more intelligently.

—Henry Ford

Even without the fear of punishment, some people are afraid that they will be embarrassed by trying something unsuccessfully. Instead of PDSA, we might observe the following dysfunctional cycles in an organization:

■ **P-D:** Plan-Do—not studying to see if the change was really an improvement; just assuming things are better as the result of a change
■ **P-D-J-R:** Plan-Do-Justify-Rationalize—knowing, but not being willing to admit, that our change did not lead to improvement

It is sometimes said that Toyota is successful on a larger scale because they have a high tolerance for failure in small improvement initiatives. In the long run, using a failure as an opportunity to learn creates a stronger organization.

We know we've turned the corner [with Kaizen] when staff get excited about a PDSA test failing.

—Ray Seidelman
Manager of performance improvement, Iowa Health System

Changing Back Can Be Better for Babies

In early 2008, the Franciscan maintenance department replaced the manual paper towel dispensers in the NICU with hands-free automatic paper towel dispensers. One automated dispenser located near a group of babies made a loud grinding noise each time it dispensed a paper towel and nurses noticed babies flinching when this happened. Occasionally, the noise would wake one of the babies and the nurses knew how important rest was for recovery. Most of Paula Stanfill's nurses chose a career in the NICU because of their passion and compassion for babies.

After some debate, her nurses suggested they go back to the manual dispensers. Paula wondered if she should let them because it seemed as though they were going backward. Then, her staff measured the decibel level of the automatic paper towel dispenser and found it was greater than 50 decibels. Paula was convinced. She approved having the automatic dispenser removed and replaced with the old manual paper towel holder. It was not as fancy, but it was better for the babies under their care. The babies were happier and healthier, which led to happier staff, which made Paula happy. Their Kaizen Report is shown in Figure 1.5. Paula learned that she needed to listen carefully to her staff and that sometimes going back is the way to go forward.

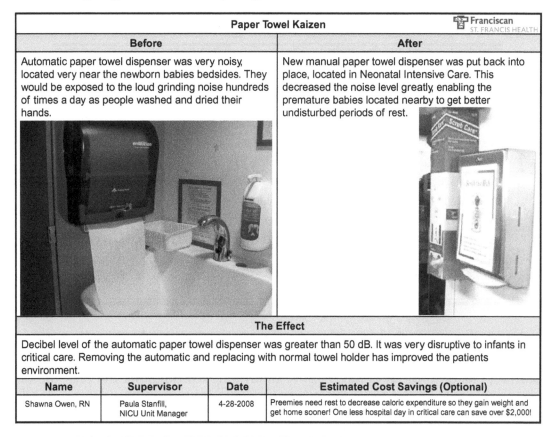

Figure 1.5 contents:

Paper Towel Kaizen	Franciscan ST. FRANCIS HEALTH
Before	**After**
Automatic paper towel dispenser was very noisy, located very near the newborn babies bedsides. They would be exposed to the loud grinding noise hundreds of times a day as people washed and dried their hands.	New manual paper towel dispenser was put back into place, located in Neonatal Intensive Care. This decreased the noise level greatly, enabling the premature babies located nearby to get better undisturbed periods of rest.

The Effect
Decibel level of the automatic paper towel dispenser was greater than 50 dB. It was very disruptive to infants in critical care. Removing the automatic and replacing with normal towel holder has improved the patients environment.

Name	Supervisor	Date	Estimated Cost Savings (Optional)
Shawna Owen, RN	Paula Stanfill, NICU Unit Manager	4-28-2008	Preemies need rest to decrease caloric expenditure so they gain weight and get home sooner! One less hospital day in critical care can save over $2,000!

Figure 1.5   A Kaizen that reversed a previous change in a NICU.

Kaizen = Continuous Improvement

Again, one common translation of Kaizen generally means "change for the better." These changes can include team projects, such as "Kaizen Events" or "Rapid Improvement Events" (RIEs). As we will discuss in Chapter 3, there is certainly a time and place for these events, which typically occur over the course of four or five days, but, as Kaizen guru Masaaki Imai emphasizes, Kaizen should be practiced by everybody, everywhere, every day.[9]

> *Our own attitude is that we are charged with discovering the best way of doing everything, and that we must regard every process employed in manufacturing as purely experimental.*[10]
>
> **—Henry Ford**

In this book, we will use the term Kaizen in the context that is often least practiced and least appreciated in healthcare (as well as other industries)—continuous improvements that happen without the formal structure of a large team or a major project. ThedaCare, a healthcare organization in Wisconsin, refers to this Kaizen and PDSA process as Continuous Daily Improvement (CDI). ThedaCare conducts weeklong RIEs, but they also use daily Kaizen methods to reach their goal of every person being a problem-solver each and every day.[11]

Newton Medical Center (Kansas) has recognized the value of employee engagement, saving $1.7 million in a year as the result of 121 ideas that came in after leadership asked people for improvements that would reduce costs or eliminate waste. For example, two surgeons met with the OR teams to find several thousand dollars' worth of supplies that were redundant. Val Gleason, the senior VP of physician services emphasized, "It was not management imposing its will; it was management saying, 'Here's the problem we face, here's the external environment, how are we going to respond to this?'" Furthermore, a hospital spokesperson said, "The ideas allowed them to save money, protect patient care, and protect the integrity of the work force by not having to have any layoffs."[12]

Kaizen should not be just a one-time flurry of ideas, nor should it be just a one-time reaction to an organization facing financial pressures. A so-called "burning platform" or crisis might prove motivating to some, but the pressure of a crisis might also harm creativity and have people hold back ideas if they fear they could be associated with job cuts that might occur in a tough economic environment. Ideally, the crisis would be an opportunity to learn and practice Kaizen methods that would continue even after the crisis has subsided.

Kaizen Starts with Small Changes

Within the theme of continuous improvement, Kaizens tend to be small, local changes at first. In many organizations, the focus of improvement is on innovation or larger scale improvements, or home runs, to use a baseball analogy. An organization might traditionally focus energy on one major initiative or innovation, such as a new building or a new electronic medical record (EMR) system, which gets positioned as the solution to most of the hospital's problems. Remember—when a baseball player swings for the fences in an attempt to hit nothing but home runs, he usually strikes out a high percentage of the time.

> *The secret of getting ahead is getting started. The secret of getting started is breaking your complex overwhelming tasks into small manageable tasks, and then starting on the first one.*
>
> **—Mark Twain**

A Kaizen organization supplements necessary and large, strategic innovations with lots of small improvement ideas—the equivalent of singles and doubles in baseball. The expectation is that a large number of small changes leads to an impressive impact to an organization's core measures. Small changes, which can be completed more quickly than major projects, can build enthusiasm and problem-solving skills that people can then apply to larger problems.

> *There are no big problems, there are just a lot of little problems.*
>
> **—Henry Ford**

In many large organizations, employees can feel intimidated by the overwhelming number of people with whom they must coordinate to make large-scale improvements. Kaizen encourages employees to start with small changes that do not require coordinating with a large number of people—changes focused at the worker level and the space in which their work is performed.

> *Be the change you want to see in the world.*
>
> **—Mohandas Gandhi**

In a Kaizen approach, we do not start by trying to improve what others do. Instead, we start by improving what we individually do. Start with something that is quick and easy. Often, a good place to start is simply moving something in the workspace closer to the work, making each day easier. Once benefits accrue from a few small improvements, motivation and confidence will grow, allowing people to tackle more difficult, more time-consuming improvements. The best way to get started is to make it quick and easy and then just do it.

Figure 1.6 An angel sign that warns against intruding on grieving families.

A Small Kaizen with Great Meaning

At Riverside Medical Center (Kankakee, Illinois), housekeeping, dietary, or maintenance staff would sometimes face the awkward situation of entering a patient room to find a grieving family with a patient who had just passed away. During an initial Lean and Kaizen program, Darlene, a member of the housekeeping team, made a simple yet effective and beautiful suggestion to prevent that from occurring again. She created an angel sign, pictured in Figure 1.6, that could be placed on the door when a patient passed away. Ancillary departments were instructed to look for the sign so they could remain respectful of the deceased and their family. The sign was also a subtle way to maintain privacy and dignity for the families, because other visitors might just think the sign was a decoration.

Kaizen = Engaging Everybody in Their Own Change

Kaizen allows leaders to get everybody involved in continuous improvement—this means front-line staff as well as leaders at all levels. Kaizen is not an approach that is limited to managers or improvement specialists from a central department. Kaizen is for everyone. Kaizen is the improvement of anything, anywhere. When applied in organizations, Kaizen is a way to improve the way the work is performed, while also improving employee morale. When embraced as a philosophy, people inevitably find opportunities to apply Kaizen in their personal lives and work lives, at home (see Chapter 12) and on the job.

> *The Kaizen philosophy assumes that our way of life—be it our working life, our social life, or our home life—deserves to be constantly improved.*[13]
>
> **—Masaaki Imai**

A common workplace cliché, often used by managers, is that "people hate change." The expression often goes unchallenged, as leaders use it to complain that people will not do what the boss wants them to do. This cliché can become an excuse and something to hide behind. With Kaizen, we learn that people love their own ideas and they love change when they initiate it.

While some people are happy and find comfort in eating the same food at the same restaurants as part of a routine, many people like trying new things, like new restaurants and new vacation destinations. Think of a time you chose a new restaurant. You were probably excited to try it. Now, think of a time when a coworker forced you to go to a new restaurant with an unfamiliar type of cuisine without getting your input. Totally different experiences, right?

The great management thinker Peter Scholtes said simply, "People do not resist change, they resist being changed."[14] This book will show you some of the necessary mindset and practical mechanisms for engaging people in improving their own work, showing leaders how to collaborate with people in a way that benefits all healthcare stakeholders.

Kaizen Upon Kaizen Upon Kaizen

Kaizens can be improved upon over time, like stair steps, with each improvement moving you closer to your work being flawless—the best it possibly could be. The following examples illustrate how staff-driven Kaizen can be iterative and cumulative over time.

In July of 2008, staff in the Franciscan NICU added Velcro® brand hook and loop fastener strips to tie back the privacy curtains when not in use, which prevented them from getting in the way of staff, while improving the aesthetics of the unit, as shown in Figure 1.7.

In June of 2009, they improved on the idea by adding signs to the curtains, as pictured in Figure 1.8.

Then, in February of 2011, they added black clips to ensure the curtains did not have gaps that could reveal a mom breastfeeding her baby, a Kaizen that is documented in Figure 1.9. Over four years' time, the NICU staff members continuously made simple improvements to change their privacy curtains for the better. This series of Kaizens nicely demonstrates the compassionate concern the NICU nurses have for continually improving the care experience for both babies and parents.

It would be counterproductive to look at the final improvement from 2011, and then ask, "Why didn't you come up with all of those improvements back in 2008?" Improvements often seem very obvious in hindsight, but the opportunities may be less obvious when mixed into the busyness of our daily work. All three of the above Kaizens should be celebrated in their own right. It goes to show when you embrace Kaizen, it can be very difficult to stop improving—at home or in the workplace. One small improvement begets others in a positive cycle.

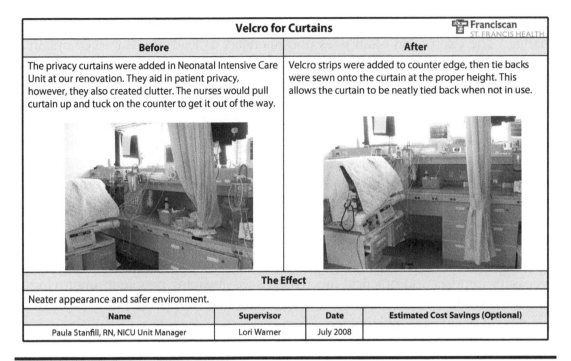

Velcro for Curtains	▣ Franciscan ST. FRANCIS HEALTH
Before	**After**
The privacy curtains were added in Neonatal Intensive Care Unit at our renovation. They aid in patient privacy, however, they also created clutter. The nurses would pull curtain up and tuck on the counter to get it out of the way.	Velcro strips were added to counter edge, then tie backs were sewn onto the curtain at the proper height. This allows the curtain to be neatly tied back when not in use.

The Effect			
Neater appearance and safer environment.			
Name	**Supervisor**	**Date**	**Estimated Cost Savings (Optional)**
Paula Stanfill, RN, NICU Unit Manager	Lori Warner	July 2008	

Figure 1.7   A Kaizen that improves patient privacy.

Kaizen Closes Gaps between Staff and Leaders

In a primary care clinic that was once a client of coauthor Mark, staff members complained that they spent too much time searching for the thermometer. Yes, *the* thermometer. Surprisingly, in a clinic with five or six nurses, three physicians, and 10 exam rooms, everybody was wasting time looking for the one and only digital thermometer.

This thermometer was supposed to be kept at the central nurses' station, which was inconvenient for all, because it meant walking from an exam room to get the thermometer when needed. It was a greater frustration, causing delay for patients, when the thermometer was inevitably being used by another nurse or medical assistant. In the course of brainstorming small improvements, the clinic team asked for a thermometer for each room, which would reduce the walking, waiting, and frustration for under $100 per room.

When senior leaders were given this proposal for spending approval, they expressed their shock and surprise. "What do you mean there is only one thermometer for that entire clinic?" asked one director. The clinic staff said they had never thought to ask for more thermometers, because they generally were never asked for their ideas on improving clinic operations, and they knew budgets were tight. The leadership team was not aware of the problem because they were rarely, if ever, present in the clinic and were unfamiliar with the details of the clinic's daily work.

Thanks to this discovery, the story did not end with only the approval of a $900 purchase request. This moment helped health system leaders realize that they also needed to apply Kaizen to their own schedules and management

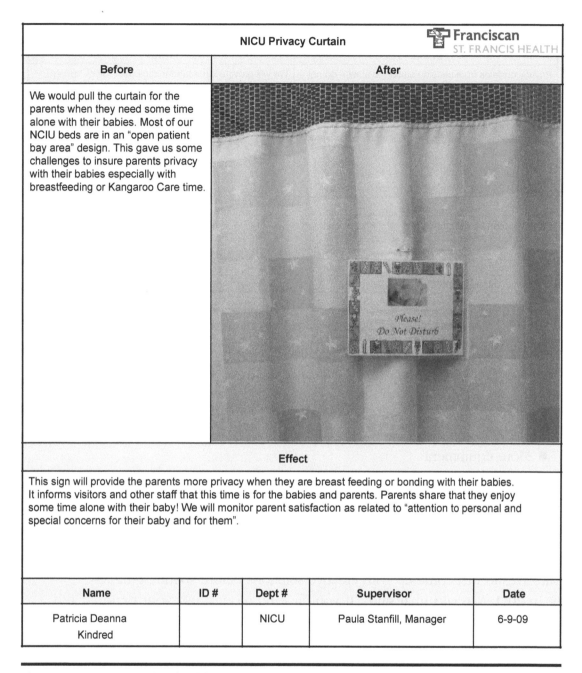

Figure 1.8   A Kaizen that builds upon previous privacy improvements.

priorities. This would help ensure they could continue closing the awareness gap to better support clinic staff and their patients over time.

Creativity before Capital

There is a commonly used expression in the Lean management approach that says we should value "creativity over capital."[15] Kaizen thinking emphasizes finding simple, low-cost countermeasures and solutions. Shigeo Shingo, one of the creators of the Toyota Production System, chastised "catalog engineers" who

Ensuring Our Patients' Privacy		Franciscan ST. FRANCIS HEALTH
Before	**After**	
Privacy curtains from bedside station to station do not completely surround moms and babies for breastfeeding or skin-to-skin sessions. Sometimes moms position their chairs to have their backs to the 3-4 inch opening between curtains. Passers-by in the open room unit can see into what should be a private space for couplets.	We will provide large binder clips (aka "black spring clips") in the top drawers of each bedside station. When moms want privacy, 1 or 2 clips can be easily accessed to clip the curtains together to ensure privacy for the families of newborns. 	
Effect		
Parents are happier knowing that no one can see them while disrobed. Having the clips accessible at the bedside means moms don't have to wait to breastfeed until their nurse returns with a clip to secure the curtains. It also saves staff time in locating clips.		

Name	ID #	Dept #	Supervisor	Date
Donna Palmer		NICU	Paula Stanfill	4/15/2010

Figure 1.9   A Kaizen that reduces staff walking and improves patient privacy.

simply bought solutions out of catalogs. In healthcare, there is a long-standing bias that the solution to problems automatically requires one or more of the following:

- More people
- More space
- More equipment

All of those options require more money. The Kaizen mindset does not mean we never spend money—sometimes, you do need more thermometers, for example, as the bare minimum requirement for effectively treating patients. We need to ensure people have what they need to provide proper patient care. But, we can challenge ourselves to first come up with creative solutions before spending money.

In 2011, Masaaki Imai said, "If you have no money, use your brain … and if you have no brain, sweat it out!"[16] The vast majority of Kaizens at Franciscan were implemented for less than $100. People working on Kaizen are requested to use their creativity to find and test low-cost solutions before they resort to spending substantial sums of money.

In one hospital lab, the technologists requested that the manager purchase a "rocker," a mechanical device that repeatedly tilts tubes of blood back and forth to keep the specimens ready for testing. Instead of just approving the request, which would have cost approximately $500, the manager asked why the rocker was needed. The team replied it was because specimens sat too long before testing. The manager asked why that was, and the team replied that the specimens are carried back to the testing area in large batches. The large batches and long delays—not the lack of a rocker—were the real root of the problem. The team was able to change its processes and work assignments to have the specimens delivered more frequently, eliminating the delay and the need for the rocker. In the long term, the lab's physical layout was changed to shorten the distance to the testing area, reducing the amount of labor time required to transport the small batches.

A different hospital considered purchasing an electronic bed and patient tracking system that would include software and multiple plasma screens. Before selecting one of the competing systems, leaders encouraged the team to manually simulate bed tracking by using a whiteboard and magnets. The intent was to use the manual board to learn, in an iterative way, what information would be needed and how that information would be used by the unit. The thought was this experience would guide the team toward a better software decision than if they had not used a manual method first. As it turned out, the unit decided they liked the simple usability, visibility, and flexibility of the magnetic board. If they wanted to make a change, it could be done immediately, rather than waiting for a change order (or being told "no" by the vendor).

Many of the examples in this book are cases where staff members were creative in making something that met their needs and solved a problem instead of buying something expensive that may not solve the problem perfectly. Figure 1.10 is an example from Akron Children's Hospital (Akron, Ohio) where an X-ray technician created an adjustable patient shield from items they already had in the hospital.

On a larger scale, there is a growing literature of cases where hospitals have used process improvement methods to avoid expanding their facilities or building

X-ray		Akron Children's Hospital
Before	**After**	
When completing diagnostic, upright radiographs, Technologists were forced to wrap Velcro straps around patient waists to place appropriate shielding devices on patients. This not only required a considerable amount of time, but also increased the risk of spreading infections from patient to patient.	An IV pole stand was modified to support a shield which could be raised and lowered according to patient height.	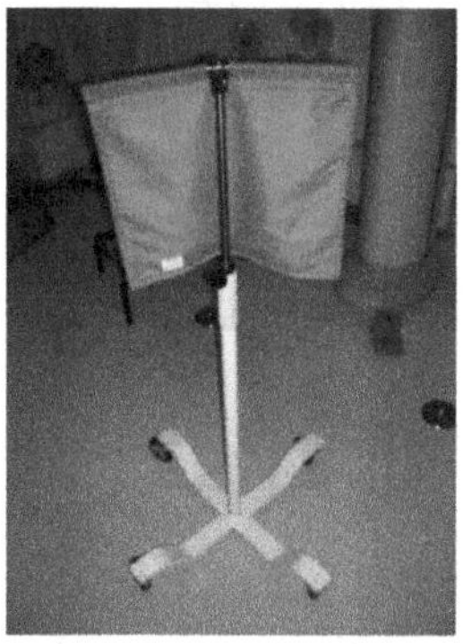
Effect		
The device does not require contact with the patient to be effective and is much faster than the traditional method. This type of device was available in a catalog, but the department was able to quickly build two of them for a fraction of the cost.		
Name	**Dept #**	**Supervisor**	**Date**
Russell Maroni, RT	Radiology/X-ray	Ron Bucci, Director	7-8-11

Figure 1.10 A Kaizen that demonstrates the practice of "creativity over capital."

new space. One such example is Seattle Children's Hospital (Seattle, Washington), which has avoided $180 million in construction costs by improving throughput and capacity through process improvement.[17] Delnor Hospital (Geneva, Illinois) was able to eliminate a planned $80 million expansion by making process improvements that prevented discharge delays, thereby reducing length of stay and freeing up capacity in a far less expensive way than the construction would have been.[18]

Expensive Mistakes Made without the Kaizen Mindset

At one hospital that Mark visited a few years back, the chief medical officer described how she had forced through the acceptance of a construction project to expand the number of emergency department exam rooms as an attempt to deal with overcrowding and having patients waiting in the hallways. Once the rooms were built, patient flow did not improve. At best, patients now had a room to wait in instead of a hallway. The executive admitted that her change (more rooms) did not lead to the improvement she desired (better patient flow). Hers was an example of rushing into an expensive, "big bang" solution. She considered it to be an expensive lesson learned, one she wished other hospitals would not repeat.

A Kaizen approach would have involved clinicians and staff members instead of being just a top-down executive decision. Through Kaizen, a hospital could experiment with a number of small-scale changes in a series of inexpensive and low-risk tests. A cross-functional team might learn that the root cause of emergency department waiting time was found far away—it is often the inpatient discharge process that is full of dysfunctions and delays.

Kaizen and Lean: Related and Deeply Interconnected Concepts

Over the past ten years, Lean methods and mindsets have been embraced by healthcare organizations around the world, with some of the most highly regarded Lean healthcare organizations including ThedaCare, Virginia Mason Medical Center (Seattle, Washington), Seattle Children's Hospital, Denver Health, Flinders Medical Centre (Australia), and the Royal Bolton Hospital NHS Foundation Trust (England).

Lean is often considered to have Japanese roots, but core elements of the approach came from Americans, such as Henry Ford and Dr. W. Edwards Deming, as well as other historical writers, philosophers, and industrialists from around the world. It cannot be said that Lean and Kaizen are strictly a Japanese system, because Toyota has spread its corporate culture to factories around the world, and many others have successfully adopted these methods.

People Are the Ultimate Competitive Advantage

While Toyota has facilities, capital equipment, and software that make its company work, Toyota's people and their role in Kaizen make a difference. Toyota's website once stated: "Every Toyota team member is empowered with the ability to improve their work environment. This includes everything from quality and safety to the environment and productivity. Improvements and suggestions by team members are the cornerstone of Toyota's success."[19]

A Toyota group leader from the Georgetown, Kentucky, factory said, "Toyota has long considered its ability to permanently resolve problems and improve stable processes as one of the company's competitive advantages. With an entire workforce charged with solving their workplace problems, the power of the intellectual capital of the company is tremendous."[20] While it is a cliché to say employees are your greatest asset, Toyota invests in people and their development because Toyota views its people as "an appreciating asset,"[21] while machines and buildings only depreciate over time.

In recent years, Toyota leaders have often referred to their approach as the "Thinking Production System,"[22] as they teach that every employee has two jobs:

1. Do your work.
2. Improve your work.

In hospitals, staff members complain far too often that they are expected only to show up, keep their heads down, and do their jobs. By not engaging healthcare professionals in the improvement of their work, leaders waste a huge opportunity to improve patient care and the organization's bottom line. Hospitals can all hire the same architects, buy the same diagnostic equipment, and outfit operating rooms in the same way as some other leading hospital. Ultimately, however, healthcare performance is about people—not just their clinical skills, but also their participation in ongoing quality and process improvement.

Kaizeneer: Franciscan uses the term "Kaizeneer" for staff members who practice Kaizen—a term that is a combination of the words Kaizen and engineer. Engineers are designers, and those who do Kaizen are essentially designing or redesigning their world around them. If Disney has "Imagineers" who design their theme parks, why can't healthcare have Kaizeneers who redesign the healthcare work environment?

High-Level Kaizen Principles—The Kaizen Mindset

Kaizen uses a defined set of principles that guides the problem-solving and improvement processes. Kaizen requires more than just putting a group together in a room and telling them they have time to make improvements. Ideally, leaders at all levels should be able to coach and guide employees and lower-level managers about these principles and mindsets to ensure the most effective and most sustainable improvements. The best way for leaders to learn how to coach others on Kaizen is to practice it in their own work.

Pascal Dennis, author and former Toyota manager in Canada, defines "Kaizen spirit" as:

1. **Cheerfulness:** the conviction that things will be better tomorrow, no matter how tough they are today.
2. **Go See:** The desire to get out of the office and experience things first hand; the willingness of leaders to work with front-line staff with humility and openness.
3. **Get Your Hands Dirty:** We roll up our sleeves and try improvements with our colleagues.[23]

Kaizen is not a series of tricks, tips, or techniques that can be copied easily; it is primarily about a culture and a way of thinking. Kaizen is not a matter of chasing external targets and performance benchmarks; it is about your employees' internal drive to come up with their own improvements that allow them to be the best they can be.

At a high level, Kaizen is about:

■ Asking all employees to search for and identify improvement opportunities
■ Empowering all employees to implement small improvements to their daily work
■ Recognizing employees for those improvements
■ Sharing and spreading improvement ideas throughout the organization, along with lessons learned

Principle 1: Asking

The title of Norman Bodek's 2005 book, co-authored with Chuck Yorke, is instructive: *All You Gotta Do Is Ask*. There are additional things that leaders need to do to encourage Kaizen, but it starts with asking people to come up with ideas to make their work easier. As they bring those ideas forward, they participate in improving the broader system in which they work.

As one of Mark's clients was getting started with Kaizen and Lean, a nurse said she was happy that the organization was starting to seriously engage front-line staff members in improvement. Yet, she shared some frustration that this seemed to be a new concept in the organization, saying, "I've worked here for six years and this is the first time anyone has asked me what I think about anything." There might have been a bit of hyperbole in the statement, but she thought it was generally true.

Principle 2: Empowering

Kaizen is a mechanism to empower all employees to make improvements in their work environment. After asking all employees to make improvements, leaders need to allow people to take action. Early in Kaizen efforts, supervisors and managers might be uncomfortable, for a number of reasons, with allowing their employees to make changes. Empowerment should not be viewed as a win–lose equation for managers. Leaders can (and should) be involved in these improvements in a collaborative way. In a Kaizen culture, managers look good when their employees make improvements. Kaizen also requires leaders to get involved when their employees require assistance, including times when they want to make improvements that go beyond the scope of their own work or their own team.

Principle 3: Recognizing

Recording an improvement and displaying the results allows the person or team who made the improvement to receive the recognition they deserve. Various methods for documenting, displaying, and sharing Kaizen improvements will be described throughout this book. Managers and supervisors may recognize improvements locally in their departments. Selected ones might be posted prominently in high-visibility areas for others to see, such as in hallways or in the cafeteria. Many leaders often think first about direct financial rewards to employees who participate in Kaizen, but there are other ways to provide recognition that might avoid some of the possible dysfunctions that occur with financial incentives, a topic we will discuss in Chapter 10.

Principle 4: Sharing

The real power of Kaizen occurs when ideas are shared. Sharing enables others to benefit from the ideas and realize that they, too, can make similar improvements to their work. This helps spread good ideas throughout the organization, engaging everyone in improvement. Ideas can be shared by posting Quick and Easy Kaizen reports on bulletin boards or by highlighting ideas in hospital-wide emails, as we will show in Chapter 5. There are other methods for documenting Kaizens, as illustrated in Chapter 7, that also allow people to "steal shamelessly" (as Bodek would say) and take good ideas back to their own work areas.
A growing number of healthcare organizations, including Franciscan, are using web-based software platforms make sharing easier across the entire hospital or broader health system, as described in Chapter 10.

This Is Not a Suggestion System—It Is an Improvement System

Sometimes when people hear about Kaizen, they say, "We already do that—we have a suggestion box!" The Kaizen approach is very different from traditional suggestion box systems in many ways. In a traditional suggestion system, someone writes down an idea on a form and drops the form into a box that hangs on the wall. Sometime later, someone else opens the box, collects the papers, and puts them in a place for managers to review. The suggestion may sit for a long period of time before it is reviewed, if it is reviewed at all.

Additionally, some staff suggestion programs are framed as a "winner takes all" contest, where one idea is selected for implementation, with a prize awarded. Unfortunately, in a setting like that, all of the other great ideas are deemed losers, which is bound to be demotivating to those who did not have their valid ideas acted upon. With Kaizen, an organization can implement virtually every idea, large or small, and everybody can receive recognition for each of his or her improvements.

At one hospital Mark worked with in the early days of a Lean journey, he found a suggestion box on the wall of the laboratory. Mark took the box down from the wall so the team could talk about what, if any, ideas had come in from employees in the past. One of the team members left to go find the key to the locked box, returning 20 minutes later to announce that none of the managers could find the key! This story became a very clear illustration to the laboratory staff and leaders about why the suggestion box did not work and how their new approach to Kaizen would have to be different.

> *Why is there a lock on your suggestion box? Are you afraid that the competing hospital across the street is sending people over to steal your good ideas?*
>
> **—Mark Graban**

Ray Seidelman emphasizes that Kaizen is not a suggestion system, where proposals might include "I need another computer." Rather, it is an approach where people identify problems that get in the way of ideal care, or what they call "signals." An example might be a staff member saying, "I couldn't find the information I needed about this medication in the record," and then responding by following the scientific method for improvement.[24]

Kaizen Has an Impact on People and Performance

At Franciscan, the adoption of Kaizen grew gradually, yet impressively, over the first few years since the launch of the Kaizen program in 2007. In the year 2011, 46% of the staff had participated during that year, and 53% of the staff had participated sometime since the launch. In 2011, 82% of all departments had at least

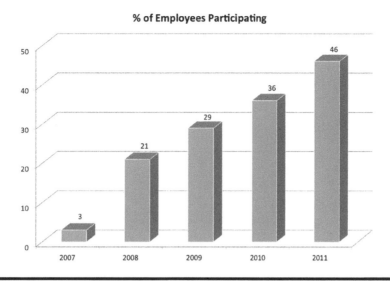

Figure 1.11   Number of employees at Franciscan St. Francis Hospitals with a formally submitted Kaizen in each year.

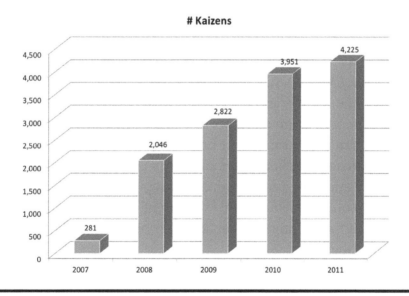

Figure 1.12   Number of formally submitted Kaizens each year.

one person participate in Kaizen. The growth in employee participation is shown in Figure 1.11.

As a benchmark, Toyota receives an average of 10 improvement ideas per person each year, after decades building their culture.[25] The number of Kaizens implemented each year at Franciscan has increased, as shown in Figure 1.12, up to 1.7 per full-time equivalent in 2011. The number at Franciscan is significantly higher than most healthcare organizations and they work to increase participation each year.

At Franciscan, the Kaizens in 2010 resulted in a total documented savings of over $3 million. Of that, about $1.7 million in savings was money that flowed directly to the "bottom line," and about $1.4 million of that was "potential" dollar savings through, for example, the saving of someone's time. Beyond these documented savings are the benefits from small Kaizens, where it is hard (or not

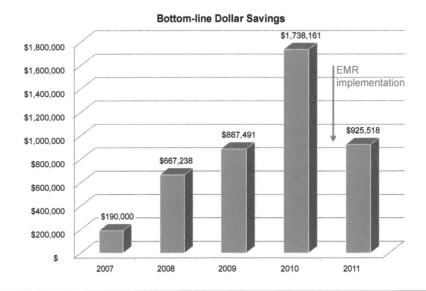

Figure 1.13   Bottom-line "hard" dollar savings from 2007–2011.

worth the time) to calculate a savings. The last four years of savings are shown in Figure 1.13. It should be noted that, while participation increased in 2011, total savings decreased as Franciscan staff were busy upgrading 12 computer systems to one system-wide EMR system.

Again, bottom-line savings and return on investment (ROI) are not the only things that matter, but they are an important part of the picture for healthcare organizations that are under significant financial pressures.

The most significant benefit at Franciscan has been the difference Kaizen makes for patients and staff, as the Kaizen examples in this book will demonstrate. The softer benefits related to patient safety, outcomes and satisfaction, along with staff safety and satisfaction, can be hard to quantify but cannot be emphasized enough.

Baptist Health Care (Florida) has a Kaizen program called "Bright Ideas" that was established in 1995 to engage all employees in improvement and innovation. Since 2008, every employee has had the expectation of implementing three ideas per year that will improve patient outcomes, save time, or improve safety. More than 50,000 ideas have been implemented since 2000, and although cost savings is not the primary goal, there has been a total estimated cost savings and avoidance of $50 million. In 2008 alone, almost 14,000 ideas were implemented, or more than two per employee, contributing $10.5 million in cost avoidance and $5.5 million in cost savings. Additionally, turnover is relatively low, at just 11% annually, and the system has been on the FORTUNE 100 Best Places to Work for in America for the last seven years.[26]

Conclusion

Both co-authors have seen first hand and believe strongly that healthcare professionals:

- care deeply about their patients
- want to provide the highest-quality ideal care to each patient
- have the ability and the desire to use their creativity to improve their workplace

Healthcare, as an industry, has a 100-year-long track record of trying to adopt and emulate quality improvement methods from manufacturing, aviation, and other industries. Yet, daily continuous improvement, or Kaizen, seems to be more a goal than a reality in a vast majority of healthcare organizations.

People want to improve. Rather than pointing fingers at individuals—front-line staff, managers, or senior leaders—leaders should understand the systemic barriers and the oft-unspoken mindsets that interfere with making continuous improvement a reality. Your organization may have tried other improvement methodologies in the past, including Total Quality Management and Six Sigma. If past attempts at continuous improvement did not work out, it might be helpful to stop and reflect upon the systematic root causes of those struggles before moving forward with this book or with Kaizen.

This book shares some of the methods, along with the required management mindsets, for facilitating effective Kaizen. We hope you are inspired by the examples shared in this book and that you will build upon, rather than copy, the methods described herein. Your patients, your colleagues, and your organization depend on it.

Discussion Questions

- If your organization has tried other improvement programs that did not work, what are some of the root causes of that?
- Does the word "Kaizen" cause problems or discomfort to people, to the point where you have to call it something else in your organization?
- What do you think is a reasonable goal for the number of Kaizen ideas implemented per person each year in your organization?
- How do you strike the proper balance in talking about benefits to patients and staff, which are sometimes hard to quantify, and cost savings or other financial benefits?

Endnotes

1. Kato, Iaso, and Art Smalley, *Toyota Kaizen Methods: Six Steps to Improvement* (New York: Productivity Press, 2010), 102.

2. Jacobson, Gregory H., N.S. McCoin, R. Lescallette, S. Russ, and C.M. Slovis, "Kaizen: A Method of Process Improvement in the Emergency Department," *Acad. Emerg. Med.* Dec;16(12), 2009, 1341–1349.

3. York, Clay, Personal interview, July 2011.

4. IU Health Goshen Hospital, "GHS Colleagues Meet Challenge; CEO Shaves Head," January 1, 2010, http://www.goshenhosp.com/main.asp?id=983 (accessed July 8, 2011).

5. Dague, James, personal interview, July 2011.

6. IU Health Goshen Hospital, "Health System among Best Places to Work in Indiana," May 6, 2009, website, http://www.goshenhosp.com/main.asp?id=942 (accessed July 8, 2011).

7. Graban, Mark, *Lean Hospitals: Improving Quality, Patient Satisfaction, and Employee Engagement: 2nd edition* (New York: Productivity Press, 2011), 2.

8. Rother, Mike, *Toyota Kata: Managing People for Improvement, Adaptiveness and Superior Results* (New York: McGraw-Hill, 2009), 139.

9. Imai, Masaaki, "Masaaki Imai—The Definition of KAIZEN," *YouTube*.com, January 19, 2010, http://www.youtube.com/watch?v=jRdTFis4-3Q (accessed August 15, 2011).

10. Zarbo, Richard, J. Mark Tuthill, et al., "The Henry Ford Production System: Reduction of Surgical Pathology In-Process Misidentification Defects by Bar Code–Specified Work Process Standardization," *American Journal of Clinical Pathology*, 131, 2009, 468–477.

11 ThedaCare Center for Healthcare Value, *Thinking Lean at ThedaCare: Strategy Deployment*, DVD, 2011.

12. Shideler, Karen, "Staff's Ideas Save Money at Newton Hospital," *The Wichita Eagle*, November 24, 2009, http://www.kansas.com/2009/11/24/1068956/staffs-ideas-save-money-at-newton.html#ixzz1N1kSo77u (accessed July 8, 2011).

13. Imai, Masaaki, *KAIZEN: The Key to Japan's Competitive Success* (New York: McGraw-Hill, 1986), 3.

14. Scholtes, Peter, Brian L. Joiner, and Barbara J. Steibel, *The Team Handbook* (Madison, WI: Oriel Incorporated, 2003), 1–7.

15. Isao and Smalley, *Toyota Kaizen Methods*, 102.

16. DeClaire, Joan, "Late to the Party: Confessions of a Lean-Hesitant Manager," *DailyKaizen*.org, July 8, 2011, http://dailykaizen.org/2011/07/08/late-to-the-party-confessions-of-a-lean-hesitant-manager-by-joan-declaire/ (accessed August 15, 2011).

17. Weed, Julie, "Factory Efficiency Comes to the Hospital," *NYTimes.com*, July 11, 2010, http://www.nytimes.com/2010/07/11/business/11seattle.html?_r=2&emc=eta1&pagewanted=all (accessed August 15, 2011).

18. Jones, Del, "Hospital CEOs Manage Staff Time, Inventory to Cut Costs," *USA Today Online*, September 10, 2009, http://www.usatoday.com/news/health/2009-09-09-saving-money-hospitals_N.htm (accessed August 15, 2011).

19. Robinson, Alan G., and Dean M. Schroeder, "The Role of Front-Line Ideas in Lean Performance Improvement," *ASQ QMJ* vol. 16, no. 4, 2009, http://www.landesassociates.com/pdfs/front-line-ideas.pdf (accessed August 15, 2011).

20. Rother, 14.

21. Liker, Jeffrey K. and Timothy N. Ogen, *Toyota Under Fire: Lessons for Turning Crisis into Opportunity* (New York: McGraw-Hill, 2011), 33.

22. Public Affairs Division Toyota Motor Corporation, "The Toyota Production System," website, October 8, 2003, http://www.toyotageorgetown.com/tps.asp (accessed August 15, 2011).

23. Dennis, Pascal, "What is Kaizen Spirit?" *Lean Pathways Blog,* March 24, 2011, http://leanpathways.blogspot.com/2011/03/what-is-kaizen-spirit.html (accessed August 15, 2011).
24. Seidelman, Ray, personal interview, July 2011.
25. Liker, Jeffrey K., and David Meier, *The Toyota Way Fieldbook* (New York: McGraw-Hill, 2006), 261.
26. Brophy, Andy, and John Bicheno, *Innovative* Lean (Buckingham, England: PICSIE Books, 2010), 138.

Chapter 2

The Roots and Evolution of Kaizen

Kaizen is about changing the way things are. If you assume that things are all right the way they are, you can't do Kaizen. So change something![1]

—Taiichi Ohno
Co-creator of the Toyota Production System

Kaizen and continuous improvement are not new ideas, nor are these uniquely Japanese concepts. People have been trying to engage employees in improvement for hundreds of years, if not longer. However, some of the historical and traditional examples are not always in agreement with modern Kaizen principles.

Benjamin Franklin is often cited as an early Kaizen thinker, having said:

- "Without continual growth and progress, such words as improvement, achievement, and success have no meaning."
- "He that is good for making excuses is seldom good for anything else."
- "When you're finished changing, you're finished."

Early Suggestion Programs

The first modern employee suggestion program was instituted in the British Navy in 1770. Before naval leadership recognized the need to listen to all personnel, even speaking an idea that contradicted a captain's or admiral's opinion could be punished by hanging.[2] A modern-day version is depicted in Figure 2.1.

The first physical suggestion box was used in Scotland, circa 1880, at the William Denny & Brothers shipyard. The intent was to solicit ideas from all employees, paying them a "fair" reward for implementable ideas, focusing on extrinsic motivation.[3]

Figure 2.1 Dilbert's boss is not a Kaizen leader (licensed from United Features Syndicate).

In 1892, National Cash Register Company (NCR) was the first U.S.-based company to implement a company-wide employee suggestion program described as the "hundred-headed brain" by their CEO, John Patterson. While Patterson realized that employees had valuable ideas, the system fell into disuse over time as new leaders took over. The system did not fail because workers "stopped having good ideas," but rather because "the predominant view of the workplace became one in which managers were expected to do the thinking and workers were expected to do what they were told."[4]

Norman Bodek wrote that Kodak, in 1898, had the first employee suggestion system. The first suggestion submitted said, "clean the windows," as the factory was lit by natural light, and this simple, inexpensive suggestion created a better work environment.[5] When the Kodak system shifted toward a cost-savings focus, participation dropped off dramatically.[6]

Suggestion boxes became more popular in manufacturing during and after World War II, and today most companies have some form of physical or electronic means for collecting customer ideas, including Starbucks and its "My Starbucks Idea" web site for customers.[7] Many of these box systems or customer voting systems are not the same as Kaizen and the principles we will describe in this book, because in these systems outsiders are making suggestions for others rather than employees bringing forward ideas they can implement themselves.

Downsides of Suggestion Box Programs

There are a number of dysfunctions that occur with suggestion box systems. Suggestions often sit for weeks or months in a locked box. Even when not so slow, employees are often not happy with the communication they get from managers. One major academic medical center described in 2011 how staff ideas submitted to their online suggestion box were reviewed by a committee who gave feedback to the employees whose suggestions have been accepted. Kaizen emphasizes implementing most ideas or, at the least, giving timely and collaborative feedback to every employee who has an idea, not just those that are deemed accepted by a far-off committee.

When Mark worked as an industrial engineer at a General Motors factory in the mid-1990s, he submitted a triplicate carbon copy form into a suggestion box. After Mark left for graduate school, he received a letter from GM. Nine months after he submitted the suggestion, they had mailed a pink copy of the suggestion, marked as "rejected." Since the process was so slow, they never had a chance to talk to Mark about the idea before he left, leaving it as a lost opportunity for improvement (in Mark's mind).

In a Kaizen approach, an idea is the starting point for a dialogue between employee and supervisor, working together to understand the real problem to be solved. Along with having a general bias for action, leaders should also have a bias toward finding *something* to implement that solves the identified problem. Often, that original idea, even if not implemented as such, sparks a new idea that *can* be implemented. When it is said that Toyota implements more than 90% of their employee ideas, that means that they found *something* to implement, not necessarily the original ideas.

Another problem with suggestion systems is that the completed forms end up going to a manager, getting added to the manager's long list of tasks. Since managers are typically very busy people, with other higher-priority items regularly popping up, an idea often gets buried in the pile.

Even when ideas are reviewed and approved in a timely manner, the manager may assign a suggestion to someone other than the original submitter to review or implement. Is that person as passionate about the idea as the person who had the suggestion? Likely not. Both authors are grateful to Bodek for his clarity in teaching that suggestions are something *you* (pointing at another person) should do for me, while ideas are something that *I* can do for myself. With Kaizen, the person who identifies the problem works with the supervisor and other appropriate people to identify solutions and then leads the implementation of the best solution.

One other common dysfunction is the tendency of suggestion systems to pay out some percentage of any cost savings to employees. While this sounds good in principle, studies have shown that organizations that have larger payouts for suggestions actually get fewer suggestions.[8] It may seem counterintuitive, but suggestion payouts can hamper teamwork in a number of ways:

1. If the suggestion system only pays the person who originally had the idea, there's little incentive to work with others or there can be conflict about whose idea it was.
2. It can be incredibly time consuming to work to quantify the impact of a suggestion.

3. There can be a lot of controversy about how much a suggestion is really worth especially if the payout is a percentage of the idea's value.
4. People will tend to focus only on large "home run" ideas or those that have a clearly quantifiable cost savings.
5. Payouts have often been based on merely having an idea as opposed to actually implementing anything that provided value or savings.

In the Kaizen approach, the ideal state would be to not pay staff for ideas, as we want to tap into people's natural intrinsic motivations. People feel pride when their ideas are listened to and when supervisors work together with them to drive change. In addition to just wanting to be heard, people are generally happy to make improvements that make their own work easier or provide better care for patients. A great number of improvement opportunities cannot be easily translated into a financial benefit, something that is especially true in healthcare. In Chapter 10, we will discuss pros and cons of incentive systems for Kaizen. Franciscan does have some financial rewards, in addition to recognition that is given in different non-monetary ways. The rewards at Franciscan are small, based on the documented implementation of an idea. The rewards are inclusive of all people who worked on a Kaizen team, not just the person with the original idea.

Another dysfunction is that suggestion boxes tend to attract anonymous complaints instead of constructive ideas for improvement. These complaints are sometimes personal attacks against others, which is one reason cited for having locks on suggestion boxes, as complaints about others become HR issues that require confidentiality. Kaizen is an approach where people act professionally and constructively, meaning we can have transparency in our system.

> Even with an active and transparent Kaizen program, there still may be a role for a locked suggestion box. While Kaizen requires transparency, some issues do require sensitivity and confidentiality. A suggestion box should be used as a safety net for instances where people need to point out violations of policy and fear doing so in a public way or in any way in which they can be identified. A healthcare organization may, for these cases, rely on a centralized process (often electronic) rather than a local suggestion box.

The differences between the traditional suggestion box and Kaizen are listed in Table 2.1.

While often well intended, the classic suggestion box has more downsides and dysfunctions than success stories. Kaizen and modern improvement systems are based on a different philosophy. Instead of putting the entire approval

Table 2.1 Difference between the Traditional Suggestion Box and Kaizen

Suggestion Box	Kaizen
Things you want somebody else to do	Things that I will do (or we will do together)
Emphasis on "what to do" or "what we want"	Equal emphasis on problem statement and proposed countermeasures
Opaque (ideas hidden in box)	Transparent (ideas on display on wall or open electronic system)
Often focused on that one big idea with a huge payback	Lots of little ideas, from everybody, every day
ROI or cost focus	Employee morale and engagement focus; cost will follow
Leaders approve or reject ideas in a conference room	Leaders work together with people in the workplace (or "gemba") to find things that work
Many or most ideas rejected	Almost all (>90%) ideas lead to some change that addresses the identified problem
Slow, periodic process (monthly or quarterly reviews)	Daily discussion and fast action taken on new ideas
Often focused on internal needs	More likely focused on customer/patient needs
If you try something, it had better work (or don't admit it doesn't)	If you try something and it doesn't work, learn from that and try something different
Poor feedback loop about what actually worked and what impact it had	Focus on the full PDSA cycle, including measuring or gauging results

burden on supervisors, Kaizen is much more collaborative and more respectful of the contribution that everybody can make toward improvement.

> *Many companies assume that the failure of the suggestion box approach is with employees that don't care, but if we dig a little deeper we find it is the system itself that squashed enthusiasm.*[9]
>
> **—Bruce Hamilton**
> *President of GBMP*

Recovering from Taylorism

Many industries, including manufacturing, are still recovering from the outdated notion that working and thinking should be separated, an idea popularized by Frederick W. Taylor (1856–1915), one of the fathers of industrial engineering. As an early efficiency expert, Taylor stood over workers, timing them and devising ways for them to do their work differently. Although many of Taylor's analysis and work improvement methods, such as time and motion studies, are still in use today, the difference is in the mindset and how these methods are applied.[10]

*[If] the new standard has been set up by the worker's own volition,
he takes pride in the new standard and is willing to follow it. If, on the
contrary, he is told to follow a standard imposed by management,
he may not be as willing to follow it.[11]*

—Masaaki Imai

Taylor was a proponent of expert-driven improvement because he taught that workers were not capable of improving their own work, saying, "The duty of enforcing the adoption of standards and enforcing this cooperation rests with management alone."[12] He insulted workers by writing that a man who did manual work was "sufficiently phlegmatic and stupid to choose this for his occupation," meaning they were incapable of thinking about improvement.[13]

That seems like an archaic, century-old viewpoint. At one hospital, as Mark was teaching hospital employees how to analyze their own work in a modern, participative way, he was introduced to an elderly patient and described how they were studying the work to improve patient care. The woman responded, "Oh, you're the time study man," using a term from a bygone era.[14]

Even today, some health systems run the risk of using outdated mindsets, where the outside expert, sometimes a young industrial engineering student, will shadow clinicians, even timing how long they are in the bathroom. This practice seems to be the polar opposite of the collaborative Kaizen approach that engages people in their own improvement.[15] In one hospital where Mark served as a consultant, a nurse lamented how she had previously tried to collect data for improvement and was told, "…to just do my job and to quit wasting my time on that analysis stuff." Furthermore, she was accused of "creating a negative work environment" by trying to make things better, as stated on her annual performance review. Arguably, the negative work environment was being created by the leaders who were not listening to her.

While we teach today that people should improve their own work, there can be value in getting the view of an outsider. Frank Gilbreth, a contemporary of Taylor, filmed surgical procedures in the first decade of the twentieth century, looking for waste and improvement opportunities (as the expert). He observed that surgeons spent more time searching for instruments than performing surgery. His improvement idea? Have a "surgical caddy" who handed instruments to the surgeon, allowing the surgeon to focus on their patient. Perhaps as evidence of the idea that "people hate being changed," Gilbreth presented the caddy idea to the American Medical Association conference in 1915, but the AMA waited 16 years to accept this as a best practice.[16]

Even with the striking differences in mindsets, the industrial engineering work analysis and improvement methods of Taylor and Gilbreth are powerful, especially when utilized in a way that allows people to improve their own work, rather than being told what to do by an expert.

James Dague, CEO of IU Goshen Hospital, emphasizes that you have to involve the people who actually do the work every day in improvement activities. Dague recalls how he previously worked in health systems where engineers would come in for a day to observe in a nursing unit, "generalizing the staffing patterns" based on that one day, and he has "never seen that work well." He adds, "I think not involving people, having changes are going to be imposed on you, will get you a lot of resistance and negativity right off the bat."

The American Roots of Continuous Improvement—TWI and Deming

In his first book, published in 1986, *KAIZEN: The Key To Japan's Competitive Success,* Masaaki Imai described how the "Japanese suggestion systems" actually came from the U.S. Air Force and the American program from World War II called "Training Within Industry," or TWI. The Kaizen system built upon TWI concepts and evolved to focus more on the "morale-boosting benefits of positive employee participation."[17]

TWI was created by the U.S. Department of War and its War Manpower Commission. Between 1940 and 1945, the TWI program was instrumental in training new factory workers who replaced those who went to fight overseas, including the iconic "Rosie the Riveter," who represented women who were new to the workplace. Effective training and management of factories was crucial to ramping up production of airplanes, weapons, and war materiel. TWI included the following three "J programs":[18]

- **Job Instruction Training (JI):** Training workers how to do jobs in the most effective way possible; large emphasis on teaching supervisors how to effectively train workers
- **Job Methods Training (JM):** Training employees and supervisors how to improve their own work; focused on improving quality and productivity
- **Job Relations Training (JR):** Training supervisors and workers how to resolve personnel problems through analytical and nonemotional methods; taught supervisors to treat all people as individuals and getting results through better understanding of people

By 1944, TWI training materials were adapted and used within healthcare to help train an influx of new personnel. Job Instruction methods were used, for example, to train nurses how to best prepare a thermometer for use.[19] Job Methods instruction proved helpful in teaching hospital clerks how to reduce wasted trips

Figure 2.2 World War II-era US Government Poster featuring Thomas Edison.

Figure 2.3 World War II-era US Government Poster asking for more improvement ideas.

through the hospital[20] and helping nurses improve the way catheterization trays were set up.[21]

Figure 2.2 is a World War II–era United States government poster that shows an early example of asking for small ideas, showing the connection between TWI, creativity, and Kaizen.

Figure 2.3 is another war poster that suggests that each person make one idea per year, a very modest goal.

Alan G. Robinson and Dean M. Schroeder's research provides further clarification about the influence of TWI (particularly the Job Methods program) on Kaizen and suggestion systems, writing that TWI "had a major effect in expanding the suggestion system to involve all workers rather than a handful of the elite … as supervisors taught workers how to perform job modifications, they learned how to make changes and suggestions."[22]

In recent years, the broader Lean community, and hospitals in particular, are rediscovering the applicability of TWI methods, including Virginia Mason Medical Center.[23] Sarah Patterson, chief operating officer at Virginia Mason, describes the importance of TWI as a way of engaging people, emphasizing on-the-job training and coaching, saying, "You don't just do a training session and let people go out and do it," adding, "You actually are there with them as a leader … observing and giving them feedback."[24]

TWI methods were brought to Japan after the end of the war, and Dr. W. Edwards Deming, an American statistician, gave a series of lectures on management in 1950 that so influenced the country that their annual quality prize is called The Deming Prize. Deming's insights on quality improvement and, more broadly, on managing and leading people were greatly influential in the development of the Toyota Production System and Kaizen methods.

What Deming called "continual improvement" included the use of the PDSA cycle to improve quality and reduce cost by improving the system. Deming emphasized that up to 96% of the problems and defects in a workplace were attributable to the system, not the poor work of an individual. Deming also taught core lessons such as removing fear from the workplace and not relying on empty slogans, as illustrated in his "14 Points for Management."[25] Deming also wrote that these 14 Points applied to healthcare with "a little modification,"[26] including the incorporation of some hospital terms and the following elaboration on his point about driving out fear:

> Drive out fear. We must break down the class distinctions between types of workers within the organization—physicians, nonphysicians, clinical providers versus nonclinical providers, physician to physician. Discontinue gossip. Cease to blame employees for problems of the system. Management should be held responsible for faults in the system. People need to feel secure to make suggestions. Management must follow through on suggestions. People on the job cannot work effectively if they dare not enquire into the purpose of the work that they do, and dare not offer suggestions for simplification and improvement of the system.[27]

It is often said that the Toyota approach to management and improvement is an amalgamation of the technical and engineering lessons of Henry Ford, Frederick Taylor, and others, combined with Deming's philosophy on people.

Some of Deming's key themes are found often in healthcare environments where Kaizen flourishes, including the elimination of barriers between departments, a focus on preventing errors instead of detecting them through inspection, and ongoing programs of training and self-improvement. Other lessons from Deming have been embraced less enthusiastically, as most healthcare organizations have not even considered eliminating annual performance ratings or merit pay systems.

Kaizen: One of the Two Pillars of The Toyota Way

Formally published as an internal company document in 2001, "The Toyota Way" documented the two pillars of the automaker's management philosophy:

- **Continuous Improvement:** Ongoing improvement in a structured and scientific way, in alignment with a long-term vision, by finding the root cause of problems and building consensus amongst a team.
- **Respect for People:** Engender mutual trust and respect amongst all levels and stakeholders, challenging others to improve and maximize their abilities, encouraging personal and professional growth, and recognizing our inherent human limitations.

As previously discussed, the term Kaizen is often translated from Japanese as meaning "continuous improvement." The term Kaizen spread through Toyota in the 1950s and 1960s.[28] As Jeffrey Liker wrote in his book *The Toyota Way*, Kaizen "is the process of making incremental improvements, no matter how small, and achieving the Lean goal of eliminating all waste that adds cost without adding value." Liker describes Kaizen as a "total philosophy" where employees are taught "skills for working effectively in small groups, solving problems, documenting and improving processes, collecting and analyzing data, and self-managing within a peer group."[29]

> From a 2010 Toyota publication: "Continuous Improvement implies that all employees must not let themselves become complacent about the status quo, but put forth their best ideas and efforts to seek greater added-value. In accordance with the second principle, 'Respect for People,' Toyota respects all stakeholders and believes that the success of its business is created by individual efforts and growth."[30]

"Respect for people," at Toyota, applies broadly to employees, customers, suppliers, and their communities. Respect toward employees is a richer, more complex concept than just being nice to everybody. Respect means, for one, that people are constructively challenged to perform to the best of their abilities and to improve over time. Highlighting the importance that the company places on this culture over Lean tools, the "respect for humanity system" was the original name for what would now be recognized as the "Toyota Production System."[31]

In healthcare settings, respect for people can include the following practices and mindsets, adapted from an article by Art Smalley, an American who worked for Toyota in Japan:[32]

- Providing a safe healthcare environment, for patients, employees, and clinicians
- Providing a well-organized and clean (and germ-free) environment
- Providing the equipment, supplies, and infrastructure that are needed to provide high-quality care
- Allowing for time to solve problems, rather than forcing people to cut corners on quality due to overwork or working around the same problems every day
- Neither wasting employees' time or professional abilities, nor wasting the time of patients
- Developing the latent talents and abilities of all employees and caregivers
- Having thorough and constructive dialogues in employee reviews, being honest and sincere in the leader's desire to help an employee improve
- Asking people to improve their work and providing methods for improvement

Smalley says this last point "shows the ultimate form of respect," demonstrating that management trusts their people and expects them to have a hand in the organization's long-term survival.

One way that leading hospitals show respect for people is the recognition that they should never put employees in a position where their Kaizen ideas lead to layoffs. Several hospitals, including ThedaCare, Denver Health, Avera McKennan (Sioux Falls, South Dakota), and Akron Children's Hospital, have a formal "no layoffs" or "no layoffs due to Lean" philosophy.[33] These organizations will retrain, reassign, or redeploy any displaced employees to other departments or create opportunities to work in a central Lean or Kaizen group. If employees feared losing their jobs, "Nobody would get very enthusiastic about improvement in that world," says Dr. Dean Gruner, the chief executive and president of ThedaCare.[34] IU Health Goshen Hospital has gone "17 years without layoffs" in the midst of their aggressive Kaizen program, says CEO James O. Dauge.[35]

These two mindsets, continuous improvement and respect for people, work together in a virtuous cycle. For example, if improvements are not made in quality or waiting times, that is disrespectful to the patients. If bad processes force employees to run around chasing supplies and medications or force them to constantly work around bad systems, that is disrespectful because they are not allowed to focus on their patients, nor are hospitals maximizing the use of their clinical training.

Organizations strive for continuous improvement out of respect for people, but it is that basic respect for people that helps make continuous improvement

Figure 2.4   The balancing principles of Lean and the Toyota Production System.

possible. If we do not truly listen and seek to understand the perspectives of all people in the workplace, regardless of their title or position, people will not collaborate constructively in improvement. If people feel ignored, disrespected, or devalued, they are likely to disengage from any attempts at improvement.

The way to ensure a sustained continuous improvement culture is to ensure each leader and each participant in the healthcare system practices respect for people—all stakeholders—each and every day. The principles must remain in balance, as illustrated in Figure 2.4.

Former Toyota leader Gary Convis summarized the connection by saying an environment for continuous improvement can "only be created where there is respect for people."[36]

Masaaki Imai and the Spread of Kaizen (1986)

The word Kaizen was popularized in the West by Masaaki Imai. Imai learned about Kaizen and Lean from luminaries such as Taiichi Ohno. Imai wrote simply, "Kaizen means improvement" and "Kaizen is everybody's business,"[37] expanding on that to talk about the role of employee suggestions as well as higher-level management practices required to initiate and align innovation and improvement.

Imai emphasized the human side of continuous improvement, writing, a "Japanese-style suggestion system emphasizes morale-boosting benefits and positive employee participation," while Western-style systems emphasized economic and financial incentives.[38] Herb DeBarba from the Cancer Treatment Centers of America says that, with their Kaizen approach, "stakeholder (employee) loyalty is a huge benefit," and their nurses have said "this is the first place that empowers me to make improvements."[39]

Imai also wrote that Kaizen is people oriented and process oriented, while Western management tended to focus on measures and results. The results-focused approach is still the predominant model taught in most MBA and MHA programs. One exception is a relatively new program from The Ohio State University called the Masters of Business of Operational Excellence for Healthcare, which devotes a major part of its curriculum to Lean, Six Sigma, and other process improvement models.[40]

Especially important in healthcare, Imai wrote that Kaizen efforts should focus on quality as a primary objective (as opposed to productivity), because "nobody can object when management asks for labor's cooperation by saying, 'Let's talk about quality.'" Imai emphasized, as Lean healthcare data shows today, that better quality leads to improved productivity.

> ThedaCare has published data that shows the strong correlation between improved quality, patient outcomes, and cost. For example, the health system reduced mortality from cardiac surgery from 12 deaths in 2002 (4% of cases) to just 1 death in 2009, while simultaneously reducing length of stay and cost per case by more than 20%.[41] These improvements came as the result of engaging clinicians in the redesign and improvement of their inpatient care model.

Imai's core Kaizen concepts were summarized in a 2009 article written by Gregory Jacobson, MD, and others for the journal *Academic Emergency Medicine* that described key Kaizen mindsets in a hospital setting, including the following:[42]

- Continually improve, with no idea being too small.
- A major source of quality defects is problems in the process.
- Focus change on common sense, low-cost, and low-risk improvements, not major innovations.
- All ideas are addressed and responded to in some way.
- Collect, verify, and analyze data to enact change.
- Empower the worker to enact change.

What are the high-level organizational goals that Kaizen should support? Imai wrote that, beyond the goal of long-term financial viability, Kaizen and all other management functions should support the balanced objectives of Quality, Cost, and Scheduling (QCS). In modern Lean management, these goals are often described as Safety, Quality, Delivery, Cost, and Morale (SQDCM).[43] Safety was probably self-evident and implied in Imai's view, so it was not necessary to call it out specifically. In healthcare, we can translate "Delivery" to the term "Access" and the availability of care for patients. In the SQDC framework, if an organization focuses on safety, quality, and delivery (or access), then costs will follow. This illustrates how Kaizen and Lean are different from a limited "cost-cutting" view.

> Patrick Hagan, former COO of Seattle Children's Hospital, says, "We rarely talk about cost. We talk about waste, quality, and safety, and we find our costs go down."[44] James Dague says, "If you focus on your people and high quality patient care, then the money follows."[45]

Imai followed up his first book with *Gemba Kaizen: A Commonsense, Low-Cost Approach to Management* in 1997 and still works as an active consultant worldwide in 2012.

Dr. Donald M. Berwick's Call for Kaizen (1989)

During this wave of the West's initial interest in Kaizen, a small number of healthcare leaders took notice. Dr. Donald M. Berwick is legendary in healthcare quality and patient safety improvement circles, thanks to his advocacy and education work done as the founder and chairman of the Institute for Healthcare Improvement and as the former administrator of the U.S. Centers for Medicare and Medicaid Services. In 1989, Berwick published a piece called "Continuous Improvement as an Ideal in Health Care" in the *New England Journal of Medicine*, where he wrote that continuous improvement "holds some badly needed answers for American health care."[46]

Berwick cited Imai with the definition that Kaizen is "the continuous search for opportunities for all processes to get better" and emphasizing that the self-development and the pursuit of completeness are "familiar themes in medical instruction and history." In highlighting what is different with Kaizen, Berwick criticized disciplinarian-style leaders who look to punish "bad apples" instead of improving processes. He also argued that a leader cannot be "a mere observer of problems," but instead needs to lead others toward solutions.

Berwick highlighted a number of themes, including:

■ Leaders must take the lead in continuous quality improvement, replacing blame and finger-pointing with shared goals.
■ Organizations must invest managerial time, capital, and technical expertise into quality improvement.
■ Respect for healthcare professionals must be reestablished, highlighting that they are assumed to be trying hard, acting in good faith; "people cannot be frightened into doing better" in complex healthcare systems.

While he mentioned technical quality improvement tools in the article, Berwick's summary of continuous improvement emphasized the culture change required to have everybody work together—removing fear, shame, and finger-pointing from the healthcare system.

"Medicine's Need for Kaizen" (1990)

Building on Berwick's work, Richard Smith, senior assistant editor of the noted journal *BMJ*, also cited Imai along with Deming and Joseph Juran, leading quality gurus of the time, writing, "there is every prospect that Kaizen might do for health care what it has done for Japanese industry."[47] Smith wrote, "The idea at the heart of Kaizen is that poor quality arises from bad systems rather than bad people." This idea is more widely accepted in healthcare today, thanks to the landmark 1999 study from the Institute of Medicine, *To Err is Human,* and the modern patient safety movement.

Smith's article also proposed that, to make Kaizen work, managers "must create an environment in which people are enthusiastic to identify deficiencies and work together to right them." Borrowing an idea from Deming, Smith wrote that leaders must abolish fear from the workplace, because people must be able to openly admit there are problems, as "every defect is a treasure." Smith concluded that "Kaizen should be more attractive to health workers than the pursuit and punishment of bad apples" and that Kaizen encouraged continual learning and improvement, not just reacting after a problem occurs.[48]

> In a well-known Toyota story, a Japanese leader told a North American manager that "no problems is a problem," emphasizing that a culture of openness and transparency is a critical starting point for improvement.[49] Healthcare still struggles with the open reporting of problems, as an Agency for Healthcare Research and Quality (AHRQ) study suggested more than 50% of healthcare professionals did not report any medical errors over a 12-month period due to a "blame-and-shame culture."[50] Furthermore, in a survey of 1,000 incident reports, 89% were submitted by nurses, with 2% coming from doctors;[51] 60% of these incidents were deemed preventable. So hiding problems interferes with improvement and the prevention of future errors.

Norman Bodek and American Kaizen

Norman Bodek is an American author who has played a critical role in the further spread of Kaizen practices and philosophies from Japan to the rest of the world. In the early 1980s, Bodek founded Productivity Inc., which translated and published many of the early books on Lean from Japan. He also brought several former Toyota Kaizen experts from Japan to conduct improvement sessions called "5 days and 1 night" at companies throughout the world. These sessions were a precursor to what became known as a Kaizen Blitz or Rapid Improvement Event, as described in Chapter 3.

As co-author of the 2001 book *The Idea Generator: Quick and Easy Kaizen*, Bodek shared a method for employees to document small changes they could make to their own work. He has authored two other books on Kaizen, *All You Gotta Do Is Ask* and *How to Do Kaizen*, and was the publisher of the English translation of an early book that studied Kaizen at Toyota called *40 Years, 20 Million Ideas: The Toyota Suggestion System*.

The Kaizen program at Franciscan is based upon this Quick and Easy Kaizen method, with its emphasis on documenting and sharing all of the small staff-driven improvements that are made in the workplace. Quick and Easy Kaizen emphasizes that we want (and often need) to start with Kaizens that are simple. If we start with the simple ones, we will then be more likely to adopt the habit of continuous improvement in all aspects of our life, as we learn about Kaizen and build confidence in our ability to improve. Over time, we will be able to tackle more aggressive and substantial improvements, such as Kaizen events or larger improvement projects.

Conclusion

The framework for a successful Kaizen culture was not an overnight invention. The roots of Kaizen thinking date back hundreds of years, if not longer. Today's healthcare organizations are learning from Toyota and other manufacturers that use adaptations of Lean and the Toyota Production System. Much as Toyota leaders build upon the teachings of those who came before them, healthcare organizations can, and should, allow their Kaizen philosophy to evolve, given other influences and inputs. Healthcare organizations have been talking about Kaizen for more than 20 years. Our hope is that healthcare is moving into a new era where Kaizen will be embraced more widely and more successfully.

Discussion Questions

■ What are some dysfunctions that you have experienced with suggestion boxes?
■ What are some behaviors to not repeat in a Kaizen program?
■ What are some reasons that Kaizen has not been embraced more widely in healthcare over the past 20 years? What are some of the specific reasons within your organization?
■ Why is a no-layoffs approach important for Kaizen to be successful? Is that realistic for your organization? Why or why not?
■ How would you define "respect for people" in your organization? Is the idea widely practiced?

Endnotes

1. Fujimoto, Takahiro, and Koichi Shimokawa, *The Birth of Lean: Conversations with Taiichi Ohno, Eiji Toyoda, and Other Figures who Shaped Toyota Management* (Cambridge, MA: Lean Enterprise Institute, 2009), 42.
2. O'Brien, Michael, "Suggestions, Please," Human Resource Executive Online, September 2010, http://www.hreonline.com/HRE/story.jsp?storyId=531781396 (accessed August 6, 2011).
3. Robinson, Alan G., and Sam Stern, *Corporate Creativity: How Innovation and Improvement Actually Happen* (San Fransciso: Berrett-Koehler, 1997), 67.
4. Robinson and Stern, 72.
5. Bodek, Norman, and Bunji Tozawa, *The Idea Generator: Quick and Easy Kaizen* (Vancouver, WA: PCS Press, 2001), 88.
6. Bodek and Tozawa, 90.
7. Schultz, Howard, *Onward: How Starbucks Fought For Its Life Without Losing Its Soul* (Emmaus, PA: Rodale Books, 2011), 259.
8. Robinson, Alan G., and Dean M. Schroeder, *Ideas Are Free: How the Idea Revolution Is Liberating People and Transforming Organizations* (San Francisco: Berrett-Koehler Publishers, 2006), 60.
9. GBMP, "Thinking Outside The Suggestion Box: How To Create An Idea System That Works," DVD, August, 2010.
10. Graban, Mark, "Time & Motion Studies Are Not 'Discredited,' Just How They Are Used," LeanBlog.org, May 25, 2011, http://www.leanblog.org/2011/05/time-motion-studies-are-not-discredited-just-the-way-they-are-used/ (accessed August 27, 2011).
11. Imai, Masaaki, *KAIZEN: The Key to Japan's Competitive Success* (New York: McGraw-Hill, 1986), 15.
12. Taylor, Frederick W., *The Principles of Scientific Management* (New York: Harper, 1913), 229.
13. Montgomery, David, *The Fall of the House of Labor: The Workplace, the State, and American Labor Activism, 1865–1925* (Cambridge, England: Cambridge University Press, 1989), 251.
14. Graban, Mark, "You're the Time Study Man," LeanBlog.org, November 16, 2007, http://www.leanblog.org/2007/11/youre-time-study-man/ (accessed August 15, 2011).
15. Graban, Mark and Amit Prachand, "Hospitalists: Lean Leaders for Hospitals," *Journal of Hospital Medicine*, Volume 5, Issue 6, pages 317–319, July/August 2010, http://onlinelibrary.wiley.com/doi/10.1002/jhm.813/abstract (accessed August 15, 2011).
16. Graban, Mark, *Lean Hospitals: Improving Quality, Patient Satisfaction, and Employee Engagement: 2nd edition* (New York: Productivity Press, 2011), 67.
17. Imai, 112.
18. Dinero, Donald, *Training Within Industry: The Foundation of Lean* (New York: Productivity Press, 2005), 3.
19. Graban, Mark, "Training Within Healthcare: It Is Just As Relevant in 2009 As It Was in 1944," , TWI News, January 2009, http://www.markgraban.com/wp-content/uploads/2011/04/TWI-0109Graban.pdf (accessed August 6, 2011).
20. Adele, Sister M., "Wasted Hours," Hospitals, August 1943, http://twi-institute.com/documents/healthcare_wastedhours.pdf (accessed August 6, 2011).
21. Brigh, Mary, "We Cannot Afford to Hurry," *The American Journal of Nursing*, March 1944, http://twi-institute.com/documents/healthcare_wecannotaffordtohurry.pdf (accessed August 6, 2011).
22. Robinson and Stern, 81.
23. Kenney, Charles, *Transforming Healthcare: Virginia Mason Medical Center's Pursuit of the Perfect Patient Experience* (New York: Productivity Press, 2010), 153.

24. Kenney, 154.
25. Deming, W. Edwards, *Out of the Crisis* (Cambridge MA: MIT CAES Press, 1982), 23.
26. Deming, 199.
27. Deming, 202.
28. Kato and Smalley, 4.
29. Liker, Jeffrey K., *The Toyota Way: 14 Management Principles from the World's Greatest Automaker* (New York: McGraw-Hill, 2004), 24.
30. Toyota Motor Corporation, "Relations with Employees," website, 2010 http://www.toyota-global.com/sustainability/sustainability_report/pdf/sr10_p59_p67.pdf (accessed August 15, 2011).
31. Liker, Jeffrey, and Michael Hoseus, *Toyota Culture: The Heart and Soul of the Toyota Way* (New York: McGraw-Hill, 2008), 326.
32. Smalley, Art, "How Do You Define 'Respect'?, ArtofLean.com, November 4, 2010 http://artoflean.com/blog/2011/01/05/respect-for-people/ (accessed August 15, 2011).
33. Graban, Mark, "How Lean Management Helped Hospitals Avoid Layoffs," FierceHealthcare.com, October 1, 2010, http://www.fiercehealthcare.com/story/how-lean-management-helped-hospitals-avoid-layoffs/2010-10-01 (accessed August 15, 2011).
34. Boulton, Guy, "ThedaCare's 'No Layoffs' Practice May Improve Firm," *Journal Sentinel Online*, Dec 20, 2008, http://www.jsonline.com/business/36477214.html (accessed August 15, 2011).
35. Dague, James, personal interview, July, 2011.
36. Dague.
37. Imai, xxix.
38. Imai, 112.
39. DeBarba, Herb, personal interview, July 2011.
40. The Ohio State University, "Courses," Online, http://fisher.osu.edu/mboe/curriculum/courses/ (accessed August 6, 2011).
41. Toussaint, John, and Roger Gerard, *On the Mend: Revolutionizing Healthcare to Save Lives and Transform the Industry* (Cambridge, MA: Lean Enterprise Institute, 2010), 3.
42. Jacobson, Gregory H., Nicole Streiff McCoin, Richard Lescallette, Stephan Russ, and Corey M. Slovis, "Kaizen: A Method of Process Improvement in the Emergency Department," *Academic Emergency Medicine*, Volume 16, Issue 12, pages 1341-1349, December 2009.
43. Liker, Jeffrey, and James K. Franz, *The Toyota Way to Continuous Improvement: Linking Strategy and Operational Excellence to Achieve Superior Performance* (New York: McGraw-Hill, 2011), 263.
44. Hagan, Patrick, Presentation, Healthcare Value Network event, February 3, 2011.
45. Dague.
46. Berwick, D.M., "Continuous Improvement As an Ideal in Health Care," *New England Journal of Medicine*, 1989 May 25;320(21):1424–1425.
47. Smith, Richard, "Medicine's Need for Kaizen; Putting Quality First," *BMJ*, Volume 301, 3 October 1990, 679.
48. Smith, 679.
49. Graban, Mark, "No Problems Is a Problem—Video," LeanBlog.org, May 15, 2010, http://www.leanblog.org/2010/05/no-problems-is-problem-video/ (accessed August 6, 2011).
50. Leonhardt, Kathryn, "Comprehensive Program to Promote 'Fair and Just Principles' Improves Employee Perceptions of How a Health System Responds to Errors," AHRQ website, http://www.innovations.ahrq.gov/content.aspx?id=2588 (accessed August 6, 2011).
51. AHRQ, "Patient Safety and Quality: Hospital Incident Reporting Systems Often Miss Physician High-Risk Procedure and Prescribing Errors," AHRQ website, http://www.ahrq.gov/research/mar08/0308RA2.htm (accessed August 6, 2011).

Chapter 3

Types of Kaizen

Such is the delicacy of man alone, that no object is produced to his liking. He finds that in everything there is need for improvement.

—Adam Smith

The word Kaizen is usually used in the context of continuous improvement or small incremental changes to an existing process. Over the past 20 years, however, the word has also become associated with episodic workshops, often called "Kaizen Events," which typically last for three to five days. That may seem puzzling to the reader. If a hospital department holds two or three weeklong events per year, how is that the least bit continuous? Do these events really lead to sustained improvement?

On the other hand, there is another Japanese word, "Kaikaku," which can be translated to mean "a rapid and radical change process."[1]

Kaizen = small, low-cost, low-risk continuous improvements

Kaikaku = larger, more radical changes

One can argue that the "Kaizen Event" should have really been called a "Kaikaku Event" or just an "Innovation Event," but the name has stuck. Some healthcare organizations have adopted terms like "Rapid Process Improvement Workshop" or "Rapid Improvement Event," both arguably being more accurate than "Kaizen Event." But what happens after the event? Do people go back to the old way of doing things? Are people continually improving upon that step function improvement of Kaikaku?

If we use the translation of Kaizen that means "change for the better," then we can perhaps broaden its definition to include improvements of varying size, length, and complexity. Healthcare, at times, badly needs radical change such as the complete transformation of processes or the design of an entire building.

But, as this book shows, there are also great opportunities to make thousands of small improvements, as well. We need both types of change—radical and continuous—and once we make a radical change, our patients and staff will be better served if we layer continuous improvement on top of that innovation.

The Continuous Improvement of a Lifesaving Innovation

One day in 2008, a man named Greg woke in the middle of the night with intense pain in his chest. Greg recalled, "Much like someone is standing on your chest, you know at that point you're having a heart attack." After arriving at Franciscan St. Francis Hospital, he remembers, "My whole body was shaking. I was thinking … I may not make it. I remember saying goodbye to my wife … and lots of tears … and pain." After receiving a percutaneous coronary intervention (PCI) well within the critical first 90 minutes, a procedure that opens an artery that feeds the heart muscle, he lived to talk about his experience. "My life was saved purely by the quick work of the heart physicians," he said.[2]

Greg benefited from a new protocol, EHART®, that was developed at Franciscan St. Francis Health. With this protocol, the average "door-to-balloon time" was reduced from 113 minutes to just 75 minutes. Patients receiving treatment within 90 minutes increased from 28% to 71%. Since "time is muscle," as some say,[3] the average heart attack size was reduced by 40%, and the average length of stay was reduced by two days[4] as the result of clearing the blockage sooner. Much of the overall improvement came from physician-driven systemic improvements to the process, including activation of the catheterization lab by an emergency physician (instead of waiting for a cardiologist) and the immediate transfer of the patient to the "cath lab" by an in-house transfer team.[5]

> More than 1 million Americans have heart attacks each year. About half will die. Of those who die, about half do so within one hour of the start of symptoms and before reaching the hospital. Prompt treatment of a heart attack, or myocardial infarction (MI), can help prevent or limit lasting damage to the heart and can prevent sudden death.[6]

The creation of the EHART protocol, a radical innovation (not formally driven by a Lean or Kaizen process) was not the endpoint for improvement. Rather, it was just the beginning. Thanks to dozens of Kaizen improvements, the health system not only sustained its improvements but also continuously improved door-to-balloon times and patient care. Kaizen does not involve committees or slowly unfolding projects; these small Kaizens add up to a major impact for patients, caregivers, and our healthcare organizations.

EHART Blood Pressure Cuffs	Franciscan ST. FRANCIS HEALTH
Before	**After**
Taking time digging through the bucket on top of the crash cart to try to find the correct size blood pressure cuffs. This can be problematic during an EHART® when you want to get a blood pressure (BP) in a hurry so that you can get medications in the patients.	Place a small strip of Velcro® brand hook and loop fasteners on the wall with different sizes of BP cuffs. Staff is able to quickly visualize the different sized cuff and get the proper size for the patient, and the blood pressure can be obtained quicker. 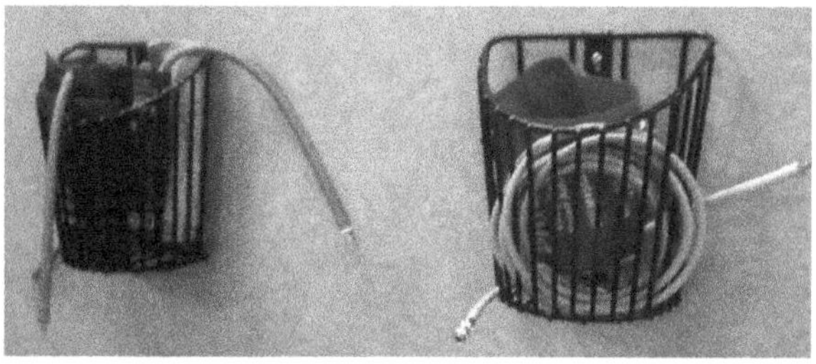

The Effect			
Improved quality of care and faster response to the needs of the patient in an acute setting.			
Name	**Supervisor**	**Date**	**Savings**
Elizabeth Black	Diana Brown, Manager	12-10-2008	Quality

Figure 3.1 EHART Blood Pressure Cuffs.

How did Kaizens at Franciscan further improve patient care? In one example, Nathan Lowder, an ER nurse, developed a Kaizen that saved more than 20 minutes during the typical patient transfer from his ER to the cath lab by having all necessary medications given to the patient while being transported in the ambulance.

In another example, Elizabeth Black, a nurse in the cath lab, noticed she was wasting valuable time during an EHART because she was always digging through a pile of different blood pressure cuffs. To reduce this waste, she quickly found some Velcro® brand hook and loop fasteners that she used to mount and organize the blood pressure cuffs of various sizes so they could be retrieved quickly. Later, maintenance ordered and installed more permanent holders, as pictured in Figure 3.1.

It is important that Kaizens are taking place on an ongoing basis, with the goal being continuously improving door-to-balloon times, improvements that help save lives.

Three Levels of Kaizen

Toyota has taught us that there are different levels of Kaizen that are practiced in a high-performing organization, as illustrated in Figure 3.2. All three types of Kaizen are based on the same Plan-Do-Study-Act (PDSA) problem-solving model and mindset.

Organizations often focus on a small number of large initiatives or projects, represented in the top portion of Figure 3.2. We need large innovations and

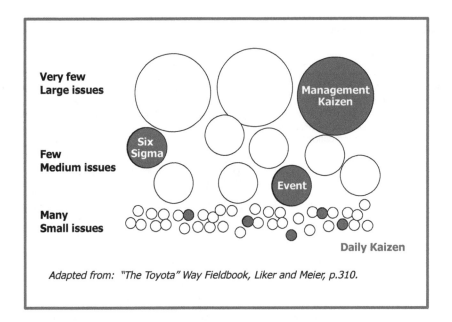

Figure 3.2   Illustration of the three levels of Kaizen improvements.

major projects, but healthcare organizations also need smaller improvements, such as weeklong improvement events and daily Kaizen.

You might know the story about a classroom demonstration by a philosophy professor where a large jar is filled with a few rocks.[7] The professor asks if the jar is full, and the students all agree that it is. In the context of healthcare improvement, these rocks might represent large improvement initiatives in an organization, such as building a new patient tower or implementing a new electronic medical records (EMR) system. Any given organization typically only has the capacity to work on a few of these problems at any given time. Many of these major improvements are, even if managed well, high cost and high risk—the opposite of small Kaizen improvements. Yet, these improvements are often very necessary. This level of improvement is often referred to as "management Kaizen" or "system Kaizen" in the Toyota framework.

Yet, as with the jar in the philosophy class, room for additional improvement still remains. In the story, the professor adds handfuls of smaller pebbles into the jar, shaking it and making room for more pebbles. What originally seemed full now has additional capacity for the right kinds of improvements. These smaller pebbles represent a middle range of problems of smaller scope and lower complexity than the large management Kaizen changes. In healthcare organizations, these can be represented by Rapid Improvement Events or Six Sigma projects.

Six Sigma is a quality improvement methodology that was created at Motorola in 1986[8] and was popularized by General Electric and their former CEO, Jack Welch, in the 1990s.[9] While Six Sigma is, like Lean, an approach for continuous quality improvement, Six Sigma is characterized by its focus on statistical analysis and the formal training of "belts" (such as lower-level Green Belts or more advanced Black Belts or Master Black Belts), people who lead defined improvement projects in an organization. To reach a "Six Sigma quality level," a process can have no more than 3.4 defects per million opportunities for error.[10] GE defines Six Sigma more broadly as a "highly disciplined process that helps us focus on developing and delivering near-perfect products and services."[11] While some healthcare organizations, such as The Johns Hopkins Hospital, use Six Sigma as part of a "Lean Sigma"[12] or "Lean Six Sigma" approach, some criticize Six Sigma as being an "elitist"[13] approach where improvement is limited to a select few who have the proper training and credentials. By comparison, Kaizen methods can be used by everybody in an organization.

A jar containing large rocks and small pebbles might once again seem full, but the professor disproves that by pouring in sand to fill the small cracks between the rocks and the pebbles. Different versions of the story end with a student pouring in water (or beer) to complete the demonstration that shows the definition of a full container depends on our context and the way we view a system.

Organizations have certain capacity for large projects and events, but there is always more capacity for daily continuous improvement. The small Kaizens done by front-line staff and their managers are represented by the sand and the water in that philosopher's jar.

The top part of Figure 3.2 represents the handful of major initiatives an organization might take on at any given time. These projects are typically owned by a senior leader and encompass an entire site or organization.

The middle range of opportunities includes issues that impact the entirety of a department or a single patient value stream. These issues are less complex than management Kaizen, yet more complex than daily Kaizen. These are problems that might need to be solved by a cross-functional or cross-departmental team who is assembled for a small project. The methods used to address these opportunities can include weeklong events, of which a large organization might have five to ten occurring in any given week, Six Sigma projects, GE work-outs, or "A3 problem solving" reports, a method being used more often in healthcare.[14]

An A3 refers to an international size of paper that is approximately 11 inches by 17 inches in size. More significantly, it is the name given to a planning and problem-solving reporting methodology that is "core to the Toyota management system."[15] An A3 is a single-page report that guides one through a structured PDSA-based problem solving approach.

Some other A3 examples appear in Chapter 7, and the A3 methodology will be discussed further in Chapter 11. One place to see and discuss A3 documents is the Lean Enterprise Institute's "A3 Dojo" site at http://www.lean.org/a3dojo/

At the bottom of Figure 3.2 are the smaller, more local problems and opportunities that can be addressed by the daily Kaizen methods presented in this book, including Quick and Easy Kaizen (Chapter 5) and Visual Idea Boards (Chapter 6). There are a "virtually unlimited"[16] number of these small improvements that can be made in an organization. Regardless of the size of the opportunity and the method used to address it, the same PDSA and Kaizen mindsets apply.

Table 3.1 shows some examples of these different levels of Kaizen in healthcare.

Table 3.1   Examples of Different Levels of Kaizen

Level	Quantity	Method(s)	Example
Large opportunities	Few	Large projects	New hospital "Lean design" effort[17]
		Major initiatives	Selection and "Lean implementation" of new electronic medical records system[18]
		12- to 16-week "Lean transformation" project	Complete renovation of a hospital laboratory, physical space, and processes[19]
Medium opportunities	More	Rapid Improvement Events (aka Workshops)	Improving patient flow for ischemic stroke patients[20]
		Six Sigma project	Reducing surgical site infections[21]
		A3 problem solving	Increasing the number of patients, hospital wide, who receive proper discharge planning[22]
Small opportunities	Most	Daily Kaizen	Adding a new gel dispenser outside of the intensive care unit
		A3 problem solving	Increasing availability of working fiber-optic endoscopes[23]
		Quick and Easy Kaizen	Updating the phone communication to parents the day before a child's surgical procedure

Imai's Three Levels of Kaizen

Masaaki Imai introduced three "segments" of improvement activity: management-oriented Kaizen, group-oriented Kaizen, and individual-oriented Kaizen.[24] There are clear parallels to the Toyota framework.

Management-oriented Kaizen are the small number of "most important and strategic issues"[25] involving large-scale systemic redesign and improvement.

Group-oriented Kaizen involves a team that is formed to work on improvements in their site. Imai wrote about the use of Kaizen to develop people, a common theme in Toyota and the Lean management philosophy, saying the Kaizen groups "were often initially formed for the purpose of stimulating cross-development among its members."[26]

Individual-oriented Kaizen includes the "almost infinite opportunity" for individuals to make local improvements by working with supervisors to implement their own suggestions. According to Imai, the starting point for Kaizen is "for the worker to adopt a positive attitude toward changing and improving the way he works," as Kaizen is considered a "morale booster."[27]

Complementary Nature of the Levels of Kaizen

These different levels of Kaizen are complementary and supportive of each other. David Meier, a consultant, author, and former group leader at Toyota's plant in Georgetown, Kentucky, teaches that he was involved in only "a handful" of formal improvement events during his ten years working at Toyota. When Toyota did conduct events, the purpose was not short-term return on investment or even the improvement itself. According to Meier, the purpose of an event was for management to *learn* about Kaizen.[28] By learning about Kaizen, this same PDSA process could be applied to larger problems (system Kaizen) or smaller problems (daily Kaizen).

In *The Toyota Way Fieldbook*, Meier emphasized, "Many organizations fail to develop an effective process for capturing opportunities from all three categories. Quite often, the small category is overlooked entirely because these opportunities are viewed as 'insignificant' or offering 'not enough bang for the buck.' In addition, the medium and large opportunities are not fully exploited due to the small number of people being trained or qualified to resolve issues."[29]

At the Cancer Treatment Centers of America (CTCA), their hospitals started with daily continuous improvement, done through the framework of an A3 problem-solving model, to build capabilities that then allowed them to also conduct larger improvement events. Herb DeBarba, vice president at CTCA said they would "rather have 1000 little improvements than one big one." DeBarba says "There are a lot of healthcare institutions doing a great job with Kaizen weeks, but it's the grassroots effort that's making us most successful and allows us to help run better Kaizen events. We have very engaged front-line staff." DeBarba added, "When we pull the teams together to run 3- to 4-day events, we rarely have to do any training on the tools and principles. We can go right to work because they've practiced Kaizen on a small scale."[30]

Three Types of Kaizen at Children's Medical Center Dallas

The core laboratory at Children's Medical Center Dallas started its Lean journey in 2007 with an initial project led by coauthor Mark. The team, comprised of six laboratory professionals (medical technologists and laboratory assistants), studied their existing layout and process flows over the course of an initial 8-week phase. The team worked with their leaders and colleagues to design a new "core cell" layout that would represent a major overhaul of the lab's physical space and work processes.[31] This radical change in the layout represented a "system Kaizen" improvement effort.

While the lab expected that the system Kaizen efforts would benefit patients (faster turnaround times), staff (a better work environment), and the hospital (better financial performance), there was interest in changing to a Lean management system, embracing Lean and Kaizen as a way of thinking toward the broader goal of creating a "learning organization."[32]

While they were working on the system Kaizen efforts, the laboratory's leaders and staff started working on small daily Kaizen improvements in their existing processes and existing space. Their methodology and many of their examples and lessons learned are shared in Chapters 6 and 7. The lab also conducted some improvement events using the GE "work-out" methodology,[33] covering the middle range of Kaizen.

The business case for the initial project was made based on the system Kaizen improvements. But, daily Kaizen was incorporated from the start, which helped build confidence in the team that they could make meaningful changes at a larger level. Once the system Kaizen was completed and the new layout was in place, the culture of continuous improvement that had developed led laboratory staff members to make small daily Kaizen improvements of that new layout.

In many traditional organizations, a major change, such as a brand new layout, would be something that people dare not challenge or criticize. Yet, at Children's, the team and leaders embraced the PDSA mindset, allowing for small Kaizens to tweak the new process. The system Kaizen layout had been well thought out and had been simulated in a number of ways, so everybody had been confident that it would work. Yet, with nearly any major change, there were small details that could not be anticipated until the new layout was really in place. The "study" phase that was conducted after the "plan" and "do" phases allowed the team to "adjust" the layout and workflow in a way that provided even better care to patients. Jim Adams, senior director of laboratory operations commented, "Every operational improvement allows you to see new barriers that you couldn't see before, which is why we encourage and celebrate the ongoing improvement of our process."[34]

Events Alone Will Not Make You Lean

It is common in healthcare, as well as other industries, that the word Kaizen is always associated with the word "event." These team-based improvement events, typically lasting three to five days, can be powerful, often resulting in dramatic changes and impressive results. Surely, weeklong improvement events have their place; however, some organizations get the impression that conducting these episodic events is the only path to improvement, as their consultant has perhaps taught them that the only way to learn Lean is by doing events. More mature Lean organizations have learned that they need to supplement events with other types of Kaizen, namely daily continuous improvement.

As Imai says, organizations cannot rely on intermittent projects. He said, in 2001, that doing a project and then "taking it easy for three months … is not every day improvement."[35] In Imai's book *Kaizen*, the idea of weeklong events or workshops did not appear at all.

Mike Rother, in *Toyota Kata*, states it directly: "Projects and workshops ≠ continuous improvement,"[36] adding, "Relying on periodic improvements and innovations alone—only improving when we make a special effort or campaign—conceals a system that is static and vulnerable."[37] This vulnerable system might include the traditional top-down organizational culture that impedes daily improvement. Projects and events do not "require any particular managerial approach," says Rother, and "this may explain some of the popularity of workshops."[38]

The best Kaizen organizations, including those in healthcare, are improving each and every day not only by changing the way front-line staff operate each day, but also changing the behaviors of leaders at all levels.

The Origins of Kaizen Events

The consulting firm Shingijitsu was founded in Japan in 1986 by a group of former Toyota engineers. Many of them had worked directly for Taiichi Ohno, one of the creators of the Toyota Production System. In 1987, the manufacturing company Danaher became the first U.S. client of Shigijitsu.[39] At Jacobs Engine Brake, one of the Danaher companies, Kaizen Events were held every six weeks. Some sources cite Masaaki Imai's Kaizen Institute as conducting the first event at Jacobs Brake in 1988.[40]

When Art Byrne left Danaher to become the CEO of Wiremold in 1991, he "personally trained hundreds of employees in Lean principles and then personally facilitated dozens and dozens of Kaizen events."[41] Even with the positive results from their events, Wiremold found that it was necessary to supplement events with an internal group who led more continuous Lean improvement efforts.[42] Reflecting upon his experience, Byrne later wrote, "While Kaizen events are an extraordinary continuous improvement delivery and deployment mechanism, it is important to make the distinction that they do not equal Lean. In fact, many people mistakenly and myopically believe that because they are doing Kaizen events, they are 'doing' Lean. This couldn't be further from the truth."[43]

Basic Structure and Format of an Improvement Event

A classic improvement event starts on Monday, ending on Thursday or Friday. Some events have their work continue through Friday, while many, like those at ThedaCare, are four-day events that have a combined "report out" meeting on Friday where each team shares its event with an audience of about 200 people.[44]

An event is a team-based approach, with the ideal size of no more than eight to ten participants. Team members should represent a diversity of different roles, departments, and experience levels, including physicians and other clinicians. The team should include some outsiders (from another department or even a patient) who can ask good questions and provide a different perspective than those who are in the middle of the work every day, in addition to those who are experts in the current process. Events are often led by outside consultants or by facilitators from an internal department, sometimes referred to as a Kaizen Promotion Office.

A typical weeklong event might have the following schedule (adapted from *The Kaizen Event Planner*[45]):

- **Monday:** Event kickoff, team training, observe and document current state process
- **Tuesday:** Design future state, brainstorm improvement ideas, select and prioritize ideas
- **Wednesday:** Design improvements, create standardized work, test the new process, get input from other stakeholders
- **Thursday:** Continue design and test cycles, gain buy-in from others, finalize standardized work, prepare training materials
- **Friday:** Train other workers, create sustainability plan, complete report, hold presentation and celebration

Events are generally action oriented, with the aim of making and testing improvements during the week. To make best use of the event time, the event week is actually part of a longer planning, execution, and follow-up cycle that might last seven to ten weeks. This time includes team selection, data collection, and other activities that help the event week run more smoothly, as well as post-event follow-ups to look at measuring improvement and updating standardized work. Many organizations measure results after the event at 30-, 60-, and 90-day intervals to ensure that the new process is being sustained.

> Improvement events have traditionally lasted a week, but they do not have to last that long. One challenge with events is the ability to free up schedules so team members can be 100% dedicated to the event for an entire week. This can be particularly difficult with physicians who would have to give up patient volume to participate, a sacrifice that impacts their paycheck in a fee-for-service environment. Some organizations have gotten creative with that challenge. For example, Barnes-Jewish Hospital (St. Louis) has created what they call a "6/3 event" where participants, particularly physicians, are only required for six hours on one day and then three hours on a day a week later. Some participants might continue working in the interim before the project is completed with the physicians. Barnes-Jewish has to choose projects with a smaller scope, given the limited time, but they have found this to be more effective than not having events at all.[46]

Additional Challenges with Weeklong Events

Even with the success of events, there are some criticisms of this approach or, at least, an overreliance on events as a transformation strategy.

For one, the schedule usually says that a dedicated event team creates standardized work on Wednesday or Thursday. What about the people who were not working that day? Most hospital departments run 24 hours a day, seven days a week and there are many part-time employees who might not be working during an event week. It is difficult or impossible to get sufficient input from all staff and stakeholders in a single day. Post-event follow-up discussions might raise an issue that some staff are "resistant" to the new standardized work, but this is quite understandable if some staff did not have a say or did not even get trained properly on the new process. In some settings, such as a small primary care physician practice, a weeklong event could more easily involve everybody who works in that area. The event team can get input from others and gain agreement on the new process in meetings after the workday is over.

Additionally, one could argue that an improvement event schedule that says "plan for sustainability" on Friday has already waited too long for any changes to be sustainable. The time to plan for sustainability is at the beginning of the project. The traditional model of an 8 to 5, Monday through Friday, event might have to evolve for a 24/7 workplace. An effective event might need to run for more than a week and it might need to run on nights and weekends to get the right input from everybody. That sort of approach might gain more "buy-in," leading to more sustainability than would a desire to force people to follow a new process that was created by others.

Another major challenge with events can be the lack of sustainability of improvement ideas generated during that week. Many organizations find that, after an event, people go back to the old way of working. You might ask, "Why would people go back to the old way of doing things if it was really better for patients and the organization?" Reverting to old methods could mean that a change was forced through, it was not really an improvement, people were not properly trained on the new process, or there is a lack of leadership to work through the difficulties of creating change in an organization.

Even Virginia Mason, with all of its success, has struggled to sustain improvements that came out of RPIWs. As reported in 2004, they were "only holding the gains on about 40% of those changes, partially because it is easy to slip back into old ways of doing things if there is a lack of accountability and follow-through."[74] One could say they applied Kaizen to their RPIW process; by 2011, their leaders reported that 90% of projects showed sustained results after 90 days, but only 50% held results and methods 6 or 12 months out.[75] It is still far from ideal to be repeating the same improvement event, because the first did not lead to a result that was embraced and sustained by staff.

There is nothing inherently bad about the weeklong improvement event structure, but the details of its use should be thought through carefully in complex healthcare settings.

Impressive Results from Kaizen in Healthcare

One reason many in healthcare equate Kaizen with events is the success of organizations like ThedaCare and Virginia Mason Medical Center, both of which have used weeklong events and daily continues improvement in their Lean journeys.

Virginia Mason Medical Center

Virginia Mason Medical Center (VMMC) has been recognized for using Rapid Process Improvement Workshops (RPIWs) as a cornerstone of its "Virginia Mason Production System" (VMPS), one example of a hospital that learned how to conduct events directly from Shingijitsu.[47] Thanks to the improvements that come from its RPIWs, VMMC providers are able to spend more time with patients, leading to better care as well as higher patient and staff satisfaction.[48] Additionally, bedsores were reduced from 8% to 2%, meaning that 838 patients each year avoided a type of harm that is increasingly considered to be preventable.[49] As a result of these quality and safety improvements, the hospital's professional liability insurance rates fell almost 50% from 2004 to 2009, a clear indicator of the program's quantifiable improvements.[50]

While receiving less publicity than the RPIWs, Virginia Mason has also used an approach to daily Kaizen called the "Everyday Lean Idea" (ELI) program. This program was started in 2005, while RPIWs were being started and before the formal VMPS name was adopted. The approaches work together, as Jennifer Phillips, innovation director said, "We have a range of improvement systems, but ELI is designed for small problems. It's not the only method and neither is RPIW." She added, "We're getting better at triaging problems to the right approach" as issues arise.[51]

One RPIW was focused on reducing operating room turnaround times from the baseline average of 30 minutes, allowing them to increase the utilization of existing rooms. The workshop team studied the existing work to find activities that were done in the room that could be safely performed outside the operating room. This allowed some prep or recovery steps to take place while another patient was in the room.

One activity that took time was the movement and positioning of patients from a gurney to the OR table. The team identified a type of bed that was versatile enough to be used for prep, procedure, and recovery, saving time and the need for staff to lift patients.[52] While that Kaizen required spending money, it was the type of case where the improved OR productivity more than paid for the beds.

Other RPIW-driven improvements include the creation of a safe anteroom next to the OR where instrument prep could take place before a patient was brought in. The anteroom has its own air flow and exchanges required to ensure sterility and to get approval from the State of Washington. To reduce the time required to connect a patient's multiple leads, VMMC started using what they call "the brick," a product that allows the patient's leads to be connected in advance to the brick which would then be connected to the machines, again saving time.[53]

After the RPIWs, VMMC was able to perform 140 cases a week in four rooms, compared to 100 previously—a 40% improvement. Turnover time was reduced from more than 30 minutes to less than 15. Surgery prep time, from setup to suture, was reduced from 106 minutes to 85.[54]

Phillips says she describes the Everyday Lean Idea program as an approach for "workshop avoidance," as, again, certain types of improvement do not require the full structure of an event or an RPIW, so "you just tackle it."[55] Because "staff see the problems every day,"[56] the ELI program is focused on the small-scale problems that people can address quickly in their own work area. One ELI improvement involved staff members taking a small action to improve communication about patients who had fallen previously or were generally a higher fall risk. A small laminated red star was added to the fall alert flags that were already being used outside of patient rooms. The idea worked and was spread to other floors after that initial testing.[57] Phillips added, "We're trying to create a culture where staff have permission and the capability to just fix things and make it better—to make it part of their everyday work."[58]

The scope of ELI improvements is intended to be "something within your control," said Phillips, adding that it "can be a challenge" when an improvement opportunity is outside of your control. VMMC sees some collaborative ELI efforts across departmental boundaries, but they are still working to improve communication about ideas that cross silos. "VMMC is working to create a strong culture of readily accepting feedback from another department and finding the time to work together on improvement," Phillips added.[59]

Using ELI with other Kaizen methods (including weeklong RPIWs), Kaizen Events (which are shorter in duration at VMMC), and "3P" exercises[60] (for designing physical spaces) allows VMMC to create a culture where improvement is both top-down and bottom-up. Ana Anurdhika, a Kaizen specialist, said that there has been an "evolution" at their hospital from thinking about imposing RPIWs on people "to meet my own agenda" to thinking more about "getting ideas from the staff."[61] With Kaizen, leaders can set directions and goals for improvements that contribute to high-level strategic aims; Kaizen is not a traditional top-down approach, where leaders dictate improvements or actions to their employees.

ThedaCare

ThedaCare has been using Lean principles since 2003. Initially, Lean education and training was done exclusively through the use of weeklong Rapid Improvement Events (RIEs), leading to $27 million in savings over the first four years.[62] Through a series of RIEs over a number of years, ThedaCare reduced the "door-to-balloon" time for Code STEMI patients from an average of 92 minutes to just 37 minutes, and CyberKnife waiting time was reduced from 26 days to just 6, showing that Kaizen methods could not only reduce costs and improve quality but could also improve access and reduce waiting times for patients.

ThedaCare's consultants initially insisted, "The only way to learn Lean is to get out to 'gemba' and do Kaizen [event] work."[63] ThedaCare's leaders realized, however, that with 5,500 employees in 40 sites, "getting each employee onto an RIE… proved impossible even after seven years of nonstop Kaizen. Another method had to be found. The RIEs could not do all the teaching and training."[64] ThedaCare eventually moved beyond a sole reliance on weeklong events.

> **Gemba:** A Japanese word meaning the "actual place," used for the place where value-adding work is done,[65] such as an exam room, the laboratory, an operating room, or the cafeteria.

To supplement the learning from RIEs, ThedaCare created Lean and Kaizen awareness training for all staff members. They have also created a leadership development curriculum and mentoring program that helps teach people to be "Lean leaders." Kim Barnas, a senior vice president at Thedacare, said, "The ultimate arrogance is to change the way people work, but not to change the way we manage."[66] ThedaCare's goal is to develop people and leaders to be able to solve problems and improve performance every day, not just through RIEs.

As ThedaCare's improvement system matured, it became more of an ongoing management system that focused on what they call "continuous daily improvement" (CDI). As of 2011, it is expected that 80% of their improvement comes from CDI activities.[67] ThedaCare reports that there were 3663 documented improvements in 2010, with a goal to double that number in 2011, which would be about 1.2 improvements per employee.[68] They ended 2011 with 9104 improvements, far more than their goal.

Examples of CDI improvement activities that were initiated by staff include:

- Designating a standardized location for storing open patient care items in their room
- Finding an easier way to ambulate patients who need oxygen
- Creating a better list of medications for discharged patients to avoid confusion
- Figuring out how to have palliative care or hospice available on the weekend
- Teaching or reminding housekeeping where isolation signs are supposed to be stored[69]

John Poole, senior vice president for the ThedaCare Improvement System, said CDI is "the hard work in the Lean world: culture change, day by day."[70] He reflected further on their evolution, saying:

> For several years, we were harvesting the low-hanging fruit, doing kaizen events and RIEs that took obvious waste out of value streams. It felt gut wrenching at the time, but in hindsight, it was the easy 20 percent of needed change. We hadn't yet created a culture of continuous improvements. We didn't have good development plans for those who would manage and supervise in the new environment, and we didn't know what the new environment would look like. We had the mechanics down, but we did not have a sustainable, reliable system. Now, the whole human side of Lean is unfolding before us.[71]

Dean Gruner, MD, the chief executive officer of ThedaCare talked about staff members generating ideas for improvement and then helping categorize them into one of the following types of improvements, depending on how complicated they are, requiring either:

- Just a few hours of work
- More thought and a complete A3 (or, as they call it, a PDSA)
- A full Rapid Improvement Event cycle[72]

ThedaCare leaders coach their employees to connect each improvement to one or more of the organization's "true north" objectives, which are customer satisfaction, safety and quality, people, and financial stewardship.[73]

Not All Kaizen Organizations Use Events

Some organizations have embraced Kaizen and have achieved great results from Lean management practices without relying on weeklong events or, in some cases, not using any at all.

Avera McKennan Uses System Kaizen and Daily Kaizen

Avera McKennan Hospital and University Health Center (Sioux Falls, South Dakota) is a 510-bed facility that is part of Avera Health. The hospital started its journey in 2004 in its laboratory, as many hospital labs in that period were early adopters of Lean methods.[76] Avera McKennan embraced a two-pronged approach of large multi-month transformation projects along with ongoing continuous improvement, including an approach they call "Bright Ideas." All employees at Avera McKennan have received training in Lean methods, and their "Excellence in Service and Process" program is a major part of their organization's strategy. Avera McKennan has conducted Lean transformation improvements in other departments, including the emergency department, pharmacy, women's center, and inpatient units.[77]

Fred Slunecka, formerly the regional president of Avera McKennan Hospital and now the chief operating officer of Avera Health, argues that improvement events are most effective when used after a more thorough system Kaizen effort. Slunecka says a longer project is the only way "you can gather all the relevant data, test all the alternatives, and achieve the buy-in of a large group of employees" for major change.[78] Slunecka argues that health care redesign is too complex to accomplish in a week, saying, "I believe that doing *just* Kaizen Events is like applying so many Band-Aids." Slunecka says he is aware of only one event that was attempted in the Avera McKennan pharmacy. He was unimpressed with the results, saying, "After a solid week of work by the brightest and most expensive minds in the building, the only change that was successfully maintained over a month's time was the relocation of a printer!"

Kathy Maass, director of process excellence, whose team runs the longer Lean transformation projects internally, commented:

> Most health care processes are complex and the implementation methodology we use grants staff the time needed to incorporate safety, quality, and efficiency into the standard work.
>
> We have experimented some with the implementation methodology and have done some shorter projects. While this takes fewer resources from a busy department, employee engagement can be a challenge,

since the front-line staff is less involved with data collection. The most successful projects are the ones where the front-line staff gathers the data and develops the standard work.[79]

Avera McKennan's experience shows how different levels of Kaizen fit together into a cohesive whole. Avera McKennan started with a kaikaku [radical change] improvement of their laboratory's layout and processes, followed by ongoing Kaizen improvements, said Leo Serrano, director of laboratories at Avera McKennan. Serrano recounts how the lab started with their large system Kaizen project in 2004. This was followed by a number of 6- to 8-week projects, or group Kaizens in Imai's framework, in 2005, conducted with the full participation of staff. Serrano says the lab conducts a formal evaluation every two years as a small group Kaizen, with individual Kaizens being done continuously (using "Bright Ideas"), with team members implementing their ideas after being evaluated together with lab leadership. Serrano concludes, "We now have a group of Lean trained individuals, and we are all committed to maintaining the hard won gains. It is a cultural change, and now our staff do individual Kaizens without realizing that it is a Kaizen; it's simply the way we do things around here."[80]

Kaizen Leads to Innovation at Franciscan

Franciscan, to date, has not done many RIEs, but they plan on using that approach more often in the future in conjunction with other modes of Kaizen. Their Kaizen leaders wanted to build maturity and experience with daily Kaizen before taking on larger events. Franciscan's view is that methods like Six Sigma, Lean, RIEs, and Quick and Easy Kaizen all need to support and encourage continuous daily improvement and building a Kaizen culture as a way of life. Kaizen needs to be taught and integrated into everyone's thinking from the top level to the front line.

> *We define innovation as the successful implementation of creative ideas within an organization.*[81]
>
> **—Theresa Amabile**
> *Professor and Director of Research*
> *Harvard Business School*

At Franciscan, Kaizen got the innovation flywheel spinning. Keith Jewell, COO, said, "Kaizen started the innovation journey for us. We were innovative 'in pockets.' Now we have 4,000 people whose job is to innovate every day—to reduce costs, and improve quality, productivity, safety, and satisfaction."

When people think of innovation, they think of major breakthroughs. Although many may not realize it, daily Kaizen is a form of incremental innovation—it is just that the innovations are usually small.

Charles A. O'Reilly III, professor at Stanford University, and Michael L. Tushman, professor at Harvard Business School, studied 35 recent and significant breakthrough innovation attempts, and they conclude, "to flourish over the long run, most companies need to maintain a variety of innovation efforts."[82] They claim that for organizations to be most successful at innovation, they need to pursue not only breakthrough innovations, but also incremental innovations, which they define as small improvements in existing products and operations.

Studies at Procter & Gamble, Lego, and other organizations have shown that a distinguishing characteristic of highly innovative organizations is their willingness to try things and fail.[83] Highly innovative organizations are made up of people who are more willing to try something to learn and see if it will make them better. They look at failure as an important way to learn. They are also much faster at making adjustments to those things they try that are not working as well and much less likely to give up on improvement efforts. This is the PDSA cycle in practice.

In innovative organizations, employees are more willing to:[84]

- deeply understand customer desires
- look for opportunities, especially to better serve customers
- identify solutions, from anyone and anywhere
- test those solutions and learn from failure
- adjust quickly and rethink solutions through iterative cycles
- decide on and institutionalize the current best solution

At its core, Kaizen is about developing a culture of innovation, as the goals of large-scale innovation and continuous improvement are similar—to make something better. If Kaizen is used as a core of cultural transformation, it can develop a workforce that rethinks and improves the products and services that an organization provides in ways both large and small.

Conclusion

Kaizen is proving to be an increasingly important part of Lean transformation efforts and healthcare improvement. When an organization takes a narrow view of Kaizen, such as equating it only with small improvements or only with weeklong events, success may be limited or unsustainable. We see that "change for the better" can come in different forms, ranging from major initiatives to daily continuous improvement. More importantly, these modes of improvement are compatible and mutually sustaining, because they are all based on the PDSA process and the scientific method. There are many different paths on the Kaizen journey, where some organizations start with smaller daily Kaizen improvements and then progress to larger changes, like the CTCA, while others have taken the opposite approach, such as Avera McKennan. Finally, as organizations like ThedaCare are demonstrating, these Kaizen activities should be tied to the strategy and goals of the broader organization, in addition to individuals making their own work easier.

Discussion Questions

- How would you determine if a Kaizen idea leads to a large "system Kaizen" initiative, a weeklong RIE or RPIW, or a small "daily Kaizen" improvement?
- Has your organization faced any challenges related to weeklong improvement events?
- For your organization, does it seem better to start with events and large initiatives, working toward daily continuous improvement or to start with small changes, working up to events?

Endnotes

1. Bodek, Norman, *Kaikaku: The Power and Magic of Lean* (Vancouver, WA: PCS Press, 2004), 363.
2. St. Francis Hospitals, "St. Francis Heart Center Shares Greg's story," website http://www.stfrancishospitals.org/Heart/DesktopDefault.aspx?tabid=49 (accessed July 8, 2011).
3. Toussaint, John, and Roger Gerard, *On the Mend: Revolutionizing Healthcare to Save Lives and Transform the Industry* (Cambridge, MA: Lean Enterprise Institute, 2010), 51.
4. Toussaint, 51.
5. Khot Umesh N., Michele L. Johnson, Curtis Ramsey, Monica B. Khot, Randall Todd, Saeed R. Shaikh, and William J. Berg, "Emergency Department Physician Activation of the Catheterization Laboratory and Immediate Transfer to an Immediately Available Catheterization Laboratory Reduce Door-to-Balloon Time in ST-Elevation Myocardial Infarction," *Circulation* 2007, 116:67–76: originally published online June 11, 2007, http://circ.ahajournals.org/content/116/1/67.full.pdf?keytype=ref&ijkey=Js7FdI4iizHXh0N (accessed August 7, 2011).
6. St. Francis Hospitals, "Heart Attack Care, website http://www.stfrancishospitals.org/DesktopDefault.aspx?tabid=426 (accessed July 8, 2011).
7. Author Unknown, "Rocks in the Jar," website, http://syque.com/stories/discovered/rocks_jar.htm (accessed August 7, 2011).
8. Motorola, "Six Things to Know About the History of Six Sigma," Motorola.com, 2004, https://mu.motorola.com/six_sigma_lessons/contemplate/assembler.asp?page=history_been_around (accessed August 7, 2011).
9. Process Quality Associates, "The Evolution of Six Sigma," website, http://www.pqa.net/ProdServices/sixsigma/W06002009.html (accessed August 8, 2011).
10. Pyzdek, Thomas, "Motorola's Six Sigma Program," *Quality Digest Online*, 1997, http://www.qualitydigest.com/dec97/html/motsix.html (accessed August 8, 2011).
11. General Electric, "Making Customers Feel Six Sigma Quality," website, http://www.ge.com/sixsigma/makingcustomers.html (accessed August 8, 2011).

12. Johns Hopkins Medicine, "Applying Lean Sigma," website, http://www.hopkins-medicine.org/innovation_quality_patient_care/areas_expertise/lean_sigma/ (accessed August 8, 2011).
13. Micklewright, Mike, "Black Belt for Sale," *Quality Digest Online,* http://www.qualitydigest.com/print/4366 (accessed August 8, 2011).
14. Jimmerson, Cindy, *A3 Problem Solving for Healthcare* (New York: Productivity Press, 2007), 35.
15. Shook, John, *Managing to Learn* (Cambridge, MA: Lean Enterprise Institute, 2008), vi.
16. Liker, Jeffrey, and David Meier, *The Toyota Way Fieldbook* (New York: McGraw-Hill, 2005), 313.
17. Wellman, Joan, Howard Jeffries, and Pat Hagan, *Leading the Lean Healthcare Journey* (New York: Productivity Press, 2010), 217.
18. Bowman, Dan, "Talking Lean Management and EMRs with Simpler's Mike Chamberlain," Fierce Healthcare, June 24, 2009, http://www.fiercehealthcare.com/story/q-mike-chamberlain-simpler-healthcare/2009-06-24 (accessed August 8, 2011).
19. ValuMetrix Services, "Midland Memorial Hospital Uses Lean to Speed Testing As Much As 42%, Frees Up 5 FTEs and 775 Sq. Ft. of Floor Space," case study, 2008, http://www.valumetrixservices.com/sites/default/files/client_results_pdf/CS_Midland_Lab_OC10257.pdf (accessed August 8, 2011).
20. Toussaint and Gerard, 51.
21. AHRQ, "Six-Sigma Inspired Workflow Redesign Leads to Better Adherence to Evidence-Based Protocols and Fewer Infections for Surgery Patients," *AHRQ Innovations Exchange,* http://innovations.ahrq.gov/content.aspx?id=2102 (accessed August 8, 2011).
22. Jimmerson, Cindy, *Value Stream Mapping for Healthcare Made Easy* (New York, NY: Productivity Press, 2010), 98.
23. Jimmerson, *Value Stream Mapping,* 110.
24. Imai, Masaaki, *KAIZEN: The Key to Japan's Competitive Success* (New York: McGraw-Hill, 1986), 81.
25. Imai, 82.
26. Imai, 97.
27. Imai, 111.
28. Graban, Mark, "The Purpose of Kaizen Events," LeanBlog.org, November 5, 2009, http://www.leanblog.org/2009/11/purpose-of-kaizen-events/ (accessed August 8, 2011).
29. Liker and Meier, 309.
30. DeBarba, Herb, Personal Interview, July 2011.
31. Adams, Jim and Mark Graban, "CMCD's Lab Draws on Academics, Automakers, and Therapists to Realize Its Own Vision of Excellence," *Global Business and Organizational Excellence*, DOI: 10.1002/joe.20383, May/June 2011, 17.
32. Adams and Graban, 17.
33. Ulrich, Dave, Steve Kerr, and Ron Ashkenas, *The GE Work-Out* (New York: McGraw-Hill, 2002), 1.
34. Adams, Jim, personal interview, September 2011.
35. Imai, Masaaki, "Definition of Kaizen," *YouTube,* January 19, 2010. http://www.youtube.com/watch?v=jRdTFis4-3Q&feature=related (accessed August 8, 2011).
36. Rother, Mike, *Toyota Kata: Managing People for Improvement, Adaptiveness and Superior Results* (New York: McGraw-Hill, 2009), 11.
37. Rother, 11.
38. Rother, 26.

39. Hamel, Mark, *Kaizen Event Fieldbook: Foundation, Framework, and Standard Work for Effective Events* (Dearborn, MI, Society of Manufacturing Engineers, 2009), xv.
40. Superfactory, Lean Manufacturing History and Timeline, http://www.superfactory.com/content/timeline.html (accessed November 30, 2011).
41. Hamel, xvi.
42. Hamel, xvi.
43. Hamel, xvi.
44. Toussaint, John, "John Shook Visits ThedaCare," website, http://www.createhealth-carevalue.com/blog/post/?bid=40 (accessed August 7, 2011).
45. Martin, Karen and Mike Osterling, *The Kaizen Event Planner: Achieving Rapid Improvement in Office, Service, and Technical Environments* (New York: Productivity Press, 2007),103.
46. Graban, Mark, "LeanBlog Podcast #76—Dr. David Jaques, Lean in Surgical Services," October 14, 2009, http://www.leanblog.org/2009/10/leanblog-podcast-76-dr-david-jaques/ (accessed August 7, 2011).
47. Shigujitsu USA, "Interview with Dr. Gary Kaplan, Virginia Mason Medical Center," website, http://www.shingijutsuusa.com/testimonials.html (accessed August 7, 2011).
48. Virginia Mason Medical Center, "VMPS Facts," website, 2010, https://www.virginia-mason.org/workfiles/pdfdocs/press/vmps_fastfacts.pdf (accessed August 7, 2011).
49. Brophy, Andy, and John Bicheno, *Innovative Lean* (Buckingham, England: PICSIE Books, 2010), 141.
50. Virginia Mason Medical Center, "Innovation in Health Care," website, http://www.virginiamasoninstitute.org/body.cfm?id=136&fr=true (accessed August 7, 2011).
51. Phillips, Jennifer, personal interview July 2011.
52. Kenney, Charles, *Transforming Healthcare: Virginia Mason Medical Center's Pursuit of the Perfect Patient Experience* (New York: Productivity Press, 2010), 99.
53. Kenney, 100.
54. Kenney, 101.
55. Phillips, Jennifer, Personal interview, July, 2011.
56. Kenney, 162.
57. Kenney, 163.
58. Kenney, 163.
59. Phillips.
60. Grunden, Naida, *Lean-Led Hospital Design: Creating the Efficient Hospital of the Future* (New York: Productivity Press, 2012), 36.
61. Kenney, 162.
62. Toussaint and Gerard, 3.
63. Toussaint and Gerard, 127.
64. Toussaint and Gerard, 128.
65. Marchwinski, Chet, and John Shook, *Lean Lexicon* (Brookline, MA: Lean Enterprise Institute, 2003), 23.
66. Barnas, Kim, "ThedaCare's Business Performance System: Sustaining Continuous Daily Improvement Through Hospital Management in a Lean Environment," The Joint Commission Journal on Quality and Patient Safety, September 2011, Volume 37, Number 9, 390.
67. ThedaCare Center for Healthcare Value, "Thinking Lean at Thedacare: Strategy Deployment, DVD (Appleton, WI: ThedaCare Center for Healthcare Value), 2011.
68. Barnas, 390.
69. Graban, Mark, visit to ThedaCare, June 24, 2011.

70. Tonkin, Lea A.P., and Michael Bremer, "ThedaCare's Culture of Continuous Daily Improvements," *Target*, Volume 25, Number 1, 2009, 8.

71. Tonkin and Bremer, 7.

72. Graban, Mark, "Podcast #119—Dr. Dean Gruner, Strategy Deployment at ThedaCare," LeanBlog.org, May 31, 2011, http://www.leanblog.org/124 (accessed August 27, 2011).

73. Toussaint and Gerard, 177.

74. St. Martin, Christina, "Seeking Perfection in Health Care: Applying the Toyota Production System to Medicine," Performance and Practices of Successful Medical Groups: 2006 Report Based on 2005 Data, Medical Group Management Association, 20.

75. Patterson, Sarah, presentation, Institute for Healthcare Improvement National Forum, December 7, 2011.

76. Graban, Mark, *Lean Hospitals: Improving Quality, Patient Satisfaction, and Employee Engagement: 2nd edition* (New York: Productivity Press, 2011), 217.

77. Graban, 218.

78. Slunecka, Fred, Email correspondence, 2009.

79. Maass, Kathy, Email correspondence, 2009.

80. Serrano, Leo, Email correspondence, 2011.

81. Amabile, Teresa M., Regina Conti, Heather Coon, Jeffrey Lazenby, and Michael Herron, "Assessing the Work Environment for Creativity," *Academy of Management Journal*, vol. 39, No. 5 (Oct., 1996), p. 1155.

82. O'Reilly, Charles A., III, and Michael L. Tushman, "The Ambidextrous Organization," *Harvard Business Review* (April 2004), pp. 74–81.

83. Lafley, A.G., and Ram Charan, *The Game-Changer: How You Can Drive Revenue and Profit Growth with Innovation* (New York, NY, Crown Business, 2008), p. 15.

84. Lafley, 243–245.

Chapter 4

Moving Toward a Kaizen Culture

Employee ideas are key to building a culture of high performance.

—Alan G. Robinson and Dean M. Schroeder[1]

Jenny Phelps, a nurse on the Franciscan 8-Tower nursing unit, noticed a breakdown in communication with food services personnel regarding whether or not a patient could have food. She decided to create a sign to signal when patients under her care could eat. After a brief chat with her supervisor, she presented the idea to the unit staff council, and they approved the idea. Jenny had the hospital print shop print and laminate some signs and tested them on her off day. Other nurses in the department liked them right away because the signs could remain at the doorway of the patient's room, being flipped over to change from "food allowed" to "NPO" (a Latin abbreviation for nothing by mouth), as shown in Figure 4.1.

Within a week, the entire 36-bed nursing unit was using the new signs. The unit's manager, Christa Smiley, said, "In the past this wouldn't have happened so fast. It would have taken weeks and months and committee meetings, and convincing and selling. Now my nurses are getting used to seeing a good idea and quickly adopting the change. We now have a culture where improvement and change can happen faster and more effectively because everyone is part of the change culture."

The Real Goal—Cultural Transformation

When coauthor Joe joined Franciscan as an employee in 2006, he asked Dr. Paul Strange, the vice president of quality services, what he envisioned as the goal for their Lean Six Sigma program. Dr. Strange said, "The real goal is a cultural *transformation* of our organization to one which *constantly seeks to improve* the

Figure 4.1 NPO signage-employee initiative helps prevent nutrition errors.

quality of medical outcomes, make our processes safer, and to make our care more cost-effective."

They set about understanding the organization's current state, what the future state needed to be, and how to create the required cultural change. In the past, improvement was the domain of certain personnel, such as performance improvement specialists. The new Lean Six Sigma program at Franciscan was poised to expand involvement much more widely, but it was not going to the entire organization anytime soon. A year into that program, there were two full-time Lean Six Sigma Black Belts and a few part-time belts. The Six Sigma projects were four to six months in length and averaged 15 participants. The Lean events were shorter, but still required considerable preparation and follow-up time. Franciscan could only complete about ten Lean or Six Sigma projects each each year, and, at that rate, it would take 26 years to involve all 4,000 employees.

The healthcare environment was getting more competitive. If Franciscan stayed on its current course, the future looked troubling, and leadership was concerned. Furthermore, changes were coming to healthcare faster and faster each year. They looked five years out and realized that the existing project-based Lean Six Sigma program could not grow fast enough to make the needed changes.

To make the long-term changes required at Franciscan, it was clear that everyone needed to be engaged in improvement. If a cultural transformation was needed, that meant a transformation of all employees. Franciscan's leaders were aware that transforming others is an illusion, and they realized that people must willingly transform themselves. So how do you get 4,000 people to want to do that? Kaizen was part of the answer.

Transformation starts by rethinking one's view of the world. Kaizen is more than something that is done—it is a way of thinking. Once the way of thinking permeates an organization and is practiced daily, it becomes part of the organization's culture. This chapter will explore what a culture of Kaizen looks like, some of the vital skills of a Kaizen culture, and how to start creating that culture.

What a Kaizen Culture Feels Like

"When we first started our Kaizen journey, it didn't strike me as terribly impactful that some people were organizing their supply drawers," said Keith Jewell, COO at Franciscan. "What convinced me about the importance of Kaizen was the culture that I started to see forming. Getting people to think differently and to focus on improvement as a way of life was a worthwhile goal. It was the culture we needed to create in order to prepare ourselves for the coming changes in our healthcare environment. We are significantly changing our organization to respond to those changes and Kaizen is a vital part of our transformation."

You know you work in a Kaizen culture when:

- Everyone is engaged.
- Everyone is relentlessly searching for opportunities to improve.
- You have control over your workplace.
- Patients and families are happy.
- Staff and physicians are happy.
- Work and patient care flow like clockwork.
- The workplace is clean, orderly, and safe.
- Everyone works together.
- Everything gets questioned.

Everyone Is Engaged

Kaizen is about engagement. Engagement is a term that describes a combination of employee loyalty, commitment and motivation. A recent report defines full engagement as "an alignment of maximum job satisfaction ('I like my work and do it well') with maximum job contribution ('I help achieve the goals of my organization')."[2] The report estimates that only one in three employees worldwide is engaged, with one in five being actively disengaged, meaning they are "disconnected from organizational priorities, often feel underutilized, and are clearly not getting what they need from work."[3] Employees become more strongly engaged when they contribute to making the organization better. Studies show that people want to be involved in decisions related to their work and workspace.

As a BlessingWhite study says, "Engaged employees are not just committed. They are not just passionate or proud. They have a line-of-sight on their own future and on the organization's mission and goals. They are enthused and in gear, using their talents and discretionary effort to make a difference in their employer's quest for sustainable business success."[4] A Kaizen culture has this level of engagement, personal mastery, and alignment.

A 2011 survey found that 32% of workers in the United States are "seriously considering" leaving their organization—up significantly from 23% in 2005. Another 21% are not necessarily planning to leave, but they have an unfavorable view of their employers, and they have low scores on key measures of engagement.[5] With the healthcare industry facing major shortages of key personnel, including pharmacists, primary care physicians, nurses, and medical technologists, it is imperative to increase employee engagement to help attract and retain people. A 2007 study showed 13% of registered nurses had switched jobs in the first year of their career and 37% "felt ready to change jobs."[6] Money not spent on turnover can be invested into patient care and existing employees.

James Dague, CEO of IU Health Goshen Hospital, focuses on improving retention, because it can cost $65,000 to replace an employee and much more than that for a nurse or a physician. Increased retention can be the best form of cost reduction, and Dague says, "That's how you can justify honing people's skills to make them more satisfied."[7]

According to an oft-cited 1946 study[8] that has been replicated more recently with similar results,[9] the top two things employees want are appreciation and involvement. The Kaizen methodologies described in this book increase involvement and emphasize appreciation and recognition (which, again, does not necessarily mean financial recognition). Table 4.1 shows the top ten things that employees want in the workplace. The practice of Kaizen directly addresses most of those employee desires.

Table 4.1   Top Ten Things That Employees Want in the Workplace

What Employees Want
1. Full appreciation for work done
2. Feeling "in" on things and involved
3. Sympathetic help on personal problems
4. Job security
5. Good wages
6. Interesting work
7. Promotion and growth opportunities
8. Personal loyalty
9. Good working conditions
10. Tactful discipline

Drivers of Engagement

A 2005 Towers Perrin worldwide survey of more than 86,000 employees gives the top ten drivers of workplace engagement, as shown in Table 4.2.[10] Drivers four and eight in the list indicate that employees want to be involved in decisions about their work. Drivers one and two indicate that employees value learning new skills. Kaizen enhances both learning and involvement, especially when an organization is focused on driver five—customer and patient satisfaction.

Before this culture change took place at Franciscan, certain people were in charge of improvement, certain people were in charge of quality, certain people were in charge of finance, and everyone had their own siloed interests to look after. With a Kaizen culture, everyone is implementing improvements,

Table 4.2   Top Ten Drivers of Workplace Engagement

Top Engagement Drivers
1. Opportunities to learn and develop new skills
2. Improved my skills and capabilities over the last year
3. Reputation of organization as a good employer
4. Input into decision making in my department
5. Organization focuses on customer satisfaction
6. Salary criteria are fair and consistent
7. Good collaboration across units
8. Appropriate amount of decision-making authority to do my job well
9. Senior management acts to ensure organization's long-term success
10. Senior management's interest in employees' well-being

and everyone is accountable and takes ownership for their part in making the healthcare organization extraordinary in multiple dimensions, including quality, patient safety, and cost. Masaaki Imai stresses that real culture change occurs when Kaizen is practiced daily by everyone in an organization, "from the CEO to the janitor."[11]

Franciscan COO Jewell said, "Employees want to make contributions, but sometimes they feel they need to be asked. I wanted them to know they are empowered to make change. I wanted them to know we want to give them the structure and infrastructure to make the necessary improvement to their work."

It is our opinion that the 2011 BlessingWhite Research Employee Engagement Report is correct in its statement that employees who are the most disengaged "didn't start out as bad apples." Rather than blaming individuals for being disengaged, we must look at systemic causes. Dr. W. Edwards Deming said that employees typically started their career or a new job with very high intrinsic motivation, but that level of engagement goes nowhere but down over time. Deming said this is due to the way dysfunctional organizations systematically "squeeze out from an individual, over his lifetime, his innate intrinsic motivation, self-esteem, dignity"[12] through the way people are managed (or mismanaged). Thankfully, both coauthors have seen examples where the disengaged have become reengaged in their work, thanks to their participation in the early stages of a Kaizen program. "Bad apples" can regain their original "good apple" appearance and attitude.

Everyone Is Relentlessly Searching for Opportunities to Improve

Fiona Wood, MD, was named Australia's most trusted citizen three years in a row. She invented a patented spray-on skin culturing technique and led the care of 28 burn victims of the 2002 terror bombing in Bali, some of whom had suffered burns over 98% of their body's dermis and fought deadly infections. Dr. Wood says, "I firmly believe that everyday we go to work we should be looking for opportunities to improve the outcomes such that tomorrow is a better day. The day you think that it is as good as it gets … is retirement day."[13]

Franciscan's culture also changed from one with a few people searching for improvement opportunities to one in which everyone is relentlessly looking for opportunities. People are starting to see improvement opportunities where they did not see them before. One of the fundamental mindset differences that has been observed is that the most effective Kaizeneers were searching for improvement opportunities much more frequently than most. Kaizen permeated their lives as they were searching at work and at home (as you will see in Chapter 12).

Table 4.3   Eight Types of "Waste"

Type	Example
Defects	Wrong medication or dose given to patient
Overproduction	Collecting "rainbow tubes" of blood specimens from a patient, just in case they will be used
Transportation	A cancer patient walking from building to building in the course of a single visit
Waiting	Patients waiting to be discharged once medically ready to go home
Inventory	Medications or supplies have expired due to over-ordering
Motion	Nurses walking 5 miles in a single shift
Overprocessing	Charting "long form" (typing too much information) when the EMR calls for "charting by exception"
Human talent	Staff not being given an opportunity to improve a process.

When searching for ways to improve, the Lean framework of the "eight types of waste" can be helpful, as shown in Table 4.3.[14]

Before being exposed to Lean, people often confuse activity and motion with real value to the patient. "Value" is the activity that directly helps diagnose or treat a patient.[15] Patients ultimately value their health and quality of life, so one needs to look closely to see if daily activities contribute to that goal or not. If it is not adding value to the patient, it is waste.

People often gauge their own personal value in the workplace as "being busy," while Lean thinkers realize that much of the motion, searching, and work-arounds in healthcare are actually waste, contributing no value to the patient and can, therefore, be eliminated.

> *Most people spend more time and energy going around problems than trying to solve them.*
>
> **—Henry Ford**

After learning to distinguish waste from value, healthcare professionals start seeing waste where they never saw it before. Running around to search for a missing instrument is no longer unnoticed as a part of the everyday routine. It is now something that should be eliminated by making systemic improvements to prevent instruments from going missing. Once people start improving, they get swept up in the positive cycle of wanting to make more improvements, which means noticing and bringing forward more problems.

Laura Pettigrew, manager of medical records at Franciscan, said, "Staff are more aware of different ways of doing things because of being exposed to so many improvement ideas from the rest of the department and organization. They are now noticing opportunities for me and saying, 'that's a Kaizen.'"

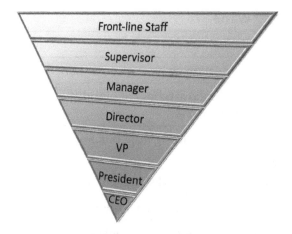

Figure 4.2   Inverted pyramid showing front-line staff on top of the organization.

Nancy Mosier, manager of pediatrics at Franciscan, said, "Kaizen supports the inverted pyramid" model of an organization chart, where staff members are shown at the top, as shown in Figure 4.2. In Kaizen, our "staff searches for and finds improvement opportunities and works with their supervisor and manager to help them see the opportunities," she said. In Kaizen, staff members learn to enroll their peers and their leaders in their own ideas. Managers at all levels are involved in the model of "servant leadership."[16]

The Two Parents of Transformation: Pain and Possibility

Coauthor Joe learned from Fred Oaks, a pastor and speaker, that the two parents of transformation are pain and possibility.[17] Either can be used as motivation for Kaizen. The most powerful driver of transformation is a combination of both—continually focusing on and moving toward what is possible, with a reminder in the back of our mind of the pain that can result if we do not improve.

Pain

Personal transformation is often preceded by a significant emotional event or trauma, such as the discovery that one has a terminal illness like cancer, a tragic accident resulting in the death of a loved one, or being downsized by an organization. Pain can be a powerful motivator to change or transform. Pain teaches us great life lessons.

In healthcare, pain and horrific tragedies have helped lead to improvement and culture change. The tragic death of a patient, Mary McClinton, who was mistakenly injected with a topical disinfectant instead of contrast dye, was the "essential catalyst for change," leading to the "patient safety alert" system at Virginia Mason Medical Center.[18] At Johns Hopkins Medical Center, the tragic and preventable death of 18-month-old Josie King was a catalyst for systematic patient safety improvement efforts, including improved communication between providers and families, as well as the use of checklists to prevent errors.[19]

Possibilities

> *"No use trying," Alice said, "one can't believe impossible things." "I daresay you haven't had much practice," said the Queen. "When I was your age, I always did it for half-an-hour a day. Why, sometimes I've believed as many as six impossible things before breakfast."*

> **—Lewis Carroll**
> *Alice's Adventures in Wonderland*

Transformation does not have to be preceded by pain. The good news is that transformation can be preceded by seeing a great possibility for a future that is better than today.

Franciscan focused on the possibilities that Kaizen could create for their organization. Keith Jewell, COO, said, "When we rolled out the Kaizen program, our staff was excited by the possibilities." Franciscan conveyed the possibilities by continually sharing success stories at meetings, by email, through bulletin boards, and on its website.

One of the core principles of *Lean Thinking* is the continuous pursuit of perfection.[20] Rather than aiming to be in the top quartile or top 10% of a benchmark, the Lean and Kaizen philosophies drive organizations to aim for perfection. Paul O'Neill, former chair of the Pittsburgh Regional Health Initiative, has pushed healthcare to work toward theoretical limits of absolute perfection, including zero infections and zero patient harm. While it used to be viewed as a "God-given fact that 2% of the people who go through intensive care units are going to get an infection," Allegheny General Hospital (Pittsburgh, Pennsylvania), proved that "it's possible to eliminate hospital-acquired infections that occur in intensive care units by setting the goal at zero, and then establishing a process of continuous learning and continuous improvement so that, when there is an infection, you learn where there was a break in protocol so you can go back and eliminate the possibility that you're going to have breaks in protocol going forward."[21]

> *Perfection is not attainable, but if we chase perfection we can catch excellence.*

> **—Vince Lombardi**
> *Professional football coach*

Some leaders hesitate to set goals of zero infections or other instances of perfect patient care. The pushback on perfection often comes from the idea that, for example, zero infections is something so far away from the current performance of the system, that it might seem unattainable and, therefore, discouraging to healthcare professionals. Leaders often do not want to set goals or expectations that will lead to disappointment or frustration.

> *Start by doing what's necessary; then do what's possible; and suddenly you are doing the impossible.*

> **—Saint Francis of Assisi**

A Kaizen culture is a positive, forward-looking culture that dreams up and pursues great possibilities, such as healthcare without infections. At the same time, these far-reaching goals are not viewed as targets that must be reached immediately with the fear of punishment for not hitting targets hanging over everyone's heads. Kaizen is a culture where everyone is empowered to take actions everyday to continually move toward those possibilities, with goals of perfection being inspiring and showing the right direction for the organization.

You Have Control over Your Workplace

> *We all seek to control our lives: our careers, our relationships, our reactions to events and situations. People who gain control automatically become more productive.*

> **—Robert F. "Bob" Bennett**
> *Former CEO of Franklin Quest and former United States Senator from Utah[22]*

Have you had a day in which you ran into one problem after another and everything seemed to be spinning out of control? How did it make you feel? Do you get tired of always having to react to top-down directives? If these mandates conflict with each other, are you told to figure it out anyway? Feeling out of control can be frustrating and exhausting.

Researchers have shown that office workers who have control over their workplace decor outperform those who have the placement of artwork dictated to them. A psychology study set up three scenarios. First, subjects in the study worked in a very spartan workplace with no decorations. The second group worked in an "enriched" workplace that had plants and artwork, a change that led to a 15% increase in productivity without harming quality. The third group was allowed to place and arrange those same plants and art pieces where they wanted, and their productivity was 30% higher with, again, no decrease in quality. In another interesting yet unsurprising lesson, when subjects in the third group were given control and then had it taken away, productivity declined.[23] It was not the decorations themselves that made a difference; it was the level of control that people had over the decorations. Remember what Scholtes said, as referenced in Chapter 1, about people resisting "being changed."

An additional study from 1986 showed that a sense of being in control is a more important aspect of the human personality than researchers previously thought. For the elderly in nursing homes, an increased sense of control led to increased happiness and alertness. More importantly, their mortality rate was lowered by 50% over a period of eighteen months.[24]

The Kaizen culture is about gaining control of one's work, workspace, work life, attitude, and destiny. It is about creating a safe and secure future for you and your organization. It is about enabling your organization to become and remain the service provider of choice in an area. It is about thinking and learning how to make the world a better place in every way—starting with healthcare practices, not broadly, but in a specific department and workplace. When people gain more control of their world, they are happier.

Figure 4.3 shows a Kaizen from a hospital in the Midwest. The nurses' station in a unit did not have enough workspace for social workers or case managers to sit and work. The team freed up space to allow the addition of a small worktable. This Kaizen required spending a small amount of money, but leaders quickly gave approval when they saw that the workspace was a basic requirement for staff to work efficiently. The Kaizen led to improved teamwork, without staff fighting for space, and better patient care, as support functions could be more responsive to patient needs, including more timely discharges.

Patients and Families Are Happy

The purpose of business is to create and keep a customer.

—Peter Drucker
One of the best-known writers on management

In healthcare, the primary customers are patients and their families. Within a Kaizen culture, they are happy with the services being provided because the customers have been studied and understood and the value they want and need is delivered to them each time, exactly when it is needed. Furthermore, as the engagement studies earlier pointed out, a top-ten engagement driver is an organization that focuses on customer satisfaction. Employees define success as high-quality care and great service to patients and families. Employees realize that, if they can deliver better service to patients, they are contributing to revenue growth and the long-term strength of the organization, as well as their own job security.

Studies suggest that high employee satisfaction correlates with patient outcomes and lower rates of medical errors.[25] A Towers Watson study concluded, "It was found that employees' views of empowerment, career development opportunities

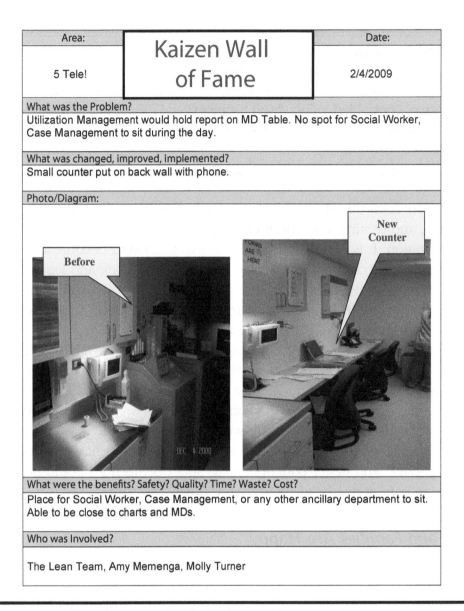

Area:	Kaizen Wall of Fame	Date:
5 Tele!		2/4/2009

What was the Problem?

Utilization Management would hold report on MD Table. No spot for Social Worker, Case Management to sit during the day.

What was changed, improved, implemented?

Small counter put on back wall with phone.

Photo/Diagram:

Before

New Counter

What were the benefits? Safety? Quality? Time? Waste? Cost?

Place for Social Worker, Case Management, or any other ancillary department to sit. Able to be close to charts and MDs.

Who was Involved?

The Lean Team, Amy Memenga, Molly Turner

Figure 4.3 A small work counter that led to improved teamwork.

and teamwork influenced engagement. Further, employee engagement was a key predictor of patient satisfaction, leading to an increased likelihood that patients would recommend the network's hospitals to others."[26] It might seem reasonable to conclude that there is causation, not just correlation between these factors.

At Franciscan, when dietician Jennifer Smith worked with staff to ensure that breastfeeding moms had the privacy they needed, she was advocating for the patient's family, and it produced happier moms, as illustrated in Figure 4.4.

Mischelle Frank, manager of business transformation at Franciscan, led a team to redesign how food was delivered to patients in the postpartum nursing unit, with a focus on creating a "Wow Dining Experience." Her team turned in numerous Kaizens related to that redesign, such as several new recipes, how the food was presented, and the order in which the meals were prepared and delivered, as the Kaizen illustrated in Figure 4.5 demonstrates.

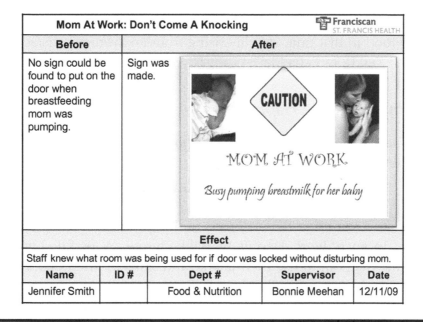

Mom At Work: Don't Come A Knocking		Franciscan ST. FRANCIS HEALTH
Before	**After**	
No sign could be found to put on the door when breastfeeding mom was pumping.	Sign was made.	
Effect		
Staff knew what room was being used for if door was locked without disturbing mom.		

Name	ID #	Dept #	Supervisor	Date
Jennifer Smith		Food & Nutrition	Bonnie Meehan	12/11/09

Figure 4.4   A Kaizen that improves privacy for mothers and babies.

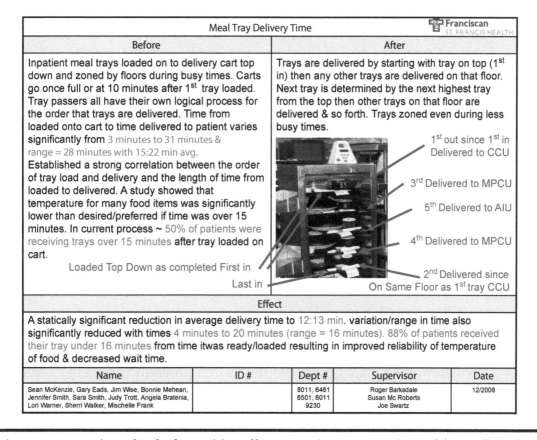

Meal Tray Delivery Time	Franciscan ST. FRANCIS HEALTH
Before	**After**
Inpatient meal trays loaded on to delivery cart top down and zoned by floors during busy times. Carts go once full or at 10 minutes after 1st tray loaded. Tray passers all have their own logical process for the order that trays are delivered. Time from loaded onto cart to time delivered to patient varies significantly from 3 minutes to 31 minutes & range = 28 minutes with 15:22 min avg. Established a strong correlation between the order of tray load and delivery and the length of time from loaded to delivered. A study showed that temperature for many food items was significantly lower than desired/preferred if time was over 15 minutes. In current process ~ 50% of patients were receiving trays over 15 minutes after tray loaded on cart.	Trays are delivered by starting with tray on top (1st in) then any other trays are delivered on that floor. Next tray is determined by the next highest tray from the top then other trays on that floor are delivered & so forth. Trays zoned even during less busy times. 1st out since 1st in Delivered to CCU / 3rd Delivered to MPCU / 5th Delivered to AIU / 4th Delivered to MPCU / 2nd Delivered since On Same Floor as 1st tray CCU

Loaded Top Down as completed First in
Last in

Effect	
A statically significant reduction in average delivery time to 12:13 min. variation/range in time also significantly reduced with times 4 minutes to 20 minutes (range = 16 minutes). 88% of patients received their tray under 16 minutes from time itwas ready/loaded resulting in improved reliability of temperature of food & decreased wait time.	

Name	ID #	Dept #	Supervisor	Date
Sean McKenzie, Gary Eads, Jim Wise, Bonnie Mehean, Jennifer Smith, Sara Smith, Judy Trott, Angela Bratenia, Lori Warner, Sherri Walker, Mischelle Frank		8011, 6461 6501, 6011 9230	Roger Barksdale Susan Mc Roberts Joe Swartz	12/2008

Figure 4.5   A Kaizen that had a positive effect on patients' perceptions of the quality of the food in a unit.

These Kaizens had a positive effect on the patients' perceptions of the quality of the food in that unit, steadily rising from an average satisfaction score of 74% to 82% over 12 months.

Staff and Physicians Are Happy

Management's job is to create an environment where everybody may take joy in his work.[27]

—W. Edwards Deming, Ph.D.

When people are involved in the decisions in their workplace, they can experience more joy. In *Joy at Work*, Dennis W. Bakke wrote, "A joy-filled workplace gives people the freedom to use their talents and skills for the benefit of society, without being crushed or controlled by autocratic supervisors."[28]

Kaizen enables people to reduce frustrations in their workspace. According to Jewell, "It is frustrating to have an inefficient system. Having a role in fixing their processes has a role in improving employee satisfaction. Encouraging employee engagement and involvement in running the hospital is making it better and that ability to contribute in a real way brings joy to the staff and into the workplace."

Kelly Butler, NICU Supervisor at Franciscan, said, "Kaizen does make staff happier. One time, when I came home from work in a happy mood, my husband asked if it was because I did another 'Happy Kuzie' that day, which made me laugh because he didn't remember the word Kaizen."

Kim Siegfried, a nurse in the pediatric specialty offices, noticed the physicians she worked with were frequently thirsty and hungry. Unfortunately, satisfying their thirst or hunger was inconvenient because they were two buildings away from the cafeteria. Kim ordered snacks and drinks and stocked them in the staff refrigerator, starting an honor system to cover the costs. It made a nice difference, as she noticed physicians and staff were happier, as shown in Figure 4.6.

Medical records has been the top-performing Kaizen department at Franciscan for three years in a row. When they started their Kaizen journey, their employee satisfaction was at the 4th percentile in the nation, meaning that 96% of employees surveyed across the country were more satisfied. Three years into the program, their employee satisfaction had improved to the 63rd percentile.

Laura Pettigrew, their manager, credits the Kaizen program with being a significant reason for that improvement; as she said, "Staff used to rely on management to make all the decisions. Through Kaizen, we kept putting the onus on them to take ownership for their work and their work environment. We did a lot of coaching early on, and when they started to see that they could make better decisions than management, because they were closer to the work, and they started seeing

Happier Physicians Make Happier Patients	
Before	**After**
We are located in the Pediatric Specialty Clinics at Indianapolis Campus in the Medical Office Building #2, far from the cafeteria.. Our Doctors are always thirsty and hungry! **Franciscan** ST. FRANCIS HEALTH	We brought soda and sell it for 40 cents and we take turns bringing in snacks! 
Effect	
Happy Doctors.............This is Dr. Fuqua one of our Pediatric specialists. He looks happy with his candy and a diet coke.	

Name	ID#	Dept#	Supervisor	Date
Kim Siegfried		7911	Paula Stanfill	12/1/08

Figure 4.6 Happier physicians make happier patients.

the benefits, they were sold. Kaizen is how we gave our employees more power, control, and autonomy, and that translated into improved employee satisfaction."

My staff are really alive now.

—Paula Stanfill
Manager, Franciscan NICU

At Children's Medical Center Dallas, staff satisfaction increased in the core laboratory when measured 12 months into their Lean journey and their use of Kaizen methods, as shown in Table 4.4.[29] The satisfaction was measured on a scale of 1–5, with 5.0 being the highest. The shift to a Kaizen culture in their lab is featured later in Chapter 6. Even with their improvements, Jim Adams, senior director of laboratory operations says, "You can't expect a consistently upward trajectory of these engagement scores as you develop this culture. There are going to be times when these new ways of operating make people uncomfortable and they choose to leave. Unless this is managed and communicated properly, there can be a perception that somebody was 'forced out,' which can harm morale for some periods, unfortunately."[30]

Table 4.4 Staff Satisfaction Scores 12 Months into a Lean Journey (out of 5.0)

	Before Lean	12 Months After Starting
I have the opportunity to do what I do best every day.	3.11	3.92
I feel free to make suggestions for improvement.	2.84	3.48
I feel secure in my job.	2.32	3.42
Stress at work is manageable.	2.43	3.23
I am satisfied with the lab as a place to work.	2.51	3.43
I would recommend my work area as a good place to work to others.	2.38	3.46
Grand Average of All Questions	2.96	3.69

In the Utah North Region of Intermountain Healthcare, the employee score for "my opinion seems to count" increased from 3.68 to 3.89 (out of a 5-point scale, with 5.0 being the highest) with the introduction of a staff idea system, their version of Kaizen. While they plan on continuing the annual staff surveys, the number of implemented staff ideas becomes a continuous measure of staff engagement, says Bart Sellers, regional manager of management engineering. Through this measure, they can gauge their progress toward their goal of every employee being a problem solver. "How better to engage employees than to have them involved in improvement?" asks Sellers.[31]

Work and Patient Care Flow Like Clockwork

With Kaizen and in a Lean process, work flows seamlessly, like clockwork. Materials, information, and resources are exactly where you expect them to be, each and every time. The Lean healthcare literature is now filled with examples of organizations that have improved patient flow, such as the examples of Franciscan and ThedaCare improving their door-to-balloon times, as mentioned in Chapter 3. Both organizations improved flow not by working faster, but by reducing waste and minimizing avoidable interruptions and delays in their processes. A Kaizen culture is constantly working toward minimizing delays in patient care, because reducing waste through Kaizen benefits both patients and staff.

For example, Alisa Daniels, a nurse in the Franciscan NICU, consolidated discharge information from three locations into one location to streamline the discharge process, as illustrated in Figure 4.7.

The Workspace Is Clean, Orderly, and Safe

In a Lean environment, cleanliness, order, and safety go together. Lean methods like 5S, as explained in Chapter 11, are often misconstrued as being focused on just looking neat and tidy, but 5S is really about creating a safe, effective

Discharge Cabinet		Franciscan ST. FRANCIS HEALTH
Before		**After**
Discharge supplies, such as pamphlets and other information we send home with parents, were kept in 3 different places, usually scattered & disorganized. 		All discharge supplies are kept in one file drawer in the middle of the unit for organization and easy access. Extra supplies are kept in the parent resource cabinet. 
Effect		
This should help to further streamline and organize discharges in the NICU		

Name	ID #	Dept #	Supervisor	Date
Alisa Daniels	050698	NICU	Paula Stanfill	7-9-10

Figure 4.7   Discharge cabinet.

workplace where problems are readily visible. In this culture, problems occur less often because people are continuously working to prevent problems through better systems and processes. When problems do occur, they are investigated and resolved immediately or very quickly.

Ronda Frieje, pharmacy manager at Franciscan, noted, "Kaizen drove people to recognize the power over their own work environment to make change. Kaizen has driven positive changes in our department. Things just work better now. Our workspace is clean and orderly, and everything is where we've designed it to be. We separated look-alike, sound-alike, and different-strength drugs. I sleep better now knowing how much Kaizen effort we've put in over the last few years to ensure our patients are safe."

Figure 4.8 shows a Kaizen from a hospital's radiology department. Staff members noticed that access to safety supplies was often blocked by the storage of collimator servers, including one that had not been used in years. Making this change would help prevent a potential delay in recovering a patient in distress.

When a patient developed an infection after a foot surgery, Sandy Dennis, a nurse in surgery at Franciscan, did some research and discovered the best practice of using chlorhexidine wipes and presented the information at a monthly infection control meeting. After gaining agreement, Dennis implemented the practice immediately to reduce the likelihood of a future infection, as shown in Figure 4.9. Nurses are happier because the patient outcomes are improved, and the practice also demonstrates compassionate care.

Everyone Works Together

People in a Kaizen culture have accepted their expected role in workplace improvement. Supervisors and managers accept that they are no longer expected to have all

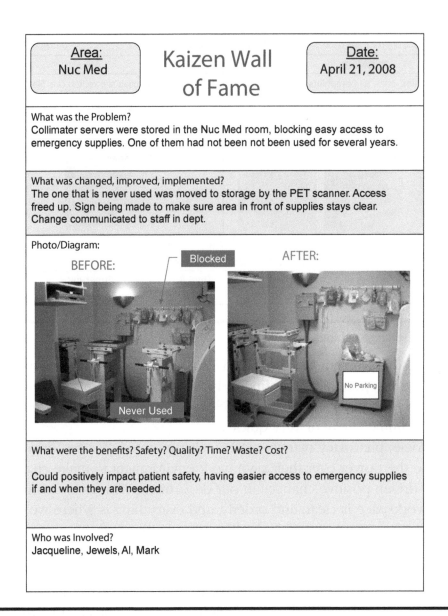

Area: Nuc Med	Kaizen Wall of Fame	Date: April 21, 2008

What was the Problem?
Collimater servers were stored in the Nuc Med room, blocking easy access to emergency supplies. One of them had not been not been used for several years.

What was changed, improved, implemented?
The one that is never used was moved to storage by the PET scanner. Access freed up. Sign being made to make sure area in front of supplies stays clear. Change communicated to staff in dept.

Photo/Diagram:

BEFORE: Blocked   AFTER:

Never Used   No Parking

What were the benefits? Safety? Quality? Time? Waste? Cost?

Could positively impact patient safety, having easier access to emergency supplies if and when they are needed.

Who was Involved?
Jacqueline, Jewels, Al, Mark

Figure 4.8 Nuclear Medicine's safety supplies.

the answers and their new role is to help employees shine. Improvement does not just happen unless everyone works together to make it happen every day.

The pharmacy at Franciscan has experienced an impressive cultural change since starting its Kaizen journey. Ronda Freije, manager at the Indianapolis campus, said, "One of the biggest benefits Kaizen has brought to the pharmacy is a team culture. We work as a team now. Before, we tended to be split into cliques. The pharmacists would hang out with the pharmacists, the techs with the techs. Now, they are connected. Kaizen also developed our cross-shift teaming and cross-department teaming abilities. We work better with everyone now."

Laura Pettigrew, manager of medical records at Franciscan, noticed a similar shift in collaboration, saying, "Our staff used to depend on leaders for day-to-day decision making on things like staffing and coverage. I knew, as a manager, I needed to get out of the day-to-day business so I could focus on developing the

Foot Scrubs	Franciscan ST. FRANCIS HEALTH
Before	**After**
We had a discussion during an Infection Control Meeting concerning foot and/or toe infections following surgery.	Implementation of foot scrubs prior to surgery. In a tub of water, scrub with CHG sponges prior to procedure. 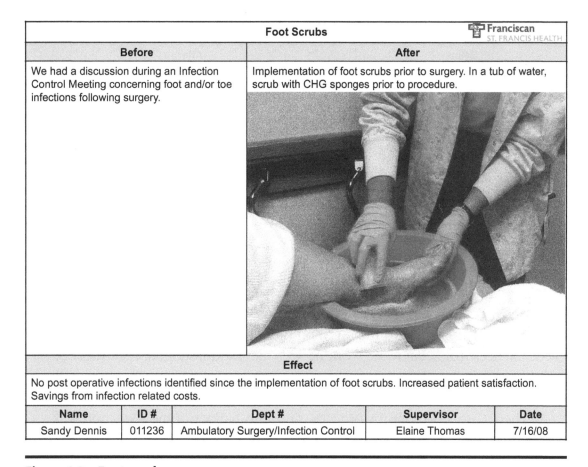

Effect
No post operative infections identified since the implementation of foot scrubs. Increased patient satisfaction. Savings from infection related costs.

Name	ID #	Dept #	Supervisor	Date
Sandy Dennis	011236	Ambulatory Surgery/Infection Control	Elaine Thomas	7/16/08

Figure 4.9 Foot scrubs.

future of our department. I questioned what we could have our employees do. Now they work together to arrange staffing and coverage. If someone wants to take time off, it is up to them to work with others to get coverage. If they can't do it themselves, they come to me. Now, their communication is better." Laura said they now lead each other. "With Kaizen, they remind each other." Laura has noticed also that early on most Kaizens were solo, whereas now there are many more completed by small teams.

At one hospital Mark worked with, the patient care techs struggled for a long time with uneven workloads due to the difficulty in predicting which patients would require the most assistance during the day. It seemed impossible for any charge nurse to make assignments in a way that was fair and even, or consistently even, throughout the day. During their initial Kaizen work, the techs decided to manage their own workloads as a team. Instead of top-down assignments, the techs started self-managing and reassigning patients to help level each other's workloads, in addition to the normal practice of temporarily helping with each others' patients, as needed.

ES Mop Buckets		Franciscan ST. FRANCIS HEALTH
Before	**After**	
The ES staff had been throwing away the toilet brush buckets in the rooms when they were soiled or in an isolation room.	Although the brushes are thrown away when soiled or in an isolation, ES staff now cleans the buckets with our hospital disinfectant. After the 10 minute kill time, they can be ready for use again.	
Effect		
The cost of the buckets are $2.00 per bucket. The savings is about $2,000 per year by disinfecting and re-using the buckets.		

Name	ID #	Dept #	Supervisor	Date
Greg Kello		ES	Elena Weathers	6/24/2010

Figure 4.10   ES mop buckets.

Everything Gets Questioned

In a Kaizen culture, it is no longer acceptable to accept "Well, we've always done it that way" as an answer to the question of "Why do we do things this way?" Even practices that seem to be working well can be questioned, regardless of how big or how small the improvement is. We do not have to change everything, but nothing should be off limits from being questioned.

At ThedaCare, one contributor to the "door-to-balloon" time reduction was questioning why cardiologists had to consult and provide a second opinion if an emergency room physician saw signs of a "Code STEMI" event in the EKG print-out. Waiting for the cardiologist would cause up to a 30-minute delay in that vital patient care. After allowing the emergency physicians to make the determination on their own, the next step was to question why a properly trained EMT could not make the determination in the ambulance.[32]

In another instance, Greg Kello, an environmental services supervisor for Franciscan, questioned why they were throwing away so many mop buckets. He discovered that they could clean and reuse those that had not been in isolation rooms, as documented in Figure 4.10. Many Kaizens come from asking the question "why have we always done it this way?"

Small Successes Lead to Bigger Successes

If we start with the small improvements first, we will then be more likely to adopt the habit of continuous improvement in all aspects of our life. With practice, you will be ready to tackle more aggressive and substantial Kaizens. Small changes are easier to implement and sustain. Making small changes is also more fun and satisfying than trying to make one large change.

In the Kaizen improvement shown in Figure 4.11, Kelly Butler from Franciscan redesigned the nursing logbook to change it for the better.

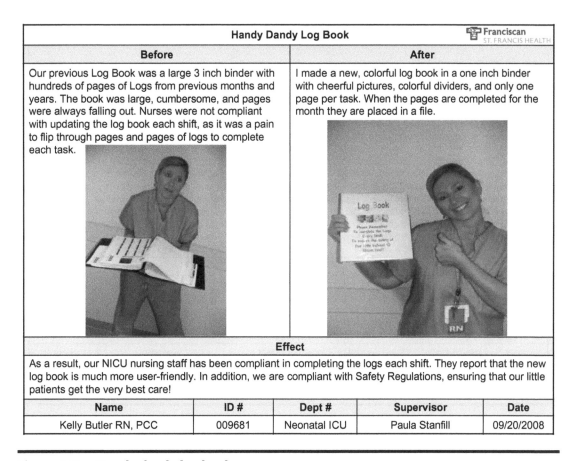

Handy Dandy Log Book		Franciscan ST. FRANCIS HEALTH
Before	**After**	
Our previous Log Book was a large 3 inch binder with hundreds of pages of Logs from previous months and years. The book was large, cumbersome, and pages were always falling out. Nurses were not compliant with updating the log book each shift, as it was a pain to flip through pages and pages of logs to complete each task.	I made a new, colorful log book in a one inch binder with cheerful pictures, colorful dividers, and only one page per task. When the pages are completed for the month they are placed in a file.	
Effect		
As a result, our NICU nursing staff has been compliant in completing the logs each shift. They report that the new log book is much more user-friendly. In addition, we are compliant with Safety Regulations, ensuring that our little patients get the very best care!		

Name	ID #	Dept #	Supervisor	Date
Kelly Butler RN, PCC	009681	Neonatal ICU	Paula Stanfill	09/20/2008

Figure 4.11   Handy dandy log book.

Starting small with Kaizen has these attributes:

■ They are small changes.
■ They are within an employee's span of control.
■ They are simple ideas.
■ They do not negatively impact other departments or patients.

Kaizen is the process of taking baby-sized steps on one's improvement destination. Pam Fugate, a former nursing manager at Franciscan, was hiking with her husband to the 80-foot-tall Rainbow Falls in the Smokey Mountain National Park. The hike to Rainbow Falls is a 5.4-mile round trip hike that is rated moderate in difficulty, gaining about 1,500 feet in elevation. She struggled to make the steady climb to the falls, stopping numerous times. Finally, she told her husband, "I can't make it any further," and promptly sat down on the side of the trail. After a few minutes of coaxing, it was obvious to her husband that Pam was done. He continued to hike to the falls, counting the steps. Once at the falls, he called Pam on her cell phone and said, "You have to see this … it is only 1,000 steps … you can do it … let's count them off together." She stood and, holding her phone to her ear, began counting, "1, 2, 3, …"

Standardized Blood Distribution Process	Franciscan ST. FRANCIS HEALTH
Before	**After**
• Lab personnel worked in one specific department within the lab (micro, blood bank, chemistry or hematology) and at only one specific campus. • Each unit/area had different expectations of how the Blood Bank was to communicate when blood products were ready and how to send the products to the unit/area. • Because of all the different communication processes/expectations, communication had the tendency to break down and blood products were being missed and therefore had to be destroyed. • Blood product were left in the tube system. • Blood Bank was making many additional calls. • Pink slip was to be returned in 5 minutes. • 2008 discarded units of PRBC's was 56.	• Lab personnel now work in all areas within the lab (micro, blood bank, chemistry or hematology). They also work between all campuses. A standard process for all lab and nursing personnel was needed so that everyone understood the process clearly. • All blood products that are sent via the tube system are now sent with a send secure function. No phone call required. '0000' is the universal code to release the product from the tube system. The send secure function sounds an alarm on the receiving unit/area prompting someone to remove the product. • Blood Bank now make phone calls less frequently. • Pink slip is now to be returned within 10 minutes of being delivered via the tube system. • 2009 discarded units of PRBC's was 27.

Effect				
• Standard process/expectations for both lab and nursing. • Decrease number of phone calls therefore an increase in time and productivity. • Also with an increase in the expected return time of the pink slip, lab is now spending less time following up, leading to an increase in time and productivity. • Saving $220 per unit of PRBC for a total saving of $4,180 plus the added time and productivity above.				

Name	ID #	Dept #	Supervisor	Date
Lab/Nursing Process Committee Stacy Dickerson & Debra Orange		6050 7010	Marianne Benjamin Deb Berner	April 2010

Figure 4.12 Standardized blood distribution process.

She made it to the falls to sit with her husband and share the scenery of the deep woods punctuated by water free falling 50 feet to the rocks below.

Pam sat there thinking of the parallels of this walk to her weight-loss journey. She discovered that she could go farther than she thought she could. So, when times get difficult—when she thinks she cannot possibly go one step further and considers straying from her diet—she recalls her hike to Rainbow Falls, and she starts counting the steps. She thinks about making it to the next day and simply puts one foot in front of the other. It was a valuable lesson for Pam that she uses frequently.

As people get better at making small improvements, they naturally try larger improvements. Over time, staff members become more comfortable with change as it becomes a way of life. Staff learn new skills, become more highly developed in problem solving, and gain confidence in making changes. Practicing with small changes makes the larger changes seem more possible.

At Franciscan, the lab and nursing committee has adopted Kaizen as their problem solving and improvement methodology, even for their big efforts, such as developing a standardized blood distribution process, as shown in Figure 4.12. Deb Orange, manager of patient safety, said, "Kaizen was something everyone on our team had experience with, and it made our improvement process simple and straightforward to do and document."

Three departments at Franciscan worked together to reduce denial of payments from insurance companies. They surprised themselves with the results, saving the organization over $250,000 per year, as illustrated in Figure 4.13.

Reduction/ Elimination of Denials and Write-offs			Franciscan ST. FRANCIS HEALTH
Before	**After**		
Current ED form (chart) did not have significant documentation to avoid denials and/or write-offs.	Indicators for Radiology were added to the ED form to determine why a test was run. An indicator for 'Long Term Use of Anticoagulants' was also added.		
Effect			
This will help eliminate approximately $250,000 per year of denials and/or write-offs for the ED due to 'lack of documentation.'			
Name	**Dept #**	**Supervisor**	**Date**
Lisa Swift, Merredith Basham, Mary Pease, Heather Taillon , Alan Manning, Marilyn Gaddy, Karen Bledsoe	Integrate Case Management	Kim Kolthoff	7-29-09

Figure 4.13   Reduction/elimination of denials and write-offs.

When Kaizen was initiated at St. Francis, nearly all the Kaizens turned in were small improvements. Four years into the program, about 20% of the Kaizens turned in could be classified as medium to large improvements.

Yard by yard, life is hard. Inch by inch, life's a cinch.

—Anonymous

Nancy Mosier, manager of pediatrics at Franciscan, said, "It is important to note that Kaizen is not just small changes for the better—it can be big improvements. However, we want our staff to start small and take baby steps so they can develop their skills and abilities over time to do Kaizen." Nancy's point is well taken. Kaizen can be used for large-scale improvements when those improvements are broken into bite-size chunks.

We can do no great things, only small things with great love.

—Mother Teresa

You know the old saying about how to eat an elephant—one bite at a time. The same holds true for Kaizen. Any size project can be more easily completed if it is broken down into a series of small tasks. At the same time, one needs to be cautious that focusing on small tasks does not lead to losing sight of the overall process or needs of patients.

Imai's Three Stages of Kaizen

It is easy to say that you want to have a Kaizen culture in your organization. Changing an organization's culture may take a year in a single department, but it can take many years or a decade to change the culture of a larger organization. Starting small with baby steps can lead to larger improvements and culture change. Masaaki Imai shares a framework that includes three separate stages that one might expect to go through in a Kaizen journey.

In the first stage, supervisors must make every effort to help employees bring forward improvement ideas, no matter how small. The initial focus is on improving one's own job and area. Leaders need to say yes to virtually every idea in order to build interest and enthusiasm for Kaizen.

In the second stage, which might be a year or two into this journey, the organization starts to provide more education for staff on problem-solving skills, so people can provide better quality suggestions.

Imai emphasizes that "only in the third stage" should managers be concerned about the financial payback or ROI of improvements, once employees are interested and educated about Kaizen. He writes that organizations tend to struggle with Kaizen when they want to jump immediately to the third stage instead of thinking of the development of a Kaizen culture over a "five to ten-year span."[33]

Conclusion

Kaizen systematically creates an environment where change becomes the normal way of life. This results in a culture where people embrace change instead of being mislabeled as "resistant." Kaizen leads to greater adoption of change, of all types, as small changes lead to bigger changes. A Kaizen culture becomes a culture that is more responsive to the changing demands and landscape of healthcare. Healthcare professionals in a Kaizen culture are not just happy; they find more meaningful engagement in their important work.

The role of leaders is critical in creating a Kaizen culture. The behaviors and mindsets that are required, at all levels, to encourage Kaizen are described more fully in Chapter 9 and throughout the book. Transforming a culture requires that we advance beyond the status quo by driving toward the possibilities of perfection.

Discussion Questions

- Does your organization currently have some of the attributes described in this chapter? If not, do you think Kaizen can lead to that culture?
- How engaged are the people in your workplace? Other than surveys, how can you gauge overall engagement? How can you tell if an individual is highly engaged?
- Why did Deming say that people get disengaged in the workplace over time? What can leaders do to prevent this?
- How do you know when your organization's culture has changed?

Endnotes

1. Robinson, Alan G., and Dean M. Schroeder, *Ideas Are Free: How the Idea Revolution Is Liberating People and Transforming Organizations* (San Francisco: Berrett-Koehler Publishers, 2006), 262.

2. Blessing White 2011 report, 5.

3. Blessing White, 6.

4. Blessing White, 5.

5. Mercer, LLC, "One in Two US Employees Looking to Leave or Checked Out on the Job, Says 'What's Working Research," website, http://www.mercer.com/press-releases/1418665 (accessed September 17, 2011).

6. American Association of Colleges of Nursing, "Nursing Shortage Fact Sheet," website, http://www.aacn.nche.edu/media/factsheets/nursingshortage.htm (accessed September 17, 2011).

7. Dague, James, personal interview, July 2011.

8. Labor Relations Institute of New York, "Survey: Foreman Facts," 1946, http://www.apcointl.org/institute/emd_pdf/EmployeeRetention.pdf (accessed September 17, 2011).

9. Ken Kovach (1980); Valerie Wilson, Achievers International (1988); Bob Nelson, Blanchard Training & Development (1991); Sheryl & Don Grimme, GHR Training Solutions (1997–2001).

10. Towers Perrin HR Services, "Winning Strategies for a Global Workforce: Attracting, Retaining and Engaging Employees for Competitive Advantage," 2006, http://www.towersperrin.com/tp/getwebcachedoc?webc=HRS/USA/2006/200602/GWS.pdf.

11. Imai, Masaaki, "Definition of KAIZEN," http://www.youtube.com/watch?v=jRdTFis4-3Q&feature=related.

12. Deming, W. Edwards, *The New Economics*, 2nd ed. (Cambridge, MA: MIT CAES, 1994), 121.

13. FranklinCovey, "Leadership Training Solutions," http://www.franklincovey.com/tc/solutions/leadership-solutions.

14. Graban, Mark, *Lean Hospitals: Improving Quality, Patient Satisfaction, and Employee Engagement: 2nd edition* (New York: Productivity Press, 2011), 38.

15. Graban, 32.

16. Greenleaf, Robert K., and Larry C. Spears, *Servant Leadership: A Journey into the Nature of Legitimate Power and Greatness, 25th Anniversary Edition* (New York: Paulist Press, 2002), 21.

17. Rendle, Gilbert R., *Leading Change in the Organization* (Herndon, Virginia: Alban Institute, 1997), 88.

18. Kenney, Charles, *Transforming Healthcare: Virginia Mason Medical Center's Pursuit of the Perfect Patient Experience* (New York: Productivity Press, 2010), 62.

19. Pronovost, Peter J., *Safe Patients, Smart Hospitals: How One Doctor's Checklist Can Help Us Change Health Care from the Inside Out* (New York: Hudson Street Press, 2010), 8.

20. Womack, James P., and Daniel T. Jones, *Lean Thinking* (New York: Free Press, 2003), 90.

21. Africal Society for Quality in Healthcare, "In a Perfect World," 2009, http://www.asqh.org/threads/375-In-a-Perfect-World.

22. Bennett, Robert, *Gaining Control* (Salt Lake City: Franklin International Institute, 1987), xi.

23. Haslam, S. Alexander, and Craig Knight, "Cubicle, Sweet Cubicle: The Best Ways to Make Office Spaces Not So Bad," *Scientific American Mind*, September 2010. http://www.scientificamerican.com/article.cfm?id=cubicle-sweet-cubicle.

24. Goleman, Daniel, "Feeling of Control Viewed as Central in Mental Health," *The New York Times*, October 7, 1986, http://www.nytimes.com/1986/10/07/science/feeling-of-control-viewed-as-central-in-mental-health.html (accessed August 8, 2011).

25. Rathert, C. and D.R. May, "Health Care Work Environments, Employee Satisfaction, and Patient Safety: Care Provider Perspectives," *Health Care Management Review*, 2007 Jan–Mar;32(1):2–11.

26. Towers Watson, "Committed to Health: A Large Hospital Network Links Employee Engagement With Patient Satisfaction to Maximize Competitive Strength," Case Study, 2010, http://www.towerswatson.com/assets/pdf/1549/Healthcare_Case-Study_4-12.pdf (accessed September 17, 2011).

27. Neave, Harry R., *The Deming Dimension* (Knoxville, SPC Press, 1990), 198.

28. Bakke, Dennis W., *Joy at Work: A Revolutionary Approach to Fun on the Job* (Seattle: PVG, 2005), 19.

29. Graban, 11.

30. Adams, Jim, personal interview, September 2011.

31. Sellers, Bart, personal interview, September 2011.

32. Toussaint, John, and Roger Gerard, *On the Mend: Revolutionizing Healthcare to Save Lives and Transform the Industry* (Cambridge, MA: Lean Enterprise Institute, 2010), 43.

33. Imai, Masaaki, *KAIZEN: The Key to Japan's Competitive Success* (New York: McGraw-Hill, 1986), 113.

2

KAIZEN METHODOLOGIES

Chapter 5

Quick and Easy Kaizen

At first I had difficulty finding Kaizen opportunities, but over time, as I practiced, it became easier and easier for me to see them.

—Melissa Horne
Pharmacy Technician, Franciscan St. Francis Health
Completed 109 Kaizens in 2010

Two nurses in Franciscan's endoscopy department rethought the bronchoscopy kits. It turned out that 65% of the items in the kit were not needed, so the kit was streamlined, resulting in a small cost savings and a very large reduction in nonbiodegradable plastics, as shown in Figure 5.1.

This Kaizen was forwarded by managers to staff across the entire Franciscan system to show the power of small, staff-driven improvements. This Kaizen went beyond "win–win" by benefitting:

- **Staff**—by saving time with the handling of fewer items
- **Patients**—by simplifying the items required for a procedure, minimizing the probability of a delay
- **Organization**—by saving costs and by having happier staff and patients
- **Society**—by reducing plastic waste

How to Do Kaizen

Welcome to your new role as a "Kaizeneer," or one who does Kaizen. Reading this book is a good first step. However, to become a Kaizeneer, you must apply what you have learned. This chapter will introduce you to how to do Kaizen, through a specific method called "Quick and Easy Kaizen." We will show you how to create a "Kaizen Report" like those in the examples you have seen in the

Beech Grove Endoscopy Waste Savings	Franciscan ST. FRANCIS HEALTH
Before	**After**
Bronchoscopy kits contained supplies that were frequently not used and were discarded. 	The staff of the Endoscopy unit in Beech Grove reviewed the contents of pre-packaged bronchoscopy kits we receive from a local company. 

The Effect
We were able to eliminate approximately 65% of the products, including a very large amount of plastic. Therefore, in addition to some cost savings, we were able to make a significant reduction in non-biodegradeable waste.

Name	Supervisor	Date	Savings
Jayne Harris, RN, BSN Toni Perkins, RN	Loretta Hall	3/20/08	65% less waste. ~$300/year.

Figure 5.1 Reducing wasted endoscopy supplies.

book so far. Then, after reading this chapter, we will ask you to practice Kaizen with a real improvement in your own workplace.

We will introduce you to a few examples of simple kitchen improvements in addition to Kaizens in healthcare settings. We have found that using examples from both home and work can help make Kaizen more accessible to everyone.

Quick and Easy Kaizen

Quick and Easy Kaizen simply asks you to stop for a moment and look for opportunities to improve.[1]

—Bunji Tozawa and Norman Bodek

Norman Bodek was the first to use the term "Quick and Easy Kaizen" in the United States. There are five basic steps to Quick and Easy Kaizen:

1. **Find:** Search for opportunities for improvement or problems to solve.
2. **Discuss:** Discuss the idea with your team and your supervisor.
3. **Implement:** A change for the better must be implemented to be a Kaizen.
4. **Document:** Document the Kaizen by creating a simple report called a "Kaizen Report."
5. **Share:** Post it, review it, and discuss.

It is important to go through all of these steps. Some people might be tempted to cut corners, thinking, "We don't have the time to stop and document our improvements; we have so much to do, and so little time!" Others may think, "I'm not

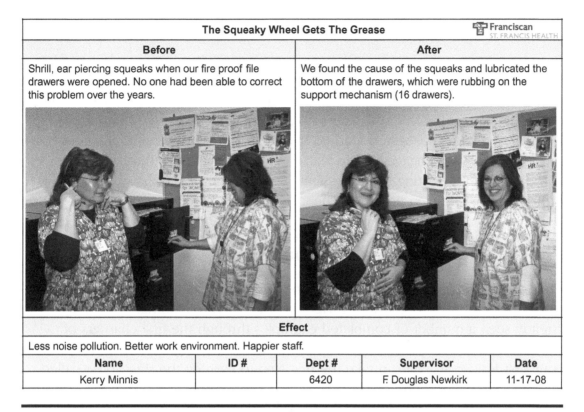

Figure 5.2 The squeaky drawer gets the grease.

going to talk to my supervisor about this, I'll just do it," but effective Kaizen is a nonbureaucratic interaction with a supervisor or manager. The power of Quick and Easy Kaizen comes from following all of these steps in a disciplined and consistent manner, as Franciscan has experienced. Kaizen might seem daunting at first, but it is a skill that grows and a practice that gets easier over time.

You can't learn how to ride a bike by reading a book on physics.

—Unknown

As we introduced in Chapter 3, Kaizen does not have to be a big project. Kaizen is best represented by small changes that people make in the workplace, or continuous improvement. Figure 5.2 shows one such improvement that was documented at Franciscan.

As the example illustrates, Kaizen can be quick and easy. By simply lubricating the file cabinet drawers, the nurses made a small change for the better. This did not require a project, a charter, a team, or an event. The nurses simply took the initiative, with cooperation from their supervisor. This small improvement makes their workplace better and helps create an environment in which they can make more changes and, eventually, also make bigger changes. Documenting even the smallest improvements is important, because it prompts reflection by the person who made the improvement, helps share and spread ideas, and gives recognition to those who are making improvements.

Starting the Franciscan Kaizen Journey

Franciscan started their Kaizen journey in April of 2007, when they brought in Norman Bodek, or "Norm" as they call him, for a day. At 8:00 a.m. Norm met with their senior leadership team for an hour, and at 10:00 a.m. he met with 300 of their leaders, ranging from managers up to the CEO. In this two-hour workshop, Joe Swartz and his colleagues learned the meaning and value of Quick and Easy Kaizen and how to engage staff in Kaizen efforts. The rest of the day, Norm met with Franciscan's existing Lean Six Sigma team to coordinate the nuts and bolts of how to run a Kaizen program. Then, they launched the program.

The Quick and Easy Kaizen Process

The best way to learn Kaizen is to do one. We encourage you to follow the five steps and do your first Kaizen right now as you are reading. You have already seen a number of completed examples through the first chapters of this book. Pick a simple idea and use the form here, in Figure 5.3, to complete your first Kaizen so you can take the first step to earning the right to be called a Kaizeneer. Feel free to photocopy this blank form, or you can download a template at www.HCkaizen.com.

Title:				
Before		**After**		
Effect				
Name	**ID #**	**Dept #**	**Supervisor**	**Date**

Figure 5.3 Quick and Easy Kaizen Form—download at www.HCkaizen.com.

Step 1—Find

The first of the five steps of Quick and Easy Kaizen is to search for and find an opportunity for improvement or a problem to resolve.

Start Small

At Franciscan, the confidence to implement Kaizens did not just suddenly appear. It took several years of practice, trial and error, and coaching for our stronger Kaizeneers to grow their Kaizen skills and to gain enough confidence to become really proficient at Kaizen. Nancy Mosier, manager of Pediatrics at Franciscan said, "I start where they are. If they are a beginner to Kaizen, I encourage them to take baby steps and start small. I approve their Kaizens right away to get wins, especially if their Kaizen only impacts them. I want them to gain confidence in the process." As people gain confidence in their abilities, leaders can challenge them and push them to improve their problem-solving skills. Early on, the focus should be on building enthusiasm and confidence.

> *It's lack of faith that makes people afraid of meeting challenges, and I believed in myself.*
>
> **—Muhammad Ali**
> *World champion boxer*

Laura Pettigrew, manager of medical records at Franciscan said, "Now staff members are taking more initiative because they have more self-confidence that they can take control over improving their job duties."

Start with You

Kaizen often starts by focusing on the frustrations you experience each day. Kaizen builds on your own intrinsic motivation to make improvements for your own benefit. Later, with experience, you will grow beyond focusing on you.

You can start generating Kaizens by searching for ideas that make your work any or all of the following:

■ Easier
■ Safer
■ More interesting

Or look for any improvements that would build skills, capabilities, and knowledge.

Make Your Work Easier

If you start by focusing on making your work easier, good things will follow for yourself and for others. Who knows the details of your work better than you?

This focus on you and making your work easier is a fundamental difference from other improvement programs that might focus only on generating cost savings for the organization.

> *Progress isn't made by early risers. It's made by lazy men trying to find easier ways to do something.*

> **—Robert Heinlein**
> *American science fiction writer*

One way to make your work easier is by finding something that is cluttering your workspace that you do not use often. Could it be moved and stored outside your workspace? If so, that could be a Kaizen. It is that simple—now you have started. Alternatively, is there something that you use every day that should have a home in your workspace, or should be moved closer to you? That too could be a Kaizen.

For example, at Franciscan, Rhonda Miller, a coordinator in the medical records department, noticed that envelopes were inconveniently located, requiring their retrieval and transportation each time they were needed. She relocated them to a more convenient location, as illustrated in Figure 5.4. Kaizen can be that simple.

If you succeed in making your work easier, time is gained each day to do Kaizen, and the benefits will begin accumulating like interest, compounded daily.

For example, when Christa purchased two linen carts, as documented in Figure 5.5, she knew the carts were a one-time cost, but the time savings to her nurses would accrue continually for years to come.

Move It, Move It, Move It			Franciscan ST. FRANCIS HEALTH		
Before			**After**		
Staff would have to step away from front desk and patient to obtain envelopes to place copies of medical records.			Reorganize front desk and moved envelopes to front desk area.		
Effect					
Eliminate the staff from walking away from patient to obtain envelopes – better customer service.					
Name	**ID #**	**Dept #**	**Supervisor**		**Date**
Rhonda Miller		7680	Laura Pettigrew		8/1/08

Figure 5.4 Move it, move it, move it.

Saving Time Getting Linens		Franciscan ST. FRANCIS HEALTH
Before		**After**
All linen was kept in a centralized linen room on 8 tower. Staff were walking several extra feet to obtain linen, especially if they were working on the west wing of the floor.		Two small linen carts were purchased for the 2 substations in rooms 806 and 866.
The Effect		
This reduces the amount of walking everyday for staff, saves time, and creates higher staff satisfaction.		

Name	Supervisor	Date	Savings
Christa Smiley	Rhonda Anders	9/5/08	

Figure 5.5   Saving time getting linens.

Make Your Work Safer

Are there electrical cords hanging that could get in the way or items on the floor that someone could trip over? Using a tie to organize the cords, or finding a home for the items on the floor would be a Kaizen, as shown in Figure 5.6. Notice that cords are still hanging down a bit after the improvement, but they are much better organized. As the expression says, do not let perfect be the enemy of good. The initial fix can spur further improvements.

Make Your Work More Interesting

> *Why not make the work easier and more interesting so that people do not have to sweat? The Toyota style is not to create results by working hard. It is a system that says there is no limit to people's creativity. People don't go to Toyota to "work" they go there to "think."*
>
> **—Taiichi Ohno**

Many Kaizens involve the reduction or elimination of boring or repetitive tasks, freeing up time for more rewarding or creative work, like direct patient care activities or more Kaizen. In one hospital lab, highly trained medical technologists would spend an hour or more putting individual caps onto specimen tubes after testing. A team member suggested using plastic covers that could be placed across an entire tray of tubes at once, a timesaving step that seals the tubes and maintains safety.

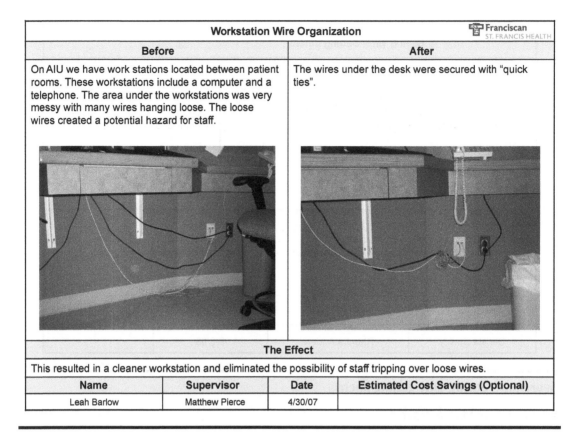

Figure 5.6 Workstation wire organizations.

Build Your Skills, Your Capabilities, and Your Knowledge

> *You cannot hope to build a better world without improving the individuals. To that end, each of us must work for our own improvement and, at the same time, share a general responsibility for all humanity.*
>
> **—Marie Curie**
> *Nobel Prize winner*

Is there an opportunity to learn something new about your work? If you can demonstrate how you applied your new learning to your work, it could be a Kaizen. One of the purposes of Kaizen is to develop the skills, capabilities, and knowledge of all employees. Franciscan received many Kaizens that have made their office-based employees more effective and efficient when using computers, like the one from Craig Whitaker, a financial analyst, shown in Figure 5.7. In this example, he learned something about making better use of the software in the course of making an improvement.

See an Opportunity or a Problem

A problem is the difference between what is happening now and what "should be" or what "needs to be." An opportunity is the gap between our current state and

Displaying the File Location in Excel 2007		Franciscan ST. FRANCIS HEALTH
Before	**After**	
Tara pointed out to me that there was no file location field at the top of Excel 2007 like there is in Excel 2003. Tara uses the location field to copy the file path (location) from Excel 2003 into Outlook when sending document links. Tara would have to switch back from 2007 to 2003 to send a file link via email.	Not having used Excel 2003 much, I hadn't noticed this missing function in Excel 2007. Like most functions in 03 that can't be found in 07's ribbon, I realized this function had to be added manually in the customize window. "Document Location" must be added to the quick access toolbar in order to have the file path displayed within Excel.	

Effect
Tara no longer has to switch back to Excel 2003 to use this function. Time has been saved (about 10 minutes per month or 2 hours per year.)

Name	ID #	Dept #	Supervisor	Date
Craig Whitaker, Tara Baer		Finance	Rosemary Tucker	5/2/2011

Figure 5.7 Displaying the file location in Excel 2007.

an "ideal condition." An issue or situation can be framed as a problem (patients are waiting longer than our current goal) or an opportunity (reducing waiting times to be closer to the ideal of zero).

Seeing good opportunities or problems takes practice. Many things that would be seen as problems to an experienced Kaizeneer are hidden to healthcare professionals who are new to this approach. Back to our simple examples—you might not have thought twice about all of those trips to the linen cart before being encouraged to practice Kaizen. What used to feel like just a necessary part of your job now looks like waste, which is something you can fix. Learning to see these wastes in the area in which you work will help you identify opportunities to do Kaizen. You can refer back to Chapter 4 for a refresher on the eight types of waste.

Identifying problems and opportunities presents a challenge for beginning Kaizeneers. In the workplace, we have problems and opportunities for improvement. Seeing both types of situations takes focus, practice, and experience. Many Kaizens involve a situation that could be viewed as a problem or an opportunity, depending on our viewpoint.

Problems

A problem is a barrier or obstacle that drags down your performance—negatively impacting quality, safety, or efficiency. Often, problems will be obvious, such as when we receive a complaint about cold food from a patient or a family member. At other times, they might be unspoken, such as nurses crawling on the floor under the countertop to plug in a computer cart.

Some types of problems you might notice:

■ A customer complaint (patient or internal customer)—this can include patients complaining the unit is too noisy at night or a surgeon complaining that an instrument was missing in the operating room.
■ An error that was made, such as the wrong meal being delivered to a patient.

■ The potential for something being done incorrectly, such as two laboratory specimens being mixed up during labeling.

■ Things you do every day that consume time, are frustrating, or do not work consistently, such as not being able to find a wheelchair when you need one.

People can often identify problems in their own work. But, by going to the "gemba," leaders or people from other departments might see problems not complained about for one reason or another. These outside perspectives are often referred to as "fresh eyes." It may be that some problems, like a missing instrument or a noisy drawer, have been brought up many times before, but people have given up and do not mention them anymore because things did not get fixed. We cannot just ask about problems, we also have to also try to observe and see first hand.

Perceptual Blindness to Problems

A challenge in finding problems is the ability to see them. Scientists have discovered that we as humans suffer from a condition known as inattentional blindness or perceptual blindness.[2] When our attention is focused on one thing, we often do not see the other things around us. Also, when we see something frequently, such as a picture on the wall, we tend to take the picture for granted, and our mind blanks the picture out. In other words, we see the picture so often we stop seeing it. Many of you may have already viewed a fun training video where you are told to count the number of times a group of people passes a basketball to each other.[3] During the team's passing (and your counting), a man in a gorilla suit walks through the frame, stops to wave, and continues walking. In most groups, 50% of people report not having seen the gorilla.[4]

> *The range of what we think and do is limited by what we fail to notice. And because we fail to notice that we fail to notice there is little we can do to change until we notice how failing to notice shapes our thoughts and deeds.*
>
> **—R. D. Laing**
> *Scottish psychiatrist*

With so much sensory overload in our world, it is human nature to block out and not notice small things that might be right in front of you. Sometimes, you need a pair of fresh eyes to see problems that have become accepted as just "par for the course" by those who do the work every day. A good way to see things you have never noticed before is to look at them through someone else's eyes. Asking someone to watch you and document the steps in your work can do this, or you can have someone videotape you doing the activity, for you to watch and review.[5]

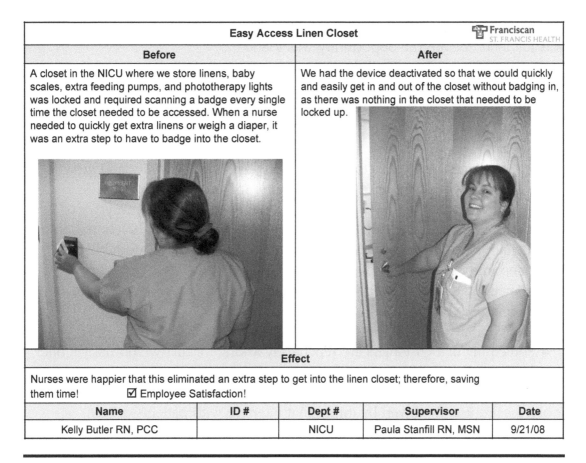

Easy Access Linen Closet		Franciscan ST. FRANCIS HEALTH
Before	**After**	
A closet in the NICU where we store linens, baby scales, extra feeding pumps, and phototherapy lights was locked and required scanning a badge every single time the closet needed to be accessed. When a nurse needed to quickly get extra linens or weigh a diaper, it was an extra step to have to badge into the closet.	We had the device deactivated so that we could quickly and easily get in and out of the closet without badging in, as there was nothing in the closet that needed to be locked up.	

Effect				
Nurses were happier that this eliminated an extra step to get into the linen closet; therefore, saving them time! ☑ Employee Satisfaction!				

Name	ID #	Dept #	Supervisor	Date
Kelly Butler RN, PCC		NICU	Paula Stanfill RN, MSN	9/21/08

Figure 5.8   Easy access linen closet.

Question Everything

Another way to help you see what you possibly are not seeing is to ask yourself why you do each of the things you do. If you question everything, you will begin to notice things that you had not noticed before. For example, Kelly Butler, a lead nurse in the Franciscan NICU, questioned why a supply closet was locked. For years, nurses had to badge in to get into the closet to get supply items. Occasionally, a nurse would have their hands full, making it difficult to open the supply closet door. The lock was a problem that got in the way of ideal patient care, yet it went unnoticed. Once noticed, it was easy to get the lock removed, and, as a result, nurses just push open the closet door, as illustrated in Figure 5.8. A seasoned Kaizeneer may even question the purpose of the door.

Opportunities

Opportunities describe how the world would be better if we could do things in a different or fresh way. Opportunities are not as obvious as problems because we do not always compare our work and results against an absolute ideal condition, such as zero infections or zero wasted motion. The earlier Kaizen about the locked closet door was both a problem (the locked door) and an opportunity (more efficient entry into the supply closet saves time). In that case, the problem was identified before the opportunity was found.

A study of more than 70 of the greatest innovators of all time found that innovators tended to search for and find opportunities first; then they identified the problems that needed to be surmounted to maximize their improvement.[6]

At Franciscan, some of the most powerful opportunities have been those that better serve patients. Better service leads to repeat business, which sustains or grows the business and leads to long-term organizational viability and growth. Some examples of patient-related opportunities might include noticing:

- An unmet customer need, such as seeing a parent sleeping uncomfortably in a chair, illustrates the opportunity to provide parents a comfortable place to sleep in their child's hospital room.
- Something that we could do better, such as being faster to respond to a patient who pushes a call light button or being 100% compliant to washing hands prior to entering or exiting a patient room.
- Something that customers are repetitively asking for that we do not yet offer, such as offering their favorite brand of coffee or offering their favorite dessert.

Problems are usually driven by things that interfere with patients or staff. Opportunities might be driven by strategic directions and priorities that are set by the senior leadership team, such as finding opportunities to improve clinical outcomes in a measurable way. Patients might not be filing complaints that infection rates are too high, but there is likely an opportunity for improvement in that area.

Problem, Opportunity, or Both: Some people prefer to define every problem as an opportunity, because the word "problem" often has negative connotations like doubt, difficulty, and uncertainty associated with it. If you never want to use the word problem, that might work just fine in Kaizen. However, Franciscan does not shy away from the word problem.

Kitchen Example

In your kitchen, how far is your dishwasher from the cabinets where you keep the dishes? Do you have to walk any distance to put cups away? If you are like most people, you may have been walking many feet each time to put something away, and you may have been doing that for years without noticing. The movement may have been unnecessarily consuming your time, and you may have never considered or known that there might be a better way. The opportunity is to save yourself time each time you do dishes. The problem is the distance separating the dishwasher from the cabinet.

Defining the Opportunity or Problem

If I had an hour to solve a problem, I'd spend 55 minutes thinking about the problem and 5 minutes thinking about solutions.

—Albert Einstein

In this first step of Quick and Easy Kaizen, it is important to spend some time defining the opportunity or problem clearly. The more clearly it is defined, the easier it will be to seize the best opportunity or to solve the right problem most effectively. Defining the opportunity or problem includes investigating and understanding its underlying nature, or what we might call the root cause. The way we define the problem impacts the types of countermeasures or solutions we may go looking for.

The opportunity or problem can be ideally defined in a few simple words. It can be defined as an opportunity, such as, "we could save two minutes each time we staple something we've printed if the stapler was located next to the printer." We can also define it in terms of the problem, such as "the stapler is five feet from the printer causing us to walk from the printer to the stapler each time we need to staple something."

In 2010, Kelly Butler was struggling with how a problem was defined. Pediatricians claimed that NICU nursing was not giving them enough notice when a circumcision was needed. Her nurses were criticized for not communicating, and it was becoming hurtful. When she investigated, she found that her nurses were consistently giving the pediatricians more than the 24-hour notice that they required.

It turned out the problem was that pediatric practices did not transfer that information immediately to the pediatrician. Kelly then defined the problem as "a breakdown in the pediatric office communication practices." However, she struggled to make headway with the practices because the offices were independent businesses outside the hospital.

Kelly decided to redefine the problem as "nursing is not involving pediatricians in circumcision timing decisions as early as they could be." With the problem statement focused on something within their control, her team quickly designed a solution that worked.

Her team now communicates directly with pediatricians by using a visual board in the NICU. As soon as a baby gets a bed in the NICU, the baby's name goes up on the board along with a predicted date of circumcision. Now, when pediatricians round in the unit, they generally assess the baby for circumcision earlier than they did before.

Because Kelly spent time to reframe the problem into something she could take action on, she and her staff could implement a Kaizen that enabled circumcisions to take place closer to their predicted date. Now, parents and physicians are happier, which makes the staff happier.

Your First Kaizen Report: Have you identified a problem or an opportunity you would like to address in your own job? If not, try to think of one now. Remember, start by thinking of something very small that you likely have the power to fix locally. Sometimes, the best Kaizens are the smallest. We are not trying to save a million dollars with a Kaizen—we are just trying to get the ball rolling. At this point, you can write a "before" statement that summarizes the problem or opportunity. Take a "before" picture or, for now, write up something in 25 words or less. You might not have a title for the Kaizen until you are done, so it is acceptable to leave that blank for now if you want.

Step 2—Discuss

After identifying a problem or opportunity, it is time to discuss the idea with your team and your supervisor. With Quick and Easy Kaizen, leaders certainly encourage employees to generate and take action on ideas, but that does not mean that supervisors or other managers are left completely out of the loop. Kaizen is not slow and bureaucratic, like a traditional suggestion box, nor is it a "free-for-all" where everybody just takes actions in isolation of their teammates and leaders. Individuals are creative, but ideas tend to be better when we involve other people.

In this phase of the process, a person with an idea should:

- Discuss the idea with their direct supervisor
- Discuss the opportunity, problem, or idea with team members
- Quantify the expected benefits of the idea, where possible

Discuss with Your Direct Supervisor

Before you implement your Kaizen, it is important to review your Kaizen with your direct supervisor. Completing the "before" section of the Kaizen Report can help communicate your idea to your supervisor. Your supervisor will help you ensure your Kaizen fits well in the context of the organization and the customers being served and will help you think through and strengthen your Kaizen. Chapter 9 covers the role of front-line supervisors in more detail. Some of the following guidelines apply, however, for any leader at any level who is reviewing a Kaizen from an employee. For example, it might be a vice president reviewing the Kaizen written up by a director who reports to them.

The Supervisor Should be a Coach

It is the supervisor's role to be both a coach and a cheerleader to Kaizeneers who report to them. The supervisor is a vital part of the Kaizen process.

Coaching is accomplished by questioning the Kaizeneer in order to help think through the Kaizen enough to implement it successfully. The supervisor is not supposed to take control and do the Kaizen for the Kaizeneer. Responsibility for implementation of the Kaizen should remain with the Kaizeneer, so they learn firsthand how to implement each Kaizen.

The Role of Supervisors and Their Judgment

A key job for a supervisor is to manage risk by ensuring that Kaizens do not adversely affect quality, procedures, policies, or safety.

The supervisor ensures the change:

- Introduces no risk to the safety of patients or staff
- Will not have side effects or cause problems beyond what the Kaizeneer can see
- Has buy-in from other team members and departments that the change could affect
- Will be cost-effective, quick, and easy to implement.

For example, if the supervisor suspects that there is a problem that would be created by a Kaizen, such as the introduction of a new patient safety risk, the supervisor should focus on educating the employee who had the idea, rather than punishing them. In cases like this, the supervisor should work with the implementer to adequately resolve these issues prior to implementation or come up with an alternative idea that addresses the issue in a better way.

Say "Yes"

The supervisor's job is to discover how to say "yes" to the Kaizen. As much as possible, supervisors should approve Kaizens. In one of Masaaki Imai's benchmark companies, Aisin-Warner, 99% of ideas were accepted and implemented.[7] The process and the experience helps to develop someone's thinking and builds enthusiasm for Kaizen.

Some of Masaaki Imai's guidelines for approving or rejecting Kaizen ideas are summarized in Table 5.1.

Many Kaizens can be easily undone or reversed if the change does not turn out to be a demonstrated improvement. Again, as long as safety or quality will not be impacted, the tendency should be to say "yes, let's try this idea." Following the Plan-Do-Study-Act (PDSA) cycle, we can evaluate, after some experimentation with the idea, if we should stick with the change, or go back to the old method, or try something altogether different.

In cases in which the proposed change cannot be implemented, the supervisor helps the Kaizeneer modify her Kaizen into something workable. In Franciscan's pharmacy, where every Kaizen is strictly scrutinized for any possible patient safety ramifications, more than 89% of Kaizens are implemented, yet many do get modified. Unlike the old suggestion box process, in which managers and leaders voted "yes" or "no" in a very disconnected way, Kaizen is

Table 5.1 Masaaki Imai's Guidelines for Approving or Rejecting Kaizen Ideas

Ideas are accepted if one of the following are true:[i]	Ideas tend to be rejected if they are:[ii]
Making the job easier	Grievances
Removing drudgery from the job	Repetition of previously submitted ideas
Removing nuisance from the job	Statements of well-known facts
Making the job safer	Platitudes
Making the job more productive	Complaints about others
Improving product quality	Too vague or impossible to implement
Saving time and cost	Idea had already been submitted
Saving in energy, material, and other resources	
Ideas for new products (services)	

[i] Imai, *KAIZEN*, 112.
[ii] Imai, 115.

about dialogue between employees and their supervisors, working together to find something that can be done to solve their problem.

If an idea involves spending a lot of money, then leaders may need to work with the Kaizeneer to find a more creative or less expensive approach that addresses the underlying problem or opportunity. Although return on investment (ROI) is not the most important thing and we want to encourage Kaizen, supervisors and managers do need to be cognizant of the short-term financial and cultural realities in their organization, meaning that Kaizen cannot be a "blank check" to staff members.

Lynne Meredith, director of revenue management at Franciscan, coaches her staff on Kaizens that are not as workable as they could be by saying, "That is a great idea, but let's take that one step further," and she helps them think through a better solution.

At Franciscan we discovered that, if you disallow one Kaizen idea, you may turn that person off from the process altogether in early stages. People can get discouraged when Kaizens get blocked or delayed. If enough Kaizens are turned down, the Kaizen program can die, like older suggestion box programs tended to do for so many organizations. As Imai wrote, "When a worker's suggestion cannot be implemented, management promptly explains why."[8]

Supervisors Assess Broader Impact

If the Kaizen will impact the entire unit or department, the manager may need to be involved in approving and helping with the Kaizen. Alternatively, organizations seeking or already at Magnet Nursing status may require Kaizens that impact the entire unit to undergo Unit Council review. At Franciscan, once Kaizens are approved, managers use email, and sometimes a daily huddle, to communicate Kaizen changes that have wide impact to all personnel in the unit.

Tray Towelettes				🏛 Franciscan ST. FRANCIS HEALTH
Before	**After**			
Wash cloths provided on patient food trays must be laundered.	 In view of the importance of hand washing and infection control issues, I suggest that every meal tray have a disposable towelette to encourage patients, family members and visitors to wash their hands prior to eating.			
Effect				
Working with Infection Control and Food Services we've received approval from Keith Jewell (COO) and Susan McRoberts (CNO) to make this improvement. **Costs:** $0.02 each *300,000 trays per year = $6,000 per year. **Benefits:** Disposable towelettes are convenient and there when you need them. Reduction in Hospital Acquired Infections, and improvement in patient, family, visitor and staff safety is priceless.				

Name	ID #	Dept #	Supervisor	Date
Wilda "Billie" Golden, Claire Roembke, Sean McKenzie		6192	Jan Rubush	7/30/08

Figure 5.9   Tray towelettes.

Supervisors Coordinate Cross Department Impact

If the Kaizen involves personnel, resources, or processes from other departments, the supervisor may need to help the Kaizeneer communicate and coordinate across departments. Coordinating Kaizens across departments is more challenging than local Kaizens, but the benefits are often greater.

For example, at Franciscan, a nurse worked with the infection control and food services departments to provide disposable towelettes on trays to encourage patients to wash their hands before eating meals, as shown in Figure 5.9.

Discuss with Your Team Members

Before you implement your idea, it is important to talk with the team members who could be affected by your improvement idea. If the idea is likely to impact your team members directly, it is best to begin discussions while you are still investigating ideas so that you can get their input and ideas. Do your best to objectively consider all ideas, not just your own ideas.

Kitchen Example

Who would be affected by rearranging your kitchen? Would a significant other be affected? Have you tried to rearrange your kitchen in the past without involving your significant other? If you are like most of us, you likely experienced some repercussions from your actions. Therefore, be sure to involve those people prior to implementing improvements. If they were not at least aware of the changes, they would likely be frustrated with the change. Thinking back to our kitchen example, if they did the dishes, they would need to understand where the dishes should be placed and why they should be placed in new locations for them to be willing to place them in their new locations.

Figure 5.10   Example of an online database of Kaizens for easy searching.

Identify More Than One Idea

The best way to have a good idea is to have lots of ideas.

—Linus Pauling
Scientist and Nobel Prize Winner

During your discussion with others, do your best to search for more than just one idea or solution. As a general rule of thumb, if you want to find the best idea, then identify many workable ideas. The more workable ideas you identify, the more likely you will be to find a best idea or solution. A good way to generate multiple ideas is to ask multiple people. At Franciscan St. Francis Health, any employee can search the organization's online database of thousands of Kaizens that have been turned in after being implemented, as pictured in Figure 5.10. For example, an employee can search for "stapler" and find all the Kaizen improvements that had something to do with a stapler. Chapter 10 has more detail about electronic systems at Franciscan and other organizations.

Expand Your Vision

During your discussions with others, see if you can refine your idea to one that goes beyond your own personal benefit to one that also has benefits for patients. Then, you will have a win–win—an idea that is good for you, your department, your organization, and your customers.

For example, Angela Collier, a nurse at Franciscan, noticed that parents periodically asked her when their baby had its last bath. So she started posting the bath time on a Post-it® note. Then, when she started talking with other nurses in

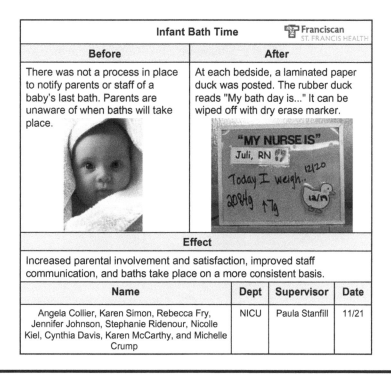

Figure 5.11 Infant bath time.

the unit, she noticed that many of them experienced the same thing. She realized that by expanding her vision and getting others involved, her idea could not only improve the process for herself, but also for all of the nurses in her unit. Working together, the nurses added a laminated duck to the communication board at each bedside, as shown in Figure 5.11. On the laminated ducks, they wrote the date of the last bath, creating a win–win for the staff and the parents of the babies.

Levels of Impact

There are many levels of impact when considering an improvement idea. These levels of impact are:

1. Self
2. Department
3. Organization (hospital or health system)
4. Customer
5. Community
6. Society

The levels can be thought of as concentric circles, as shown in Figure 5.12.

Recycling is an example that has an impact across multiple levels. The idea to recycle may come from an individual who wants to feel good by having an impact on the environment. The initial thought to recycle may also lead to ideas that reduce waste or encourage the appropriate reuse of office supplies, such as 3-ring binders, or the reuse of cardboard boxes in a laboratory—changes that save

Figure 5.12   The many levels of impact when considering an improvement idea.

the organization money. The pathology department at Children's Medical Center Dallas moved from recycling aluminum and batteries to recycling the chemical xylene. The $16,000 cost of the recycler would be recouped in three years, and the recycling unit also reduced fumes and exposure to laboratory technologists.[9] Although it might require a little extra time and effort by staff or initial investment from a department and health system, initiatives like these are better for the community and the world and, if done well, can be cost neutral or reduce costs.

In the Kaizen shown in Figure 5.13, Therese Staublin, a pharmacist at Franciscan noticed that nonrecyclable items were finding their way into recycling bins. Rex Marling, a pharmacist, had a small tool shop in his garage, so she asked him to make a top for the bin that allowed only cans to enter. Some nonrecyclables still enter, but the amount was reduced dramatically.

Recycling Enhancements		⚕ Franciscan ST. FRANCIS HEALTH
Before	**After**	
Staff would inadvertently put trash in the recycling bin. Someone would have to sort the trash out before taking the cans for recycling.	Therese suggested and Rex designed and manufactured an insert for the recycling can with a visual reminder that it is for cans only. Recycling bin now contains only cans. Template could be made from our insert to make inserts for other areas in the hospital.	
The Effect		
No time wasted sorting trash out of the recyling bin. No risk to sorter of being exposed to something hazardous in the trash		

Name	Cost Center	Supervisor	Date	Estimated Cost Savings (Optional)
Rex Marling and Therese Staublin	730	Karen Blanford	8/30/2007	Decreased wasted time

Figure 5.13   Recycling Enhancements.

The best ideas are good for all levels. However, when you first start with Kaizen, start with making things better for you. As we mentioned earlier, it is easier for most people to begin by considering themselves and their own scope of work. As you do more Kaizens, you will get better at making improvements that are good for more levels of impact. If you are leading Kaizen in your area, it is important to allow and encourage new Kaizeneers to pursue Kaizens that might appear to be self-interested. Even mature Kaizeneers turn in some Kaizens that appear to be self-centered. Kaizen efforts are usually not as selfish as they might appear, because making things more efficient for staff members usually leads to benefits for patients and the organization.

For example, if a staff member asks for a plasma screen to be put up in the lab, a manager in a traditional suggestion system might say "no" because there is no budget or because they think people want to watch TV at night. In a collaborative Kaizen discussion, the manager would learn that the larger plasma screen, used as computer monitor, would make it easier to monitor the timeliness of test orders. The manager can help make a business case for how the screen would help, or they can work together to find other ways of solving that same problem.

Common Benefits by Level of Impact

1. **Self:** Makes work easier, better, safer, more interesting, or builds your skills, your capabilities, and your knowledge
2. **Department:** Reduces waste, saves time, reduces frustrations, improves workflow, or improves staff satisfaction
3. **Organization:** Improves staff or patient safety, quality, outcomes, productivity, or costs
4. **Customer:** Improves patient safety, patient satisfaction, customer experience, or family and friends' experiences
5. **Community:** Educates community or improves community health
6. **Society:** Saves resources, reduces wastes, reduces consumption, or recycles materials

Quantifying Benefits When Possible

One cannot be successful on visible figures alone ... the most important figures that one needs for management are unknown or unknowable, but successful management must nevertheless take account of them.

—W. Edwards Deming, Ph.D.[10]

The focus of Kaizen is not and should not be primarily on monetary gains, although monetary gains are a by-product of Kaizen. At Franciscan, less than 6% of Kaizens are quantified and verified with finance personnel as directly saving

Busy Aprons	Franciscan ST. FRANCIS HEALTH
Before	**After**
Our geriatric population was in need of restraint alternatives. Most of these items can be expensive to order from the Posey manufacturer. One such item was a "busy apron". It cost around $45.	Chris Pierle, Quality Manager, arranged for the St. Francis Auxiliary to make these aprons out of scrap material, for free. Our 8 Tower nursing unit received 9 of these aprons to use for our patients.

Effect				
Saved money: 9 aprons x $45 per apron = $405. Patients/staff have alternatives to keep patients out of restraints.				

Name	ID #	Dept #	Supervisor	Date
Christa Smiley		8T	Rhonda Anders	2/7/08

Figure 5.14   Busy Aprons.

bottom-line money for the organization. The vast majority of Kaizens improve the work or work environment and improve the customer experience, but are difficult to quantify in immediate savings or increased revenue.

So if you have trouble quantifying the benefits, simply write down what the Kaizen does for you and others. Be sure to note the difference the Kaizen makes for your customers. It can be helpful, though, to ask the person with the idea to state, qualitatively, how the improvement benefits areas such as waiting time, quality, or staff or patient satisfaction, even if hard numbers are not available.

Kaizen would not be quick and easy if each one required a quantified dollar savings. Furthermore, it may be wasteful to always try to calculate a monetary savings for every idea. There may be a threshold dollar amount, above which it is worth the time and effort to estimate the cost savings. Franciscan works with Kaizeneers to quantify Kaizens that have the potential to save over $1,000.

A simple example of a Kaizen cost savings calculation occurred when we asked our Franciscan volunteers to use their creativity and skills, as shown in Figure 5.14. The savings was simply the number of aprons used times the cost saved per apron.

In another example, when pharmacists partnered with cardiac surgeons at Franciscan, albumin use was reduced during open-heart surgeries, resulting in a savings of over $90,000 per year, as illustrated in Figure 5.15. The albumin cost savings was more involved than the aprons Kaizen, but simply was the difference in albumin usage before versus after the Kaizen.

Lowered Albumin Usage			Franciscan ST. FRANCIS HEALTH
Before	**After**		
Albumin was used to expand blood volume for patients during open heart surgeries.	A change in philosophy and approach was introduced. Volume replacement orders were changed on the post operative orders and the result has been dramatic with regard to cost savings. The overall effect on blood product savings for the healthcare system, although not measurable, per se, is thought to be great, as well.		
The Effect			
Albumin usage for the 10 months prior to the change averaged 6.9 units per open heart case, based on 323 surgeries. Albumin usage for the 10 months after the change averaged 2.4 units per open heart case, based on 387 surgeries. Resulting in a savings of about $250-300 per open heart case, with an annual savings of $90,843.			
Name	**Supervisor**	**Date**	**Savings**
Christopher W. Gregory, R.Ph, Clinical Pharmacist	Ronda Freije, R.Ph., Manager	10/01/07	$90,843

Figure 5.15   Lowered Albumin Usage.

He that expects to quantify in dollars the gains that will accrue to a company year by year for a program for improvement of quality expounded in [Out of the Crisis] will suffer delusion. He should know before he starts that he will be able to quantify only a trivial part of the gain.[11]

—W. Edwards Deming, Ph.D.

Kitchen Example

Benefit Calculations: (20 cups / 2 cups per trip) × (4 seconds per trip)
= 40 seconds saved for just the cups

For example, let us look at how you would calculate the time savings if you were in your kitchen and had 20 cups to put away. Let us split the calculation into two parts. First calculate the number of trips: if you could carry 2 cups per trip, you would have to make 10 trips.

Then, estimate the time spent walking per trip, which in this case might be observed as being 4 seconds per trip. Finally, you can put the calculations together and multiply the number of trips by the time per trip to give you the total time of 10 trips × 4 seconds per trip or 40 seconds.

So if you could rearrange your kitchen so that the cabinet for the cups was just above or next to the dishwasher and you did not have to travel to put the cups away, you could save 40 seconds each time just for the cups. If you saved five minutes each time you did all dishes, not just the cups, that would give you five minutes that you could devote to more important things, such as your family or friends. This is the way experienced Kaizeneers think. When appropriate, they try to quantify the improvement potential before making the improvement.

Our website (www.HCkaizen.com) contains a more detailed explanation of how to quantify benefits of Kaizens.

Every Little Improvement is Worth Doing

Some Kaizens may not be worth doing from a purely financial perspective. For example, if the cost far exceeds the quantifiable benefits, then it might be difficult to get the money approved to spend on the Kaizen. In a traditional return on investment (ROI) view, spending might get rejected if the benefits do not exceed the cost within a certain period, such as one year.

However, because most Kaizens should require little to no out-of-pocket expense, the cost of improvement is often just a matter of people's time and effort. If, over time, those Kaizens save time and effort, and most do, there will be a longer-term payback, and every little improvement that built up the employees' ability to do Kaizen will have been worth doing.

Giving approval for Kaizens that do not have a short-term payoff may help build confidence and enthusiasm of staff members to keep generating ideas. As Imai suggests (and we mentioned in Chapter 4), the first phase of Kaizen is built around saying yes to most ideas. During later, more mature, phases of Kaizen, we can start challenging people more on their problem-solving skills and the financial impact of Kaizens.

Kitchen Example

A supervisor with experience helping others with Kaizen might help you think out the solution. They could also challenge your thinking to improve the solution. For example, they might ask you to ponder how you could get at least 80% of the dishes into one cabinet rather than the three cabinets you were thinking about. You may have been thinking of putting all the cups that you own into one cabinet, whereas your spouse or roommate may challenge you to think about separating the most commonly used cups from those that are less commonly used and put just the most commonly used cups in the cabinet next to the dishwasher. That would give you more room for other dishes. If the cabinet closest to the dishwasher contained only those most commonly used dishes, there would be enough room for most of the dishes in the dishwasher, leaving very few items that would require walking any distance to put away.

Your First Kaizen Report: At this point, you have thought more about your Kaizen, and hopefully, you have discussed it with some colleagues and your supervisor. Did they help you refine your understanding of the "Before" situation? If so, you can update that section. What different solutions or countermeasures did you consider? Because you have not implemented yet, you can write your proposed solution in the "After" section, but this might get edited later. You should be thinking of a hypothesis—if you do this, then what will happen? You will be testing this hypothesis during Step 3—Implement. Remember the PDSA cycle.

Step 3—Implement

After identifying and discussing the idea with our supervisor and our colleagues, we implement the change as part of the PDSA cycle. An idea must be implemented to qualify as a Kaizen. Keep in mind that we will test to see if the change is actually an improvement and if things changed the way we suspected in our hypothesis.

> *I have been impressed with the urgency of doing. Knowing is not enough; we must apply. Being willing is not enough; we must do.*
>
> **—Leonardo da Vinci**

In this phase of the process, Kaizeneers do the following:

- Enroll others to help
- Implement the idea
- Give a seven-day grace period for any new idea

Enrolling Others to Help

Some Kaizens can be done on your own, and some require the help of others to implement. Identifying the people you will need help from is an important step prior to implementing. Sometimes it is as simple as asking for their help. Often, you will need to explain how it benefits them and others. If you are new at Kaizen or need help outside your department, you should ask for your supervisor or manager to help you enroll others.

Joe and the team at Franciscan have found there are four levels of help needed, increasing in complexity.

1. I can do the Kaizen myself.
2. I need the help of one or more other people in my department in my discipline (i.e., nurse to nurse).
3. I need the help of others in my department that are outside my discipline (i.e., nurse to physician).
4. I need the help of others in and outside my department.

If others help you with your Kaizen, it is a good idea to add their name to your Kaizen Report when you write it. This way, they get recognized for their contributions, and they will be more likely to help you again in the future. A Kaizen Report can list several people. As a standard practice, place the name of the Kaizeneer who lead the Kaizen or originated the idea first in the list.

Table 5.2   Length of Time to Implement Kaizens

Kaizen	Length to Implement
Switch location of gauze and adhesive bandages in drawer	Minutes
Get a digital thermometer for each exam room	Minutes to order, days to arrive
Cut and round off the corner of the nurses' station counter so people do not bump into it.	Minutes to create work order, days or weeks to get a carpenter, minutes or hours to do the work.

Implement the Improvement Idea

Ideally, the person who initiated the idea should be the one to implement the idea. You plan out how to implement, who to involve, and where to start. Then, you just do it (because you have already talked with teammates and your supervisor). Some Kaizens are implemented in minutes; others may take a few days or weeks, depending on how extensive the improvement is, as shown in Table 5.2.

Seven Days Grace

Franciscan has learned that Kaizens should be given "seven days' grace." That means everyone affected by a Kaizen gets to try it for a week before weighing in on whether it should be continued or not.

Initially, when Ronda Frieje, manager of pharmacy, launched Franciscan's Kaizen program, she experienced cases in which some people did not want to try changes that others had implemented. Ronda found that, in most cases, the Kaizens in question were good Kaizens, if allowed to work. Often the issue was that some people were challenged by change and preferred to do things their old familiar way. Ronda created a practice she called, "seven days grace." She explained, "we have to be willing to try something new for seven days." She told her staff, "I'm not afraid to go back" if the idea does not pan out. Her staff felt more comfortable going forward if they knew they could go back. Ronda had to revert back only a few times in the past three years.

For example, one pharmacy Kaizen was intended to improve the productivity of assembling custom medication trays by organizing medications in locations based on the tray type. So they grouped open-heart medications together and labor and delivery medications together, and they tried it for seven days. After seven days, the analysis concluded that the productivity of tray assembly did improve, but not enough to overcome the negative effects of duplicate stocking locations that caused additional restocking effort and the greater potential of mixed medications. So they went back to the previous method of storing each medication in only one location.

Your First Kaizen Report: At this point, you have put your idea into place, testing the change through the "Do" phase of the PDSA cycle. Through the seven days' grace, you will have studied the impact of the changes. Did you get the results you expected? Were there any side effects or unintended consequences in your area or others? Talk to your supervisor and colleagues and, after this "Study" phase, decide how you are going to "Act" or "Adjust." Is this a change that you will accept, or do you need to go back and try something else? Remember, in the PDSA mindset, it is acceptable if you tried something that did not work the way you expected. If that happened, what can you learn from the experience?

Step 4—Document

Make everything as simple as possible, but not simpler.

—Albert Einstein

Documenting implemented Kaizens is a critical step in spreading improvement throughout the department and the organization. In this phase, we:

- Finalize the write-up about what was done in a simple Kaizen Report (see Figure 5.16)
- Submit the Kaizen Report

Figure 5.17 is a good example of a Kaizen Report. First, it was given a catchy title. Next, the nice use of pictures made the difference between the before and after conditions very obvious. It also described the before condition from the point of view of the customer—the patients and, especially in this case, their families. It nicely explained what was done to create the improvement. The effect section describes the benefit to staff and customers in a simple way. Finally, it gives credit to those to whom credit is due: the Kaizeneer and their supervisor.

Kaizen Report Title	
Before: ● We had this problem	**After:** ● We did this
Effect: ● These were the benefits	

Figure 5.16   The most basic Kaizen Report template.

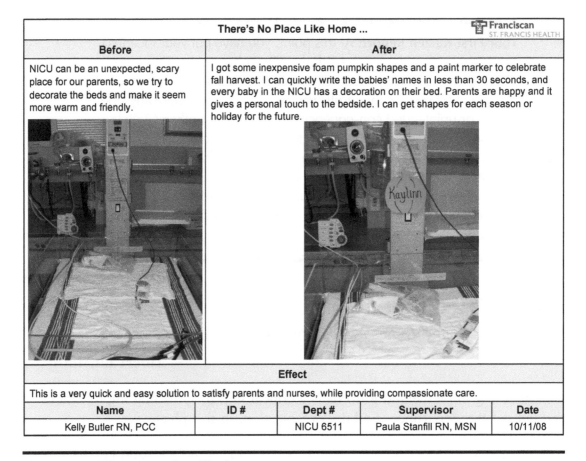

There's No Place Like Home ...			Franciscan ST. FRANCIS HEALTH
Before	**After**		
NICU can be an unexpected, scary place for our parents, so we try to decorate the beds and make it seem more warm and friendly.	I got some inexpensive foam pumpkin shapes and a paint marker to celebrate fall harvest. I can quickly write the babies' names in less than 30 seconds, and every baby in the NICU has a decoration on their bed. Parents are happy and it gives a personal touch to the bedside. I can get shapes for each season or holiday for the future.		
Effect			
This is a very quick and easy solution to satisfy parents and nurses, while providing compassionate care.			

Name	ID #	Dept #	Supervisor	Date
Kelly Butler RN, PCC		NICU 6511	Paula Stanfill RN, MSN	10/11/08

Figure 5.17 There's no place like home.

Finalize the Kaizen Report

The Kaizen Report typically includes five main pieces:

1. **Title:** The title should appear at the top of the Kaizen Report and convey what the Kaizen is about in 10 words or less.
2. **Before:** This describes what the problem or situation was before the Kaizen. Pictures or hand drawings are often better than words in this section.
3. **After:** This conveys what change took place or how it was improved. Again, pictures or hand drawings are better than words.
4. **Effect:** Here, list the benefits or results of the improvement.
5. **Credits:** The credits section should list the Kaizeneer and anyone that helped, the department name or number, the supervisor, and the date the Kaizen was completed.

When Franciscan first started its program, they had a place in the lower right of the Kaizen Report to enter the financial savings. Later, leaders realized that this overemphasized cost savings to the staff, so they removed it.

Summarize the Kaizen by using the fewest words possible. Try to use less than 75 words total to document the entire Kaizen. It should take fewer than

Pill Cutters & Pill Crushers		Franciscan ST. FRANCIS HEALTH	
Before		**After**	
In bin in compounding area.		On shelf opposite the tube station.	
The Effect			
Time and steps savings. Within easy reach of placing in tube.			
Name	**Supervisor**	**Date**	**Savings**
Cynthia Fonts	Ronda Freije	9/07	

Figure 5.18 Pill cutters & pill crushers.

10 minutes to document a Kaizen when you get good at it. Simple ones should take less than 3 minutes to complete. For example, Figure 5.18 shows a Kaizen received at Franciscan that demonstrates how simple a Kaizen Report can be.

The documentation does not have to wait until the end. For example, Kaizeneers often create the Kaizen Report as they progress through steps one through three. You can start the report when you have just an understanding of the current condition to document in the "Before" section. The report may get modified as colleagues and managers give input and feedback.

The most valuable of all talents is that of never using two words when one will do.

—Thomas Jefferson

Handwritten Example

The first Quick and Easy Kaizen Report ever turned in at Franciscan came from Debbie in environmental services, shown in Figure 5.19. She noticed that coffee filters on a nursing unit that she cleans were getting soiled and were often thrown away. She asked the nursing unit manager to purchase a plastic container for her, so the coffee filters would be protected. She labeled the container so that it would be obvious that it was for the coffee filters.

Quick & Easy
KAIZEN

Before Improvement	After Improvement
Coffee Filters were getting contaminated in 8Tower kitchen and some had to be thrown away.	Coffee filters remain clean + dry and are not wasted.

The Effect: Improved environment, cost savings with purchasing fewer coffee filters per month.

Date 4/16/07 Name Debbie Brokamp

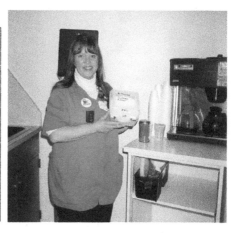

Figure 5.19 The first Quick and Easy Kaizen Report from Franciscan.

Looking back at her first Kaizen, the only thing Debbie could have added to the Kaizen Report was what she did to create the "after" condition, specifically that they purchased a plastic container.

Even though Franciscan has an electronic database so employees can submit Kaizens electronically, they allow employees to turn in Kaizen Reports in handwritten form because this keeps the process simple and easy for anyone to do, including those who are not as computer savvy as others. The paper Kaizen Reports are scanned so they are available electronically.

Electronic Example

Franciscan also allows employees to use a Microsoft PowerPoint template to create Kaizen Reports. They can either be emailed to the Kaizen Coordinator or uploaded to the database. Figure 5.20 is an example of a Kaizen that used a nice combination of words and pictures to convey the message simply. It was notable for the following reasons:

1. The four-word title is concise and clearly communicates what the Kaizen is about.
2. The before and after explanations are concise and clear.
3. The pictures help bring understanding to someone unfamiliar with the environment in which the Kaizen was done.
4. The results connect to the higher-level impacts of customers and community.
5. Overall, it is a high-impact Kaizen that is documented concisely and clearly.

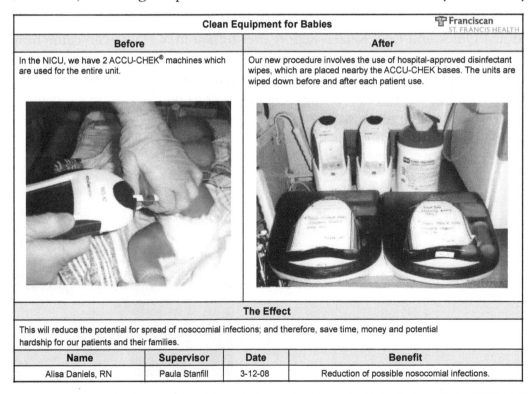

Figure 5.20 Clean equipment for babies.

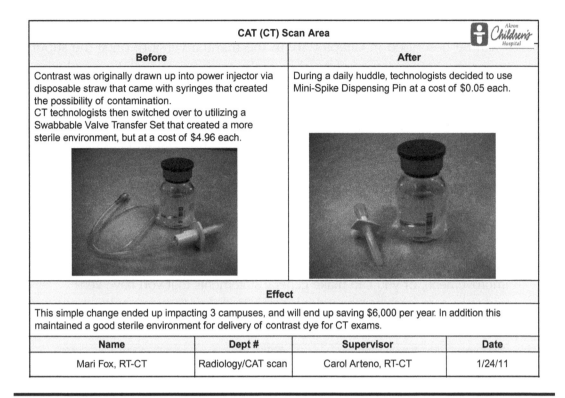

Figure 5.21   CAT (CT) scan area.

Akron Children's Hospital has started documenting their small improvements in the Kaizen Report format, including Figure 5.21, an improvement that saves a bit of money but also reduces the risk of contamination. The idea was shared and spread across three campuses.

Submit Report for Approval

Prior to submitting your Kaizen, verify that everything is completely implemented and does not contain suggestions that someone else should do. Then, submit the Kaizen Report to your supervisor. Keep in mind the agreement to implement the idea came earlier in the process when the Kaizeneer and the supervisor initially discussed it. Therefore, at this point in the process, the supervisor is either approving the write-up or asking the submitter to do another revision.

Once your supervisor receives your completed Kaizen Report, they will verify that what is documented has been completely implemented and is working, keeping in mind the seven days' grace. After seven days, the supervisor or manager should solicit positive and negative feedback on the Kaizen and its effects. At that time, anyone can approach the manager with valid reasons to revert back to the previous method or ways to improve on the idea. The manager makes the final determination whether the Kaizen stands or is withdrawn so the team can try a different improvement idea. After the Kaizen is verified to be working at the end of that period, the supervisor will approve the Kaizen Report.

Franciscan has two approval processes, manual and electronic. The electronic process will be described in Chapter 10. In the manual version, once the supervisor verifies the Kaizen is complete, they make two copies, one for employee records to reference during annual evaluations and one to send to the regional Kaizen coordinator. The original is posted in the department. The regional Kaizen coordinator reviews, approves, and enters it into the electronic system for record keeping, and decides which Kaizens are best to share hospital-wide in various ways.

Your First Kaizen Report: Congratulations! At this point, you will have completed your first Kaizen, with a before and after statement (possibly with pictures) and a description of the effect and benefits. You can state the benefits in a quantitative way (with hard numbers or financial improvement), or you can make general statements that you have verified to be true, such as "the work is easier to do" or "patients enjoy the change." Be sure to list others who contributed along the way.

Step 5—Share

The final step of Kaizen is to share the improvement. That means to post it, review it, and discuss it. This is done to give recognition to Kaizeneers and to spread good ideas more broadly.

Leveraging Improvement Ideas from Others

Most people are inherently creative and can come up with ideas for process improvement. However, it is acceptable to borrow others' ideas. This is one reason step 5, sharing ideas, is such a critical component of Kaizen.

If you borrow someone's idea, it is a good practice to give that person credit by noting on your Kaizen Report where you got the idea. However, your unique application of the other person's Kaizen idea to your work environment is your Kaizen to take ownership of discussing, implementing, documenting, and sharing.

The Kaizen shown in Figure 5.22 came about after a nurse at Franciscan heard that another nursing unit was putting all the supplies they needed for a particular procedure in a kit. She borrowed the idea to save time setting up IVs on patients.

"When we first started our Kaizen program staff thought copying was cheating," said Ronda Frieje, manager of pharmacy at Franciscan. "They thought that they couldn't adopt a Kaizen idea that a pharmacy at another campus implemented." Ronda had to explain to her staff that it is the intention of Kaizen to share and spread best practices from one another, when appropriate. Ronda said, "it was a key learning point for us." You can take someone else's Kaizen idea and uniquely customize it to your work before implementing it. By doing so, you can submit that Kaizen Report as your own. Sharing ideas is a critically important aspect of Kaizen.

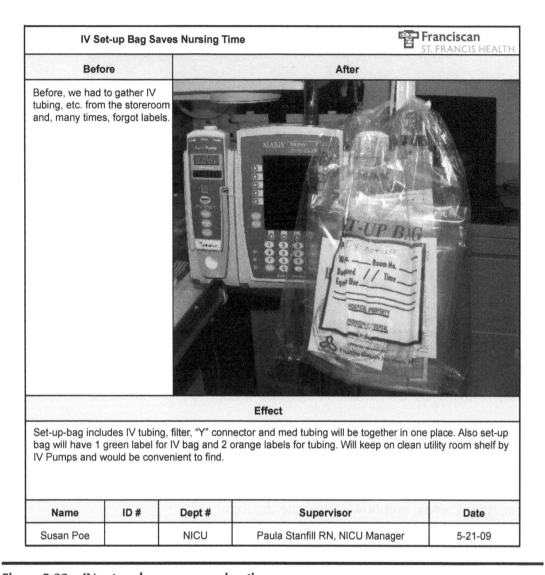

IV Set-up Bag Saves Nursing Time		Franciscan ST. FRANCIS HEALTH
Before	**After**	
Before, we had to gather IV tubing, etc. from the storeroom and, many times, forgot labels.		
Effect		
Set-up-bag includes IV tubing, filter, "Y" connector and med tubing will be together in one place. Also set-up bag will have 1 green label for IV bag and 2 orange labels for tubing. Will keep on clean utility room shelf by IV Pumps and would be convenient to find.		

Name	ID #	Dept #	Supervisor	Date
Susan Poe		NICU	Paula Stanfill RN, NICU Manager	5-21-09

Figure 5.22 IV set-up bag saves nursing time.

Sharing Kaizens

There are a variety of ways to share Kaizens—including public cafeteria display boards, intranet database, email, and web solutions.

> *The improvement of understanding is for two ends: first, our own increase of knowledge; secondly, to enable us to deliver that knowledge to others.*
>
> **—John Locke**

Post on Department Bulletin Boards

It is a good practice to post Kaizens in the department as a form of recognition for the Kaizeneers. Some departments use a dedicated Kaizen bulletin board, whereas other departments use a wall so they can keep adding Kaizens continuously over time, without running out of space as quickly.

Figure 5.23 A colorful Kaizen bulletin board for sharing ideas and recognizing staff.

For example, the frog-themed board shown in Figure 5.23 came from the NICU at Franciscan. It was notable because it had:

1. A participation chart with all employees listed and their individual number of Kaizens turned in
2. Staff recognition
3. An educational element that described the Kaizen program, how to document a Kaizen, and how to use the database
4. Effective communication
5. Central placement in the department
6. Effective use of space
7. Good use of color
8. Visual excitement

Post in Cafeterias

At Franciscan, each campus public cafeteria has a dedicated Kaizen Board where "notable Kaizens" are posted each month, as shown in Figure 5.24. By "notable," they mean Kaizens that are one or more of the following:

- Interesting to read
- Can be adopted by many others
- Are heartwarming
- Convey the organization's mission nicely
- Represent the Kaizen program well

Kaizens with photos or drawings have a better chance of appearing on this board because they tend to capture more attention.

Figure 5.24 Public Kaizen boards help share ideas more widely.

Having my Kaizen on the bulletin board made me smile at work for the month it was posted.

—Diana McClure
Analyst, revenue management, Franciscan

Share Via Email

Kaizens that are notable are shared at Franciscan through the emails sent by the chief operating officer to all staff. A nice example is a Kaizen Report that saved some money by evaluating what items nurses placed out in the sterile field during surgeries. This was sent to all employees, and over the next few months, Franciscan received additional Kaizens based on the same idea, with the one with the largest savings shown here in Figure 5.25. The improvements were all identified and driven by their surgical staff.

Some other examples of electronic sharing will be discussed in Chapter 10.

Conclusion

The five basic steps to Quick and Easy Kaizen are:

1. **Find** an opportunity to change something for the better.
2. **Discuss** the opportunity and potential improvements with your team members and your supervisor.
3. **Implement** the best improvement.
4. **Document** a Kaizen Report.
5. **Share** the Kaizen Report with others.

Surgical Services Mooresville		Franciscan ST. FRANCIS HEALTH
Before	**After**	
Cases are usually pulled by the surgeon's preference card. As a result, considerable quantities of suture would be not used and then got thrown away.	All preference cards updated, with only minimal amounts of suture being placed into the sterile field until more is needed.	
The Effect		
Huge cost savings for department.		

Name	Supervisor	Date	Savings
Staff Involved: Stacy Jo Bumpas, Bethany Day, Angie Adams, Erin Crowe, Donna Dietz, Matt Weaver, Darla Owens, Gretchen McKinney, Debra Banich, Ruben Ramirez, Jeanie James, Abby Snodgrass, David Wortman.	Jackie Klika, OR Manager, MV	1/4/08	$57,000 per year

Figure 5.25 A Kaizen about updating surgeon preference cards.

These five steps are simple and easy to learn and teach. Furthermore, they fit well in the healthcare environment; as Susan McRoberts, chief nursing officer at Franciscan said, "I am surprised at how well Kaizen has integrated into everything we do. Our nurses are applying Kaizen to their daily routine, and now they are finding more opportunities, discussing more ideas with their colleagues, implementing more improvements, documenting more of those improvements, and sharing more than they ever have. Kaizen has become an integral part of our nursing culture."

The real power of Kaizen occurs over time when everyone in an organization is empowered to apply these five steps to improve their daily work, developing their skills and abilities to make improvement. Nancy Mosier, manager of pediatrics at Franciscan said, "Kaizen has made our staff look at their work environment more closely, to see their workflow from a new perspective, and it has empowered them to make their own changes." To Nancy, the specific process of Kaizen is not as important as what Kaizen has enabled her staff to do. One afternoon, Joe walked with Nancy around her unit as she pointed out the hundreds of Kaizens she and her staff have done over the last few years. Joe agreed with Nancy when she said, "they might seem like little things, but they have added up to make all the difference."

Discussion Questions

- Is it always a good strategy to start with small Kaizens first that make your work easier?
- What did you discover about yourself as you applied your first Kaizen?
- Do your supervisors have the disposition to discover how to say yes to Kaizens?
- Do your supervisors have the skills to coach Kaizeneers? If not, how can the organization support and develop them?

Endnotes

1. Bodek, Norman and Bunji Tozawa, *How to Do Kaizen: A New Path to Innovation* (Vancouver, WA: PCS Press, 2009), 6.
2. Wikipedia, "Inattentional Blindness," website, http://en.wikipedia.org/wiki/ Inattentional_blindness (accessed August 8, 2011).
3. Chabris, Christopher, and Daniel Simons, "The Invisible Gorilla: And Other Ways Our Intuitions Deceive Us," 2010, website, http://www.theinvisiblegorilla.com/ gorilla_experiment.html (accessed August 8, 2011).
4. Chabris and Simons.
5. Graban, Mark, *Lean Hospitals: Improving Quality, Patient Safety, and Employee Engagement: 2nd edition* (New York: Productivity Press, 2011), 57.
6. Swartz, James B., and Joseph E. Swartz, *Seeing David in the Stone: Find and Seize Great Opportunities* (Leading Books Press, Carmel, IN 2006), 57.
7. Imai, Masaaki, *KAIZEN: The Key to Japan's Competitive Success* (New York: McGraw-Hill, 1986), 114.
8. Imai, 114.
9. Shetlar, Christina, Joy Eckhardt, et al., "A LEAN Laboratory 'Goes Green,'" Medical Laboratory Observer Online, August 2010, http://www.mlo-online.com/ features/2010_July/0710_26.aspx (Accessed June 18, 2011).
10. Deming, W. Edwards, *Out of the Crisis* (Cambridge MA: MIT CAES Press, 1982, 121.
11. Deming, 123.

Chapter 6

Visual Idea Boards

Man can put out about 1/20th of a horsepower. He has to rest at least 9 hours a day. He also has to eat and drink. As a power source, we are terrible. However, it is when man starts thinking of ideas that the difference between man and machine emerges.

—Soichiro Honda
Founder of Honda Motor Co.

During her new employee orientation at Children's Medical Center, a new microbiology technologist, Lisa, received more than three hours of introductory training about the Lean methodology. In the session, Lisa was told that her ideas were welcome and that she should expect to hold her leaders accountable for maintaining that environment. Joy Eckhardt, quality and regulatory compliance manager, says, "New people are often cautious to speak up," so it is important to teach this continuous improvement culture from day one.

In her very first week in the lab, Lisa had an idea for making her work easier. She noticed it was difficult to reach over the computer to get the "Gram stain" controls. As taught in the orientation, Lisa wrote her improvement idea on a card that she placed on a specified bulletin board. Unlike some workplaces, Lisa was not ignored because she was new, nor was she told to be quiet and just do her job; her voice was heard. As you can see in Figure 6.1, the improvement was made and completed the very next day.

Evangeline Brock, a senior technologist in virology, commented that it is very common for new employees to discover waste and problems that go unseen by those who have worked in an area for years. Instead of being satisfied with the way things have always been, the microbiology department demonstrates that they value everybody's ideas. This was a small improvement, but Lisa's enthusiasm for Kaizen, for Lean, and for her workplace is very apparent when you talk to her. One can hope that this small idea in a new employees' first week of work will lead to a career full of Kaizen.

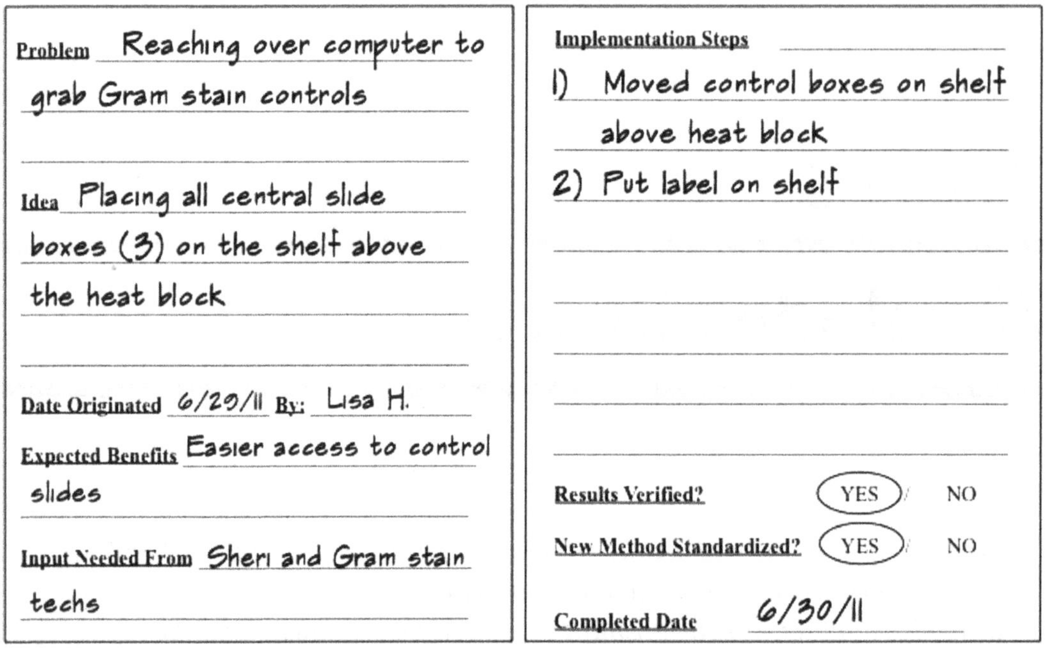

Problem Reaching over computer to grab Gram stain controls **Idea** Placing all central slide boxes (3) on the shelf above the heat block **Date Originated** 6/29/11 **By:** Lisa H. **Expected Benefits** Easier access to control slides **Input Needed From** Sheri and Gram stain techs	**Implementation Steps** 1) Moved control boxes on shelf above heat block 2) Put label on shelf **Results Verified?** (YES) / NO **New Method Standardized?** (YES) / NO **Completed Date** 6/30/11

Figure 6.1   An idea card filled out by a new staff member.

After starting with small ideas, such as moving things, employees usually move to "ideas with greater impact," says Eckhardt. Bernice Garner, the manager of the microbiology lab, noticed that after starting with "small, easier things" in initial suggestions, the team eventually gained the confidence to later propose a new department layout to her, which was delivered to her, complete with drawings. In the main lab, Eckhardt recalled how the third shift team took the initiative to move some instruments, saying, "Before Lean, people wouldn't have even thought that the layout could be better; they would have just accepted it, as is."

It took time, Garner said, for people to learn that they "owned their ideas" and that the manager is "part of the team" instead of being the only person who could make or approve suggestions. Garner emphasizes that ideas are discussed at team huddles, and it is "more a matter of team consensus" to say yes or no to an idea. Her role, as manager, is to highlight regulatory concerns or other issues that her employees might not know about. The method used at Children's Medical Center Dallas, the "Visual Idea Board," has been instrumental in building a Kaizen culture.

Making the Improvement Process Visible

The Visual Idea Board approach can be used throughout the entire lifecycle of a Kaizen—initiating, managing, documenting, and sharing improvements. In *Creating a Lean Culture*, David Mann wrote about a "visual improvement suggestion process."[1] Building upon the Lean concept of "visual management," as described in Chapter 11, this methodology provides an alternative to the suggestion box and offers greater transparency to the improvement process. Ideas are displayed on cards on a bulletin board, allowing team members and managers to view their progress from start to finish.

As a trainer and consultant, Mark has introduced this method to hospitals in the United States and the United Kingdom, spreading this approach through his first book *Lean Hospitals* and his lectures and conference presentations around the world. He has also seen this method used in other hospitals in The Netherlands, Canada, and Sweden.

In Mann's book, an idea goes through four major stages, as visualized on a bulletin board:[2]

1. Ideas are submitted.
2. Ideas are screened and advanced to a queue or rejected.
3. Ideas are actively worked on.
4. Implementation is complete.

A Visual Idea Board is managed with key Kaizen principles and mindsets, as already introduced in this book. For example, managers should rarely reject an idea outright. Instead, they should work with the person who brought forward the idea to find something that *can* be implemented. If an idea cannot be implemented at that time (because of cost or a technological challenge), the manager needs to give constructive and respectful feedback given to the person who had the idea, working with the originator to find a simpler, less expensive way to address that issue.

> The pharmacy at Franciscan St. Francis practices Kaizen with a process similar to Visual Idea Boards, a variation they went to fairly early into their use of Kaizen. They post their ideas that may affect the entire department on the board so all staff can review prior to discussion in the department meetings. Ideas are approved for implementation only after being discussed in that meeting.

The types of problems that have been addressed through this approach include the following (as written on cards by hospital staff):

■ Laboratory: "Hand writing patient information on slides takes too long and may result in identification errors."

- Radiology: "The old sign on the Magnetic Resonance (MR) room barrier is hard to read. It is an old sign that looked like it was printed on an old dot matrix printer."
- Telemetry Unit: "Old 3-hole punch sticks and does not punch all 3 holes consistently."
- Primary Care Clinic: "Forms are stored in rolling rack on the floor; we have to bend down low to get forms."

Setting up a Visual Idea Board

Identifying and documenting the problem or opportunity is the first step in any Kaizen process, including this Visual Idea Board approach. A Visual Idea Board typically has four columns to visually represent the flow of ideas as described by Mann. The board is set up with four columns, with dividing lines, labeled simply as:

- Ideas
- To Do
- Doing
- Done

A template for a board is shown in Figure 6.2.

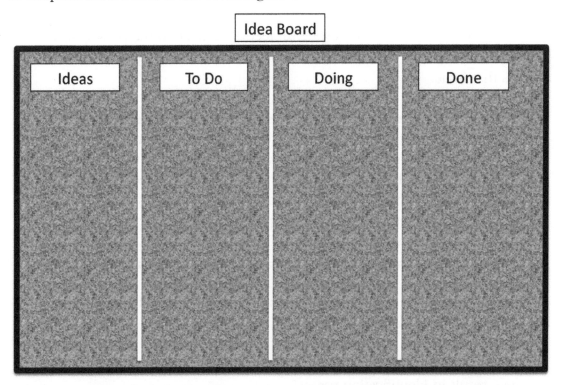

Figure 6.2 Template for a Visual Idea Board.

Figure 6.3   Visual Idea Board in the Children's Medical Center Dallas core laboratory.

Boards Should Be Highly Visible in the Workplace

Visual Idea Boards seem to be most successful when they are in a highly visible location in the workplace. Figure 6.3 shows the board in the core clinical laboratory at Children's Medical Center Dallas. The board is on a main aisle that is a high-traffic walkway in and out of the lab. As the board is used, medical technologists and other team members will often stop and look at the board, particularly those who are highly engaged. People may notice new cards, noting ideas that they want to comment on (by writing directly on the card) or noting new ideas that they can take, for example, from the core lab back into the virology area. If somebody has a concern with an idea or its implementation, they can write on the card, talk to a manager, or raise the issue in a team huddle.

A department normally uses a bulletin board or corkboard, although some have had to, out of necessity, use a whiteboard or cabinet doors for displaying their ideas. Figure 6.4 shows the board as initially set up in the pathology department at Northampton General Hospital NHS Trust (Northampton, England), where each of the four columns was a separate cabinet door. Note that they chose their own headings for the four columns, for example saying "Suggestions/Comments" instead of "Idea." This methodology certainly allows for flexibility in these implementation details.

Figure 6.4   Visual Idea Board utilizing cabinet doors at Northampton General Hospital.

Boards in Public Settings

A community health center clinic run by Riverside Health System, near Kankakee, Illinois, did not have much private space that was out of the view of patients. Some team members were concerned that their Kaizens should be hidden, but the manager's office and break room were not good alternatives because of the lack of space. Using the manager's office, even if there had been space, might have given the impression that ideas were owned and controlled by the manager, instead of the employees. Some teams, at different health systems, have expressed concern that such a board should be kept out of a break room, so people can relax and not think about Kaizen. The idea that people should not have to think about Kaizen on "their time" is common before the creation of a Kaizen culture. After people get used to making improvements, enthusiasm builds; you will find that people do not want to stop thinking about Kaizen.

The Riverside clinic, including the physicians and the office manager, decided to put their Visual Idea Board in a public hallway, but one that was out of the path of most patient traffic. As is typical, the cards did not refer to specific patients or anything that would be considered a violation of privacy rules. The team also decided that there was nothing wrong with letting patients and the community see that they were working on process improvements that would, among other things, reduce patient waiting times. Inpatient units and clinics at other organizations have made a similar decision about making these boards visible to the public.

Communication before the Visual Idea Board Is Up

Before a blank board just mysteriously appears, there are some helpful up-front communication points that can help gain acceptance and dispel any expectations that would be based on past experiences with suggestion systems.

What Happened to Our Suggestion Box?

In environments where a suggestion box has been used (or has been taking up wall space), it is important to talk to employees about what went wrong with the old method. Managers should introduce differences with the Kaizen approach, as summarized in Chapter 2. Managers should be open and honest with employees if there had been a slow review process with little or no feedback. Senior leaders can emphasize the fresh start without placing blame on front-line managers. Since Kaizen is most effective in an environment with a lot of trust, one way to build that trust is to be honest and forthcoming about what did not work in the past.

Since the Visual Idea Board process is very open and transparent, there are certain ideas that you might not want to expose to the entire team. With suggestion boxes, employees often take advantage of the privacy of the box to write up complaints about other people. Managers usually consider these submissions, such as, "Betty Sue always comes in late!" as confidential human resources department issues. Sometimes, there are complaints submitted that include information about specific patients. With a visual improvement process, team members can learn to avoid posting information that violates privacy rules.

Even with the addition of a Visual Idea Board, some organizations have left the old suggestion box on the wall as a release valve for issues that people think they have to bring up anonymously. In cases like this, the expectation should be that the box is the exception and most any idea can be brought up at a team meeting or put on the board. Other organizations have removed the box because there are still channels for an employee to make a complaint or report to senior leadership outside of their regular management chain.

What Employees Can Expect

Up-front communication about what employees and medical staff can expect with the Visual Idea Board system can set people down the right path, and it can set the proper expectations for managers and leaders at various levels. Early in a Kaizen program, leaders might be thinking about how they will hold their employees accountable, but it is fair to assume that front-line staff will have more concerns about how their managers will be held accountable for following through on the following guidelines.

The following are some common Kaizen and Visual Idea Board Guidelines:

- Post Idea Cards on the board in the left-hand column or bring cards to your supervisor or bring them to a team meeting.
- Expect a fast response from your immediate supervisor or team leader, within 2 to 3 working days.
- Expect collaboration in the improvement process (not just a yes or no answer).
- Most ideas will be accepted (in some form).
- Be able to express a problem statement as well as an idea.
- Help look for the root cause of problems.
- Be open to ideas from others that modify your idea, or be open to other ways to solve the same problem.
- Small ideas are great ideas.

A Communication Example

In 2008, the radiology department at Children's Medical Center Dallas undertook an initial Lean improvement project focused on improving outpatient MRI patient flow. Part of their approach was the use of the Visual Idea Board to harness staff ideas for improvement—both related to patient flow and other ideas that would improve the workplace. The hope with Kaizen was that engaging employees and clinicians in small improvements would lead to the confidence and enthusiasm required to tackle bigger problems.

The initial team, consisting of nurses, radiology technologists, and a representative from the front desk staff, learned about Lean and Kaizen principles in preparation for presenting to their colleagues about their improvement efforts. They created an informative, yet fun, slide (including an animated baby) that they shared in all-hands meetings. A version of the slide was used as a handout and a poster to reinforce the principles, as shown in Figure 6.5.

Formats for Idea Cards

Within the structure of the Visual Idea Board, there are different approaches and formats that can be used for the cards, and this next section will share some lessons learned from the use of different formats in multiple organizations.

Sticky Notes versus Structured Cards

It is not uncommon to start by using blank note cards or your favorite brand of sticky notes, an approach recommended in *Creating a Lean Culture*,[3] as shown in Figure 6.6.

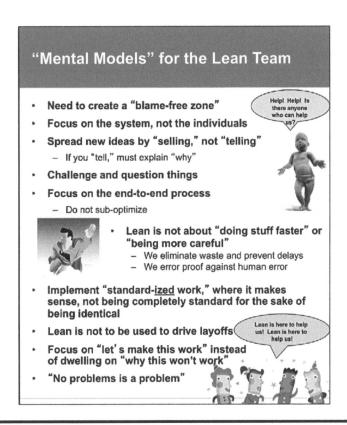

Figure 6.5 Guidelines for a Kaizen culture created by team members at Children's Medical Center Dallas.

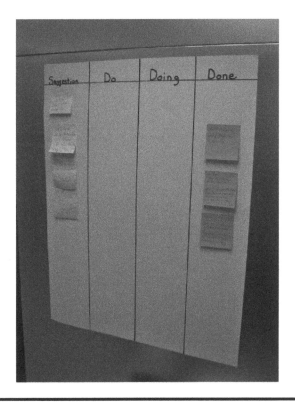

Figure 6.6 Visual Idea Board using sticky notes instead of structured cards.

Starting with a complete "blank slate" of a card can have some downsides. The lack of structure might create writer's block for a person who has identified a problem or an improvement idea. Blank cards might also attract complaints (a problem without a proposed idea) or ideas that do not have an associated problem statement.

Using a structured form or card can help create standardized work for the Visual Idea Board process and can serve as a guide for Plan-Do-Study-Act (PDSA) thinking and problem solving, leading to more effective improvement.

Idea Cards versus Suggestion Cards

When you start this process, you might be tempted to use a supply of old suggestion box cards that you have on hand. Figure 6.7 shows a format for a classic suggestion box card. Cards like these should be avoided for a number of reasons. For one, we want to focus on "ideas" (*what I can do*) instead of "suggestions" (*what others should do*). Second, this card might not prompt the type of Kaizen thinking that is more likely to lead to sustainable improvements. The suggestion box card focuses completely on the idea or the suggestion, doing nothing to prompt the submitter to think about any definition of the problem statement, let alone a root cause.

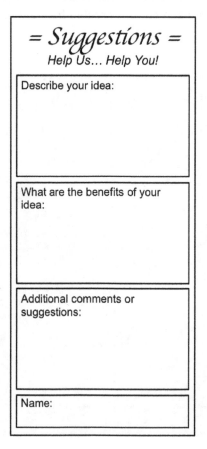

Figure 6.7   A classic suggestion box form.

Kaizen / Continuous Improvement Tracking Form

Problem Statement: What is being fixed? What was going wrong?

Suggestion / Solution: What change is being put in place? What is the expected outcome? What alternatives were considered?

☐ Safety   ☐ Quality   ☐ Turnaround Time ☐ Cost

Who Was Consulted About Change? _____

Sr. Tech / Supervisor / Manager / Director / Pathologist

Planned Period of Time to Pilot Change: _____

Documentation of Communication to Other Shifts / Employees:

What where the Outcomes from the Change?

Is the Change being Accepted as the New Process? ☐ *Yes*   ☐ *No*

Explanation:

Document Communication of Change:

Which relevant procedures / SOP's / Standard Work documents been updated?

How has the change been communicated to all who need to know?

Figure 6.8   An A4-sized Kaizen form.

Modeling the Kaizen and PDSA Process in Writing

In the first edition of *Lean Hospitals*, Mark shared an example of a form that he helped create in a hospital setting, shown in Figure 6.8.[4] The form, on an A4 (or 8.5" × 11") sheet of paper, walked a person through the PDSA cycle. This form, although helpful in structuring and guiding improvement thinking, was often unwieldy on Visual Idea Boards due to its size.

Whatever the format, capturing ideas as they arise helps ensure that they do not "get lost in the [ongoing] conversation," says Bernice Garner, microbiology manager at Children's Medical Center Dallas. Dr. Gregory Jacobson, while working as an emergency medicine faculty member at Vanderbilt University Medical Center, noticed that improvement ideas tended to be quickly lost or forgotten if not logged in a formal way. Jacobson says, "Let's say you're working in a busy emergency department at 2:00 a.m., when there are not any managers around, and you identify an opportunity for improvement. It is easy to lose track of that idea when you move on to the next patient." Capturing ideas, in some form, makes sure a moment of inspiration does not get lost. To prevent losing ideas,

Jacobson helped create a web application called the "Kaizen Tracker," where ideas could be easily submitted electronically to department leaders, as described in Chapter 10.[5]

With Visual Idea Boards, ideas do not get lost after the initial discussion with a supervisor. A manager at one hospital said, "I don't claim to remember everything that's ever told to me verbally in the hallway, so I always remind people to follow up through the formal system," including putting a card on the board to help prompt future follow-up.

Visual Idea Cards

In later trials, the form from Figure 6.9 was adapted into a double-sided card that is one quarter of an 8.5" x 11" inch sheet of paper, as shown in Figure 6.9. Some teams have made the card one-sided, using half of a sheet of paper cut down the middle vertically, which eliminates the need to flip cards around to read the content on the back, a nice example of applying Kaizen to the improvement process.

The following sections explain what gets documented on Visual Idea Cards.

Problem

It is important to have some statement of the problem or the current state situation that needs to be changed or improved upon. Without a problem statement,

Problem ____________	**Implementation Steps** ____________
Idea ____________	
Date Originated ________ **By:** ________	**Results Verified?** YES / NO
Expected Benefits ____________	**New Method Standardized?** YES / NO
Input Needed From ____________	**Completed Date** ____________

Figure 6.9 Idea Card template (download at www.HCkaizen.com).

the suggestion or idea will be missing important context. For any new idea, we should have a shared understanding of why a change needs to be made.

We want to be sure to capture and document a problem so we can celebrate the fact that somebody has raised an issue, in keeping with the "no problems is a problem" culture of Kaizen. Writing the problem statement down allows the team to further analyze it, looking for a root cause, and brainstorming countermeasures.

Looking forward in the process, if there is a case where the idea or suggestion cannot be implemented (for example, because it is too costly), then a manager can come back to the card and brainstorm other possible countermeasures to that same problem with its creator. Again, it is not necessarily as important to implement the *specific* idea that was originally on the card as it is to implement *something* that addresses the problem as we understand it.

Suggestion or Idea

While it's important to state and define a problem, it is likewise important to encourage people to write down some sort of idea, even if they are not completely sure what will improve the situation.

If a supervisor receives a card without an idea, they can constructively and respectfully ask the employee what they think could be done as an improvement, emphasizing that the idea does not have to be perfect or 100% effective. Supervisors often have to work hard at encouraging ideas because some people, given history and the current culture, have been conditioned to be very shy with their ideas. If the person is stumped for an idea, then the supervisor should not force the situation. After thanking the person for identifying the problem, the card can be brought to other team members, or the supervisor can suggest something to try.

Again, when a card includes an idea but lacks a problem statement, the supervisor can ask questions about the underlying situation to get the problem or opportunity documented on the card, so their team members can then work to solve it.

> *Don't find fault, find a remedy; anybody can complain.*
>
> **—Henry Ford**

It is sometimes said that the statement of a problem without a suggestion is just a complaint. In some organizational cultures, we see more complaining than real Kaizen. The structured cards can be a way to prompt people to develop ideas that now have a chance to be implemented. In some organizations, people just offer complaints (often anonymously through the closed suggestion box) because they think managers are not really interested in their ideas; they substitute complaints and venting for actual improvement.

Date Originated

This field allows the visual tracking of how long ideas have been on the board. It is realistic to expect that a new idea on the board will move into the "To Do" column within 72 hours of being written. Ideally, new ideas are responded to on the same day. But this might not be possible, especially if that initial review has to wait for a face-to-face discussion with the person who wrote the card.

A good measure of the effectiveness of the Visual Idea Board system is the elapsed time that occurs after the writing of the card, including:

- Time from generation to being moved to "To Do"
- Time until the card reaches the "Doing" column
- Time until the idea is "Done"

These dates when cards moved forward in the process can be tracked on the back of card under "Implementation Steps." Think of this time data as a "turn-around time" or a "length of stay" for an idea.

Created by

Since one of the dysfunctions of a suggestion box is anonymous submissions, it is important to have a name or names associated with each card. Without this, leaders are not able to follow up and collaborate with the people who brought an opportunity forward. It is worth emphasizing to employees that the Idea Card is the starting point for a collaborative discussion, which is why we need to have their name associated with their idea.

If managers find anonymous cards, they can ask the team at a daily huddle for the originator to come forward, or the manager can present the card to the team, asking for somebody to become the owner of the idea's implementation.

Expected Benefits

It can be helpful to encourage employees to think about the expected benefits of improvements from the Idea Cards. These benefits can be qualitative, such as "reduce supply expenses," or they can be quantitative, such as "reduce wasted paper by 500 sheets per day." Some organizations will list specific categories of improvement that might represent departmental goals or the organization's high-level strategic pillars. Figure 6.10 shows a completed Idea Card from the Utah North Region of Intermountain Health that lists categories of what they call "Dimensions of Care," including clinical and service excellence, employee and physician engagement, operational effectiveness, and community stewardship.

Their card has many nice features, including the prompting of "how would we measure success?" Prompting employee recognition upon the completion of the improvement is also a nice touch.

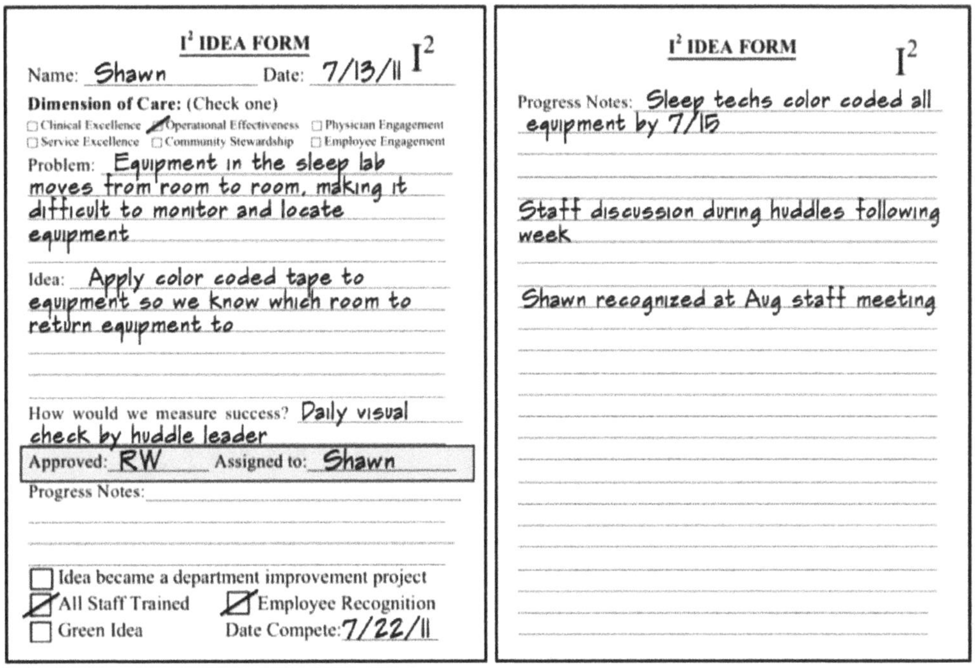

I² IDEA FORM I²

Name: Shawn   Date: 7/13/11

Dimension of Care: (Check one)
☐ Clinical Excellence ☑ Operational Effectiveness ☐ Physician Engagement
☐ Service Excellence ☐ Community Stewardship ☐ Employee Engagement

Problem: Equipment in the sleep lab moves from room to room, making it difficult to monitor and locate equipment

Idea: Apply color coded tape to equipment so we know which room to return equipment to

How would we measure success? Daily visual check by huddle leader

Approved: RW   Assigned to: Shawn

Progress Notes:

☐ Idea became a department improvement project
☑ All Staff Trained   ☑ Employee Recognition
☐ Green Idea   Date Compete: 7/22/11

I² IDEA FORM I²

Progress Notes: Sleep techs color coded all equipment by 7/15

Staff discussion during huddles following week

Shawn recognized at Aug staff meeting

Figure 6.10   Completed idea card from the Utah North Region of Intermountain Health that lists their "Dimensions of Care".

Bart Sellers, regional manager of management engineering at Intermountain, gives credit to Mann's *Creating a Lean Culture* and a DVD from GBMP titled "Thinking Outside the Suggestion Box" as the sources for their Kaizen program. Sellers also says, "one of the reasons we have been successful is that we don't have great expectations about big savings" from improvement ideas. Reflecting further, Bart adds that they kept Kaizen simple and did not require root cause analysis, saying he has seen some other organizations struggle because they "made the mistake of expecting too much too soon without first building in the cultural expectations of everybody participating every day."[6]

Figure 6.11 shows the increase in implemented ideas over time in the Utah North Region. The sudden increase in the number of ideas corresponds with "stating an expectation for participation, one idea per FTE per year, for the first time in January 2011," says Sellers. Participation fell temporarily in late 2011 due to a combination of special factors that distracted managers from their Kaizen work, but the hospital appears to be back on track in early 2012.

It is important to help align Kaizen to patient needs and organizational goals. In conjunction with the Visual Idea Board, the laboratory at Children's Medical Center Dallas started tracking and posting key performance measures every day in the lab, near their board. They started holding daily team huddles in that space. Jim Adams, senior director of laboratory operations, recalls that, within a month of starting to discuss patient-focused measures like turnaround time, "the ideas being generated shifted from 'here's what I want,' like providing a toaster or hot chocolate in the break room, to 'here's what we need to provide better patient care,' such as installing bar code scanners to help reduce clerical errors."[7]

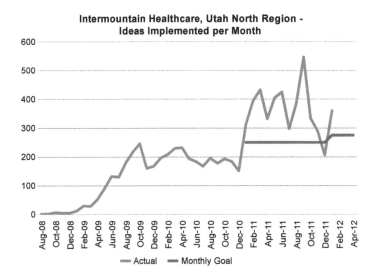

Figure 6.11   Number of ideas implemented each month in the Utah North Region of Intermountain Health.

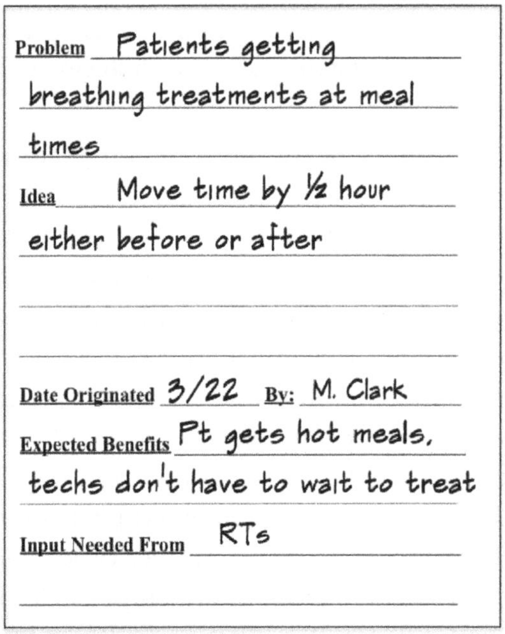

Figure 6.12   One of the first Idea Cards filled out in an inpatient unit.

The expected benefits statement on the card creates a hypothesis that is tested through the PDSA cycle. For example, by combining the problem statement, suggestion, and benefits of an Idea Card, as pictured in Figure 6.12, we might get the following statement:

> *Because some patients are getting breathing treatments during meal time, we should move the meal time by 30 minutes before or after the treatment. If we do this, the patient will get hot meals (improving patient satisfaction scores) and techs won't have to wait to treat (improving productivity).*

This hypothesis gets tested as we complete the back of the card and close out the idea.

Input Needed from

People often identify small changes that could be implemented simply and immediately on their own. For example, a laboratory technologist might want to swap the bench top locations for storing absorbent wipes and disposable pipette tips. But the person with the idea is usually not the only one who uses that bench. Rather than just immediately making the change, the Idea Card might list their team members' names as a prompt to get their input before trying out the change. If it is a small and reversible change, the person with the idea might just make the change. Use the card as a reminder for that person or the supervisor to talk with team members, including those on other shifts, to make sure they are accepting of the change.

Even with small changes, team members in the microbiology area of the Children's Medical Center Dallas lab are encouraged to discuss ideas with at least one other team member because, "Two heads are better than one," says Evangeline Brock, senior technologist in the virology area.

This space on the card is also used when a local change might affect people in another area or department, to ensure that a local change does not just sub-optimize part of the process. For example, the lab might decide to reduce costs by running a particular low-volume test just one time per day to reduce the expense of wasted reagents from a test kit. Informing those who might be affected, including the emergency department, might uncover that the local lab expense savings would actually cost the hospital far more due to delayed discharges and longer lengths of stay.

In some cases, changes may be so small and so minor that they have no impact on clinical care. In other cases, a proposed change may have a subtle or obvious clinical impact. Early in a Kaizen program, team members may be overly cautious about making changes. For this reason, it is important to have a supervisor or a clinical leader more involved. Over time, team members will get a better sense of what improvements can be made on their own and which need to be signed off by a clinician. An effective Kaizen program will strike a balance between being careful to anticipate and mitigate risks without being too slow, overly cautious, or bureaucratic.

Implementation Steps

This space on the back of the card can be used to list any of the following progress updates, with their associated dates:

- What steps are being taken to pilot or test the idea
- What requests have gone out to other departments

- What data is being collected
- What communication has taken place within or outside of the team
- Why an idea might be temporarily "on hold"

Updates on ideas can be given in team huddle meetings, department newsletters, or other formats, but the card itself remains a communication channel. As people walk by the Visual Idea Board, people can stop briefly and review the latest status of ideas in which they were interested.

There are times when an idea might be legitimately placed "on hold" for some period of time, when no action is expected to take place. For example, a card that describes a problem with a piece of software, like the electronic medical records system, might be on hold because the hospital knows they are upgrading to a new version in 60 days. Rather than making a change request for software that is going away, the team might hold the idea until they can evaluate the new version. The Idea Card might become irrelevant, which means it could move to the "Done" column, or it would be reopened as a change request to Information Systems or the software vendor.

In a variation on this method, some teams have created a separate "On Hold" column or a card holder on the wall for these ideas, maintaining visibility but separating them from ideas that are actively being worked on in the "Doing" column. Care should be taken, however, that putting an idea on hold is a relatively rare exception, rather than being a normal and easily accepted part of the process.

Results Verified?

After implementing an idea, or during an initial trial phase, it is important to gauge the success of the change in qualitative or quantitative ways. Because we are following the scientific Plan-Do-Study-Act model, we do not want to assume that all changes are actually improvements, as we discussed in Chapter 1. A well-written Idea Card should state how results are expected to improve with the change.

At this stage, check the results against the hypothesis. If the Idea Card said we should expect nurses to walk less because of the change, can we confirm that result through data or direct observation? If we said a change would reduce patient waiting times, can we confirm that? Regardless of the answer to this question, yes or no, we want to write an honest answer on the card.

If we did not get the result that we expected, we can talk about this as a team. We can ask questions such as:

- Why do we think we did not get the expected result?
- What can we learn from this experiment?
- What can we try as an alternative countermeasure to address that same problem?

New Method Standardized?

If our change did not lead to an improvement, we can revert back to the old way of doing things, or we can try something new. If, however, we did get positive results from our change, our "Act" phase of the PDSA would be to update our standardized work documentation. We will also need to communicate the changes fully to everybody in the department who is affected—those who do the work and those who interact with those who do the work.

We can help ensure sustainability of the change by being intentional about standardizing the new method, and by recording notes about how we are doing this on the card.

Completion Date

When we recorded the Date Originated on the card, we set the stage for recording the Completion Date, which allows a team to measure how long it takes to get ideas completed. Since Kaizen is not intended to be a slow, bureaucratic approach, the goal should be to have ideas completed within a week or two. The results from some ideas can be evaluated within a day or two, while more complex ideas may require a longer data collection period before we deem the idea complete—whether it has been accepted and standardized as the new process or not.

Idea Card Examples

The following section contains Idea Cards from different departments that address different staff and patient needs.

Staff and Patient Annoyances

The card shown in Figure 6.13 highlights a problem that nursing team members at Riverside Medical Center did not think they could fix on their own—a noisy door on the clean utility room, along with a loud noise that occurs when the supply cabinet is closed. A nurse submitted a card for her manager and team to discuss. Some examples like this require a manager to call maintenance, something the nurse might not know how to do on their own.

Asking for Help

Figure 6.14 shows an Idea Card that brings up an issue that could not be addressed within the department where the idea originated. Techs in a medical/surgical unit asked for additional patient transport coverage beyond 7:00 p.m. The problem statement was defined as the techs spending too much

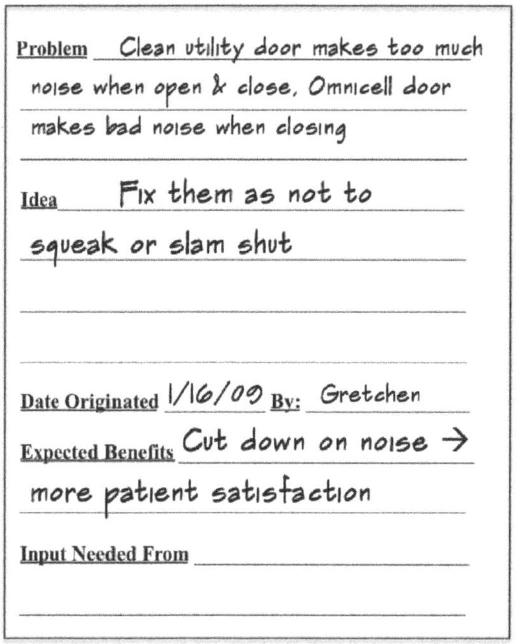

Problem Clean utility door makes too much noise when open & close, Omnicell door makes bad noise when closing

Idea Fix them as not to squeak or slam shut

Date Originated 1/16/09 **By:** Gretchen

Expected Benefits Cut down on noise → more patient satisfaction

Input Needed From

Figure 6.13 An Idea Card that required assistance from maintenance.

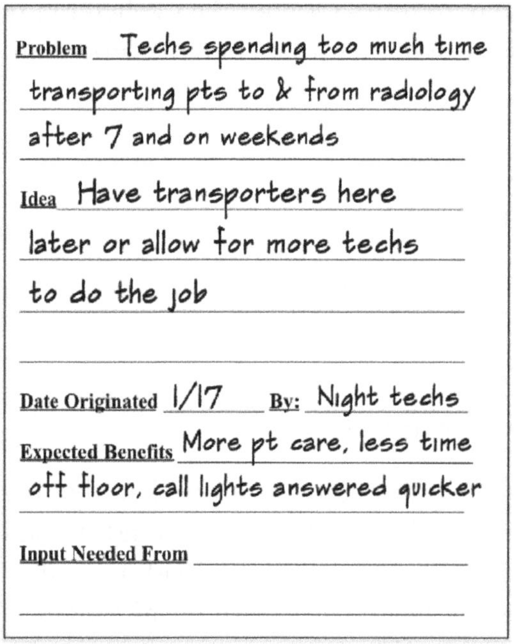

Problem Techs spending too much time transporting pts to & from radiology after 7 and on weekends

Idea Have transporters here later or allow for more techs to do the job

Date Originated 1/17 **By:** Night techs

Expected Benefits More pt care, less time off floor, call lights answered quicker

Input Needed From

Figure 6.14 An Idea Card that required managers to collaborate with another department.

time transporting patients. In discussing this card, the unit manager (possibly along with a leader from the transport department) would probe and ask how the patients are affected by techs being away from the unit. It is a good practice to always try to bring the discussion back to patient needs. The "estimated benefits" section of the card touches on the patient impact—the time required to answer call lights.

As the "idea" section begins, there are multiple ways of addressing the issue. Adding staff, either more techs or transporters, would be one way of addressing this problem. It is a good practice not to just automatically add more people when there is a problem and people say, "we need more staff." Hospitals often do not have the budget to add people, anyway. The Kaizen approach challenges us to come up with more creative countermeasures than adding more people, more equipment, and more space.

Either way, the important thing is that a front-line staff member raised the issue to be discussed. In an old suggestion box type program, managers might simply say, "no, we don't have the budget," and that would be the end of the discussion. In the Kaizen approach, everybody must work together to find a way of addressing the problem that was brought up. We do not have to always implement exactly what was submitted, but it is the role of a manager to help find a countermeasure that works.

Addressing Patient Needs

As illustrated in Figure 6.15, there are often a number of nonclinical patient needs that, if met can increase patient satisfaction. We often see Idea Cards that reflect what patients need and, in this case, what the techs need to provide the best service.

This card has an observation that comes directly from the point of patient care—these particular combs do not work well on some women's hair. The tech cannot initiate the purchasing process on her own, so it is important to raise this

Figure 6.15 An Idea Card that identifies a small improvement that improves service to patients.

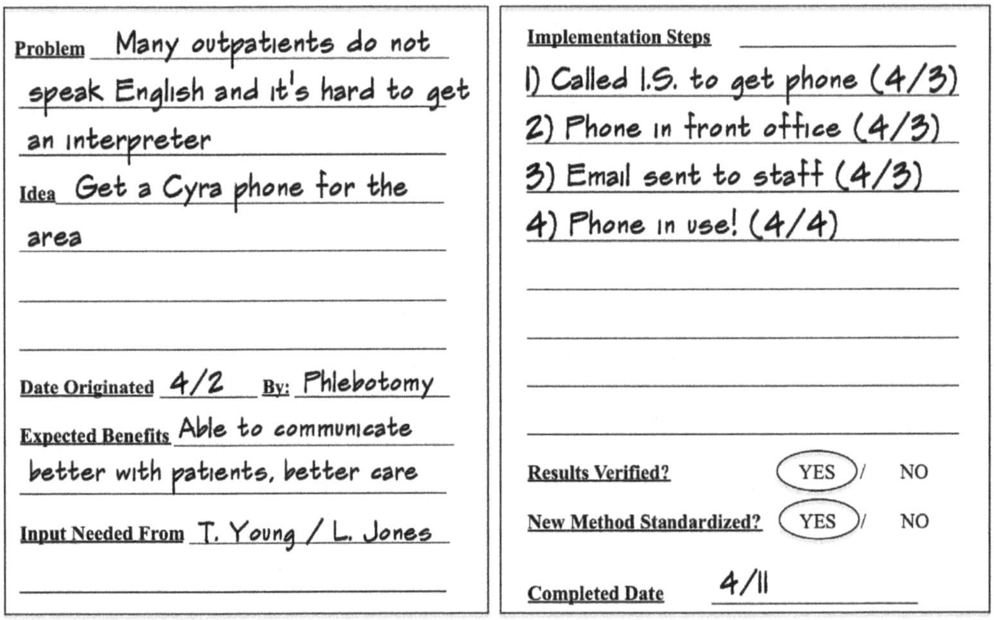

Problem __Many outpatients do not speak English and it's hard to get an interpreter__	Implementation Steps _____
Idea __Get a Cyra phone for the area__	1) Called I.S. to get phone (4/3)
	2) Phone in front office (4/3)
	3) Email sent to staff (4/3)
	4) Phone in use! (4/4)
Date Originated __4/2__ By: __Phlebotomy__	
Expected Benefits __Able to communicate better with patients, better care__	Results Verified? (YES)/ NO
Input Needed From __T. Young / L. Jones__	New Method Standardized? (YES)/ NO
	Completed Date __4/11__

Figure 6.16 An Idea Card that was implemented within a few days.

issue for the unit manager, along with purchasing and materials management, because they will have to buy and restock brushes.

Since the "expected benefits" area of the card is blank, this is a great opportunity for a team leader or manager to ask the person who wrote the card to articulate what they think the benefits would be. It might seem obvious that the benefit would be increased patient satisfaction, but it is better to ask and have that discussion rather than assume. The impact of the idea might be surprising or unintuitive. In a traditional suggestion system, a manager or senior leader might say "no" to an idea like this because buying brushes increases costs. Using the Idea Card as the starting point of a discussion (and direct observation at the point of care) might paint a more complete picture of why the idea should be implemented.

Early on in the process, it is important to be biased toward saying "yes" to ideas like this, so that "KR" will have the motivation to write more Idea Cards. If ideas like this are rejected, word will likely spread among KR's coworkers that management is not serious about improvement.

As shown in Figure 6.16, phlebotomists in the specimen collection area found it was hard to find a live interpreter. After discussing this issue with some coworkers, one of them knew that the hospital had access to a service where interpreters could be quickly reached via a special phone. The person posted the card on the Visual Idea Board, and they worked with a supervisor to get the necessary approvals. As shown on the card, the process moved along quickly from problem identification and a suggestion being made on April 2 to a request going to IS to get the special phone on April 3. This was a perfect example of how Kaizen can be faster than a suggestion box approach,

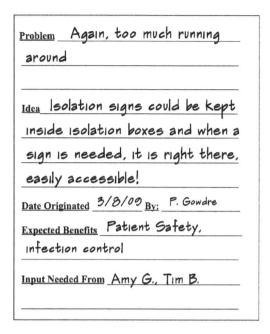

Problem _Again, too much running around_

Idea _Isolation signs could be kept inside isolation boxes and when a sign is needed, it is right there, easily accessible!_

Date Originated _3/8/09_ By: _P. Gowdre_

Expected Benefits _Patient Safety, infection control_

Input Needed From _Amy G., Tim B._

Figure 6.17   An Idea Card that required input from infection control.

where the idea might have waited in the box for weeks or months before being discussed or acted on.

Getting Input from Others

The card in Figure 6.17 shows another example of nurses looking to make process improvements that will reduce the time they spend running around, providing more time for patient care.

The card identifies a more specific aspect of the common "hunting and gathering" problem—time spent looking for isolation signs for the patient rooms. The initial suggestion seems reasonable enough, to store these laminated signs in the isolation boxes that are hung on the door.

In this case, the nursing staff was cautious to make sure that there were not going to be any infection control problems created, keeping in mind the primary goal of patient safety. The team could have taken quick initiative to make additional signs for other rooms. Instead, they posted the idea and created the opportunity for infection control to give input on this idea. Would the reused laminated signs be dirty from their earlier exposure on the door? Would the team really want to put those back into the isolation box with clean supplies?

The presence of a board does not guarantee ongoing Kaizen activity will occur. One hospital had an initial wave of improvements that were managed through boards in multiple nursing units. Over time, enthusiasm seemed to wane, and the Visual Idea Boards were eventually reclaimed as general bulletin board space. A nurse from the original team that created the board looked back and said, "The managers didn't go around asking for ideas," because they had too many other demands on their time. In other hospitals, the success of the Kaizen program has been a factor of the amount of effort put in by the supervisors and managers in each department. One cannot just put up a board and expect to get results from Kaizen if one is not willing to put in daily effort, as managers, to encourage ideas and their implementation.

Other Formats of Idea Boards and Cards

As different healthcare organizations have used methods similar to Idea Cards and Visual Idea Boards in their practice of Kaizen, we see variation in the format of the cards and even their shape.

Park Nicollet's KEEP Form

Park Nicollet Health Services (Minnesota) started a program in 2006 called Kaizen Everyday Engagement Program (KEEP) as an organization-wide initiative focused on generating small, local improvement ideas. Park Nicollet describes KEEP as a way for employees to submit improvement ideas and for managers to track and coach people through the implementation process. KEEP was presented to staff not as cost cutting measure, but as a way to make their own work easier. Park Nicollet previously initiated the use of Rapid Process Improvement Workshops, but as Jennifer Rudolph, former KEEP Administrator & Lead Specialist, states, "we realized that we had to figure out how to get every staff member engaged in improvement."[8]

The KEEP form they use to manage improvement ideas is shown in Figure 6.18. When ideas are completed, staff submit them via an internal website, a system discussed more in Chapter 10.

As referenced in the form, there are four "KEEP Coaches" from a central Quality Improvement Team (QIT) who monitor and help shepherd ideas in the areas of the hospital and clinic they support. There is also a hospital-wide KEEP Coach who works with other QIT staff members. The KEEP Coaches meet monthly to review any large improvement ideas that are beyond the scope of KEEP and to consider rewards for high impact ideas.

IDEA DEVELOPMENT WORKSHEET
Contact your KEEP coach (listed on 2nd page) at any time with questions.

Instructions:

| Got an idea? | → | Fill out this form | → | Get approval from your supervisor to implement | → | Implement & complete idea | → | Have supervisor sign & send this form to your KEEP coach | → | You are awarded Ovation points! |

Date: 15 June 11

KEEP Idea Title: Improve SW 8.1 workshop kickoff email communication

Your Name: Allison Johnson

Location/site: 5050 1st floor

List Names of potential Team Members, if any: Cynthia Sorenson
Erin Huberty

CURRENT SITUATION
- What is the current process/condition today?
- Who is involved with the process/condition today? (Departments/Locations)
- When/How often does the process/condition occur?

The current version of SW 8.1 is outdated. The template included is cumbersome to use and makes it difficult to produce a defect-free communication. It is not used according to the standard and old, random changes, have been saved into the template, creating rework and evolving the tool over time into an awkward and unwieldy tool.

NEW IDEA
- What is the idea?
- Who is affected by the new idea?
- How will the idea change the way the process condition is currently handled?
- When/How often will the idea be used?

Convene a cross-service line team to review, revise, and update the kickoff email template and accompanying standard work 8.1. Present this updated version at the leads meeting for feedback and approval, completing a PDCA cycle.

Figure 6.18   Example of an Idea Development Worksheet from Park Nicollet Health Services.

KEEP Idea Type: Cost Savings   Revenue Generating   ⟨ Neither ⟩
(please circle only one)

If you indicated this as a cost savings or revenue generating idea please fill out:

Annual Cost Savings   _____

Annual Revenue Generated   + _____

Cost of Implementation   − _____

Total   = _____

IMPLEMENTATION PLAN
- Who will implement the idea?
- How will you implement the idea? List implementation steps
- Estimate a target implementation date

Complete all items on the service line implementation checklist and make modifications to the template as suggested by the Leads group. Communicate changes via QI/IPS communication process and begin using the new template.

Please review your implementation plan with your supervisor prior to implementing your idea.

Supervisor/Leader Approval:

Supervisor Name: __Julie Clarke_____

Signature: _____ Date: __9/10/11_____
* Please sign when idea has been implemented and completed by employee and send to your service line KEEP coach for tracking and ovation awards.

KEEP Coaches Names, Numbers, & Interoffice Address:
SL 1&3 –Hospital KOT
SL 2 –Primary Care & Behavioral Health KOT
SL 4 –Specialty Services KOT
SL 5 –Corporate KOT

Figure 6.18 (continued)

Many ideas implemented through KEEP include improvements that directly enhance the patient experience:

- When we have a positive stress test in our area, patients are often overwhelmed and "zone out". I always get them a pen, paper, and folder to take notes. This helps them remember important facts and it calms them, too.

■ It would be nice to have a sign directing patients to the observation unit near the emergency center. Many of our patients get confused or lost trying to find the observation unit. I believe that placing a sign where patients can see it would be very beneficial and make the patient experience much better.

■ Having a patient struggle trying to use the bathroom is very upsetting for them when they have to ask for assistance. If a handicap button was available for the patient, he or she could access the room without any problem. The door is rather narrow, and the handle is difficult to manage. The safety and protection of the patient should be first and reduce their personal accidents.[9]

In 2010, Park Nicollet had 400 formally documented KEEP improvements, having an impact in the following areas:

■ Staff Support (116 ideas)
■ Quality/Safety (89)
■ Cost/Profit (65)
■ Patient Experience (55)

Rudolph commented that the biggest barrier with KEEP is that "people think it's a traditional suggestion system, where they want to tell us what to do and not participate themselves. We view it more as a system that enables staff to generate and implement improvement ideas, themselves."

Akron Children's Hospital

Akron Children's Hospital, having a lot of Cleveland Indians fans, created a board with a fun baseball theme, shown in Figure 6.19.

Their ideas are each represented on a baseball, with bats indicating who is working on the idea. Instead of a linear flow, the ideas round the bases, as if playing a baseball game. New ideas start off on first base, moving counterclockwise around the bases, eventually crossing home plate to score a run as they are completed.

Seattle Children's Hospital Pharmacy

The pharmacy at Seattle Children's Hospital has been using a variation on a Visual Idea Board since early 2009. After a visit to Japan, they brought back the creative idea of visualizing improvement ideas as cherry blossoms on trees that represent different types of waste, as shown in Figure 6.20.

The Seattle Children's card prompts its creator to choose a type of waste be placed on the proper "waste tree." The card also prompts for a description of the current state as well as asking, "what can you or your coworkers do to reduce this waste?" This places the focus on local ownership of ideas as opposed to just

Figure 6.19   A baseball themed Idea Board from Akron Children's Hospital.

Figure 6.20   Ideas are represented on cherry blossoms on trees in the Seattle Children's Hospital pharmacy.

making a suggestion for others. Anne Bournay, the inpatient pharmacy operations manager, says they have learned, "The best success comes when we have a check-in meeting with the person who had the idea," adding, "If we do not connect back with that person, there will be failure and they won't submit the next idea."

An example of a filled-out card is pictured in Figure 6.21.

As ideas have been implemented, the pharmacy team fills out the back of the blossom, as pictured in Figure 6.22, and continues the fun visual representation by "harvesting ideas" into paper baskets, as shown in Figure 6.23.

Since the program is called "Tend Your Own Garden," any idea that falls outside of pharmacy is submitted through the hospital's electronic system, CPIdeas, to be forwarded to the appropriate manager. The pharmacy eventually replaced the paper trees with large vinyl decals. The pharmacy has generated 138 ideas between January 2009 and September 2011. The staff ideas have resulted in a total savings of about $500,000, but not all of the ideas have quantified dollar amounts, due the complexity or time involved.

Visual Management of the Idea Boards

One major advantage of Visual Idea Boards over suggestion boxes is that the current status and health of a department's Kaizen efforts are visible to all. You can see the actual Idea Cards, the number of ideas, and the time elapsed since the idea was initially presented (if that date is recorded on the card).

If an organization has made a commitment to employees that their ideas will be accepted and worked on toward completion, the visual nature of the board allows staff members to hold their leaders accountable—or at least it provides constructive pressure for everybody to take action. By comparison, ideas left to rot in a suggestion box are hidden from all.

Senior leaders, as they conduct "gemba walks" in a department, will have a visual cue about how a specific department's leadership is fulfilling their commitment to continuous improvement. For example, they might see a board, as pictured in Figure 6.24, which has many new ideas, but limited progress in the evaluation and implementation steps. The senior leaders can ask questions of local management, looking to determine why there seems to be limited progress. It might be, as in the photo, which is just a new board, but seeing a board like this a year into a Kaizen program would be a cause for concern.

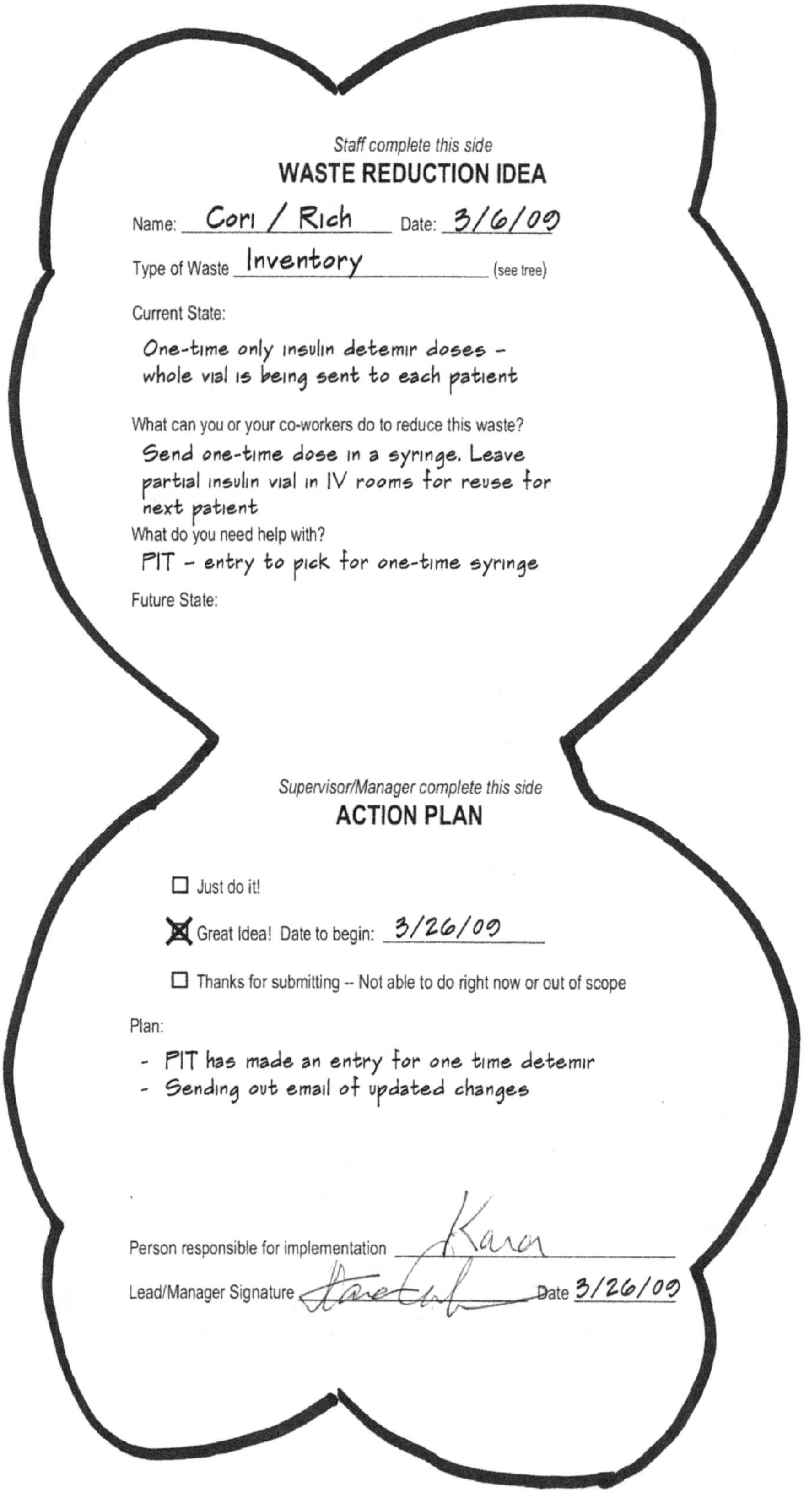

Staff complete this side

WASTE REDUCTION IDEA

Name: _Cori / Rich_   Date: _3/6/09_

Type of Waste _Inventory_   (see tree)

Current State:

One-time only insulin detemir doses –
whole vial is being sent to each patient

What can you or your co-workers do to reduce this waste?

Send one-time dose in a syringe. Leave
partial insulin vial in IV rooms for reuse for
next patient

What do you need help with?

PIT – entry to pick for one-time syringe

Future State:

Supervisor/Manager complete this side

ACTION PLAN

☐ Just do it!

☒ Great Idea! Date to begin: _3/26/09_

☐ Thanks for submitting -- Not able to do right now or out of scope

Plan:

- PIT has made an entry for one time detemir
- Sending out email of updated changes

Person responsible for implementation ___Kara___

Lead/Manager Signature _____ Date 3/26/09

Figure 6.21   Example of a completed blossom card.

WE DID IT!!

What has improved? (Quality, Cost, Delivery, Service, Engagement)

Q – Patient receives a patient-specific dose!

C – We have a savings of approximately $4,600 for month of March alone. We are not charging the patient for an entire vial

We are not wasting entire vials of insulin & creating waste in the environment

Supervisor/Manager Signature _____ Date 3/36/09

Signature of submitter _____ Date 4/17/09

Figure 6.22   The back side of a folded cherry blossom card that completes the PDSA cycle.

Figure 6.23   Completed improvements are "harvested" into the bushel baskets.

Figure 6.24   This Visual Idea Board has collected many ideas without any being implemented.

Asking "why?" in a sincere way is a more effective style and an example of a general Lean leadership principle, as in "why hasn't there been more progress with this board?" Yelling or "chewing people out" does not show respect for the managers in the area. As with other problems, we should aim to understand the systemic root cause by asking why multiple times. If "lack of time" is given as a reason, leaders should work together to free up time for Kaizen as a key organizational priority.

A different problem that might be noticed visually is shown in Figure 6.25. This is a real board that clearly has many completed ideas, but just one new idea and two improvements in progress. It looks like a single large batch of ideas came in, but leaders are not doing enough to encourage the ongoing generation of new ideas in team huddles or other settings. Seeing a board like this is, once again, an opportunity to ask why and to remind department managers that continuous improvement means that this should be more of an ongoing process.

Another situation that can occur is being stuck in the middle. The board, shown in Figure 6.26 illustrates a situation in which new ideas came in (but quit coming in) and nothing is being completed.

Seeing a large grouping of ideas stuck in the middle might indicate a department is stuck in "analysis paralysis," meaning they are constantly looking into, researching, or discussing an issue without taking anything to completion. Granted, some ideas do take days or weeks before we have a countermeasure we can try, or we might be waiting for enough data to be collected to gauge if the idea led to a real improvement or not (following the Study and Adjust stages of the PDSA cycle). Experience shows that many ideas can move to the "Completed" column within days or a week, so seeing nothing in the far right column should be a red flag that leads one to stop and investigate.

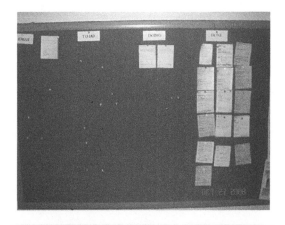

Figure 6.25   This Visual Idea Board is no longer generating new ideas.

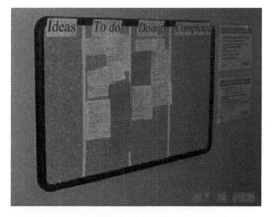

Figure 6.26   The Visual Idea Board shows a burst of ideas that were not getting completed.

Using Idea Cards to Coach People on Kaizen

As Imai emphasized, early on in a Kaizen program, it is most important to encourage people to make suggestions and implement changes without too much criticism from supervisors or managers. In early stages, we want to build confidence and enthusiasm for people to participate in Kaizen.

There are times, though, when managers might want to provide feedback or coaching about submitted Idea Cards. This discussion should not be done in a corrective tone, but rather should be a constructive, honest, and respectful dialogue about how to best orient suggestions toward patient needs and make sure we are solving the real root cause of the problem. As with any Kaizen methodology, we want to treat each idea as if it were a gift, being respectful of the person who gave us a so-called "bad idea."

In the core lab at Children's Medical Center Dallas, between 15% and 20% of submitted ideas are not implemented in the original form, according to John Burns, supervisor of the hematology area. One reason an idea might be rejected is if the change adds more steps to a process instead of reducing waste. Clay York, manager of the core laboratory, explains that some of these early ideas would introduce more waste because employees were not getting to the root cause of the situation. To help counter this, York has focused on providing improved "Lean 101" training to all employees. Even when an idea is not going to be implemented, York "appreciates that a problem was pointed out," adding, "That's what we want—problem solvers; you need people who can see problems."

When an idea is not accepted, the supervisor will write an explanation on the card rather than just saying "no" and not interacting with the originator of the card. The supervisor should also discuss the card at a team huddle or with the originator in a one-on-one setting. Unlike traditional suggestion systems, where a rejection represents the end of the process, the supervisor in a Kaizen setting demonstrates "respect for people" by continuing the dialogue with the originator. The discussion that occurs after an initial rejection "sometimes leads to a better idea" and resolution, said Burns.

One example of an idea that the team did "not move forward" with at Children's Medical Center Dallas (they avoid saying "rejected") was a suggestion from a medical technologist to reuse paper printouts from the printers at the laboratory instruments that were a backup system to electronic reporting. The supervisor thought there might be the risk of a mix up if the paper was reused on the same analyzer. Rather than rejecting the employee's idea outright, the team brainstormed and decided that it would be acceptable to reuse paper on a different instrument that runs different tests, eliminating the risk of reading the wrong test result over the phone.

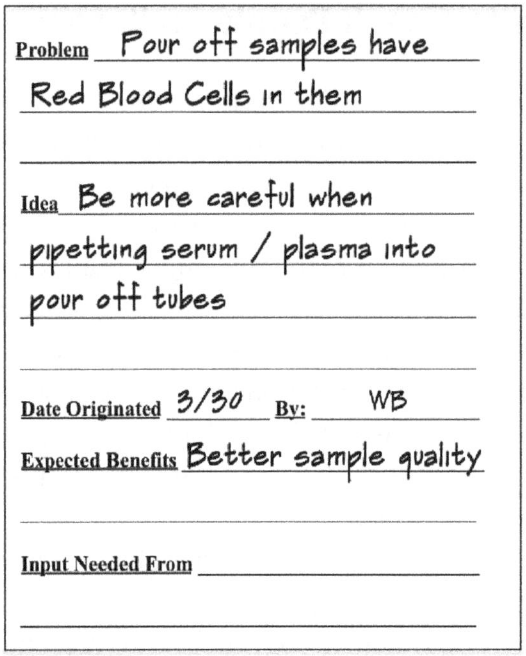

> Problem Pour off samples have
> Red Blood Cells in them
>
> Idea Be more careful when
> pipetting serum / plasma into
> pour off tubes
>
> Date Originated 3/30 By: WB
> Expected Benefits Better sample quality
>
> Input Needed From

Figure 6.27 "Being more careful" is rarely an effective countermeasure.

The Suggestion to "Be More Careful"

Figure 6.27 shows an early card submitted by an employee of a hospital laboratory.

The person who created this card defined a great problem statement, highlighting the problem that some specimens had red blood cells (RBCs) in them after being "poured off" during the preanalytical phase of the process; however, the suggestion to "be more careful" might prove to be an ineffective platitude.

A supervisor could use this card to start a discussion with "WB" and their teammates. The supervisor might ask if everybody working in the pour off area has had sufficient training. One might ask if there are different methods that make it less likely to get RBCs in the specimen. Do people working in the area know why it is important to avoid the contamination of specimens with RBCs? Are there situations where the workload is too high or not leveled, creating situations where people are rushed in their work?

In the Kaizen mindset, we assume that people want to do good work. Being careful, generally speaking, is a good start, but it is not always sufficient for quality. For example, airline pilots certainly want to avoid a crash on every takeoff and landing. That said, there are some flights that crash. Hanging a sign in the cockpit asking the pilot to "be more careful" would do nothing to prevent crashes in a highly complex and technical environment.

It would be a good practice, in this case not to just lecture people or post signs that remind people to be careful. Whatever countermeasures are tried, the team should have a way of measuring sample quality to know if they are improving the outcome of that pour off process.

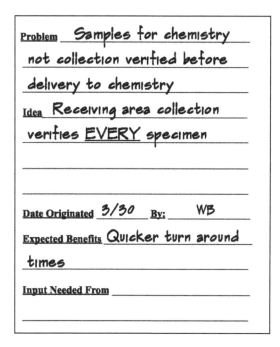

Problem Samples for chemistry not collection verified before delivery to chemistry

Idea Receiving area collection verifies EVERY specimen

Date Originated 3/30 By: WB

Expected Benefits Quicker turn around times

Input Needed From

Figure 6.28   An Idea Card that shows the need to coach staff members on problem solving.

Something's Not Happening—So Don't Forget

Figure 6.28 shows another Idea Card for which there is an opportunity to coach the author on good problem-solving approaches.

This card has a good, succinct problem statement, and it is a good problem to solve; however, the suggestion to remember to verify every specimen is unlikely to uncover the real root of the problem of some being missed. Leaders can coach the author of the card to ask why and to look for the underlying root cause or causes of this problem. Is there a technical problem with the software or one of the scanners? Are people feeling pressured into rushing through their work, causing errors?

The person who submitted the card should be thanked for highlighting and raising the issue, but should be gently coached to help come up with a better understanding of the problem, as well as countermeasures that are more likely to address this issue.

Easier for Us, but Not Best for the Whole System?

In the card shown in Figure 6.29, a nurse from an inpatient unit at a hospital identified a problem. Patients who were admitted from the emergency department between 5:00 and 6:00 p.m. arrived during the shift-to-shift nursing report period. As a result, the patient might not get seen immediately upon admission, which can delay needed medication orders or care.

The suggestion, however, would require some discussion among leaders and staff from inpatient units and emergency. Postponing admissions is one counter-measure, and it might seem to solve the problem, as stated.

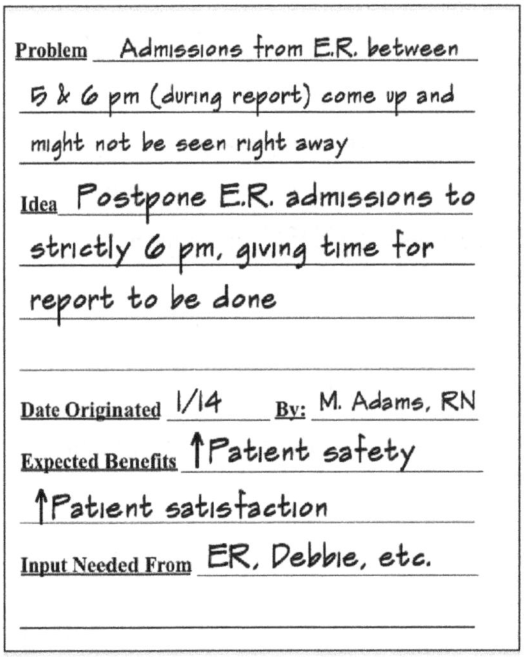

Problem ___Admissions from E.R. between 5 & 6 pm (during report) come up and might not be seen right away___

Idea ___Postpone E.R. admissions to strictly 6 pm, giving time for report to be done___

Date Originated ___1/14___ By: ___M. Adams, RN___

Expected Benefits ___↑Patient safety ↑Patient satisfaction___

Input Needed From ___ER, Debbie, etc.___

Figure 6.29   An Idea Card that shows a potentially sub-optimizing idea.

In a traditional suggestion box system, a director or vice president might read this card and reject it, saying that the hospital cannot delay admissions because it causes space and throughput problems in the emergency department. The leader or leaders might just say "no," and the nurse who submitted the card might get zero feedback, with no opportunity to discuss the root cause problem or find another way to address these problems.

In a Kaizen approach, this card is the beginning of a dialogue. A manager can talk with the nurse, or with a team from the unit, or with a cross-functional team from the unit and emergency. The mindset might shift from talking about "why we can't take patients between 5 and 6" to figuring out "how can we change things so patients *can* be seen promptly, regardless of their admission time?" This might require process or staffing level changes in the inpatient unit, but somebody should be making a decision that is best for the patient and best for the organization rather than only doing what is best for a particular unit.

One outcome of an Idea Card like this might be to initiate a Kaizen Event or a larger analysis and problem-solving effort for what is a relatively complex issue and set of circumstances.

Tracking Completed Cards

At Children's Medical Center Dallas, the microbiology team keeps completed Idea Cards in a binder that has a separate folder for each employee. At the end of each year, the number of cards created by each employee is one input into

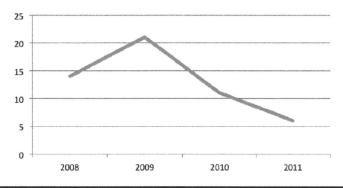

Figure 6.30 Number of Kaizens completed by a medical technologist across a 4-year period.

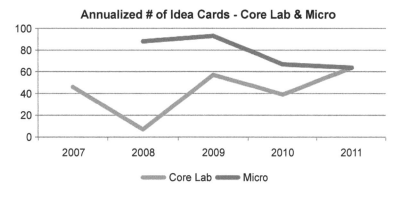

Figure 6.31 Number of Kaizens completed in the core lab and microbiology areas.

their annual employee evaluation and performance review process. If somebody helped with an Idea Card, a photocopy of the card is placed in their folder.

In a review completed in July 2011, 26 of the 30 employees in the microbiology area had created at least one Idea Card since 2008. One microbiology technologist, Dianna, submitted an average of 15 cards a year from 2008 to 2010. "A department might have a lot of improvements at first, but it can be hard to not run out of ideas after a while," said Evangeline Brock. For example, Dianna's pace of suggestions increased after the first full year, but then declined after the third year, as shown in Figure 6.30.

Figure 6.31 shows the annualized number of Idea Cards submitted in microbiology/virology (30 people) and the core lab area (33 employees).

To help encourage participation in Kaizen, the lab incorporated the understanding and application of Lean principles and tools as part of the basic expectations of all staff. All job descriptions were modified to include the statement, "Follow standard work documents and actively contribute suggestions and process improvements to eliminate waste and add value in alignment with the hospital, section, and department goals and objectives." Jim Adams adds, "We have tried to encourage staff to incorporate the Kaizen thinking into their daily routines."[10]

Conclusion

Visual Idea Boards provide an open and transparent alternative to the traditional suggestion box. Structured cards prompt staff members to follow the PDSA improvement process for defining a problem, suggesting a countermeasure, and then testing that change in a scientific way. The boards allow staff and leaders to hold each other accountable for the progress of cards, leading to faster improvement cycles and improved team communication about ideas that can improve patient care and make people's work easier.

Discussion Questions

- Why is it important to have both a problem statement and an improvement idea?
- Can you think of a fun way of representing or visualizing ideas on a bulletin board that would engage your colleagues?
- Is it necessarily true that suggestions will drop off over time? What can you do to counter that?

Endnotes

1. Mann, David, *Creating a Lean Culture* (New York: Productivity Press, 2005), 146.
2. Mann, 147.
3. Mann, 146.
4. Graban, Mark, *Lean Hospitals: Improving Quality, Patient Satisfaction, and Employee Engagement: 1st edition* (New York: Productivity Press, 2009), 195.
5. Jacobson, Gregory H., N.S. McCoin, R. Lescallette, S. Russ, and C.M. Slovis, "Kaizen: A Method of Process Improvement in the Emergency Department," *Acad. Emerg. Med.* 2009 Dec;16(12):1342.
6. Sellers, Bart, email correspondence, August 29, 2011.
7. Adams, Jim, personal interview, April, 2011.
8. Rudolph, Jennifer, personal interview, May 5, 2011.
9. Rudolph.
10. Adams, Jim, email, August 2011.

Chapter 7

Sharing Kaizen

You are forgiven for your happiness and your successes only if you generously consent to share them.

—Albert Camus
Philosopher

In February 2010, Russell Maroni was working as an X-ray technician at Akron Children's Hospital when he traveled to volunteer for the earthquake relief efforts in Haiti. Russell and his clinical skills were pulled in to help at a field hospital, performing X-rays to help triage patients who might be sent to a U.S. Navy medical ship. Faced with the need to increase the number of X-rays, along with the quality of the films, given equipment and circumstances that were far from ideal, Russell drew upon the Kaizen training he had received back home, 1700 miles away, in Ohio. One of his workplace improvements was documented in Chapter 1 as Figure 1.10.

While coaching a Haitian on running the portable X-ray machine, Russell incorporated a number of clever Kaizens, including cutting some packing Styrofoam into pieces that could be used to properly position patients. He filled some bags with gravel to act as sand bags and cut four inches off the table legs, among other small improvements. If there was ever a situation that required creativity over capital, this was it. Russell documented and shared the improvements in a handwritten A3 report that was included in a journal, later published to raise funds for Haiti relief. The A3 document and the journal can be downloaded for free at www.LeanForHaiti.org, as a great example of Kaizen thinking, acting, and sharing.

Different Formats for Sharing

As introduced earlier, the fifth and final step in the Kaizen approach is sharing and spreading improvement ideas throughout an organization or beyond. Previous chapters have introduced a few different formats for sharing completed Kaizens.

In this chapter, we share additional examples of completed Kaizens in a number of formats, including Quick and Easy Kaizen Reports, Kaizen Wall of Fame Reports, and the "A4 Report." This chapter also includes examples of different types of A3 Reports, as introduced in Chapter 3, including a variation that is structured around the Six Sigma DMAIC (Define, Measure, Analyze, Improve, Control) framework.

The intent of this sharing, as it should be within other organizations, is to inspire your own improvements. Sometimes, sharing leads to the adoption of the same Kaizen in other units, departments, or hospitals. But resist the temptation to force somebody else's improvements on others. If people see a Kaizen they choose to adopt, that is the best approach. Better yet, if they can improve upon the idea, have them do so, and share the improvement back to the original department. The ill-considered copying of another person's Kaizen does nothing to develop one's own skills and confidence.

The Kaizen Wall of Fame Format

A number of hospitals that Mark has worked with have implemented a process to give recognition for Kaizens, whether they come from the formal Visual Idea Board process or if they were small "just do its" that never went through the board process. These reports are, like the Quick and Easy Kaizen reports you see throughout this book, designed to be short, concise, and to the point, capturing the essence of the improvement in a way that is understandable to a layperson. The bulletin board where these reports are displayed, Figure 7.1, was dubbed the "Kaizen Wall of Fame" by the team in the core laboratory at Children's Medical Center Dallas.

Children's Medical Center Dallas and the other hospitals that developed this method with Mark typically did not give financial rewards or direct incentives to participate in Kaizen. The recognition and reward for Kaizen, beyond making one's work easier or the good feeling that came from helping colleagues or improving patient care, came from the wall itself. As you will see in the following examples, the names of people involved in the Kaizen were displayed on the wall. This gave people recognition amongst their peers, their managers, and senior leaders who visited the department to review the improvements that were made.

An example template is shown in Figure 7.2. This, along with other templates and forms, can be downloaded at www.HCkaizen.com. Readers will recognize this format and template as a variation on the Quick and Easy Kaizen documentation method.

Figure 7.1   Wall of Fame in the Children's Medical Center of Dallas laboratory.

In the lab at Children's Medical Center Dallas, the electronic template is available to all employees on a shared drive. While anybody is allowed to fill one out, the reports are typically filled out by supervisors or managers, with review and input given by the staff members who participated in the improvement. The supervisors often use this as an opportunity to train their employee in how to fill out an electronic report, for those who feel comfortable with the technology. In some cases, handwritten versions of the report are accepted and displayed, avoiding the waste of retyping the report.

After Lisa, the new lab employee who was featured at the start of Chapter 6, had her idea implemented and standardized as a new method, a Kaizen Wall of Fame report was created, as shown in Figure 7.3.

As with the other reports, Lisa is given credit and recognition by having her name listed and by having her photos posted on the wall. Just think of how this example could be highlighted when senior leaders visit the department, allowing them to reinforce to Lisa and the lab's management team how important it is to foster and maintain this culture and environment. Other department leaders who have not yet embraced these principles can be brought in to see the benefits of Kaizen in terms of morale, quality, and efficiency.

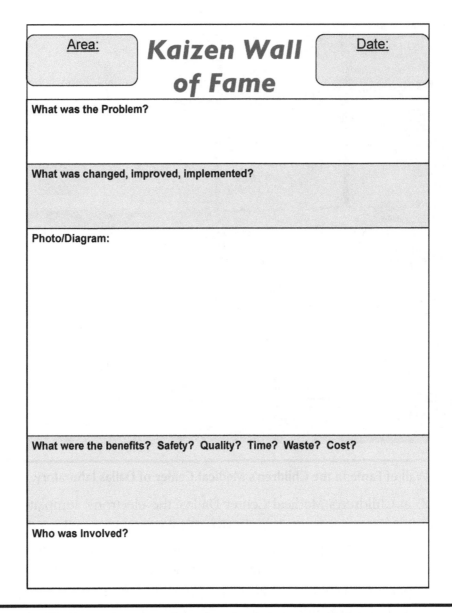

Figure 7.2 Wall of Fame form template (download at www.HCkaizen.com).

Kaizen Sharing Examples

The remaining examples in this chapter are grouped into these categories:

- Making things better for patients and their stay
- Preventing mistakes or harm
- Making work easier for staff or saving time
- Preventing delays
- Saving space or cost

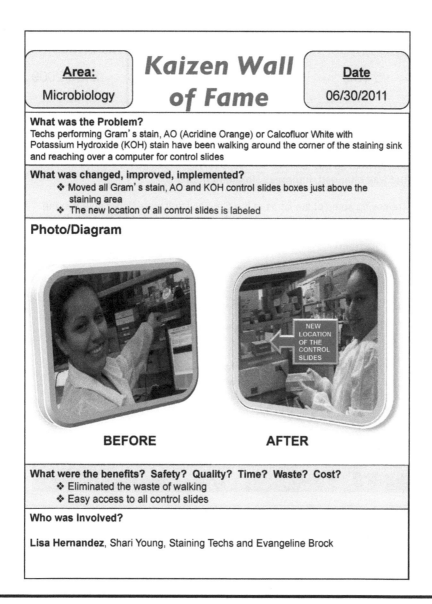

Figure 7.3 Kaizen report that was made after the Idea Card shown in Figure 6.1 was completed.

A single Kaizen will often fall into two or more categories. Saving time for staff can allow them to spend more time with patients, which leads to better outcomes and less harm. Preventing mistakes is better for patients, saves money for the healthcare organization, and reduces stress for staff members.

Making Things Better for Patients

While the emphasis with early Kaizen is often on making work easier for staff, our ultimate goal is to make things better for patients, for their clinical care and to give them a better experience during their stay.

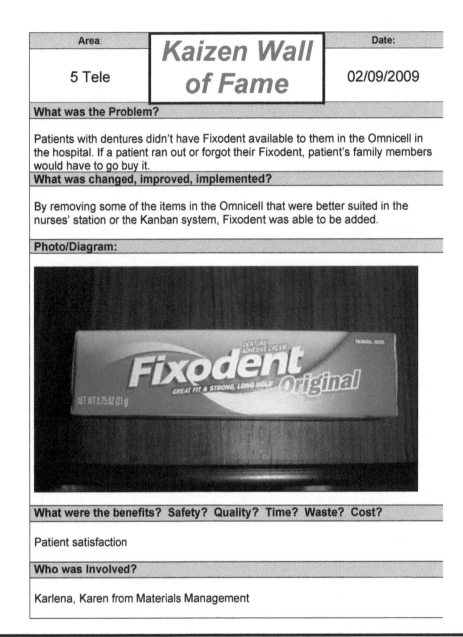

Area:	**Kaizen Wall of Fame**	Date:
5 Tele		02/09/2009

What was the Problem?

Patients with dentures didn't have Fixodent available to them in the Omnicell in the hospital. If a patient ran out or forgot their Fixodent, patient's family members would have to go buy it.

What was changed, improved, implemented?

By removing some of the items in the Omnicell that were better suited in the nurses' station or the Kanban system, Fixodent was able to be added.

Photo/Diagram:

What were the benefits? Safety? Quality? Time? Waste? Cost?

Patient satisfaction

Who was Involved?

Karlena, Karen from Materials Management

Figure 7.4   Kaizen report that leads to better service to patients.

Supplies for Patients

The telemetry unit team at Riverside Medical Center (Kankakee, IL) observed that patients often forgot to bring denture adhesive, and their family members would have to leave to buy it. By removing unneeded items from the inventory control cabinet, the department was able to make the adhesive available to the patients, as shown in Figure 7.4.

Case Study – 3.12

Northampton General Hospital **NHS**
NHS Trust

Knightley Ward: Improving Meal Rounds

The problem:

Patient meals are cooked on the hospital site, and patients are given two hot meals per day, and a cold breakfast from a choice of a range of menus. The hot meals are delivered to wards in special catering trolleys, and ward staff are responsible for giving them out and providing assistance to patients who are less able to feed themselves. Knightley Ward staff observed a number of issues relating to their patient meal times for example:

- Once the trolley is opened, meals need to be delivered quickly or the meals start to cool, and staff were concerned that this didn't always happen
- Some patient tables needed to be cleared from clutter before the meal could be given
- The open gravy jugs allowed the gravy to cool
- Other clinical tasks happened at that time, so staff were not available to assist patients
- It wasn't always clear which patients needed assistance with feeding

Actions taken:

As part of the Meals module of "Releasing Time to Care – The Productive Ward" Knightley ward staff videoed a meal round and mapped the process to analyse the issues and delays. Timings were taken to provide a baseline measure and a patient questionnaire was undertaken. The team then brainstormed ideas for improvement and tested and implemented the following:

A wipe clean place mat was introduced as a visual reminder to keep the table clear of clutter ready for the meal

1. The delivery time of the meal trolley was changed to allow more staff to assist patients at mealtimes
2. Insulated gravy jugs were purchased to keep the gravy hot throughout the meal round
3. A wipe clean place mat on bedside tables reminds patients to keep the table clear of clutter ready for their meal

Results:

Time taken between the meal trolley door being opened and the last patients dinner delivered

(bar chart with y-axis "Time in minutes" 0 to 40, x-axis Meal timings: Breakfast, Lunch, Dinner, legend: Before, After)

- After the changes were implemented, the results of patient questionnaires revealed that 100% of the patients surveyed were entirely happy with their meal times
- Utilising these changes has saved on average 25 minutes a day, which results in patients getting their meals quicker and hotter
- Yearly this amounts to a saving of 152 hours nursing time which has been released for patient care.

Contact us:

If you would like more information on this, or other lean improvements at NGH please contact the lean team on: lean@ngh.nhs.uk.

October 2010

Figure 7.5   Kaizen write-up from Northampton General Hospital.

Improving Meal Rounds

Figure 7.5 summarizes a number of improvements made at Northampton General Hospital NHS Trust (Northampton, England). Changing meal times and changing some of the equipment used led to happier patients because food was served at the correct temperature, also making things easier for staff.

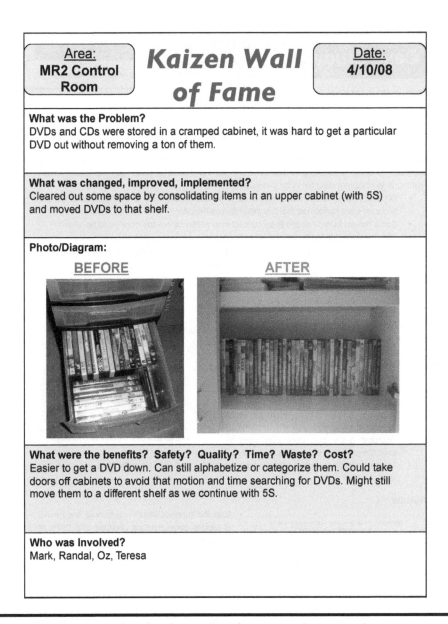

Figure 7.6   Kaizen report related to improving the MRI patient experience.

Easier to Get DVDs

In the MRI area of the radiology department at Children's Medical Center Dallas, the team made simple improvements to DVD storage, as shown in Figure 7.6, making it easier for staff to find a movie that was requested by a patient, reducing the stress of an MRI procedure.

IVF Hooks for Bathrooms				
Before		**After**		
Patient restrooms don't have a place to hang IVF while patient is using the restroom.		Install coat hooks on the walls of the patient restrooms so patients with IVF have a place to hang their IV bag.		
Effect				
Better patient satisfaction and improved pateint safety				
Name	**ID #**	**Dept #**	**Lead**	**Date**
BR			QM	7/21/11

Figure 7.7   Kaizen report about an improved inpatient experience.

Little Details for Patients

Theresa Adams, a resident, and Dr. Saralyn Williams, an attending, in the emergency medicine department at Vanderbilt University Medical (Nashville, Tennessee) suggested a small change that would increase patient satisfaction as well as helping ensure a more sterile environment, by giving patients a proper place to hang IV bags instead of setting them someplace where they might get dirty, as shown in Figure 7.7.

Preventing Mistakes or Harm

Beyond a creating a nicer experience for patients, Kaizens can have a bigger impact if they help prevent errors and decrease risk from a clinical and patient safety standpoint. Staff members can also use Kaizen to make the workplace safer for themselves and their colleagues.

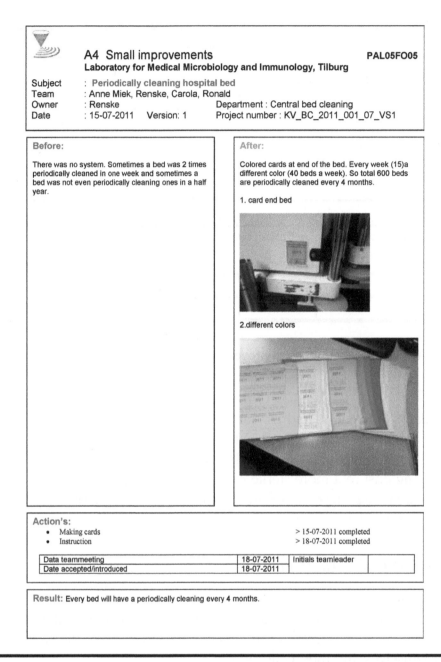

A4 Small improvements	PAL05FO05
Laboratory for Medical Microbiology and Immunology, Tilburg	

Subject   : **Periodically cleaning hospital bed**
Team   : Anne Miek, Renske, Carola, Ronald
Owner   : Renske   Department : Central bed cleaning
Date   : 15-07-2011   Version: 1   Project number : KV_BC_2011_001_07_VS1

Before:

There was no system. Sometimes a bed was 2 times periodically cleaned in one week and sometimes a bed was not even periodically cleaning ones in a half year.

After:

Colored cards at end of the bed. Every week (15)a different color (40 beds a week). So total 600 beds are periodically cleaned every 4 months.

1. card end bed

2.different colors

Action's:
- Making cards   > 15-07-2011 completed
- Instruction   > 18-07-2011 completed

Data teammeeting	18-07-2011	Initials teamleader	
Date accepted/introduced	18-07-2011		

Result: Every bed will have a periodically cleaning every 4 months.

Figure 7.8   A color coding improvement from The Netherlands.

Ensuring Proper Bed Cleaning

St. Elisabeth Hospital (Tilburg, The Netherlands) noticed that beds were not being cleaned according to a systematic schedule. To improve infection control, they instituted a simple system with color coding to help indicate which beds needed to be cleaned each week, as shown in Figure 7.8. Their improvement was written up in what St. Elisabeth calls an "A4 Small Improvements" report, which is equivalent to an 8.5" × 11" page.

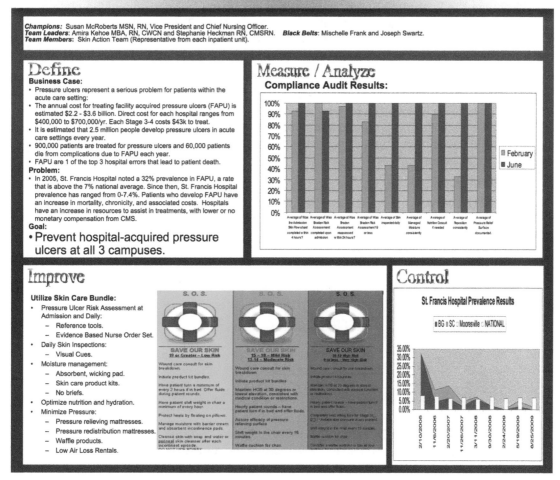

Figure 7.9   A "DMAIC" format A3 summary of patient safety improvements.

Preventing Pressure Ulcers

Figure 7.9 shows a DMAIC format A3 from Franciscan that summarizes a number of improvements that reduced the number of hospital-acquired pressure ulcers. These improvements directly benefit patients, but they also reduce the length of stay and save money for the hospital. For more about the A3 format see Chapter 11.

Area: **Microbiology**	*Kaizen Wall of Fame*	Date: 4/1/08

What was the Problem? Fungal cultures are inoculated in the middle of the plate with the specimen and cross streaked on the entire plate. This results in no isolated colonies, inability to identify a mixed culture and a delay in the patient results. Tissues for fungal culture are ground and inoculated to the fungal plates in the same way. Note: grinding is detrimental to the survival of zygmycetes fungal elements.

What was changed, improved, implemented? Streaking fungal cultures (excluding blood fungus) for isolation when they are originally inoculated with the specimen will enable the detection of a mixed culture immediately. Inoculate tissue fungal cultures with ground specimen, a small finely sliced piece of tissue embedded in the agar and streak for isolation.

Photo/Diagram:

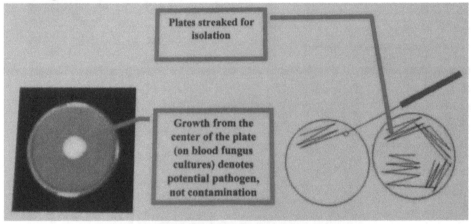

What were the benefits? Safety? Quality? Time? Waste? Cost?
This will result in a time savings and will improve the quality of patient care. Zygomycetes are very aggressive infections and a rapid accurate diagnosis is very important to patient treatment and survival.

Who was Involved?
Dianna Sage, Bernice Garner, Shari Young, Sandra Hipo

Figure 7.10   More accurate lab results through standardized work.

More Accurate Lab Results through Standardized Work

The microbiology team at Children's Medical Center Dallas identified variation in the way certain plates were set up and "streaked," a practice that could reduce the quality of some test results. The Kaizen in Figure 7.10 shows their improvement and how it was communicated visually to their colleagues.

Incomplete X-Ray Order Sets	
Before	**After**
Pt had c -spine done - only did ap/lat (had to go back to get odontiod view *caused >1 hr delay*). Ordered from off-service resident who only ordered ap/lat from wiz order and did not use common rad order (w/c includes obliques and odontiod). This is not the first time this has happened. The off-service residents were not getting a properly structured orientation when they started their month in the ED.	Improve the off-service orientation to show them the specific order sets. These guide the residents by providing the "correct" orders for patient in the ED. The two view c-spine for trauma is not adequate, as the required minimum view would be a 3 and up to a 5 view. The ED order sets only provide a three or five view.
	Also informed techs to always double check if they see incomplete x-ray series given that there are off-service residents rotating through the ED.
Effect	
Better training, less rework (and cost) from going back to do additional x-rays. Fewer delays for patients.	

Name	Dept #	Supervisor	Date
DG	Emergency	DT	2/10/2006

Figure 7.11   Ensuring correct X-ray order sets are used.

Proper X-Ray Ordering

Gregory Jacobson, MD, working as a faculty member in emergency medicine at Vanderbilt University Medical Center, noticed an off-service resident ordering an incomplete X-ray order set. Jacobson asked the resident to show him how the order was put in and discovered that the resident did not know about the emergency department order sets. The root cause of this misunderstanding was the lack of a proper orientation to the department for off-service residents. The Kaizen shown in Figure 7.11 describes the improvements that were made to increase the proper use of order sets. Root cause problem solving is discussed more in Chapter 11.

Background:

Ideally my patient would have had a properly functioning wound vac, but this time he didn't.

Current Condition:

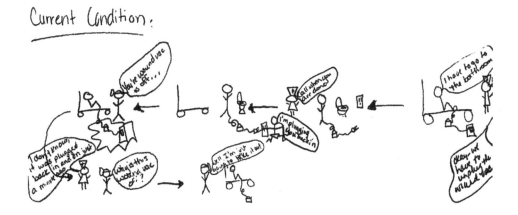

Root Cause:

My patient's wound vac suction wasn't working.

Why? The pump wasn't on.

Why? The pump did not have enough battery.

Why? The pump hadn't been plugged in properly.

Why? Nobody knew there was a specific way to plug the cord into the pump.

Rule 2

Figure 7.12a   An A3 created with the "adaptive design" methodology.

Ensuring Equipment Is Ready

Figure 7.12 shows a problem-solving A3 that was created through the "Adaptive Design" methodology used at Iowa Health System. An A3 of this style is drawn in pencil, often having plenty of eraser marks because a team creates it in real time as they work through iterations of the scientific method. In this case, they were reacting to the problem of not having a properly functioning wound vacuum. A team documented the current state and went through a root cause investigation, asking "why?" five times. With input from frontline staff, they developed and tested countermeasures to ensure that the problem would not occur again.

Ideal State

Countermeasures:

	Who	When	Done
1. Hands-on staff education about the proper way to plug in	All	July Unit meeting	✓
2. Visual cue on pump -if possible	KCI	6/14/11	
? 3. Contact FDA	Janice		
4. Educate pump specialists (KCI)	All	6/14/11	✓
5. Educate UBE's	Wound nurse	6/14/11	✓
6. Poster & pictures	Megan & Sheena	6/29/11	✓
7. Communicate with system	Megan & Liz	July Report Out	✓
8. Wound Vac team to create education	Wound nurses Staff RNs	August	✓

Signal Question:

Is my wound vac functioning properly?

Start: 6-1-11
End: 6-29-11

Owners: Sheena, Janice, Megan, Mary Wen
Mary, Nancy, Troy, SN, OD, Deb
KCI Laur
and Prot.

Figure 7.12b   An A3 created with the "adaptive design" methodology.

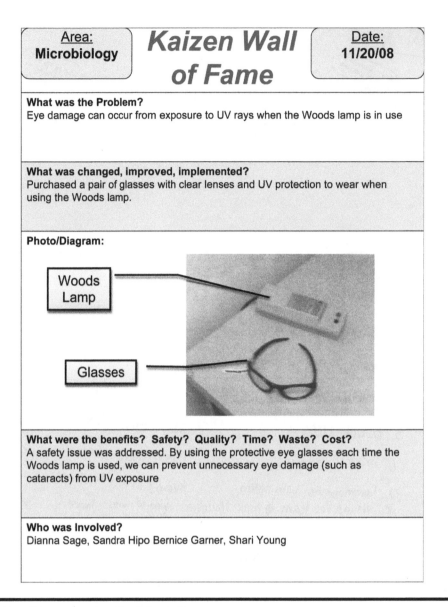

Figure 7.13   Eye protection for lab staff.

Eye Protection for Lab Staff

Kaizens can be focused on safety for staff members, as well as patients. Figure 7.13 shows an example from the laboratory at Children's Medical Center Dallas, where staff members needed UV eye protection when using a piece of equipment. Lab leadership moved quickly to get the glasses ordered.

Kaizen Wall of Fame

What was the Problem?
When using the hematoclad open ended hematocrit tubes, the critoseal would come out during centrifugation and blood would aerosolize within the centrifuge. This caused a safety issue and a time issue.

What was changed, improved, implemented? The self-sealing tube was validated as a replacement to the hematoclad brand tube. There is no need to stock the critoseal clay and the sealant in the E-Z safe brand does not allow blood to escape. Repeat set-up of the test was eliminated.

Photo/Diagram:

What were the benefits? Safety? Quality? Time? Waste? Cost?

Safety is improved because blood does not escape the tube. Time is saved from having to repeat the test. Money is saved by not having to order the critoseal clay.

Who was Involved?

Janie Rutherford presented the idea and performed the validation study.

Figure 7.14   Preventing aerosolized specimens.

Preventing Aerosolized Specimens

The Children's Medical Center Dallas lab team also found and resolved another potential safety risk, as documented in Figure 7.14. Changing the type of seal on the container had multiple benefits, including improving safety and reducing the risk of exposure of bloodborne pathogens, while also saving time and money.

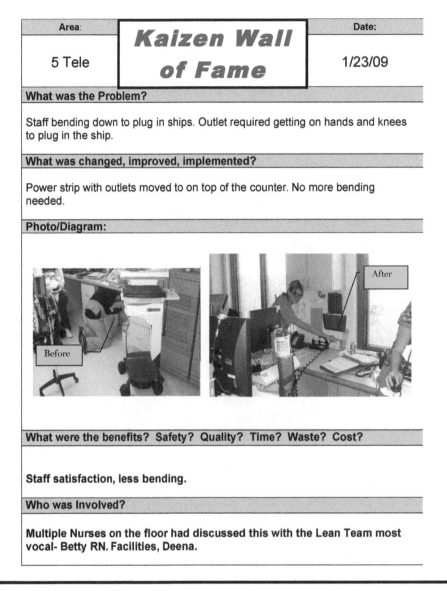

Area:	Kaizen Wall of Fame	Date:
5 Tele		1/23/09

What was the Problem?

Staff bending down to plug in ships. Outlet required getting on hands and knees to plug in the ship.

What was changed, improved, implemented?

Power strip with outlets moved to on top of the counter. No more bending needed.

Photo/Diagram:

Before / *After*

What were the benefits? Safety? Quality? Time? Waste? Cost?

Staff satisfaction, less bending.

Who was Involved?

Multiple Nurses on the floor had discussed this with the Lean Team most vocal- Betty RN. Facilities, Deena.

Figure 7.15   Easier to plug in carts.

Making Work Easier for Staff

The following examples show cases where healthcare professionals were able to save time or make their work easier. This often leads to improved patient care, because the time saved can be reallocated, as well as lower costs for the organization.

Easier to Plug In Carts

Nurses at Riverside Medical Center had portable computer carts, which they called "ships," that needed to be plugged in for charging. Before their Kaizen, it was frustrating because they had to crawl on the ground to plug them in. Power strips were installed on top of the desks in the nurses' station, as documented in Figure 7.15.

Figure 7.16 **Improved ergonomics and specimen quality.**

Improved Ergonomics and Specimen Quality

The core lab team at Children's Medical Center Dallas used 5S principles to make a printer easier to reach and also relocated frequently used items to be closer at hand, as shown in Figure 7.16. Moving the printer had a side benefit in that the printer no longer impacted a piece of test equipment that was sensitive to the vibrations caused by the printer.

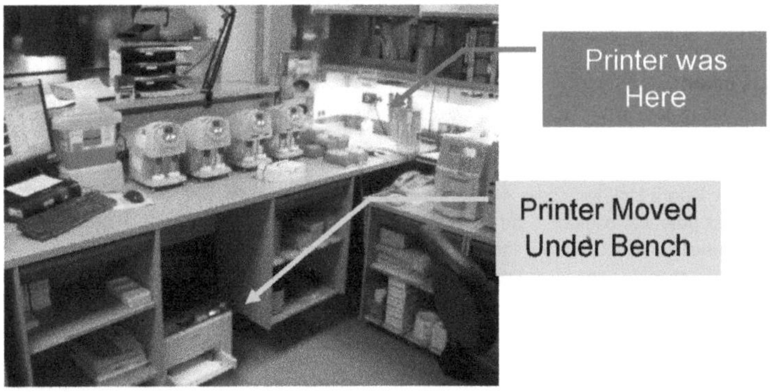

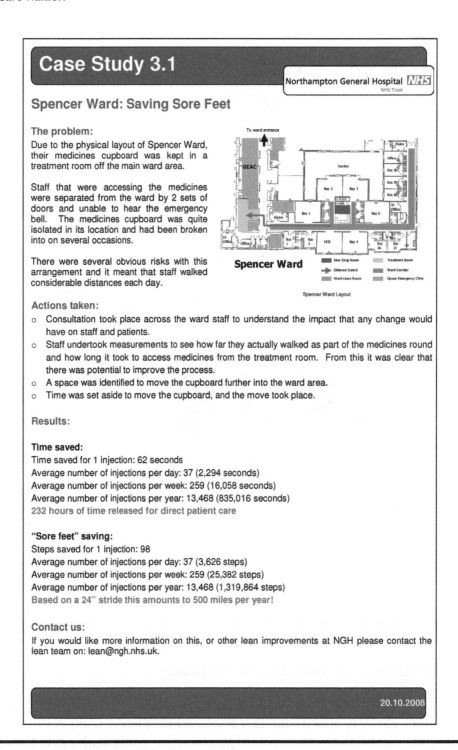

Figure 7.17   Reducing staff walking time and distance.

Saving Sore Feet

Nurses in a ward at Northampton General Hospital had to walk too far to get medications from a cabinet. Working together to find a new location reduced walking, improved security, and ensured patients got medications in a more timely manner, as documented in Figure 7.17.

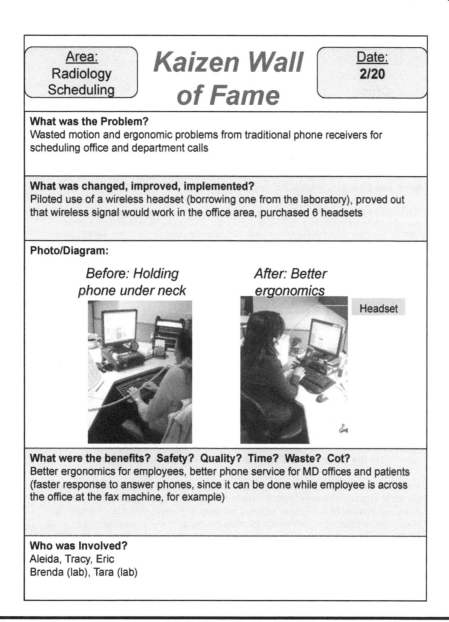

Figure 7.18 Better phone ergonomics and productivity.

Better Phone Ergonomics and Productivity

The radiology scheduling office staff at Children's Medical Center Dallas spends most of the day on the phone, and the ergonomics were far from ideal. A laboratory employee who was participating in some early Lean work told them about the wireless headsets used by customer service staff in the lab. While this change involved some expense, it greatly improved productivity of the scheduling staff because they could walk to the fax machine and still answer phone calls, reducing delays in getting procedures scheduled, as shown in Figure 7.18.

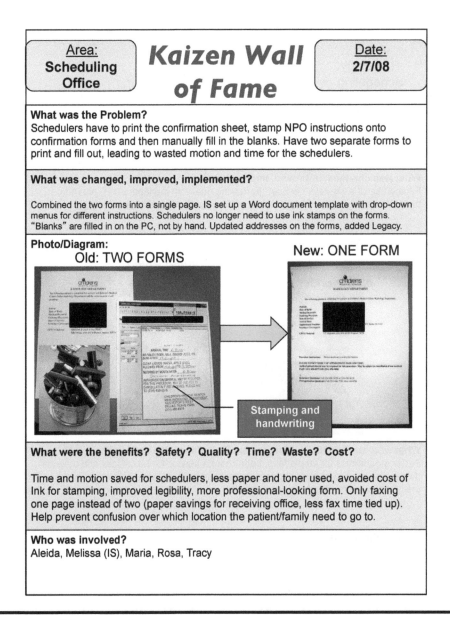

Figure 7.19   Combining two forms into one.

Combining Two Forms into One

The radiology team at CMCD also discovered that they were using two different forms during the scheduling process, including one form that was printed and modified using rubber stamps. The information services department created a new consolidated form, documented in Figure 7.19, that made the work easier and faster, while allowing the team to stop using a whole bucket's worth of stamps.

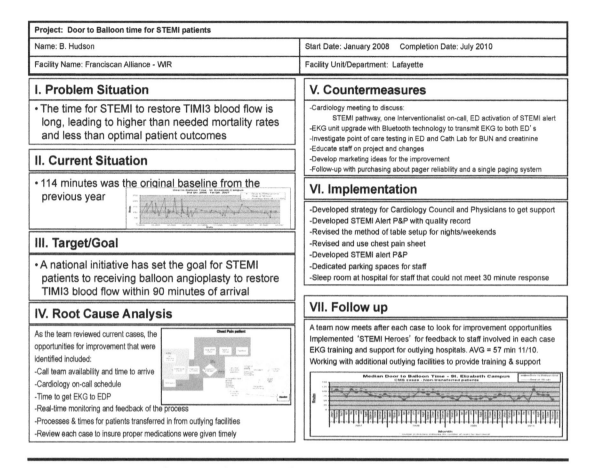

Figure 7.20   Faster codes STEMI heart attack care.

Preventing Delays

Kaizens that prevent delays can also improve patient care and reduce costs, as shown in the following examples.

Faster Code STEMI Heart Attack Care

Figure 7.20 shows an A3 report from a Franciscan Alliance hospital that summarizes improvements made in Code STEMI patient flow. The baseline time in January 2008 was 114 minutes, and, after the improvements, the average in November 2010 was 57 minutes.

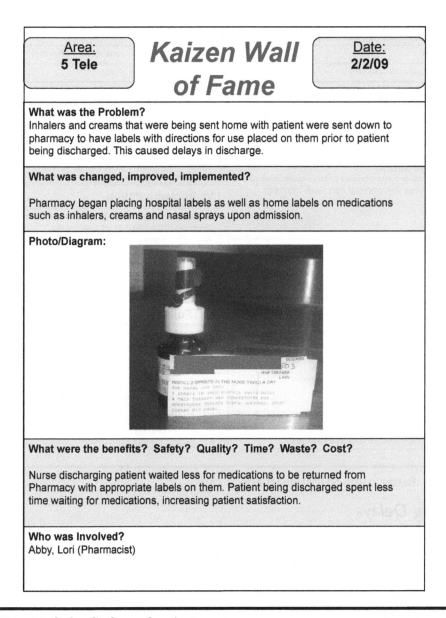

Area: 5 Tele	*Kaizen Wall of Fame*	Date: 2/2/09

What was the Problem?
Inhalers and creams that were being sent home with patient were sent down to pharmacy to have labels with directions for use placed on them prior to patient being discharged. This caused delays in discharge.

What was changed, improved, implemented?

Pharmacy began placing hospital labels as well as home labels on medications such as inhalers, creams and nasal sprays upon admission.

Photo/Diagram:

What were the benefits? Safety? Quality? Time? Waste? Cost?

Nurse discharging patient waited less for medications to be returned from Pharmacy with appropriate labels on them. Patient being discharged spent less time waiting for medications, increasing patient satisfaction.

Who was Involved?
Abby, Lori (Pharmacist)

Figure 7.21   Meds for discharged patients.

Meds for Discharged Patients

The telemetry unit at Riverside Medical Center found that patient discharges were often delayed when nurses had to wait for medications to be sent from the pharmacy. Many of these creams and inhalers were already being used by the patient, but only had inpatient labels. So, they were thrown away, being replaced by new medications that had the proper outpatient labeling causing some medications to be wasted. The pharmacy found they could change their process to initially label the medications for both inpatient and outpatient purposes. Discharge delays were reduced, cost savings were realized by the patient or payer, and labor was reduced for the hospital. The Kaizen is shown in Figure 7.21.

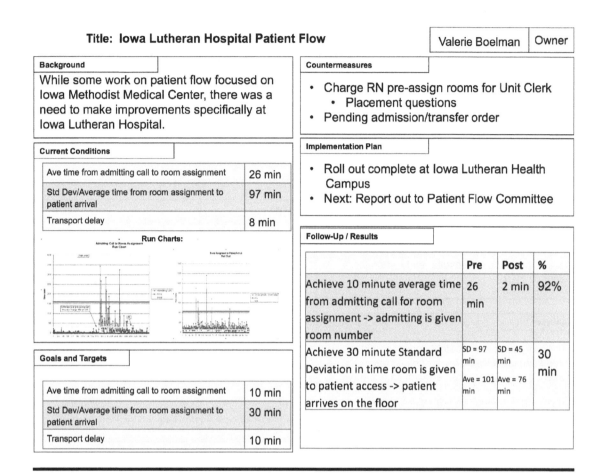

Title: Iowa Lutheran Hospital Patient Flow | Valerie Boelman | Owner

Background

While some work on patient flow focused on Iowa Methodist Medical Center, there was a need to make improvements specifically at Iowa Lutheran Hospital.

Current Conditions

Ave time from admitting call to room assignment	26 min
Std Dev/Average time from room assignment to patient arrival	97 min
Transport delay	8 min

Run Charts:

Goals and Targets

Ave time from admitting call to room assignment	10 min
Std Dev/Average time from room assignment to patient arrival	30 min
Transport delay	10 min

Countermeasures

- Charge RN pre-assign rooms for Unit Clerk
  - Placement questions
- Pending admission/transfer order

Implementation Plan

- Roll out complete at Iowa Lutheran Health Campus
- Next: Report out to Patient Flow Committee

Follow-Up / Results

	Pre	Post	%
Achieve 10 minute average time from admitting call for room assignment -> admitting is given room number	26 min	2 min	92%
Achieve 30 minute Standard Deviation in time room is given to patient access -> patient arrives on the floor	SD = 97 min Ave = 101 min	SD = 45 min Ave = 76 min	30 min

Figure 7.22　Getting patients to rooms with less delay.

Getting Patients to Rooms with Less Delay

This A3, Figure 7.22, from Iowa Lutheran Hospital shows how two different types of admission process delays were reduced.

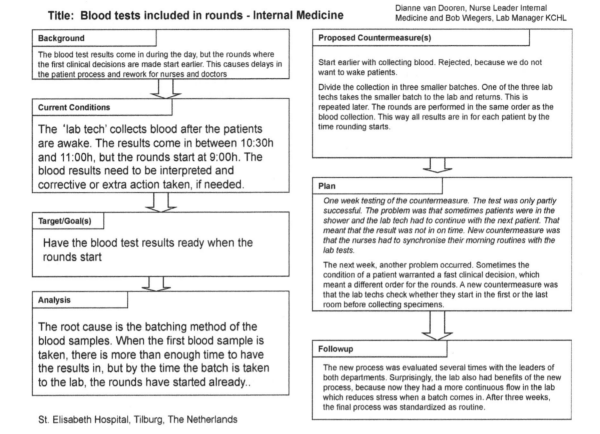

Title: **Blood tests included in rounds - Internal Medicine**

Dianne van Dooren, Nurse Leader Internal Medicine and Bob Wiegers, Lab Manager KCHL

Background

The blood test results come in during the day, but the rounds where the first clinical decisions are made start earlier. This causes delays in the patient process and rework for nurses and doctors

Current Conditions

The 'lab tech' collects blood after the patients are awake. The results come in between 10:30h and 11:00h, but the rounds start at 9:00h. The blood results need to be interpreted and corrective or extra action taken, if needed.

Target/Goal(s)

Have the blood test results ready when the rounds start

Analysis

The root cause is the batching method of the blood samples. When the first blood sample is taken, there is more than enough time to have the results in, but by the time the batch is taken to the lab, the rounds have started already..

St. Elisabeth Hospital, Tilburg, The Netherlands

Proposed Countermeasure(s)

Start earlier with collecting blood. Rejected, because we do not want to wake patients.

Divide the collection in three smaller batches. One of the three lab techs takes the smaller batch to the lab and returns. This is repeated later. The rounds are performed in the same order as the blood collection. This way all results are in for each patient by the time rounding starts.

Plan

One week testing of the countermeasure. The test was only partly successful. The problem was that sometimes patients were in the shower and the lab tech had to continue with the next patient. That meant that the result was not in on time. New countermeasure was that the nurses had to synchronise their morning routines with the lab tests.

The next week, another problem occurred. Sometimes the condition of a patient warranted a fast clinical decision, which meant a different order for the rounds. A new countermeasure was that the lab techs check whether they start in the first or the last room before collecting specimens.

Followup

The new process was evaluated several times with the leaders of both departments. Surprisingly, the lab also had benefits of the new process, because now they had a more continuous flow in the lab which reduces stress when a batch comes in. After three weeks, the final process was standardized as routine.

Figure 7.23 More timely results for rounding.

More Timely Test Results for Rounding

A team at St. Elisabeth Hospital made changes to better coordinate the timing of morning laboratory testing and morning rounding. Following the PDSA process, their initial tests confirmed that the process was improved, as documented in Figure 7.23.

Fewer Supply Chain Delays

Cardinal Health and Christiana Care Health System (Delaware) collaborated to improve their supply chain, reducing the delays in getting material received and processed through the dock to customers. Their DMAIC A3 is shown as Figure 7.24.

Better Access to Endocrinology

Akron Children's Hospital documented some completed improvements, along with some that are still in progress, that tackled the problem of long waits for endocrinology clinic appointments, as seen in their A3, Figure 7.25.

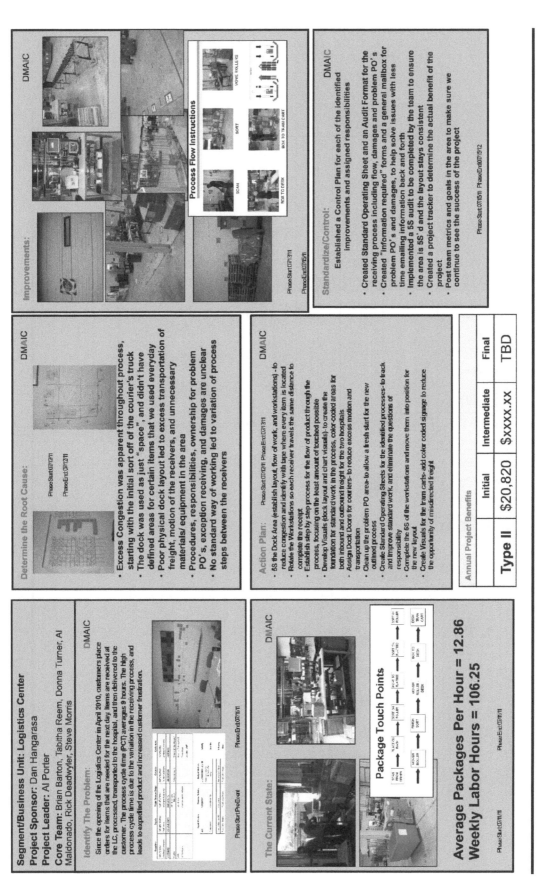

Figure 7.24 Fewer supply chain delays.

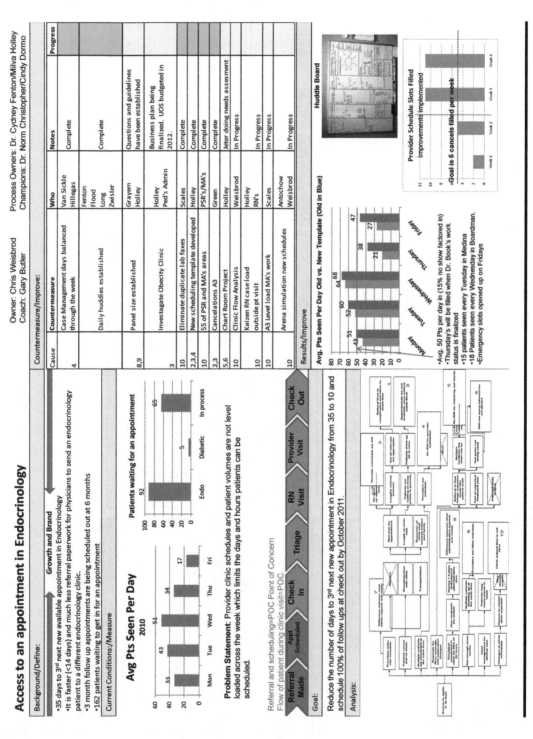

Figure 7.25   Better access to endocrinology.

Saving Space or Cost

Space and cost go hand in hand. In the Kaizen mindset, rather than just reflexively saying we need more equipment or more space, we work to find process improvements that are more creative and less expensive, as the following examples show.

Creativity over Capital in the Lab

The pathology staff at NHS Northampton General Hospital had a problem where they were running out of white "bricks" that held specimens and related paperwork that were waiting for testing. Without Kaizen thinking, the team might have just asked for more of these bricks to be purchased.

The team spent a few minutes brainstorming about what else could hold the tubes and papers. They discovered the empty patient specimen tubes were shipped in black racks. These racks were sturdy enough to hold full specimen containers, and they were the perfect size, a clever short-term countermeasure that cost them nothing, as illustrated in Figure 7.26. What used to be an item to recycle became an item to reuse. The lab was spared the expense of buying more white racks that would have only been needed for a short time before the lab's flow was eventually improved.

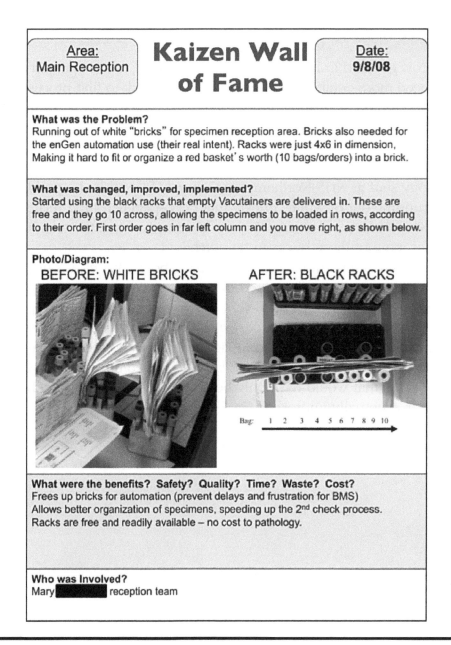

Figure 7.26 Creativity over capital in the lab.

Company Medical Clinic Costs

Figure 7.27 is an example of an A3 shared by consultant Tracey Richardson that focuses on reducing cost for a company's employee health clinic. Reading the A3 shows a more detailed PDSA problem-solving process, starting with the proper definition of the problem statement, breaking down the problem, going to see the problem first hand, understanding the root cause, and then proposing and implementing countermeasures that were followed up on over time.

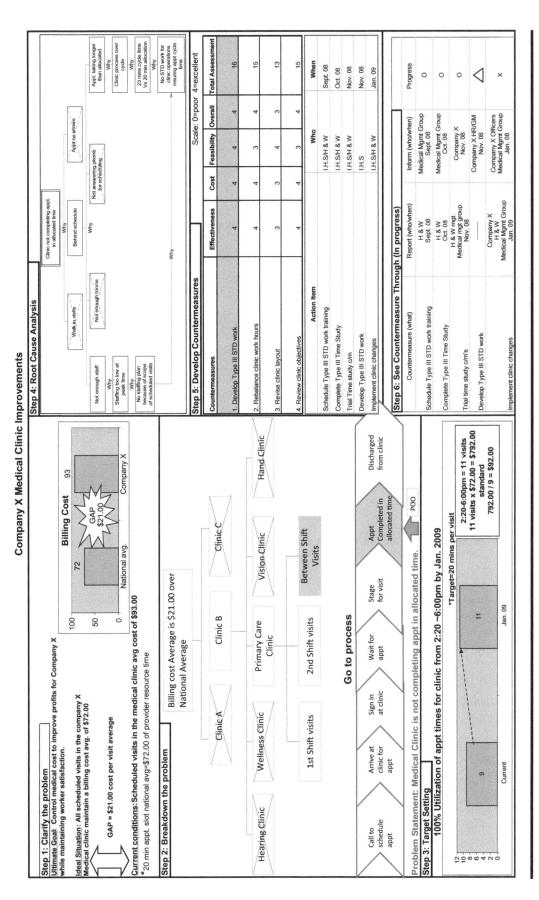

Figure 7.27 Company medical clinic costs.

Area: Bacteriology	Kaizen Wall of Fame	Date: 8/23/2010

What was the Problem?
We have an extremely large number of patient isolates that require freezing with a dwindling freezer capacity.

What was changed, improved, implemented?
Dr. Doern spoke with Infection Control personnel to determine which organisms continually require freezing. Through communication, it has reduced the number of isolates to be frozen.

Patient isolates to be frozen

Each freezer box holds 81 isolates

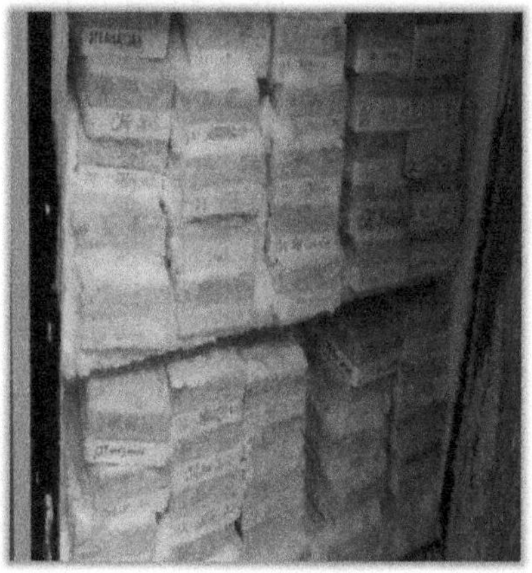

-70 °C freezer space available

What were the benefits? Safety? Quality? Time? Waste? Cost?
Cost and labor reduction, saves freezer space

Who was Involved?
Dianna Sage, Dr. Welch, Dr. Doern, Sharon Holmes, Infection Control, Shari Young, Bernice Garner, Minh Vu

Figure 7.28 Rethinking freezer use.

Rethinking Freezer Use

Rather than buying another freezer, which would have added cost and space, the bacteriology section of the Children's Medical Center Dallas lab questioned existing practices and determined they actually needed less space. The worked with infection control to ensure safety was the first consideration, as shown in Figure 7.28.

Conclusion

The process of documenting and sharing Kaizens serves a number of important functions for a healthcare organization. When people document their own improvements, it helps them reflect upon their improvements, the learning, and the benefits. Sharing examples of Kaizen gives recognition to those who have initiated and completed Kaizens by posting the improvements for others to see. Sharing Kaizens also allows others to utilize or build upon the improvements in their area or their department, inspiring them to develop their own ideas for change. Regardless of the exact format you use, the key is to take time to document improvements, to celebrate them, and to recognize the people involved.

Discussion Questions

- Why is it often difficult to put Kaizen improvements into just a single category, such as quality or cost?
- Of the different documentation formats you have seen, what do you think would work better in your organization?
- How can you encourage or teach people to document their own Kaizens?
- What do you see as some of the advantages and disadvantages of using software to write up a Kaizen versus doing it by hand?

Chapter 8

The Art of Kaizen

There is no joy other than the joy of creating. There is no man who is truly alive other than one who is creating. All others are just shadows on the earth with nothing to do with being alive. The joy of living, whether it is love or action, is the joy of creating.

—Romain Rolland
Nobel Prize Laureate in Literature

Dan Lafever, information services quality manager and one of the strongest Kaizeneers at Franciscan, has integrated Kaizen throughout his life. Dan sees opportunities so frequently that he now gifts others with his thoughts and ideas in what he calls "random acts of Kaizen."

As you might guess, not everybody is open to receiving ideas from others. For example, Dan was in a grocery checkout and noticed a grocery item fall on the floor. He asked the cashier how many times a day something falls and she replied it happens several times a day. Dan asked, "Have you ever thought about putting up a barrier so nothing falls?" She replied, "No, I haven't" and did not appear interested, so Dan did not push the conversation any further.

But, if people seem eager, Dan might bring up an idea by asking it in the form of a question, "Have you considered doing it this way?" and he will explain the new possibility. Then, he will work with that person to create a solution. Even if Dan's initial idea is a good one, this collaboration is a critical step in the improvement process.

One time, he was in a sandwich shop and noticed the breakfast sign in the window was curled, making the sign difficult to read. He asked the owner, "Did you know your sign is curled?" The owner was interested in improvement, and one Kaizen idea led to several others. Then, the owner asked Dan to come talk to his staff about Kaizen. To Dan, once you catch the Kaizen fever, you start thinking that just about anything can be improved. Dan now notices how people perform activities and asks himself, "Why is that done that way?" To Dan, random acts of Kaizen are a matter of raising awareness, asking why, jointly solving problems, and sharing those ideas that could help people find a better way. Dan said, "There is always another way. There is always a better way." The key is engaging people in change and improvement.

Barriers to Kaizen

If we agree that individuals in healthcare want to do the right thing for patients and their coworkers, why is there so little Kaizen in some healthcare organizations? Or, why do we have so many improvements that are not sustained? What are the systemic barriers to Kaizen and how can they be reduced or eliminated?

Even the most highly educated healthcare professionals sometimes express skepticism about their ability to participate in Kaizen and continuous improvement on a daily basis. This can be especially true if their workplace has not engaged them in improvement, whether that has been over the entirety of a 30-year career or just the first three years of a young employee's working life. It can take time to gain confidence, which is why the Kaizen approach encourages people to start with small, local, low-cost, and low-risk improvements.

When we talk to leaders, physicians, and front-line staff about Kaizen, the idea of continuous improvement makes sense. It appeals to them rationally and intellectually, but people then start talking about barriers to Kaizen, which include the things listed in Table 8.1.

We have some tips for dealing with some of these barriers, whether real or perceived. But, for many of these barriers, you will have to come up with your own countermeasures based on your organization. If you truly want to make Kaizen happen, then these barriers will be resolved through the creativity of your leaders and staff, applying continuous improvement and the Plan-Do-Study-Act (PDSA) cycle to the Kaizen process itself. As the radiology team at Children's Medical Center Dallas said in Chapter 6, you have to shift your mindset from talking about "why this won't work" to reframing the discussion around "let's make this work."

Whether you think that you can, or that you can't, you are usually right.

—Henry Ford

At Franciscan, coauthor Joe and other leaders have tried teaching Kaizen in the context of overcoming barriers, and it was not as effective as taking a more positive approach to making Kaizen successful. If you get a chance to take a race-driving course, the instructor will tell you that the car will automatically go where you are looking. If you look at an accident or look at the wall, you will be pulled into a crash. So, teaching Kaizen at Franciscan,

Table 8.1   Barriers to Kaizen

Others are resistant to change
Lack of time
"I get rewarded for firefighting"
Get in trouble for admitting we have problems
"We forget to follow up on ideas"
"People don't think we need to change or improve"
People give up when not getting responses
Lack of confidence in self or others
Administration only wants cost savings (real or perceived)
Lack of trust in the organization
Getting in trouble with coworkers
"It's the other people who need to change"
Fear of losing jobs
"I have people to do that for me; I delegate it"
"Perceived loss of control if I let employees do Kaizen"
"My people jump to solutions"

the wall or the barriers are a reality, but they do not believe it should be the primary focus.

Ideally, we would not have to overcome barriers, as they should not be created in the first place. If you work with people the right way, you will not create as many barriers. This is the art of Kaizen. Just as there is an art to practicing medicine and nursing, there is also an art to practicing Kaizen, especially when it involves other people changing their behaviors or what they do. Of course, it is challenging to do it all right—even the best do not always get it right.

Resistance to Change

Nothing so needs reforming as other people's habits.

—Mark Twain
American author and humorist

When people report that "resistance to change" is a problem in their organization, they can mean resistance to participating in a Kaizen program, in general, or a resistance to a specific Kaizen idea. When we feel or perceive resistance to a change, we should not blame the person or tell them simply, "don't be resistant, just get on board." Is there a legitimate problem that would be caused by the proposed change? Has there not been enough communication about the change and its expected impact? Did we not seek to get input from that person before announcing a change? Kaizen is more effective when we anticipate and try to proactively prevent "resistance" by engaging people in the right way, rather than just castigating them as being "change resistant."

90% of resistance is cautionary.

—Shigeo Shingo

Any perceived resistance should be the starting point for a discussion rather than a reason to stop talking and to stop working toward improvement.

Lack of Time—We're Too Busy

People underestimate their capacity for change. There is never a right time to do a difficult thing. A leader's job is to help people have vision for their potential.

—John Arthur Porter
Canadian sociologist

It is not at all uncommon to get push back regarding Kaizen from staff and leadership, saying things like, "this is too much work," or "you're asking too much of us," or "we're too busy for this." It comes down to a core complaint of, "we don't have enough time."

Imai wrote that managers "should spend at least 50 percent" of their time on improvement.[1] How do we create time for Kaizen? Instead of accepting "lack of time" as an excuse that immediately ends the discussion about improvement, we should use our Lean problem-solving skills to understand why we have a lack of time. When we view lack of time as a problem to solve rather than an unsolvable excuse, we can introduce countermeasures that free up time for improvement. If we have too many meetings, we can take a fresh look at what meetings should even occur and which meetings are happening just because "it's always been that way." Another thing an organization might do is introduce guidelines around how to best use email to minimize the amount of time managers are spending answering emails on which they were just "CCed," often for no good reason.

Since individual managers cannot arbitrarily decide to stop attending meetings, some organizations, including ThedaCare, have taken the approach of creating a two-hour "no-meeting zone" every morning.[2] During this window, the expectation is that managers will spend time attending team huddles in the "gemba" and coaching employees in their improvement efforts. The two hours freed up by the meeting-free zone is not intended to be used for answering email.

For staff members, we can focus initial Kaizens on freeing up time by eliminating waste. Paul O'Neill, former chair of the Pittsburgh Regional Health Initiative, said in an interview:

> *We've found in the work that we've been doing that 50% of a nurse's time is spent doing things that don't add value, like looking for medications that aren't where they're supposed to be or looking for equipment that isn't where it's supposed to be. You want to identify and have the people in the process identify every aspect of waste every day, so that people can work on systems redesign to take out the waste.[3]*

As people free up time by eliminating waste, some of that time can be dedicated to direct patient care or other value-adding activities. Some of the newly freed up time can also be used for additional Kaizen activity. Referring back to Chapter 3, some organizations have started with large-system Kaizen projects or weeklong events. One advantage of these focused efforts is that an initial large push for improvement can free up a large amount of time that can then be used for daily Kaizen. Of course, "lack of time" might be a barrier to scheduling even that first event or workshop.

Oftentimes, when somebody has a Kaizen idea, there is not immediately time available to work on the Kaizen, or there is not time to get others involved for even a quick discussion. It is important to have a mechanism for holding ideas until we have time to work on them. Using slow times at the end of the day for Kaizen might be a more productive alternative, in the long run, to sending people home early when there is no direct work to be done.

Evangeline Brock, a medical technologist at Children's Medical Center Dallas, says that they "take advantage of the slow times of year," which is the summer in the virology area, to spend more time on Kaizen improvements, especially ideas that might have accumulated on the Visual Idea Board during the year.

It is often said that the soft side of change is the hard part. At Franciscan, leaders teach their Kaizeneers the art of Kaizen by teaching a few basic principles that help mobilize the support of others. The following practices help avoid a great deal of the real or perceived resistance to change.

A Model for Mobilizing Support

Franciscan teaches a positive model for mobilizing the support of others that is based on a study of 70 of the most successful people of all time as published in the book *Seeing David in the Stone* by Joe and James Swartz.[4] After looking at the work of inventors like Edison, scientists like Einstein, artists like Michelangelo, talk show hosts like Oprah Winfrey, statesmen such as Thomas Jefferson, and businessmen such as Bill Gates, a pattern was discovered as to how they mobilized the support of others in order to accomplish great things.

The model that developed proposes approaching and involving others in the creation of solutions that move us toward the future vision, and is based on these tenets:

1. Respect others.
2. Create a vision that matters.
3. Convey the why.
4. Connect to the mission.

Tenet 1: Respect Others

Show proper respect to everyone.

—1 Peter 2:17

"Respect for people" is often called the first rule or tenet of Lean and Kaizen, as introduced in Chapter 2. If you approach every Kaizen with a deep respect for those you are working with, you will avoid the vast majority of potential barriers that are likely to surface while implementing any change initiative. People can tell if you truly respect them; it shows in how you treat them. Do you truly listen to other people, demonstrating that you seek to understand their point of view, remembering what is important to them? Do you help deliver results, through your Kaizens, that are important to them?

Courage is what it takes to stand up and speak, Courage is also what it takes to sit down and listen.

—Sir Winston Churchill

Respect involves listening to people when they identify a problem or bring up an issue that interferes with their work. In traditional settings, managers unfortunately often brush aside legitimate issues as complaining. Instead of asking people to do whatever it takes to get things done—a process that often involves costly or frustrating workarounds—managers should honor their employees by listening to their needs.

In many organizations, managers and leaders have been conditioned to be the ones with all the answers. We all take pride in solving problems and being the ones to get things done. This often leads to managers not listening to the ideas of others. In a Kaizen environment, we should not feel a sense of loss when someone else has an idea. Rather, it should be a positive reflection on the entire team.

Much of what is labeled "resistance to change" can actually be described as people reacting to a real or perceived lack of respect from their manager or colleagues. If people are pushing changes on others without getting proper input, people will naturally take issue with that. By showing respect, we can avoid these barriers and better engage people in improvement.

Tenet 2: Create a Vision That Matters

If you are working on something exciting that you really care about, you don't have to be pushed. The vision pulls you.

—Steve Jobs

One reason people are deemed "resistant" is that they either do not know the future vision that an organization is working toward, they do not agree with it, or they did not have any input into that vision. Before starting with Kaizen, leaders should work with their team members to define why the change in approach is needed. Does the organization think they need to improve? If so, how do we define improvement in terms of the patient, our coworkers, and the organization?

When Mark worked with the microbiology department at Children's Medical Center Dallas, the department was gathered for an introductory discussion and planning meeting. The first discussion defined goals for improvement in a collaborative manner. Team members were asked in a very open-ended way to define why and what they needed to improve. It turned out that the vision was incredibly well aligned between employees, the clinical and operations directors, and the hospital's leadership.

They all defined goals as:

■ Improve service (quality and response time of test results)
■ Determine proper staffing levels (not understaffed and not overstaffed)
■ Reduce overtime

Improving service to children, via the physicians who order tests that contribute to their care, was an easy goal to get alignment around. It was also easy to get everyone to agree on less overtime—the staff members were tired of working a lot of overtime to get their work done, and the hospital had a financial interest in reducing overtime. The more difficult question was around "proper" staffing levels. The team felt, especially in one key area, that they were understaffed because testing volumes had increased dramatically, yet they had the same number of people. The team committed to bring forward Kaizen ideas that would reduce waste in their day, increasing their own productivity while maintaining or improving quality. Department leaders committed to increasing staffing levels if the data showed it was required (after working to reduce waste). Ultimately, that key area was able to add one new person, a 25% increase in staffing that helped them handle what had been a 50% increase in workload, reducing waste through Kaizen and process redesign led to less overburden, less overtime, and an environment where people were happier in their work of caring for kids.

In the radiology area at Children's Medical Center Dallas, the team was very motivated by their desire to deliver better service to kids. While the hospital had a financial incentive in increasing MRI utilization and increasing throughput in the department, leaders never discussed that with staff, nor did they try to make that a primary motivation for improvement. Increasing throughput was highly aligned with the goal of reducing waiting times for outpatient MRIs. The goal of getting the right diagnostic imaging to the patients in a more timely manner was incredibly motivating to the team members. They were focused not only on the children and their care but also on the parents, as faster imaging might help rule out conditions that would cause a lot of fear and anxiety to the families.

If you want to get people to change something, get them thinking about a future condition that is better for all stakeholders. For example, Amy Macke, a nurse at Franciscan, noticed that breast milk from her patient's mothers was being wasted, and she decided to do something about it. She talked to the other nurses in her unit about how much work it took for a mother to pump the milk and how disappointing it was to mothers when milk had to be thrown out just because a due date was not properly marked.

She began talking about a world where mother's milk was never wasted, creating a powerful vision. Then, she introduced a label that could be used to identify when the milk was pumped, as shown in Figure 8.1. The nurses in the unit could immediately relate to her vision, and they helped implement and use her label.

Amy was more effective in leading change because she went far beyond what some managers might do. In other organizations, a manager might send out an email, or they might hang a sign with a very directive tone. The sign might say, "Here is the new label, you MUST all use the label, every time!" That might naturally make nurses resistant, as their unconscious reaction might say, "You can't tell me what to do!" Amy's leadership approach engaged people more constructively. She treated people with respect by helping them know why it was important to use the new labels.

Tenet 3: Convey the Why

Man will put up with any "how" if he has a "why."

—Friedrich Wilhelm Nietzsche
Philosopher

Breast Milk Stickers		Franciscan ST. FRANCIS HEALTH
Before	**After**	
We did not have a way to identify when breast milk was fresh. Since frozen milk needs to be used with 24 hours of thawing, if milk was not labeled as fresh (use with 48 hours) it would be discarded as expired.	We worked as a team to create a sticker that could be placed on the bottle which had the appropriate information on it to provide safe administration of fresh breast milk. **Fresh** Breast Milk (never frozen) Pumped @ Date____ Time____ Use or Freeze by 48 hours, Discard if refrigerated > 48 hrs.	

Effect				
This will eliminate discarding breast milk that may have been misrepresented as previously frozen.				

Name	ID #	Dept #	Supervisor	Date
Amy Macke RN, IBCLC, Juli Stenger RN, Gina Neitling NAS, US		NICU	Paula Stanfill	2-9-10

Figure 8.1　Breast milk sticker.

Another basic tenet of the art of Kaizen is to explain the "why" of what you are trying to accomplish. If you explain why you are doing your Kaizen and the benefits to those you are trying to get to adopt the Kaizen, you will be more likely to gain their engagement. People want to know "what's in it for me?" which is often abbreviated WIIFM. Healthcare professionals are naturally concerned about others—their patients and their coworkers—but it is human nature to also be concerned about the WIIFM. Good Kaizen improvements can lead to improvements that benefit patients and staff. But, if there is a conflict in those objectives, we should choose what is best for the patient.

Beyond WIIFM, healthcare professionals will generally respond positively when a change or policy is communicated in terms of patient needs and care. Traditional organizations rely far too much on formal authority and top-down direction, telling staff that they must do certain things because it is policy or because the boss says so. In a Kaizen culture, managers are far less directive, relying on the intrinsic motivation of people to enable better patient care. In cases where managers do have to be directive, there should always be an explanation of why. Explaining why shows respect for people in a very meaningful way.

Natalie Novak, director of medical records at Franciscan, engaged her entire department in a vision of a fully electronic medical records department. This would be a major change, so Natalie's leadership style was not one where she came up with a master improvement plan and then dictated all of the required changes for her staff to carry out. Natalie conveyed the many whys for going paperless. First, she told her staff, "our CEO is asking for us to go paperless." She also told them about the benefits of going electronic, including simplifying document distribution and searching, improving version control and tracking, reducing office supply costs, and enabling staff to work from home. When staff understood the reasons why, they worked together to draw out ideas that made that vision a reality.

Over the last several years, her staff implemented Kaizen upon Kaizen in the effort to go electronic. For example, one Kaizen was to store all memos in an online database so staff can search any memo they have received. This is helpful because the Franciscan email system automatically deletes emails after three months. Another was to convert all labor productivity calculation worksheets to an electronic format. Another was to perform all of their quality reviews online. A big Kaizen was to scan auditing information into an online searchable database, which dramatically cut the time required to prepare for Medicare Recovery Audit Contractor (RAC) audits.

Collectively, the small Kaizens added up to make a big difference. Because of the Kaizen work, the medical records department was able to take on an increase in volume without adding the three additional employees that they estimate would have been required without implementing Kaizen. This makes the hospital more cost competitive in an era when costs are rising and reimbursements are dropping.

The practice of explaining why can also extend to guests of your hospital. At Children's Medical Center Dallas, the staff noticed that families often brought food into the waiting area of the radiology department. Sometimes, children who were not supposed to be eating before their sedation would run over and eat some of somebody's food. If this was noticed, it would possibly lead to a procedure being canceled and rescheduled. If this was not noticed, the child might get sick while under sedation.

The department previously had a small and very directive sign inside the waiting area that just said "no food or drink." That sign was often not seen or just ignored. During the initial Lean project, one Kaizen was putting up a new sign outside the unit that explained why, in two languages, as shown in Figure 8.2.

Signs to Keep Food Out	
Before	**After**
We had a sign INSIDE the department waiting room that said "no food or drink." People always bring food in and the sign is either too late (they just keep the food) or it's not seen.	Posted English & Spanish signs OUTSIDE the door.  
Effect	
Far fewer incidents of people bringing in food. Less risk of NPO violations from a child stealing a french fry from somebody.	

Name	ID #	Dept #	Supervisor	Date
Lean Team		Same Day	Eric	March 2008

Figure 8.2 Food signs.

The sign requested that people not bring in food or drink out of respect for patients who were not able to eat. Compliance to the rule increased dramatically.

Tenet 4: Connect to the Mission

When Joe first started working in healthcare, he sat down with Dr. Chuck Dietzen to learn about medicine because he knew almost nothing about the field. Chuck explained that it would take too long to teach him the practice of medicine; however, he said he could teach Joe the *art* of medicine.

Chuck pulled out a picture from his wallet and laid it in front of Joe. "This is Abby," he said. Abby was Chuck's first patient after finishing medical school. She was a 2 1/2 year old with leukemia and was, at that point, expected to die in a few months. Chuck, however, knew his job went beyond attending to her physical needs, so he spent extra time with Abby, joking, telling stories, and giving her hope. He spent an hour every evening after his shift visiting with Abby. When he discovered that French fries were her favorite food and about the only food she would eat, he began sneaking in fries every evening. His colleagues at the hospital pulled him aside several times and cautioned him that he should not get too attached to Abby because she was going to die, and, if he got too close, he would be devastated and would not want to continue practicing medicine. Chuck's reply was, "No, you don't understand … Abby is the reason I suffered through all those years of medical school. I am called to make a difference for the Abbys of the world."

Chuck did make a difference. Abby survived and now has a family of her own. When Chuck needs to be reminded of the difference that can be made in healthcare, he pulls out his picture of Abby. To Chuck, and many other professionals, healthcare is more than a career; it is a calling.

If you have been called to the healthcare field, it is likely that you understand Chuck. Healthcare is a significantly meaningful profession. Those who need the services of healthcare professionals are often experiencing pain and trauma in their life. They are in a state of crisis and desperately hope that their health can be restored, done quickly and kindly. Healthcare providers meet people's highest physical needs in their most stressed and vulnerable state, and they make a powerful and real difference in people's lives. It is important to recognize that healthcare is a process of people serving people. Any significant change in the practice or art of healthcare must start with a deep respect for people and a deep understanding of why they were called into this profession.

Healthcare professionals like Chuck usually have an extremely high degree of intrinsic motivation—an internal drive to care for patients and their families. This drive often includes the desire to make things better—improving processes, workflows, and the workplace environment. While there are many examples like Kim, the Children's Medical Center Dallas medical technologist who was able to implement a Kaizen idea in her very first week of work, there are far more examples of hospital staff who unfortunately have that drive for improvement drummed out of them.

Like the story about Dr. Dietzen and his patient, you are more likely to get the full engagement of others if you understand why those you work with were called to their profession. If you are able to connect the improvement idea that you are proposing to what is important and meaningful to them, you will get better participation from others.

Is This about Me or Is This about the Mission?

Franciscan's Kaizeneers are taught to remember, "we, not me." To engage and enroll others in an improvement opportunity, first see the opportunity from the group's point of view. When discussing the opportunity with others, use "we," instead of "I" in your language. This can help connect what you are doing to the organization's mission to serve patients and the community.

In Mark's experience working with Children's Medical Center Dallas, leaders in the laboratory and radiology very naturally talked about how improvement efforts needed to tie back to their mission, informally stated as "taking care of kids." Clay York, laboratory operations manager, frequently emphasizes tying improvements back to the patients. Even though the lab is physically disconnected from patients, York strengthens the emotional connection to their unseen patients by talking about how turnaround times affect the ability to get children discharged and back to school. York asks, "Are we doing this for the performance measures or for the kids?" Clearly, they are doing it for the kids.

At IU Health Goshen Hospital, every meeting starts with the reading of the organization's mission or a department's mission, says CEO James Dague, along with some reflection of how well they are living those values. Dague and the other leaders help individuals connect their improvement work to their personal mission, saying:

> One of the things we talk about in healthcare is one's personal mission. Why did you get into this job and into this profession? How are you doing in completing your life's mission? We want to get out of your way, in our culture, to allow you to fulfill that mission. That's something that brings this home to the individual far more than I ever thought it would.[5]

Working with Others Based on Their Willingness to Invest

Much of the art of Kaizen involves working with others to make change happen. When an opportunity for improvement is first introduced, people's willingness to invest their time and effort in that improvement often varies widely.

People can be thought of as being in three camps. First, there are the "eager stakeholders" who are always excited about improvement opportunities and are willing to go along with changes initiated by others. Second, there are the "cautious stakeholders" who want to keep things the way they are because it seems that keeping things in the status quo is more important to them than the new opportunity. They represent the majority of people in many organizations. Finally, there are the "opposers" who will initially be against almost any improvement opportunity, or at least appear so. They are typically a small but challenging group. These groups often appear in a bell curve distribution. Working with each of these three groups requires different strategies.

One organization Mark worked with referred to a small group of employees as "CAVE people," where CAVE stood for Citizens Against Virtually Everything. One person commented, "If you offered them a $20 bill, they would complain that the bill was wrinkled or dirty, or something." It was a funny line, but when we run across "CAVE people," we should try to be respectful and understand why that negativity might have built up over time.

How can you know which of those three camps someone is in? When working on an improvement, you can periodically probe to see how engaged a person is. Ask them if they have experienced the same frustration and problem as you have. Ask them if they have thought about doing something about the problem. Before talking about your idea, you will want to assess how willing they are to invest their time and energy in the opportunity. Typically, those who are in the cautious camp will not share strong opinions about the Kaizen, while, those opposed will often voice a strong negative opinion. One may find a portion of opposers that will not voice an opinion, but they will actively resist when it comes time to implement the Kaizen. Some people will be passive aggressive, saying yes and then undercutting the idea by not taking action or by badmouthing the idea privately. It is preferable to have an environment where people disagree vocally and respectfully, because it creates fewer surprises as you go.

Strategy 1: Co-create with Those Eager for Opportunity

People support what they create.

—Kurt Lewin

Considered the founder of social psychology

The eager stakeholders are often thought of as easy to work with; however, if their idea for improvement is different than yours, they may eagerly pursue their own idea. So, a good approach with this group is to "co-create" the solution. The more you can involve this group in creating the solution, the more likely they will own the solution with you. They will be more willing to change and persuade others to adopt the new improvement idea.

Seek Their Ideas

> *Nowadays, I make it a practice to call [my workers] into consultation on any new work. I observe they're more willing to set about a piece of work when their opinions are asked and their advice followed.*
>
> **—Columella**
> *Roman landlord, 100 A.D.*[6]

Seeking the ideas of others not only expands the pool of ideas but also helps lower resistance. Using an infection analogy, an idea from inside the host is recognizable as friendly and tends to be more easily accepted. Ideas from others might be attacked as a foreign body. Therefore, if possible, let those that have to make the most behavioral changes discover and adopt their own solutions.

Laura Pettigrew, manager of medical records at Franciscan, stated, "We now pose new challenges to staff and let them solve them. Sometimes it takes a few weeks, but they typically come back with a solution to try, so they own it." In Chapter 1, we introduced the idea that people tend to like their own ideas and reject those forced by others.

Play Kaizen Catch Ball

A good way to learn to catch and throw a baseball is to practice with someone. Likewise, a good way to learn to play Kaizen is to practice with someone. You can practice with someone by playing Kaizen "catch ball." You and your partner take each idea that is thrown out, trying to improve it or refine it before throwing the refined idea back to the other person. This cycle continues until there is reasonable consensus on how to move forward in the PDSA process.

Kaizen catch ball is a form of structured brainstorming. When done well, it has the advantage that everyone feels like they contributed in tangible ways to the final solution, thereby becoming co-creators of the Kaizen. Co-creators have ownership of the idea and are generally more committed to their idea than those who were not involved. Another advantage of Kaizen catch ball is that it allows the group to anticipate and work through the many issues that could surface during implementation, so the chosen solution will be more likely to work without a hitch.

> *Two are better than one.*
>
> **—Ecclesiastes 4:9**

Joe Click, a pharmacy technician at Franciscan co-creates when he plays catch ball. His regular catch ball partner, Brenda, had talents that complemented his.

She generally saw more opportunities because she was more experienced. Also, she had a sarcastic outlook and could readily see the negative, whereas Joe was stronger at seeing the positive. Brenda was humble, got along well with everyone, and was interested in every area of the pharmacy, which helped in the implementation of their Kaizens. He was stronger at writing, so he would write the Kaizens up. Together, Joe and Brenda became prolific Kaizeneers.

Tragically, Brenda died in an auto accident. Joe was distraught for months and all but stopped doing Kaizen. It took some time, but Joe came back, and now he plays catch ball with many other people. For example, he regularly finds three or four people in the area of the pharmacy that most pertains to the Kaizen idea he has and starts out with, "There has got to be a way to do this thing better. I'm thinking this … what do you think?" Someone in the group catches his idea and throws back a refined version, and round and round it goes until they come up with the Kaizen that they implement as a group. Before submitting the Kaizen Report, he runs it by the contributors and edits it based on their suggestions.

Joe's manager, Ronda Frieje, credits him as being key to bringing the departmental shifts together because he regularly involves all shifts with his catch ball approach. She said, "By the time we are ready to implement a Kaizen that could affect the entire department, he has already talked with all the key people, and that goes a long way toward getting the buy-in to implement and succeed."

Nancy Mosier, manager of pediatrics at Franciscan, says she has four reasons why it can be more effective to do Kaizen in groups:

1. The group is sold on the idea because they contributed the creation of the idea.
2. The group brings out pros and cons and troubleshoots the idea before trying it.
3. The group becomes the critical mass needed to sell the idea to others.
4. Kaizen is more fun when done in a group.

Reigniting Everyone's Creativity

> *The greatest source of competitive advantage is not really cost or quality, but creativity.*[7]
>
> **—John Micklethwait**
> *Editor-in-Chief, The Economist*

Many people will say they are not creative people, so they cannot participate in Kaizen. Research has shown that people are naturally creative, but they, unfortunately, have this creativity drummed out of them over time in the education system and the workplace. When employees are allowed and encouraged to creatively contribute to improve their own job performance and their organization in ways that are beyond their job role and scope, it might be surprising what can be accomplished.

When Norman Bodek teaches Quick and Easy Kaizen, he always asks audience members to raise their hands if they consider themselves to be a highly creative individual. A few hands sheepishly go up, maybe 2% of the room.[8] Norman explains that, in kindergarten, almost every child we know is highly creative and they demonstrate that constantly; however, after two years of school, they lose a shockingly large amount of their creative abilities.[9] Test taking teaches kids that it is important to memorize answers and conform; thoughts and ideas that do not fit the predetermined answers are wrong. The practices of the education system, including letter grades, which usually start in the first grade, create a culture of holding back one's creative abilities for the fear of being wrong (see the discussion of PDSA and experimental nature in Chapter 1).

> *If there is no sense of trust in the organization, if people are preoccupied with protecting their backs ... creativity will be one of the first casualties.*
>
> **—Manfred F. R. Kets de Vries**
> *Clinical professor of leadership, INSEAD*

This fear of being wrong continues into the workplace, making people cautious to the point that they forget they can be creative. With Kaizen, we want and need to reverse those learned thought processes and deeply engrained habits and barriers to creativity. Leaders need to build trust by participating directly and by not punishing "failed" attempts at Kaizen.

Strategy 2: Sell Opportunity to Those Who Are Cautious

How do you work with the majority of people who may be cautious about an improvement idea? People can be cautious for good reasons. They may have experienced a change in the past that made their work more difficult or took things away from them that they felt were important and meaningful. That change might not have been an improvement to them. To sway those who are cautious, you will need to sell an idea to them by explaining why it is important and what's in it for them, connecting the change to something meaningful.

The researcher Everett Rogers[10] found five factors that determine how quickly innovations are adopted within a culture:

■ The relative advantage of the new method or technology
■ How compatible it is with adopters' existing beliefs and customs
■ How simple and easy it is to use
■ How easily it can be tried or experienced
■ The observability of the results

Likewise, to determine how fast your idea will be adopted, you can evaluate it using Everett's list. Notice that all five factors are viewed from the eyes of the potential adopter. With cautious stakeholders, it is important to be able to see the world from their eyes. They might want to wait until the opportunity has been proven before they invest. If so, it is important that you know this, so you can assure them that the idea will be tested first.

Encourage

Part of selling to those who are cautious is to encourage them to give the idea a try. If they try your idea and it works, they will be more encouraged to try their own Kaizens. Over time, they will more likely move from the cautious camp to the eager stakeholder camp. Laura Pettigrew, manager of medical records at Franciscan, said, "It took a lot of encouragement over a long period of time. We had trouble getting the staff to grasp Kaizen early on. We've been at it for four years and some just recently have finally embraced Kaizen."

She explained her success by saying, "We gave them the reins. We encouraged them to implement their ideas. We were always willing to try each Kaizen out, and we were always willing to go back. Now they feel comfortable with us. Kaizen worked for us because we trusted and encouraged our staff, because they work in the process daily—they know their work better than we, as leaders, do."

Seven Days' Grace

Seven days' grace is a practice we covered in Chapter 5, and we bring it back up here because it can help you to overcome the cautious stakeholder's desire to adopt only proven ideas. Seven days grace allows ideas that do not end up working to be withdrawn. We can all appear to be resistant to change at times. When a change gets implemented, initially there will be resistance voiced from those that have to change their behaviors, even if the idea is the best one in the world. Knowing that there will be some resistance no matter what, many departments at Franciscan have an unwritten seven days grace policy. The seven days grace policy fits the PDSA cycle well, because PDSA emphasizes "let's try it," and the success of the idea is legitimately gauged by how well it works in practice.

Measure Progress

Change is occurring around us all the time; however, often we do not notice it unless it is sudden, because change requires a comparison to something that previously existed. For example, have you noticed how distant family members seem to easily notice how much children have grown between visits? Children grow so gradually that the parents who are there every day do not recognize how much the kids have grown. The distant family member has an old mental snapshot to compare the children to and can readily see the difference

Kaizen is similar in that the improvements are so gradual over time that those working in the organization may not notice the difference, but someone who visits every year will more readily see the difference. Because we implement a lot of small changes, the overall improvement may go unrecognized. Often, it may seem like we are not making much progress on our journey of continuous improvement until we compare ourselves to an earlier time and remind ourselves by documenting the improvements that have been made. Recording before and after data points helps those cautious stakeholders to be sold on the difference Kaizen is making. Taking plenty of "before" pictures can help remind us how much change has occurred. When senior leaders visit our area on a monthly "gemba walk," they might recognize more improvement than those managers who are there every day. Before and after staff surveys can also make these culture changes more visible.

Strategy 3: Find Common Meaning and Negotiate with Opposers

The third and final camp is the people who generally oppose improvement opportunities. If you push this group, you will likely get strong pushback. If you fight, you will get a fight in return. This is especially true when those ideas cause someone to have to change their behavior or if they threaten a perceived or real benefit someone is receiving because of their status or situation. If the change will cause someone to lose something they value, whether it is perceived or real, they will defend themselves. So, if ideas naturally provoke a response, is there a way to present ideas and avoid a negative response from this group?

There are four approaches you might consider when working with those who oppose your Kaizen:

- Include opposing viewpoints
- Find common meaning
- Negotiate
- Demand change as a last resort

We will discuss each approach in the following section.

Include Opposing Viewpoints

Those who cannot change their minds cannot change anything.

—George Bernard Shaw

Consider the improvement opportunity from the opposer's viewpoint. Then, show him how the idea addresses what is important to him. By addressing the opposer's viewpoints upfront, it will disarm some of his issues, and it shows that you are considering his viewpoint in the solution. At the same time, be willing to change your idea or to give it up if proven wrong or given a better idea by others.

Find Common Meaning

Find the common meanings that you and the opposers can all agree upon. For example, since patient safety is likely important to the opposers, you can ask if the improvement opportunity has the potential to improve patient safety. If so, do your best to repeatedly communicate the difference this improvement could make on patient safety. Also, explore if the proposed change might be perceived by the opposers as reducing some meaning they have in the work they do and get their input on that.

Most of the 109 Kaizens that pharmacy technician Melissa Horn completed in 2010 required her to work with other departments throughout Franciscan's Indianapolis campus. She works to find common ground by talking with the nurses who would be affected by her proposed changes, and they flag potential problems. She finds that pharmacy techs surface half of the problems, and the nurses in the units surface the other half. She said, "The techs are always out on the floor, and we see potential problems."

She notes that finding common meaning on most of her Kaizens is easy, because many of them focus on preventing a medical error and keeping a patient from being harmed. However, when it is not a patient safety issue, she talks with nurses to understand what is important to them about the potential Kaizen. Then she emphasizes to them how the Kaizen will address what is meaningful to them. One of the most meaningful Kaizens she did for the nurses was to add little plastic bins within the larger bins in the automated medicine-dispensing machine. The bins organize pills better and keep them from floating around, saving time spent looking for expiration dates, and making it easier to sort the pills. The Kaizen was a win–win for the pharmacy techs and the unit nurses.

Negotiate

Negotiation involves searching for a win–win situation and discovering with the opposers what they need from the improvement. When Paula Stanfill, NICU manager at Franciscan, implemented a practice change with one of the point of care tests (POCT) in her department, she encountered a roadblock. Paula was told by the person responsible for the POCTs, "The ACCU-CHEK® meters are not your property. You can't make an improvement to the ACCU-CHEK processes without our approval and involvement." Paula approached the POCT person and tried explaining why the change would be helpful. When it seemed that she was facing an opposer, Paula switched to a negotiation style. Paula asked, "what could we do to support infection control efforts?" Together, they worked out a solution that revealed another option Paula did not know was available and she was able to implement the win-win change throughout the NICU.

Use Demands as a Last Resort

Never take a person's dignity—it is worth everything to them and nothing to you.

—Frank Barron
A pioneer in the psychology of creativity

Leaders should demand or require an unwanted improvement only as a last resort, because forcing an unwanted change leaves an unpleasant memory behind and can creative negative feelings toward Kaizen. If a leader forces a change that negatively impacts staff by causing them to work harder or makes the work more frustrating, this can increase the percentage of staff who are generally opposers. It is better to negotiate and seek win–win solutions. However, there are circumstances where, for the best interests of the organization, requiring the implementation and compliance to an unwanted improvement is necessary. When it does seem necessary to force an idea, leaders should go out of their way to explain why the idea is being implemented over the objections of some of the staff.

Joe Click learned early on that forcing change did not work. He says it is important to "get to know people and let them get to know you and trust you, which takes time." He noted, that when working with opposers, you should not "take rejection personally. Be both humble and thick skinned, and don't get offended if you have an idea and nobody wants it." Joe suggests that leaders be flexible and willing to negotiate with opposers to find a solution that works for all.

The mobilizing support model,[11] as introduced earlier in this chapter, is just one framework of getting others to support your Kaizen. If done well, enrolling support in your Kaizen using this model will increase the percentage of staff who are eager stakeholders and decrease the percentage of staff who are opposers.

Kaizen and Positive Deviance

A discussion about Kaizen would not be complete without mentioning an approach called "Positive Deviance."[12] Positive Deviance is an area of research in behavioral and social change that started in the area of nutrition in the 1970s. Researchers observed that some children living in poverty were much better nourished than others. They found that some parents had discovered better ways to feed their children.

In every community or organization, there are certain individuals, called "Positive Deviants," whose uncommon practices or behaviors enable them to find better solutions to problems than their neighbors who have access to the same resources.[13] So, in a sense, these are the Kaizeneers.

Franciscan used Positive Deviance as part of an AHRQ funded project with Indian University's Regenstrief Institute and seven other hospitals on preventing MRSA infections. Through the collaborative use of this methodology to engage staff, Franciscan reduced the number MRSA infections from 48 in 2006 to 8 in 2010.

Rules for Leaders

There are seven guidelines for the practice of the Positive Deviance Approach.[14]

1. **Go ask the experts.**
   The "experts" or "gurus" are those who really know the work processes—the front-line staff. This is similar to the Kaizen principle that the people who do the work are in the best position to solve problems and make improvements.
2. **Seek all the unusual suspects and the interested.**
   When working on Kaizens, invite those who normally work in the process, but also invite the unusual suspects or those participants you might not normally think about. For example, if you are the laboratory, invite in representatives from departments that send you specimens, like the emergency department or inpatient units. They might bring a different perspective to the meeting and help the team see things they had not seen before. Outsiders and fresh eyes can ask questions and see things that would go unstated or unseen by those who are in the middle of that work each day. So-called "dumb questions" can often lead to amazing insights and can break through the "we've always done it this way" inertia.
3. **Know that solutions are in plain sight.**
   Whatever you want more of already exists in the organization. There are practices living in the subconscious of people just waiting to be unleashed. Allow Kaizens that have not been considered to surface. Let people discover and adopt their own ideas, and continually ask questions to draw out the unspoken good ideas.
4. **"Nothing about them without them."**
   This means we do not talk about someone who is not in the discussion. It is too easy to point fingers at others. If you find participants blaming or pointing to those not in the meeting, curb that behavior by including those people in the next meeting.
5. **Encourage and allow discovery.**
   Allow your staff to voice and vent their concerns. Help your staff go through the discovery process, so they can see for themselves, proving or disproving the effectiveness of a change through the PDSA cycle.

6. Leave the solutions with their owners.

Allow the idea owner to own the implementation of that solution. Do not remove that responsibility or honor from them. With Kaizen, supervisors and managers are active participants, but they do not take over and own the idea.

7. People are more likely to ACT their way into a new way of thinking than to THINK their way into a new way of acting.

Model and practice the change you wish to see. Expectation shapes reality.

Conclusion

Kaizen is not easy, especially when it is rarely a solo activity. Engaging others in improvement is more of an art than a science, requiring us to get others to buy into a shared mission or, at least, to see what's in it for them and their patients. Showing respect for others includes listening to others, understanding their perspectives, and explaining why a change is necessary. It should be an unusual case where ideas are mandated in a top-down manner. Recognizing whether individuals are eager, cautious, or opposers helps us find the right style of working with people to enroll them in our important improvements.

Discussion Questions

- Can you think of a time when somebody seemed to be "resisting change?" How might you handle that situation differently?
- Do you consider yourself a "highly creative person?" Why or why not? Is it possible to rediscovery your creativity? How might you do that individually or as a team?

Endnotes

1. Imai, Masaaki, *KAIZEN: The Key to Japan's Competitive Success* (New York: McGraw-Hill, 1986), 83.
2. Barnas, Kim, "ThedaCare's Business Performance System: Sustaining Continuous Daily Improvement Through Hospital Management in a Lean Environment," The Joint Commission Journal on Quality and Patient Safety, September 2011, Volume 37, Number 9, 393.
3. Graban, Mark, "Quotes from the Paul O'Neill Podcast Interview on Patient Safety," *LeanBlog*.org, 2011, http://www.leanblog.org/2011/07/text-and-quotes-from-the-paul-oneill-podcast-interview/ (accessed August 9, 2011).
4. Swartz, James B., and Joseph E. Swartz, *Seeing David in the Stone: Find and Seize Great Opportunities*, (Leading Books Press, Carmel, IN 2006), 1–2.
5. Dague, James O., personal interview, July 2011.

6. Robinson, Alan G., "The Idea Driven Organization," Presentation at FIT Center For Innovation Management Summit, November 2007. (www3.fitnyc.edu/continuinged/CIM/CEOSummitKeynote.ppt) - accessed February 23, 2012.

7. Micklethwait, John, and Adrian Woolridge, *The Right Nation: A Study in Conservatism in America* (New York: Penguin Press, 2004), 185.

8. Bodek, Norman, personal interview, August 2011.

9. Robinson, Ken, "Sir Ken Robinson: Do Schools Kill Creativity?" YouTube.com, 2006, http://www.youtube.com/watch?v=iG9CE55wbtY&feature=related (accessed September 13, 2011).

10. Rogers, Everett, *Diffusion of Innovations*, 5th ed. (New York: The Free Press, 2003), 229.

11. Swartz and Swartz, pp. 77–129.

12. Positive Deviance Initiative, "What is Positive Deviance?," website, http://www.positivedeviance.org/ (accessed August 9, 2011).

13. Positive Deviance Initiative.

14. Integrated from several sources, including, Margaret M. Toth, *Solving Intractable Problems with Positive Deviance*, (Delmarva Foundation, 2007) and *DAD Guide for Facilitators*, (Albert Einstein Healthcare Network, 2009).

3

KAIZEN LESSONS LEARNED

Chapter 9

The Role of Leaders in Kaizen

Saying yes to Kaizen was easy for me. As a leader, I recognize my role is to lead others to create the future of our organization. I knew our future required the continuous development of the improvement skills and abilities of all our staff and their engagement in continually improving the services we provide to our patients and their families.

—Bob Brody

CEO, Franciscan St. Francis Health

For Kaizen to be effective, the role of first-level supervisors and managers has to change dramatically, as illustrated by a story from the laboratory at Children's Medical Center Dallas. John Burns, a medical technologist, had worked for Children's since 1992 and was described by his leaders as, "competent, dependable, technically superb, responsible, and known for helping colleagues," and from John's protests about those labels, you could add humble. Many times over the years, John had been offered a shift supervisor role, but he repeatedly declined. Why was that? John equated being a supervisor with "going to the dark side," because that role represented being "controlling" and "bossy," and under previous leadership, those traits were rewarded. Being a supervisor was akin to being a "police officer" in that setting.

Two years into the lab's Lean and Kaizen journey, John finally accepted that supervisor position. What had changed? The role, along with the expectations for this role from the directors, was more compatible with John's personality and his desire to help others. John said, "The only good thing about having worked under the old management approach was that experiencing that misery burned into my mind how *not* to be as a supervisor." The lab was shifting to a "no blame" culture, with everybody being more focused on processes and systems. There was a renewed focus on their mission of "taking care of kids," and leaders were expected to act as coaches and helpers, facilitating the success of others. This new approach was palatable to John, as he said, "It's a night and day difference in the culture and I would recommend my position to anyone."[1]

Leading to Create the Culture

This chapter contains an overview of the general actions and mindsets required from leaders, at all levels, in an effective Kaizen program, along with specific requirements for each level. First-level managers are involved in every Kaizen, coaching and guiding staff. Middle-level managers drive Kaizen by showing their commitment, determination, and giving guidance, so everybody is working on Kaizen. Top-level leaders see to it that Kaizen becomes a part of the organization's culture by first making it a part of their personal culture.

Franciscan has found that leadership also comes from those who are not in formal management positions. "There was resistance at the start of the Kaizen program," according to Paula Murphy, the Kaizen coordinator in their pharmacy, as "staff went to the classes but they didn't get it." Then, Paul Shoemaker, a pharmacist, spoke up in a department meeting and said, "This is to enable you, those who know your job better than anyone, to make your job more user friendly." After Paul's comment, Kaizens started rolling in. It takes leaders, from the front-line staff to the CEO, to create the right conditions for Kaizen.

Key Actions for Leaders at All Levels

The key to successful Lean implementation is that leaders have to change. We have to change from the all-knowing, being "in charge," autocratic "buck stops with me," impatient, blaming person—who is a control freak—to the person who is patient, knowledgeable, a good facilitator, willing to teach, actually willing to learn, be a helper, an effective communicator, and be humble.[2]

—John Toussaint, MD
CEO, ThedaCare Center for Healthcare Value

At Franciscan, everyone is continually reminded how much influence leaders have. The departments that are performing the best in Kaizen are those with leaders who believe in Kaizen and have decided it is important enough to incorporate into everything they do. They made a strong commitment to the Kaizen process, and it shows in their results. Some of the key things they have done include:

1. Demonstrating that they believe in the power of Kaizen
2. Participating in Kaizen
3. Asking their staff to do Kaizen

4. Using Kaizen to develop people
5. Recognizing and rewarding staff for Kaizen
6. Sharing and spreading Kaizens
7. Selling the benefits of Kaizen

Key Action 1: Believe In the Power of Kaizen

Revenue management is a top-performing department at Franciscan. According to their director, Lynne Meredith, it starts with believing in what Kaizen can do for the department. She says, "If you don't believe in Kaizen, your managers won't believe, and your staff won't believe." When Lynne noticed someone make a change, she would say, "Hey, that's a Kaizen. Make sure you write it up." Lynne also noticed that her employees needed a regular reminder of why Kaizen is important and what's in it for them. She says, "Part of believing in Kaizen is having a ready answer to the question about why we're doing Kaizen, and it cannot be because administration wants us to do Kaizen. Rather, the reason we do Kaizen—all of us—is to recreate our world around us and continually mold and transform it into the way it could and should be, and that is powerful."

Key Action 2: Participate in Kaizen

Imai's expression "Kaizen is for everybody" includes leaders at all levels. This does not mean jumping in and solving other people's problems. It means initiating and conducting your own Kaizens, working with your manager to make small improvements in your own work, before you ask others to do Kaizen. Doing your own Kaizens shows employees that you are serious about improvement, and you can use your experiences to coach them and relate to them. If it was difficult to do your first Kaizen, share that with your team.

> *The [servant] leader has a vested interest in the success of those being led. Indeed, one of our roles as a leader is to assist them in becoming successful.*
>
> **—James C. Hunter**
> *Author*

Another important aspect of Kaizen participation is to be a "servant leader" for your employees. Again, you want to empower your employees to make their own improvements, but you need to take an active role in evaluating and giving feedback on ideas, as well as following up on their implementation. There will be many cases when a staff member raises an issue that requires help from others. In those cases, leaders need to escalate the opportunity to the right level in the organization. In a traditional organizational model, the more senior a leader you are, the more decisions you get to make. In a Kaizen approach, this is not the case, because leaders push decision making down in the organization.

However, the more senior leaders tend to have a broader view of the organization or a wider managerial span, so they can help fix problems that front-line staff cannot solve on their own.

Key Action 3: Just Ask

Starting a Kaizen Program can be as simple as asking staff to do Kaizen. Keith Jewell, Franciscan COO, said, "Kaizen has something in it for everybody. I get an economic return, in the form of savings, which far exceed the investment in the program. The staff gets to make their work easier and better. We get improved service and quality for our patients. It is a program that benefits all of our customers. It really is a win–win program. There is not a lot of controversy in doing good things for others. So, I just ask staff to participate. We don't require it, but we do encourage them to participate."

Evangeline Brock, a medical technologist at Children's Medical Center Dallas, says, "Five years ago, our ideas weren't listened to." Brock said, "New employees would ask why we do things a certain way, and there wouldn't be a good answer." As the lab's leaders embraced Kaizen, they found it was necessary to continually reinforce to staff that "it's OK to speak up," because people are often very conditioned against doing so. Asking once is probably not enough; managers need to ask every day.

Leaders have to be willing to make time available to participate directly in Kaizen. Jennifer Rudolph, formerly of Park Nicollet Health Services, emphasizes to their leaders, "If you approve the idea, then you are approving the time to work on it."[3] Another large hospital's CEO had initiated a program where staff members were encouraged to call out problems to senior leaders, following the mantra of "no problems is a problem." Unfortunately, so many problems were called out, it overwhelmed the ability of leaders to react and help. The CEO later offered his apology for raising expectations for improvement and then disappointing people. The story illustrates why it is important for a Kaizen approach to ask people to not only call out problems, but to also think of improvements they can implement locally. The story also illustrates why an organization might want to pilot a Kaizen program in a single department rather than starting as an entire hospital, to learn the amount of time and support is really required.

Ask, Don't Tell

Another general tenet of Kaizen is to "ask, don't tell." In general, people do not like being told what they should and shouldn't do. In Franciscan's Kaizen program, it is optional for staff to participate. Keith Jewell noted, "It wasn't forced, and therefore we didn't experience a lot of resistance. Everyone was charged up by the potential opportunity."

Whether you are doing a Kaizen yourself or coaching someone else through one, a good way to avoid telling people what to do is to share you thoughts and ideas in question form. When Joe Click, pharmacy supervisor at Franciscan, works with staff on Kaizen, he says, "I avoid telling people what to do. Instead, I do my best to ask questions, such as, what do you think of this idea? How can we implement it?"

As David Mann writes in *Creating a Lean Culture*:

> The classic sensei (teacher) is Socratic in approach, teaching by stretching the student's thinking and perceptions through questions that stimulate the student to consider entirely new possibilities.[4]

John Toussaint, MD, former CEO of ThedaCare, shifted from being the leader who had all the answers to one who asked a lot of questions. To help staff see waste and drive improvement, Toussaint was successful by "asking staff questions, which helps staff to think about the problems themselves. The leader should never tell the staff what to do, but they instead need to be able to ask the right questions."[5]

Questions should be asked humbly, with respect, and in a thoughtful and careful way. For example, you could ask, "Could you help me understand how this process works?" Kaizen leaders should avoid asking questions they know the answer to, as if to push or manipulate the person to give a certain answer. These should be questions of inquiry or questions that get the other person to think in a new way.

Be careful of directives that are cleverly disguised as questions. When Mark's wife asks him, "Why did you throw your socks in the middle of the floor?" they both laugh about how she is not really asking a question of inquiry. She is not searching for a root cause of Mark's behavior. Her question is really a statement that says, "Please don't leave your socks on the floor."

Key Action 4: Use Kaizen to Develop People

Part of empowerment is allowing your staff to make mistakes, as discussed in Chapter 1, using those mistakes as opportunities for learning. That said, we do not want to allow reckless mistakes or changes that would obviously hurt people. However, it is also your job to ensure the learning environment is emotionally safe for your staff, being cautious with people's physical safety without being overcautious about every small change needing to have zero risk of failure. There are rare instances when somebody might truly have a bad idea that would cause harm. Instead of just rejecting the idea, take the time to develop the improvement skills of your staff by allowing them to think the risks through, under your guidance, and empowering them to find a better solution.

Key Action 5: Ensure Staff Members Are Recognized and Rewarded

The recognition through the Kaizen program has made me feel valued and lets me know I am making a real difference.

—Craig Whitaker
Financial analyst, Franciscan

At Franciscan, Lynne Meredith wants her staff to recognize that it is important to her that they take time out of the day to focus on Kaizen. So, she regularly recognizes people in her staff meetings and makes a point of explaining how those people went out of their way to coordinate with another in order to implement a particular Kaizen. Lynne said, "I have been persistent in reinforcing the Kaizen behaviors that I have wanted to see more of."

Recording an improvement and displaying the results allows the person or team to receive the recognition they deserve. At Franciscan, managers and supervisors post Kaizen Reports locally in their departments, and selected ones are posted prominently in high-visibility areas, such as in hallways or the cafeteria. Ronda Freije, pharmacy manager, shares graphs with her staff showing how her department is performing in the organization. She said her staff "are proud that they are one of the top-performing departments in total Kaizens turned in. It is a way for our techs to get recognized. It gives them a sense of achievement." Ronda also has potluck lunches where she recognizes recent turned-in Kaizens, and she occasionally brings in ice cream as a way of showing her appreciation to the team.

Key Action 6: Share and Spread Ideas

The real power of Kaizen occurs when ideas are shared. Sharing enables others to benefit from your ideas, allowing them to realize that they too can make similar improvements to their work. This helps spread good ideas throughout the organization and engage everyone in the improvement of their work processes.

At Franciscan, success comes by keeping Kaizen in front of staff. The most successful Kaizen leaders devote a portion of every staff meeting to recognizing staff, asking about recent Kaizens, and sharing ideas. They utilize staff meetings to discuss those Kaizens that will affect their entire team. They also share regularly in other venues, such as rounding huddles.

At Children's Medical Center Dallas, ideas from the core laboratory have been seen by other staff members on the Kaizen Wall of Fame, as shown in Chapter 7. In one instance, some laboratory information system comment templates were adjusted so they could be opened with fewer keystrokes. This time-saving improvement was shared and adopted throughout the other parts of the lab, including microbiology and virology.

Key Action 7: Sell the Benefits

Leaders at Franciscan regularly spend time reminding staff of the benefits of Kaizen. They communicate those benefits using examples from throughout the organization. They communicate that Kaizen enables compassionate concern for patients and their families by improving safety, quality, and customer satisfaction. Leaders also reinforce that Kaizen enables organizational stewardship by improving productivity, lowering costs, and increasing throughput. Finally, leaders remind their employees that Kaizen demonstrates respect for their fellow employees by empowering them to make a difference. Collectively, these benefits enable their organization to be financially stronger, which leads to increased job security for all staff.

It Is Not Always about Cost

The part of Kaizen that excites some senior leaders is cost savings, especially in a tough economic environment. However, if too much focus is placed on cost savings, staff may get discouraged because they want to improve quality, safety, and waiting times, while creating a better workplace. One way to address this is for administration to recognize and share a variety of types of Kaizen, not just those that reduce costs.

At the Cancer Treatment Centers of America, the objective statement for an "A3" Kaizen improvement is almost always about improving patient care, says Herb DeBarba, their vice president for Lean Six Sigma. Out of 450 A3s they analyzed, only one was financially driven.[6]

As originally highlighted in *Lean Hospitals*, Bill Douglas, chief financial officer at Riverside Medical Center, sent a powerful message to their employees early in their Lean journey by saying, "Lean is a quality initiative. It isn't a cost-cutting initiative. But the end result is, if you improve quality your costs will go down. If you focus on patient quality and safety, you just can't go wrong. If you do the right thing with regard to quality, the costs will take care of themselves."[7] Statements like this are very helpful, especially if staff members are cynical about past cost-cutting programs.

Another challenge is that it is sometimes difficult to quantify the cost or benefit of each Kaizen into dollars. Some benefits are more subjective than others, such as staff or patient satisfaction improvements. If it were difficult to get approval for Kaizens that benefit patient satisfaction, people would be understandably discouraged.

Nancy Mosier, manager of pediatrics at Franciscan, faced a dilemma and learned an important lesson—to be creative and persistent when faced with the dilemma of purchases that are tough to cost justify. The rooms in her unit had one reclining chair each, yet both parents often wanted to stay the night with their kids. She had no money in her budget, and this had been the case for several years. However, she had a heart for the parents of her little patients and did not give up. She decided to get creative and approached the hospital's foundation to apply for a grant. The foundation had some extra money from generous donors who saw the need as valid, and Nancy got her chairs. Now both parents can stay with their kids, which adds a great deal of comfort to the patients and to their parents. How would you even calculate a return on investment on making parents comfortable while their children are being treated? Nancy knew that making patients and their families happier would lead them to say good things about the hospital, which would be good for its long-term viability.

Role of Top-Level Managers

Top-level managers see to it that Kaizen becomes a part of the culture of the organization. Franciscan considers the top-level managers to include the C-level (CEO, COO, CFO, CMO, CNO), the president, the vice presidents, medical directors, and executive directors.

Leadership and Kaizen Participation Starts at the Top

James Dague, CEO at IU Health Goshen Hospital, says a critical factor in the success of a Kaizen system has been his high visibility, because he makes rounds one to three times a week, and "the constancy of it has to be there at the top level." Dague asks about improvements that people are working on and how their work perpetuates the hospital's mission and their personal missions. Dague humbly emphasizes that, while he played an important role, his employees deserve the credit for their program, as he says "they didn't have to do [so many improvements]."[8]

Dr. John Toussaint's Participation

John Toussaint, MD, was CEO of ThedaCare from 2000 to 2008. In 2003, he initiated their Lean efforts under the heading of the "ThedaCare Improvement System" (TIS). In their early years, much of the focus was placed on weeklong Rapid Improvement Events, or RIEs.

As CEO, Toussaint promoted Lean, while sponsoring and encouraging events. He "explicitly communicated to senior leaders that they were expected to participate in at least two RIEs each year, making it clear to all other leaders and managers that this meant them too."[9] Looking back, Toussaint reflected, "It took commitment and focus at the senior level to clarify that TIS was the beginning of a cultural transformation, and that everyone would be affected."[10]

Being "behind" an initiative is quite different than being in front of it [leading the initiative].[11]

—Jamie Flinchbaugh
Author and consultant

Toussaint, however, was not yet participating in events, himself. One of his mentors, George Koenigsaecker, called Toussaint and asked if he had been part of an RIE team yet. Toussaint answered, "No, but I am trying to schedule one." Koenigsaecker kept asking the same question for a few months, and Toussaint finally participated in an event.

Koenigsaecker then asked, "Did you stay for the entire time on Monday, or did you have to go to some important meeting halfway through and miss the mapping of the initial state?"[12] Toussaint admitted that he had left the event on Monday for two hours and that he had left many times throughout the rest of the week, excusing his absences as "the fire fighting that most CEOs have to do."[13]

The response from Koenigsaecker was blunt, telling Toussaint, "You're never going to learn this unless you tell your secretary you are on vacation for this week, which means you are at the entire event, participating with the staff, learning the tools, and understanding what it takes to improve a process."

It is not enough that top management commit themselves for life to quality and productivity. They must know what it is that they are committed to—that is, what they must do. These obligations cannot be delegated. Support is not enough; action is required.[14]

—W. Edwards Deming, Ph.D.

Toussaint then fully participated in the next event, better understanding the "ups and downs of the group's emotions" during the week, giving him a better appreciation for what is really involved in Kaizen. Toussaint reflected that "the staff and physicians became very curious as to why I would take a week off of my duties and work on the obstetrics unit or on the loading dock at home care. They realized we were serious about this improvement thing the more they saw me working side by side with them to fix problems or on my weekly gemba visits to their units."

Over time, Toussaint participated in 14 different weeklong events, including value stream assessments, and Lean design exercises called "3Ps" and "2Ps." Why was it important for the CEO to participate? Toussaint reflected on this, saying, "When I went to the floor as a team member on an improvement activity, it sent a loud message first that I cared about the plight of the front-line workers' and that this wasn't some fad or management trick."[15]

Leadership also plays an important role in ThedaCare's "continuous daily improvement" activities, which are expected to account for 80% of their overall improvement, Toussaint and other senior leaders spend time in the gemba daily, as does current CEO Dean Gruner, MD, and other senior leaders, asking questions and encouraging improvement of all kinds.

Going to the Gemba

At Iowa Health System, Ray Seidelman, manager of performance improvement, says that for daily Kaizen to be successful, "it needs to be the front-line staff identifying the problems and initiating improvements." Yet, senior leadership has an important role to play in driving people to improve by asking challenging and "provocative" questions to staff members, says Gail Nielsen, their director of learning and education. For example, a senior leader saw that HCAHPS (Hospital Consumer Assessment of Healthcare Providers and Systems) scores were down, so she challenged staff to find ways to improve. Rather than blaming people, senior leaders at Iowa Health System went to the floors (the *gemba*) to spend time with staff and patients, to see what the real situation was and to get ideas from staff members. Nielsen says it comes back to top leaders asking, "I wonder what the real situation is. I wonder what's going on?" This style of leadership is very different than a traditional command-and-control model, where a senior leader might mandate improvement without getting directly involved other than continuing to look at the scores.

Gruner adds that going to gemba connects him to the work the health system does and it helps him model the behaviors that he expects from his staff, saying, "Colleagues enjoy the time I spend with them as they know how precious time is and that spending it with them signals the importance of their work."

Kaizen Reports Are for Everybody

Keith Jewell, Franciscan COO, says, "Major change requires a senior leader champion and their significant involvement." He continues, "It surprises me how much people look to the leader. Staff want to know that the leader believes in the Kaizen program. So, I role model what I expect and what I want others to model. It accelerates the success of the program. If they see my Kaizens in the database, they know that it is important." Figure 9.1 is a Kaizen that Keith turned in, and it was enjoyed very much by all.

Key Actions for Top-Level Managers

Here are some actions and behaviors that are especially important for senior leaders.

Key Action 1: Communicate Expectations and Prioritize

Get your CEO to communicate the expectation that your organization wants all employees and affiliated staff to participate in Kaizen. Ensure that it is communicated several times each year in multiple media formats. Communicate the

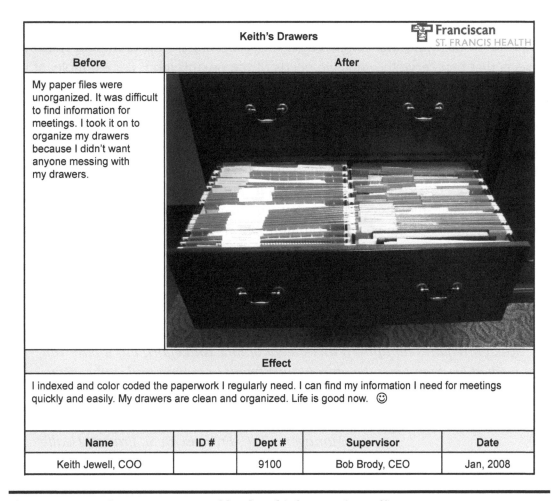

Keith's Drawers	Franciscan ST. FRANCIS HEALTH
Before	**After**
My paper files were unorganized. It was difficult to find information for meetings. I took it on to organize my drawers because I didn't want anyone messing with my drawers.	

Effect
I indexed and color coded the paperwork I regularly need. I can find my information I need for meetings quickly and easily. My drawers are clean and organized. Life is good now. ☺

Name	ID #	Dept #	Supervisor	Date
Keith Jewell, COO		9100	Bob Brody, CEO	Jan, 2008

Figure 9.1   A Kaizen report created by the Chief Operating Officer.

long-term expectation; then start slowly, such as expecting one or two improvements per person per year. Then, increase the expectation each year as appropriate, based on the amount of improvement the overall system can support.

In 2007, the CEO at Franciscan, Bob Brody, and COO Jewell challenged each employee to submit two Kaizens per month as a long-term goal. In order to get employees used to the practice of Kaizen, they asked all full-time employees in 2008 to submit at least one Kaizen during the year. Then, in 2009 they asked full-time employees to submit at least two. Employees were not punished in any way for not reaching that goal.

At the Utah North Region of Intermountain Healthcare, Bart Sellers, regional manager of management engineering, says that senior leaders set no expectations on the number of Kaizens for the first few years of their program. The initial goal was to figure out how to do Kaizen, including the roles and expectations for managers. Eventually, a "modest" goal was set at one Kaizen per employee per year. Sellers says, "Before setting the expectation, we had some departments taking off and others were ignoring it," adding that, "Setting the measure was good for awareness and getting the attention of managers," but the goal would not be used in a punitive way.[16]

Beyond setting goals for the number of Kaizens, top-level leaders are also in a position to help prioritize improvements, by selecting events or system Kaizen projects that best serve the strategic needs of the organization. For example, at the Cancer Treatment Centers of America, the C-level leaders select high-level projects, such as RIEs and Six Sigma projects, while also clearing paths and providing strategic support the for the A3 improvements that are primarily generated by staff members.[17] "The beauty of the A3 program is that it empowers front-line stakeholders to select the projects that will make the biggest impact for their patients via their processes," says Jennifer Smith, their director of Lean and Six Sigma.[18]

Generally, staff members and first-level managers will choose their daily Kaizen activities, but the general communication from top-level leaders about vision, priorities, and challenges will help people point their Kaizens in the right direction.

Key Action 2: Resource Adequately

Kaizen requires an upfront investment of time and effort, but it pays you back at least ten times the upfront investment in patient and staff satisfaction and retention.

—Paula Stanfill
Manager, NICU, Franciscan St. Francis Health

An under-resourced Kaizen program will suffer. In addition to top leadership support, an organization needs to devote some budget and some people to help facilitate the program. In Chapter 10, we share the staffing levels and organizational model that Franciscan has found to work well for their Kaizen Promotion Office.

Top-level leaders are also in a position to ensure that other leaders have enough time for Kaizen on a daily basis. At Toyota, a person in a "team leader" role has between five and seven direct reports,[19] about the same ratio of nurses with a charge nurse in a medical or surgical unit. Like a charge nurse, the team leader is a worker who provides coaching and support, but can jump in to do the actual work, if need be. In the first level of Toyota's salaried management, a "group leader" might have four team leaders reporting to them.[20]

In comparison, many hospitals (as well as organizations in other industries) have previously eliminated a layer of management to reduce their costs. A common side effect is that managers end up having such a broad span of responsibility (such as 25 or 30 employees on a shift), that they cannot devote enough time to coaching everyone. A few years into its Lean journey, one leading hospital added a layer of management back in, learning it was required to properly support improvement efforts. Increasing costs in that category allows them to all work more effectively in reducing overall system costs through various types of Kaizen.

Key Action 3: Sponsor a Recognition and Incentives Program

It is important to ensure that employees are recognized for completed Kaizens. For many people, getting public credit and recognition is more important than financial rewards. Simply putting Kaizen Reports on a bulletin board and thanking people in team meetings can create a lot of goodwill and pride in people's improvements. Employees can be recognized in a number of other channels, including hospital newsletters, intranet pages, or posters. Top-level leaders also need to provide the budget and support required for a financial reward system for employees, if one is desired. This is discussed more in Chapter 10.

Key Action 4: Share Notable Kaizens

At Franciscan, the COO forwards a "Notable Kaizen" to all 4,000 employees once or twice a month. The Kaizen is shared with a sentence or two from the COO, which is typically prepared by the Kaizen program staff for his final review to decide if it is worth sharing.

Here are a few of the Notable Kaizens that have been sent at Franciscan:

Dear Franciscan Family,
This notable Kaizen (Figure 9.2) demonstrates our value of Christian Stewardship. With all of the uncertainty in the world financial markets, now, more than ever, is the time to be financially prudent.

—Keith Jewell, Sr. VP & COO

Dear Franciscan Family,
As you've probably noticed, we've launched a hospital-wide recycling program. It is part of our continuing effort to demonstrate our value of Christian Stewardship by being good stewards with earth's resources. We refer to our larger Christian Stewardship effort as "3R" which stands for "Reduce, Reuse, and Recycle." The Kaizen below (Figure 9.3) nicely demonstrates the first R, Reduce. Reduce means to reduce usage, in this case masks that were wasted and not used.

—Keith Jewell, Sr. VP & COO

Dear Franciscan Family,
This Kaizen demonstrates our value of Christian Stewardship. Two of our Radiology Technicians took the initiative to reduce the cost of handouts for our patients. They involved others in their department along with a physician to ensure the new handout was correct and complete. Now the same basic information is being communicated in a less expensive way (Figure 9.4)

—Keith Jewell, Sr. VP & COO

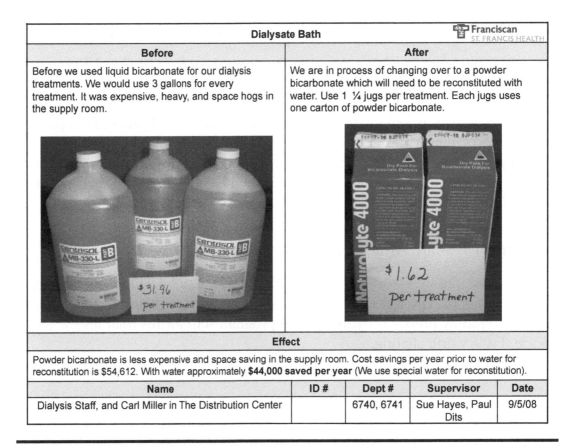

Figure 9.2   A Kaizen report shared by the COO via an all-staff email.

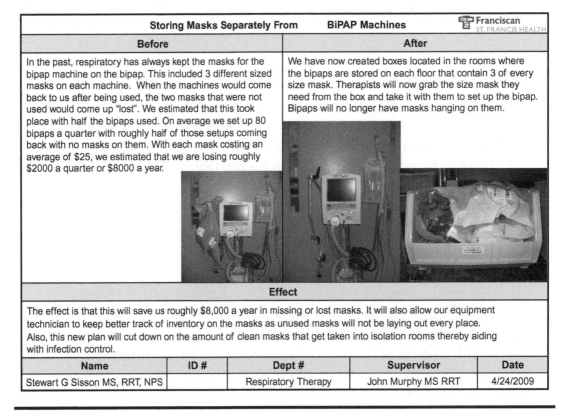

Figure 9.3   Another Kaizen report shared by the COO.

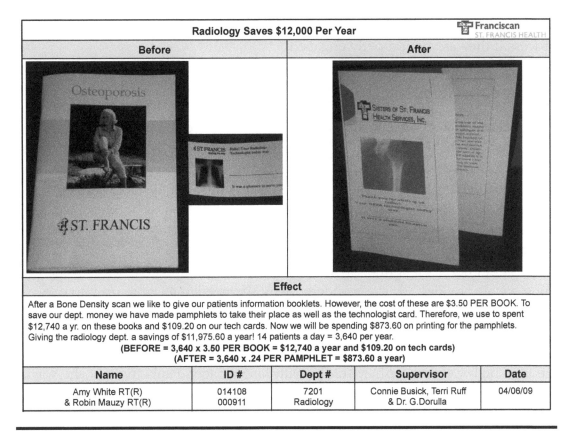

| Radiology Saves $12,000 Per Year | | | | Franciscan ST. FRANCIS HEALTH |

Before / **After**

Effect

After a Bone Density scan we like to give our patients information booklets. However, the cost of these are $3.50 PER BOOK. To save our dept. money we have made pamphlets to take their place as well as the technologist card. Therefore, we use to spent $12,740 a yr. on these books and $109.20 on our tech cards. Now we will be spending $873.60 on printing for the pamphlets. Giving the radiology dept. a savings of $11,975.60 a year! 14 patients a day = 3,640 per year.

(BEFORE = 3,640 x 3.50 PER BOOK = $12,740 a year and $109.20 on tech cards)
(AFTER = 3,640 x .24 PER PAMPHLET = $873.60 a year)

Name	ID #	Dept #	Supervisor	Date
Amy White RT(R) & Robin Mauzy RT(R)	014108 000911	7201 Radiology	Connie Busick, Terri Ruff & Dr. G.Dorulla	04/06/09

Figure 9.4 Another Kaizen report shared by the COO.

Key Action 5: Thank People Personally

In the course of rounding or going to the *gemba*, it means a lot to front-line staff to have a top-level leader stop and acknowledge their Kaizen work. A sincere question about improvements, a smile, and a handshake will go a long way toward giving recognition and encouraging people to do more Kaizen.

> *When you go to gemba, it's an opportunity to sincerely thank everyone involved for their work. The funny thing is, as the leader, I also would like to thank them for allowing me to support them. I can't give direct care, but, contrary to the old style CEO walking around to be seen, it is a privilege for me to see the team. Every time I am in gemba it reminds me of why, just like clinicians, I went into health care. It feels good.*

—Kathryn Correia
Former President of Appleton Medical Center and ThedaClark Medical Center and Former Senior Vice President of ThedaCare

Role of Middle-level Managers

Middle-level managers are the managers of the first-level managers. At Franciscan, they are at the levels of manager and director. Middle managers play a critical role in the success of Kaizen, because these managers can shut down the Kaizen process if they are not properly engaged.

Paula's Baby Steps Lead the Way

Paula Stanfill's life's passion is caring for babies. Her eyes light up when she talks about the babies she and her staff have cared for. She is the manager of the Franciscan Neonatal Intensive Care Unit (NICU), which cares for newborn babies who are struggling with serious health concerns. Paula admits she was skeptical of the Kaizen Program when it first started. She thought it was another program of the month—just another to-do being pushed on her plate—a plate that was already overflowing and overwhelming at times.

Paula did not get it at first, saying, "It seemed like improvement was something we already did," so she wondered why she needed to write up improvements after the fact. She resisted, but then recalled that she was called to healthcare to serve others, so she decided to figure out "this Kaizen thing."

It was not until she took some baby steps and completed a Kaizen report that the light bulb went on for her. Traditionally, as manager, Paula thought she was supposed to lead in a directive manner. Instead, she got directly involved and led the way for her staff by turning in most of the improvements in her department. However, most of her staff initially resisted adopting the change. She explained that, at first, it was like pulling teeth. Like so many things she had brought to them over the years, her staff, being cooperative, said, "Just tell us what to do and we'll do it," but Paula wanted them to motivate themselves.

The "Great Big Pile of Problems"

Paula admits the Kaizen program was initially more thorns than roses. It was time consuming in the beginning. Another manager commented that it was a "great big pile of problems." The piles were created when managers let a backlog of Kaizens build up because they felt the need to oversee and control each one that was submitted. While some Kaizens required coordination between departments (such as maintenance, capital expense approvals), not everything actually requires the manager's direct involvement at all stages.

Early in the program, Paula felt the need to "police" every submitted Kaizen to make sure they met her standard. At one point, she was overwhelmed and decided to put control of the Kaizens back in the employees' hands by asking the lead nurses in her department to get involved. She discovered that they would learn to coordinate their own Kaizens if she asked them to.

Over the next few months, Paula coached her lead nurses as they worked on their own Kaizens. Once those nurses became proficient, she asked them to coach the rest of the staff in her department, as her nurses were well versed in a nursing education practice called "see one, do one, teach one." Beyond lightening some of her own workload, Paula discovered the process grew self-starters in her department and sparked enthusiasm. That's when the program started taking off.

Lynne Meredith, director of revenue management at Franciscan, discovered something similar. After the first year of Kaizen, Lynne and her manager decided to get directly involved only in those Kaizens that required more than one person and especially those that affect her entire team. Lynne said, "I told them you don't need my permission to make your job more efficient."

Paula and Lynne discovered that success comes when leaders at all levels in an organization start by leading the way and then transitioning to more delegation over time by:

1. Learning and modeling the Kaizen practice themselves
2. Coaching their direct reports as they learn to model the practice
3. Asking their direct reports to coach those that report to them as they learn the practice

Leaders Drive Kaizen Success

Kaizen must be led by middle-level managers according to Ronda Frieje, the manager of the Indianapolis pharmacy within Franciscan. At the start of the Kaizen program in her department, Ronda sent a number of employees to the in-service on the "eight wastes" of Lean, as introduced in Chapter 4. Her employees initially made fun of the "Toast Kaizen" training video that was shown.[21] They did not quite connect "making toast" with their work in Pharmacy. It was not until they started seeing Kaizens implemented in their department that it started making sense to them.

> From the authors' experience, the "Toast Kaizen" DVD has been a very effective training tool in healthcare organizations. The criticism that the video is sort of silly, being based in a kitchen, is understandable. But the video can be fun, and people learn well in this scenario because they let their guard down, and creative thinking is sparked. By learning to talk about waste in this context, people become more comfortable about looking for waste in their own workplace, which can be embarrassing.

One early Kaizen that made a big difference for the pharmacy staff was when they rearranged the department to improve flow. Everything required to fill an order was arranged in the logical physical order. They had talked as a department about it for a week before making the change. Then, after the change, they tweaked things for several weeks until they found optimal locations for everything. After this improvement, staff saw a clear benefit to them and their work, because things were easier and worked better. Ronda explained that managers "have to help staff with Kaizen for a while until they start getting it. Then, the manager has to start stepping away to give ownership to staff members, coaching and supporting them over time."

Occasionally, employees will quit participating in the Kaizen program. One of Franciscan's most prolific Kaizeneers in 2007 had not submitted anything in 2011. When she was asked why, she said that her new manager did not see the Kaizen program as important. Her previous manager placed Kaizen as a top agenda item, and her department had been a top Kaizen performer. This demonstrates how important leadership is to growing and sustaining Kaizen programs.

Lynne Meredith keeps Kaizen fresh by finding different ways to encourage her staff. She explains, "You can't relax—you have to keep staff engaged by trying new things and rehashing old things in order to keep it interesting." Her leadership team has put flyers in bathroom stalls, conducted departmental contests, posted Kaizens on their bulletin board, and had potluck lunches. Lynne noticed that competition amongst staff helped early in the program. However, as her Kaizeneers matured, they were not as motivated to compete. Unfortunately, competition discouraged the lower performers, because they never seemed to measure up over time, which led them to basically give up. So, in her third year of the program, she decided to shift from competition to cooperation to raise the overall capability of the department. Lynne began having the top performers work with the low performers to get them to see one Kaizen, do one, and teach one. Now, all her staff members are good about sharing and are self-motivated to come up with unique ideas to improve their work and patient care.

The Kaizen Difference

Prior to Kaizen, Paula's staff experienced a kind of helplessness. With every new program, her nurses felt more and more overloaded with things to do. The Kaizen program was the key to a positive change in the NICU. Her staff did not understand the Kaizen process until they did a few themselves. Then, Paula enjoyed watching each staff member experience their own "aha" moments. Slowly, she watched their excitement and enthusiasm grow. It took about one year to get her lead people going. When they realized they could make change in their department, they felt empowered. They, in turn, involved other staff members in Kaizen.

Staff members used to feel powerless. Now, they feel like they can do something about almost anything. This empowerment has brought control back to their work life and a sense of joy back to their department. Paula says, "Now, staff members recognize problems on their own, and they take ownership to team up and resolve them." Instead of the manager leading with a solution, the employees tell Paula about the solutions they will be testing to resolve the problem. Paula has also noticed an increase in people working as a team to identify improvement opportunities and resolve problems.

Paula's department may not produce the most Kaizens, but the NICU has made a significant impact at Franciscan because of the quality of their Kaizens. They have had more Kaizens recognized in this book than any other single department because theirs are simple, meaningful, and fun. They strike a chord in people and, besides, people tend to have a warm spot in their hearts for babies and those who care for them.

Key Actions for Middle-level Managers

Key Action 1: Be the Departmental Owner and Develop Co-Owners or Coordinators

When you first start a program in your department, the manager should initiate and help coordinate the Kaizen activity. However, about a year into Franciscan's implementation, it became clear that the departmental managers were too busy to adequately manage the Kaizen workload. Franciscan asked each department to appoint a Kaizen coordinator if it was deemed necessary, and a few departments decided to use a small team approach. In addition, some departments that are on a nursing "Magnet" journey now use the "unit council" to review and approve Kaizens that have department-wide impact. Kaizen coordinators at Franciscan have "Kaizen program coordination" added to their job responsibilities, because it must be something they are formally expected to oversee.

Role of Departmental Kaizen Coordinators

The pharmacy department at Franciscan's St. Francis Health's Indianapolis campus appointed a departmental Kaizen coordinator. The roles and responsibilities of the departmental Kaizen coordinator are:

- Sort
- Coach and coordinate
- Receive, approve, and track
- Surface and share

These are the same duties performed by supervisors and managers in the absence of a coordinator.

Sort

Paula Murphy, a Kaizen coordinator at Franciscan, receives between 200 and 300 Kaizens per year from staff in her department. The coordinator role is only 25% of her job, and she does not have time to work with every Kaizeneer, so she sorts Kaizens to decide where to best allocate her time. For the simple ones, she has a quick discussion with the Kaizeneer and has them move forward. For the more complex Kaizens, she helps as much as she can and sometimes directs the Kaizeneer to talk with a person who can help them better, such as their supervisor or the unit manager.

Coach and Coordinate

A Kaizen coordinator takes on part of the supervisor's role of coaching by helping staff members think through the implementation of Kaizens, where appropriate, especially ones that are cross-departmental. From time to time, someone will present a problem to her without an identified solution. Paula either spends the time to help them identify a solution to the problem, or she asks them to work with their supervisor and come back with a solution.

Paula cautions staff that, "Not everything is a Quick and Easy Kaizen." For example, she was presented a Kaizen that asked for a billboard in the break room that lights up and flashes. Paula reminds staff that for it to be a Kaizen, "you do it, you start it, and you complete it." She says, "I'm not Santa Claus."

Occasionally, Paula received a Kaizen that was really an idea for another department to make an improvement. For example, one Kaizeneer wanted to put a doorbell outside the catheterization lab. When she received a Kaizen like this, she helped the Kaizeneer coordinate with other areas. If it was not a complex Kaizen, she would simply give them the contact information and let them follow through and make the contact.

Receive, Approve, and Track

A Kaizen coordinator takes on the burden of receiving, approving, and tracking Kaizen Reports for the department, as described in this chapter.

Surface and Share

A Kaizen coordinator also emails all approved Kaizen Reports to every department staff members or posts them on a Visual Idea Board, so they know what changes are being made.

Key Action 2: Use Departmental Meetings

Managers of the higher-performing departments at Franciscan regularly devote a part of meeting their time to Kaizen. For example, they ask their staff to come to the next meeting with two improvement ideas—small, quick ones. They block off some time in the meeting, such as 15 minutes, to discuss some of those ideas. They ask staff to voice their ideas, and they limit the ensuing discussion to a few minutes for each Kaizen, allocating just enough time to understand the nature of each Kaizen and any issues that would have to be overcome to implement it. These managers record each Kaizen in a simple action item list. In organizations that use the Visual Idea Board method, as discussed in Chapter 6, these ideas might go onto an Idea Card to be posted on the board, keeping the idea visible for follow-up.

Paula's "Get 'er done" Kaizen		⛪ Franciscan ST. FRANCIS HEALTH		
Before		**After**		
Staff came up with lots of ideas for improvements and Q&E Kaizens. They were often very busy with direct patient care and said they would submit them later when they had time to look up the form.		I started carrying a paper version of the forms so that they could jot them down. Then I would edit slightly and submit in typing to the Kaizen web site for review and approval.		
Effect				
We are getting a lot more staff involved and we are getting more Kaizens submitted!				
Name	**ID #**	**Dept #**	**Supervisor**	**Date**
Paula Stanfill RN		6511 NICU	Lori Warner	12-21-10

Figure 9.5   A Kaizen related to the Kaizen process itself.

Key Action 3: Encourage Staff to Participate by Asking for Their Ideas

It is the role of managers and supervisors to continuously encourage people to implement their ideas and turn them in as Kaizens. At Franciscan, the revenue management department is a top-performing Kaizen department in terms of "Kaizens per FTE." Their former director, Debbie Tocco, would periodically visit with each employee to help them think of Kaizens. She would ask if they had changed anything lately. If they had, she would ask what was changed, and often she would find herself telling them, "That's a Kaizen," encouraging them to write it up. If they had not done a Kaizen lately, she would ask them questions about their work. If she saw an opportunity, she would ask a question about it, rather then tell them what the Kaizen should be, in order to help them discover their own Kaizen. She also talked about Kaizens at her department meetings.

Paula Stanfill, the NICU Manager at Franciscan, did a similar thing to boost the number of Kaizens being done in her department. She carried blank Kaizen Reports around and asked her staff if they had made any changes lately. If so, she helped them document the changes as Kaizens on the spot. Paula explained that it helped engage her busy staff, and a few individuals got an "aha moment" when they saw how easy documenting a Kaizen can be. Paula even created a Kaizen Report, as shown in Figure 9.5, illustrating again that leaders at all levels can participate in their own Kaizens!

The Kaizen shown in Figure 9.6 shows another good idea to get staff to encourage each other to participate more, with a fun game of "tag."

Key Action 4: Create a Departmental Recognition System

Middle-level leaders can create a departmental recognition system if the broader organization does not have one, or they can supplement the overall program, as facilitated by the Kaizen Promotion Office.

Department Bulletin Board

At Franciscan, each department was encouraged to have a Kaizen Bulletin Board. The bulletin board shown in Figure 9.7 won a contest at Franciscan for its

Tag ... You're It!	Franciscan ST. FRANCIS HEALTH
Before	**After**
Need more motivation with Quick & Easy Kaizens.	Playing the game "Tag" with the staff to help motivate their creativity. I started first and then I tagged someone to be "it" and after they completed a Q&E, they tagged someone else, and so on... Quick & Easy Kaizens will be posted and shared during staff meetings.
Effect	
Motivate staff to participate in Q&E Kaizen. The "Tag" game has a had successful result for staff compliance and motivation.	

Name	ID #	Dept #	Supervisor	Date
Diana Brown		7161	Marci Bennett	10/31/08

Figure 9.6   A fun way to get more participation in Kaizen.

Figure 9.7   An example of a departmental recognition system.

creativity. The petals of the sunflowers each contained a Kaizen. In the center were pictures of Kaizeneers. The water pot contained Kaizen education, and the water drops contained their names and a count of the Kaizens turned in. The board represents the idea that people need to feed and water ideas for them to bloom into flowers, and each flower produced the fruit of more experienced, happier Kaizeneers.

Figure 9.8   A "star chart" that visually shows participation levels for each staff member.

Star Charts

The Franciscan staff often responds well to what are called "star charts," which is basically a list of names with one star posted for each Kaizen turned in that year. It visually shows how each person is performing and draws out the competitive nature in people. There are many ways to motivate people, and, depending on the department's culture, this sort of competition can invigorate everybody instead of demotivating some. The charts are displayed prominently in the departments that use them.

The Franciscan emergency department wanted to encourage off-shift staff to increase their number of Kaizens turned in, so they created a star chart, shown in Figure 9.8, that compares the day shift to the other shifts.

Date Implemented	Title	Date Reviewed	Has this solution helped?	If no, what changes are needed?
January				
01/22	Preprinted order for urine drug screen.	02/28	Yes	
01/29	Use tape to seal envelopes.	02/28	Yes	
01/30	Keep O_2 tanks by pain recovery rooms.	02/28	Yes	
01/31	Write Dr's office phone # on top of Plan of Care.	02/28	Yes	
01/31	Place how to cancel fax above machine.	02/28	Yes	
01/31	Now have process to send "cc" of Dr. dictation.	02/28	Yes	
01/31	Dr. dictation is printed at 7 am automatically.	02/28	Yes	
February				
02/07	Place nurse note tabs in chart.	02/28	Tabs ordered need to apply.	
02/07	Initial when Rx called to pharmacy.	02/28	Form changed to include nurse signature.	
02/13	Clarifying referral information.	02/28	Yes	
02/17	Clarifying pain prescriber on chart.	03/28	Yes	
02/27	Emergency drug dosage for sedation.	03/28	Yes	
02/28	Checking for co-pays.	03/28	Yes	
02/29	Looking up fax numbers.	03/28	Yes	
02/29	Ordering linens.	03/28	Yes	

Figure 9.9   A tracking sheet that shows the status of Kaizens.

Key Action 5: Put a Tracking System in Place, if One Does Not Exist

Design and put into place a mechanism to track Kaizens submitted in your department, if one is not already in place at the organizational level.

Log Sheet

If you have a paper process, then you will likely want to keep a log sheet to track Kaizens as they come in. A tracking sheet, as shown in Figure 9.9, is a good way to manually see the status of Kaizens in a department. Some departments post it in the break room for all to see, and other departments post it in the Kaizen Binder. Prior to the online Kaizen database that Franciscan developed, as discussed in Chapter 10, most departments tracked Kaizens in a manual way.

Kaizen Binders

Departments that use a paper Kaizen Report use a large binder to hold all their Kaizens, which is typically kept in the break room. Some departments use monthly tabs to organize the Kaizens by month. The Kaizen Log Sheet mentioned above can be placed in the front of the binder. An example of a Kaizen binder from Children's Medical Center Dallas was also shared in Chapter 6.

Key Action 6: Tie to Performance Evaluations

At the right point in time, Kaizen can be tied to your annual employee performance evaluations. In the second year of the program at Franciscan, one department added the expectation of two Kaizens to their performance reviews and, in the third year, several other departments added a Kaizen count expectation to their review process. The experience at Franciscan suggests that it is best to wait until you are a few years into Kaizen before creating this formal connection. Early on, you want Kaizen participation to be voluntary, and even the slightest pressure to meet an annual goal will shift the focus to goals and their compensation instead of focusing on the improvements and learning how to do Kaizen.

The pharmacy department at Franciscan had strong Kaizen growth in the first two years, but there were still individuals who would not participate. In their third year, they added Kaizen to their annual performance evaluations in order to encourage those late adopters. However, soon afterwards, staff started believing Kaizen was mandatory. Their Kaizen coordinator, Paula Murphy, had to explain to the staff that Kaizen is not mandatory—rather it is encouraged. She explained that staff does not have to do Kaizen. If a person does not turn in six Kaizens per year, they will score a little lower in their performance review, but there are plenty of other categories in which they can score higher and negate the Kaizen score. Paula gets the most pushback regarding Kaizen being part of performance evaluations from staff who score poorly across the board.

In 2008, Natalie Novak, director of Franciscan's medical records department, asked her employees to submit one Kaizen per month. She asked her managers to add it to their goals and asked each manager to ask it of their staff. Submitting 12 Kaizens per year became the standard. Her department achieved the goal and became one of the top-performing departments at Franciscan. Lynne Meredith said, "Just saying you have to turn in Kaizens and not holding people accountable doesn't work for 20% of people."

Kaizen and Annual Reviews

Although some in the quality field remain adamantly opposed to annual performance reviews,[22] often citing the teachings of Dr. W. Edwards Deming,[23] this process is a reality in most organizations. When these systems are in place,

Kaizen organizations often incorporate staff participation into annual ratings or pay increases.

There is a key distinction to make between setting a goal that is aspirational versus having a quota or a hard target that has penalties for not being met. If leaders set a goal of one Kaizen per employee per month, they need to ensure that the overall system can support such a goal, including the capability of supervisors to coach and lead the process and time being made available. If the goal is not reached, top-level managers should follow the common Lean management practice of asking why and looking for barriers to Kaizen, as discussed in Chapter 8. This will lead to more effective development of a Kaizen program than would punishment.

In a fully mature Kaizen environment, employees and managers at all levels will participate in Kaizen because it is personally rewarding, it makes their lives easier, it improves patient care, and it strengthens the organization. With this intrinsic motivation, goals would not be necessary. However, when getting started with Kaizen, goals can be helpful if done with the right approach, including having clear expectations, managers who participate in Kaizen, and fairness. When Franciscan instituted goals, it sent the message that Kaizen is important and should be tried by everybody. There was some grumbling initially, but this quickly subsided once staff members tried Kaizen and saw the benefits.

Jim Adams, the senior director of laboratory operations at Children's Medical Center Dallas, recalibrated their performance evaluation system because, "The scoring had become quite inflated over many years," he observed. Adams set the new baseline of "meeting basic expectations as described in one's job description" as a score of a 2 out of 5 (with 5 being the highest). Adams says there was no guarantee of a better rating for participating in Kaizen or other Lean methods, but it was stated as a basic expectation, and the increase of one's score depended on the value that was added through Kaizen. Placing the expectations in the job descriptions and the performance evaluation tool made it easier to positively differentiate, in a formal way, between those who adopted and operationalized Lean and Kaizen concepts from those who did not.[24]

Role of First-Level Managers

First-level managers are also critical to the success of Kaizen. They are the ones that teach and coach staff about Kaizen on a daily basis. First-level managers supervise front-line staff and have roles and titles such as supervisors, team leads, lead nurses, charge nurses, lead technologists, and patient care coordinators.

A First-Level Manager Is a Coach

Laura Pettigrew, manager of medical records at Franciscan, said, "The biggest secret to our success in being the top Kaizen department at Franciscan three years in a row is coaching, mentoring, and communication." Iowa Health System works to develop their supervisors into "master coaches" who have an increased confidence in their ability to manage change. These coaches are better able to help their employees take action on Kaizen ideas, says Sal Bognanni, the executive director for their Center for Clinical Transformation. As improvements are made, the culture improves as staff members feel more valued and empowered, which leads to better outcomes, productivity, and patient satisfaction.[25]

Key Actions for First-Level Managers

A first-level manager is the most important person, next to the Kaizeneer, because daily Kaizen is guided and coached most actively by these leaders.

Key Action 1: Coach

At first, Kelly Butler, NICU Supervisor, struggled with getting her staff to participate, remarking, "They didn't want to do Kaizen, because it sounded difficult." She helped them by starting simply, including helping staff remove a lock from a closet door, as documented in Chapter 5. Kelly kept encouraging them, but some would say, "I don't know how to do it." So, Kelly would help them think through an improvement, documenting and submitting a Kaizen Report.

Laura Pettigrew, manager of medical records at Franciscan, recognized the importance of the supervisor in Kaizen success. She involved herself in most Kaizens at the start of her program, with the purpose of modeling the coaching style she wanted to see emulated by her supervisors. She wanted to show her supervisors how to keep the responsibility in the hands of the Kaizeneer and how to lead them through solving their own problems by asking questions and helping them think through a countermeasure. She said, "I wanted to show them how we learn from mistakes and how supervisors could lead staff to work with the other employee to work it out together. Staff used to moan and gripe about someone else and not do something about it. Now they know they have to do something to work it out."

The Amount of Supervisor Coaching

The amount of coaching required depends on other factors, including the Kaizeneer's experience level, their Kaizen's level of impact, and the personal history of the Kaizeneer.

If the Kaizeneer has implemented a steady string of successful Kaizens, and the new one being proposed is similar in scope to ones they have done in the past, then the coaching can be really simple, such as asking a few questions about the solution and the implementation plan. An experienced Kaizeneer who is proposing a Kaizen that only affects her, like moving their stapler, may only warrant a 30-second discussion. Whereas, an inexperienced Kaizeneer, with few

Kaizen successes, who is proposing something that could affect everyone in a department may require hours of thorough coaching.

In Chapter 5, we mentioned the various levels of impact ranging from affecting only one person to affecting the entirety of the organization or beyond. If a change only impacts the Kaizeneer, then there might not be a need for much coaching. However, if the Kaizen could affect everyone in a department or those in other departments, then considerably more coaching will be needed for the Kaizen to be successful. Supervisors may just need to ensure the impact does not go beyond the Kaizeneer and others in their role, that the change does not introduce new safety or quality risks, and the change is likely to be successful based on the implementation plan. The supervisor also helps ensure that a "failure" of the Kaizen would not have any major repercussions, other than being a learning opportunity.

Key Action 2: Empower Staff—Do Not Do the Kaizen for Them

Some of Kelly Butler's NICU employees required her coaching a few times before they realized they were to think through the Kaizen themselves first and involve others. When it came time to implement, Kelly helped people identify the needed actions. She helped them think through with whom they needed to coordinate, and she helped them think through how to engage others in the Kaizen idea. Then she empowered them to do the actions. She did not do it for them, but instead helped them think through how they could do it on their own. Being a coach means avoiding the temptation to do the Kaizen for people, because that creates dependency (and too much work for the leaders), and it hampers learning.

Key Action 3: Use Rounding to Coach

Cherysh Getz, a supervisor of medical records at Franciscan, visits with every staff member at least once a month and uses some of that time to coach staff on Kaizens. When she sits down with a new staff member, she describes the program and shows them examples. Then, she guides them through submitting a Kaizen Report online. She keeps revisiting with them until they are comfortable creating a Kaizen Report on their own.

To get the brainstorming process going, she asks them questions about how they go about their work and where the items they need to do that work are located. She said, "Once they get started and they realize the benefits of doing Kaizens outweigh the time it takes, they realize they can do it." When Cherysh runs into a staff member who seems resistant, she uses positive encouragement. She realizes there can be a variety of reasons why staff hesitate to document Kaizens. If she discovers they are technologically challenged, she spends extra time guiding them through the online entry until they feel comfortable. Cherysh also teams up with others on every Kaizen she does, because it gives her additional opportunities to coach others.

Key Action 4: Help Set Expectations

The supervisor should also help Kaizeneers set priorities, by helping them identify the most important implementation actions and teaching the Pareto principle that 80% of the benefit will likely come from 20% of the actions. The supervisor coach should also ensure Kaizeneers are not trying to do too much on their own without including the help of others.

When the supervisor comes across a Kaizen that should not be implemented, she should carefully explain why. Ronda Frieje, pharmacy manager at Franciscan, said, "If we couldn't do a Kaizen, I felt that we owed it to the Kaizeneer to sit down with them face to face and explain why." In situations like this, the supervisor should work with the Kaizeneer to find other ideas that could be implemented to address the underlying problem or opportunity.

Key Action 5: Review and Approve Kaizen Reports

The person's direct supervisor is generally the person that approves Kaizen Reports for the Kaizeneer, as introduced in Chapter 5. The direct supervisor's main task is to verify completion of the Kaizen. Did the Kaizeneer do what she claimed to do? Do the results make sense? If so, approve the Kaizen. If not, then work out a plan with the Kaizeneer.

Concerns about Selfish Kaizens

Some leaders also wonder if employees will gravitate toward their own selfish desires when implementing Kaizens instead of serving needs of the organization. Figure 9.10 is a humorous look at an imaginary Kaizen that helps an individual while hurting the overall system.

After reviewing thousands of Kaizens, Franciscan found very few that only helped the implementer without also helping the organization. Even those that one could call selfish did, over time, lead to Kaizens that helped the organization. Peer pressure helps to limit selfish Kaizens, especially those that will impact others. The review by supervisors and managers is another important check and balance in this process, and it is one reason why people are not allowed to just make changes in isolation.

Franciscan adopted a practice to overlook those "selfish" Kaizens from new Kaizeneers that have no negative impact on others and to look at the longer-term view of developing staff. This ties into Imai's model of the three stages of Kaizen, where it is important to build enthusiasm in early stages by saying "yes" to most ideas.

Keeping with Imai's model, more mature Kaizeneers might have their ideas challenged in a constructive way, coaching them on their improvement and problem-solving skills, while approaching them with respect and not questioning their intentions. Leaders at Franciscan have learned to carefully consider approaching people who appear to turn in selfish Kaizens and to wait until it becomes

When less isn't more.

Figure 9.10 An imaginary Kaizen that helps an individual while hurting the overall system (cartoon used with permission).

an obvious pattern of behavior. Typically, initiating that discussion helped a person come up with a better idea for addressing their problem or opportunity. However, in one case, these discussions with a mature Kaizeneer caused the staff member to temporarily stop submitting Kaizens.

Concerns about Promoting a Quick Fix Solution Mentality?

There is a natural human tendency to start with solutions, especially with best practices like nursing bundles, without first understanding the problem and analyzing the root causes. With Kaizen, implementing an idea should be really easy to do, especially for new Kaizeneers. However, leaders need to develop the PDSA and scientific thinking culture into the organization as people grow and mature in their Kaizen abilities, meaning ideas should be tested before they are permanently implemented. Again, at Franciscan, the checks and balances of the supervisor, peer pressure, and management review have seemed to temper this tendency to jump to solutions.

Concerns about Suboptimization

Leaders at Franciscan had a legitimate concern that staff-driven improvements might not adequately consider system-level effects, leading to potential sub-optimization and problems for the larger system. However, after reviewing thousands of Kaizens, the number that had the potential to suboptimize the system was very small. Asking supervisors to coach staff members through their Kaizens helps reduce potential suboptimizations. Also, when Kaizens get discussed prior to implementation, the Kaizeneer often gets pushback from other staff members if it would appear to suboptimizes things.

Key Action 6: Help Document Benefits

As Kaizeneers gain more experience, first-level managers can spend more time coaching on how to evaluate the benefits of their improvements, in patient safety, staff safety, time savings, cost savings, quality, speed, patient satisfaction, and staff satisfaction.

Our website (www.HCkaizen.com) contains a more detailed explanation for supervisors on how to quantify the benefits of improvements.

Key Action 7: Make Kaizen Fun

Kelly Butler helped her employees make their Kaizen Reports more cheerful by adding pictures. According to Kelly, it took staff doing Kaizen to realize, "oh, this isn't so hard." Over time, her team found it easier to take and incorporate pictures. For example, Kelly asked one of her staff to hold up some old forms and frown to capture the mood before the improvement and then asked the staff to hold up the new colorful forms and smile to capture the mood after the improvement. Her simple photos created a fun Kaizen that was documented in Figure 9.11 and shared across the hospital.

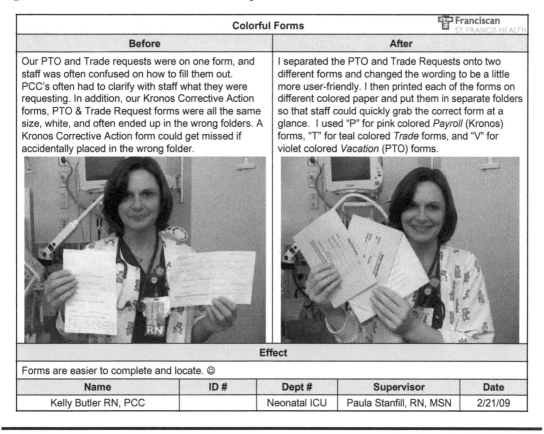

Colorful Forms		Franciscan ST. FRANCIS HEALTH
Before		**After**
Our PTO and Trade requests were on one form, and staff was often confused on how to fill them out. PCC's often had to clarify with staff what they were requesting. In addition, our Kronos Corrective Action forms, PTO & Trade Request forms were all the same size, white, and often ended up in the wrong folders. A Kronos Corrective Action form could get missed if accidentally placed in the wrong folder.		I separated the PTO and Trade Requests onto two different forms and changed the wording to be a little more user-friendly. I then printed each of the forms on different colored paper and put them in separate folders so that staff could quickly grab the correct form at a glance. I used "P" for pink colored *Payroll* (Kronos) forms, "T" for teal colored *Trade* forms, and "V" for violet colored *Vacation* (PTO) forms.
Effect		
Forms are easier to complete and locate. ☺		
Name	**ID #**	**Dept #**	**Supervisor**	**Date**
Kelly Butler RN, PCC		Neonatal ICU	Paula Stanfill, RN, MSN	2/21/09

Figure 9.11 Kaizen reports can be fun.

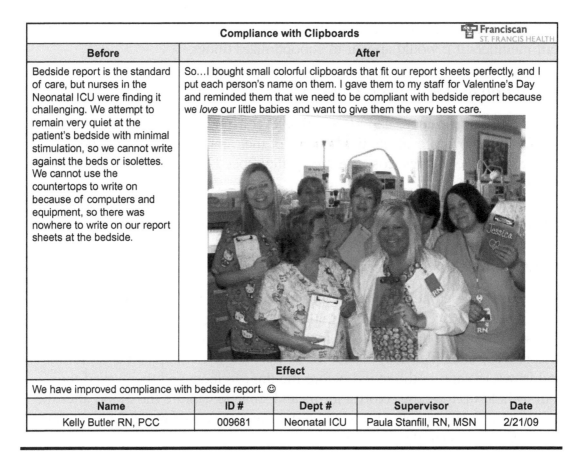

Compliance with Clipboards				Franciscan ST. FRANCIS HEALTH
Before	**After**			
Bedside report is the standard of care, but nurses in the Neonatal ICU were finding it challenging. We attempt to remain very quiet at the patient's bedside with minimal stimulation, so we cannot write against the beds or isolettes. We cannot use the countertops to write on because of computers and equipment, so there was nowhere to write on our report sheets at the bedside.	So...I bought small colorful clipboards that fit our report sheets perfectly, and I put each person's name on them. I gave them to my staff for Valentine's Day and reminded them that we need to be compliant with bedside report because we *love* our little babies and want to give them the very best care.			
Effect				
We have improved compliance with bedside report. ☺				
Name	**ID #**	**Dept #**	**Supervisor**	**Date**
Kelly Butler RN, PCC	009681	Neonatal ICU	Paula Stanfill, RN, MSN	2/21/09

Figure 9.12   Recognition and small tokens are a great way to reward staff.

Key Action 8: Recognize and Reward

See to it that those employees you coach are properly recognized and rewarded, so they will want to do it again. Ensure they get the credit that is due them. Giving recognition in front of others will encourage more people to participate.

Kelly Butler noted that, when staff got recognized for Kaizen and when they saw that it does make a difference in the daily work in the unit, her entire nursing unit became engaged. Kelly said, "Once we got the ball rolling, people got excited and started thinking up new ideas. I now catch people talking about Kaizens."

When you can, ensure that people benefit from improvements. In the Kaizen shown in Figure 9.12, each staff member received a clipboard that the supervisor picked up at the dollar store and personalized using a marker. For less than $10 total, the supervisor ensured her staff received a tangible benefit and tied the Kaizen into their personal goals of providing the best possible patient care.

Key Action 9: Share and Spread Ideas

The real strategic power of Kaizen is in the sharing and spreading of ideas. An improvement in one area could be the stimulus for staff to customize the idea

Thermometers at the Point of Use		Franciscan ST. FRANCIS HEALTH
Before	**After**	
Nurses spent too much time searching for thermometers	Have one thermometer in each room at the point of use. 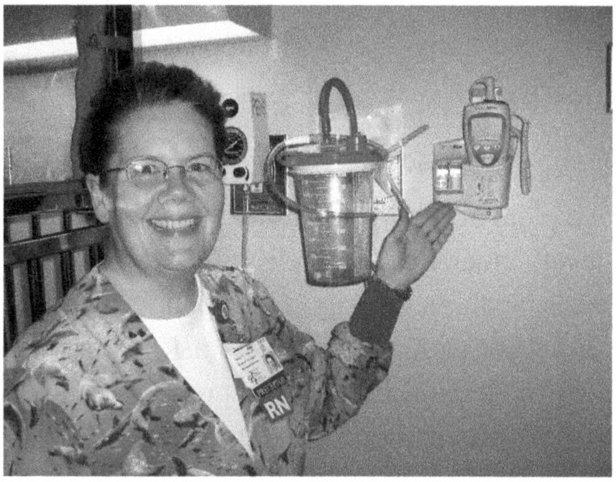 	
Effect		
Saves nursing time searching for thermometers.		

Name	ID #	Dept #	Supervisor	Date
Nancy Thompson		6301	Nancy Mosier	2008

Figure 9.13   A Kaizen that was shared across multiple departments.

and apply it in another area. One idea can lead to ten others. Part of the role of a supervisor is to share and spread ideas to others. When you see ideas used in other areas, bring them back and share them with your staff, and then encourage them to implement the ones they like.

Nancy Thompson, a supervisor in the Pediatrics unit at Franciscan, took the initiative in 2008 to create a business case to buy and place thermometers at the point of use in patient rooms, as shown in Figure 9.13. The manager of the pediatrics unit decided to help her implement her idea. Then Nancy approached the Kaizen Promotion Office (KPO) and willingly shared her idea with the entire hospital system by email, which led to widespread adoption. One idea was multiplied, which reduced the time nurses spent searching for thermometers in many sites. This reduced the nurses' frustration and stress at work and increased the joy in their work. One supervisor really can make a big difference.

Key Action 10: Be a Cheerleader

Finally, first-level managers are the daily cheerleaders of Kaizen. Growing a Kaizen program requires sustained energy and encouragement over a long period of time. The most successful departments at Franciscan have supervisors and managers who continuously encourage Kaizeneers to take action on each Kaizen idea. Even if an idea does not work, they encourage people to reevaluate things and try again. In the face of failure, supervisors remain positive and focus on what can be learned from the failed Kaizen and what can be done better next time.

Conclusion

Each level of leader, from a front-line supervisor to the CEO, plays a key role in Kaizen. Leaders at all levels define what leadership is by what they do, especially the top-level leaders. There are many key behaviors and mindsets that are the same across levels, such as directly participating in Kaizen. After creating an environment that is conducive to Kaizen, leaders ask for improvements and help create the time required to work on them. Leaders recognize and spread Kaizens, continually reminding people of the purpose and the benefits of their improvements.

Discussion Questions

■ What is your answer to an employee asking you "why are we doing Kaizen?"
■ How many ideas should you ask each employee for in a year? What is realistic this year? In ten years?
■ What level of leader is most critical to the success of Kaizen?

Endnotes

1. Burns, John, email correspondence, August 2011.
2. ThedaCare Center for Healthcare Value, "Thinking Lean at ThedaCare: Strategy Deployment," DVD, (Appleton, WI: ThedaCare Center for Healthcare Value), 2011.
3. Rudolph, Jennifer, personal interview, September 2011.
4. Mann, David, *Creating a Lean Culture* (New York: Productivity Press, 2005), 92.
5. Toussaint, John, "More Organizational Transformation Topics: Gemba," *ThedaCare Center for Healthcare Value* Blog, http://www.createhealthcarevalue.com/blog/post/?bid=159 (accessed August 9, 2011).
6. DeBarba, Herb, personal interview, July 2011.
7. Graban, Mark, "Riverside Medical Center Puts Lean in the Laboratory," *Society of Manufacturing Engineers Lean Manufacturing Yearbook 2007*, 56.
8. Dague, James O., personal interview, July 2011.
9. Toussaint, John, Unpublished manuscript, 2009, used with permission.
10. Toussaint, manuscript.
11. Flinchbaugh, Jamie, *The Hitchhiker's Guide to Lean: Lessons from the Road* (Dearborn, MI: Society of Manufacturing Engineers, 2005), 39.
12. Toussaint, manuscript.
13. Toussaint, manuscript.
14. Deming, W. Edwards, *Out of the Crisis* (Cambridge MA: MIT CAES Press, 1982), 21.
15. Toussaint, John, email correspondence, June 2011.

16. Sellers, Bart, personal interview, September 2011.
17. DeBarba.
18. Smith, Jennifer, email correspondence, September 2011.
19. Liker, Jeffrey, and David Meier, *The Toyota Way Fieldbook*, (New York: McGraw-Hill, 2005), 117.
20. Liker and Meier, 223.
21. GBMP, "Toast Kaizen," DVD (Boston: GBMP), 2004.
22. Graban, Mark, "Podcast #117—Samuel A. Culbert, 'Get Rid of the Performance Review!'" LeanBlog.org, http://www.leanblog.org/117 (accessed August 10, 2011).
23. Deming, W. Edwards, *Out of the Crisis* (Cambridge MA: MIT CAES Press, 1982), 116.
24. Adams, Jim, email correspondence, September, 2011.
25. Bognanni, Sal, personal interview, July 2011.

Chapter 10

Organization-Wide
Kaizen Programs

You have to manage a system. The system doesn't manage itself.

—W. Edwards Deming, Ph.D.

Many of the Kaizen methods shared to this point can be implemented locally at a department level, as did the laboratory at Children's Medical Center Dallas. Other organizations, like Franciscan, have moved beyond local efforts to develop and maintain an organization-wide Kaizen program. This chapter shares what Franciscan and other successful organizations have done to create a programmatic approach to Kaizen. This includes creating a central Kaizen Promotion Office, considering the use of incentives and contests, and documenting and sharing Kaizens electronically. We will also outline some expected timelines and costs associated with a Kaizen program.

Getting Started

The upfront costs can be as small as providing some initial kickoff training. As mentioned earlier in the book, Franciscan's leaders brought in Norm Bodek for a day of training and workshops. If you bring in a well-known consultant or a trainer from a local community college, the costs and fees can vary widely. You can try to create your own kickoff training, but the expertise brought by consultants can be invaluable, especially when you are bringing something new to the organization. Yet the expertise level also varies widely, and does not necessarily correlate with the cost, so shop wisely.

A timeline for an organization-wide Kaizen program includes planning, kickoff, growing, and maturing the program. At Franciscan, leaders planned for a month prior to the official kickoff in April of 2007. The kickoff event lasted for one day. In the two months after kickoff, they provided the initial "how to" training and developed an internal website with blank Kaizen Reports, instructions, and resources. Then, starting with month three, they conducted training on Lean topics on a monthly basis for the first year, as detailed in Chapter 11. In the second and third year, Franciscan's leadership brought additional training to specific departments that were struggling with Kaizen. A successful Kaizen program does not just happen—it needs to be designed, implemented, and executed well.

When Will You See Results?

Leaders often ask how fast they can expect to see results after launching a Kaizen program. The good news is that Kaizen delivers small, but real and tangible, results immediately. You will start seeing small results as soon as the Kaizens begin to roll in. At Franciscan, the first Kaizen was completed and turned in the very first day after the kickoff event, with dozens more being done in the first month. Each Kaizen provides benefits, even if they are as simple as saving two seconds of time.

It is important to understand that the greatest benefits of Kaizen are seen when the organization's culture is changed. The time required to change a culture is measured not in weeks or months, but in years or even a decade, depending on how aggressively and skillfully Kaizen is introduced and embraced. At some point, Kaizen will permeate the organization so fully that the effects cross over into every improvement activity, making it somewhat difficult to separate out the effect of Kaizens from Lean Six Sigma and other improvement approaches that are taking place simultaneously.

James Dague, CEO of IU Health Goshen Hospital, recalls, "The first three years of this program are very tough because everybody's waiting for it to go away. You're not going to take all the negatives that got you to this point, where you need an improvement program, and wash it out of your organization in one year." Leaders need to have patience, as Dague adds, "You have to just keep beating the drum. Sometimes you may feel like you're in a stadium all by yourself, but you've got to just persevere with the program. It has to have a return as you go along. But, you've got to establish that this is not a project of the month or a temporary thing, but this is the way we're going to run our culture from now on."[1]

Since the time Franciscan started their Kaizen program, it has spread through the organization each year, leading to some visible changes in the culture. For example, four years ago employees tended to regularly voice their frustrations in a loud and adamant way to administration regularly in various forums around the hospitals. Now, there is noticeably much less of that. The same forums still exist, and employees are encouraged to voice their frustrations and needs, but staff now realize they have the power to improve and redesign their workspace, and the future of the hospital is in each employee's hands, more than ever.

Senior leaders are generally the most interested in results and how Kaizen benefits the organization financially, because they are held accountable in that regard by the board of directors. Although the biggest benefits of Kaizen cannot easily be measured, financial benefits are something that can be objectively measured. According to Keith Jewell, Franciscan COO, "we took 32 million dollars of bottom-line costs out of our three hospital system in Indianapolis in the last few years." More than 12 percent of that (about $4 million over time) was achieved through their Kaizen program, another 20 percent of that resulted from the Lean Six Sigma program, and the remainder came from their supply chain value analysis initiatives. Jewell foresees the Kaizen program exceeding other programs in the future, because it engages all staff.

Tying Kaizen to the Organization's Strategy

One key method to help foster a culture change is tying the Kaizen program to the organizational strategy. Early in a program, you want Kaizen to be primarily self-directed, as ideas are surfaced and driven by staff, focused on things that are in their scope of control that matter to them. However, as Kaizeneers develop their skills and abilities, they will naturally enlarge their scope of Kaizens, and we will expect a greater portion to align with what is important to the organization. This alignment is most likely to happen after putting a formal mechanism and communication in place that ensures staff members know what the organization's vision and strategy are. This can accelerate the maturation of the Kaizen process and can ensure that a higher proportion of Kaizens are aligned to higher-level strategy.

At IU Health Goshen Hospital, CEO James Dague put a lot of effort into constantly communicating the four "focus areas" for the organization, what some might call a "true north"—customer satisfaction, quality, cost effectiveness, and best people—as well as the overall mission. This helps ensure that their staff-driven improvements naturally align with those strategic areas, in addition to making their own work easier.

Dague says, "We've got pressure through the culture of the organization to always be improving. So you implement 4,000 ideas in a year. Some of those are directed by projects from administration, flowing off of our goals, while you also get idea generation from people simply finding different ways to improve their job." Dague wants employees to be strategic, but he also tells them, "If you've got a job irritant, get rid of it. You can get rid of it through our cultural processes. Pick one and let's get at it, but don't just ignore it."[2]

Some organizations issue specific "Kaizen challenges" to staff, where leaders establish and communicate a particular goal or focus area for a period of time, like 30 days. A challenge might focus people on things like improving hand hygiene to reduce infections or improving the emergency department registration process to get patients back to an exam room faster. Generally, these challenges can be applied to other strategic pillars, such as cost or patient satisfaction. After that challenge period, a single improvement could be selected for a prize or special recognition, but all improvement ideas are evaluated and potentially implemented, with recognition being given through the usual methods. Challenges can help align an organization by ensuring improvement is both top down and bottom up.

The Kaizen Promotion Office

Many organizations have created a central Kaizen Promotion Office (KPO) that oversees the program for the hospital, a region, or a system. The KPO is vital to the program's success because it helps guide and coach the organization, while helping to create cohesiveness in the organization's approach to Kaizen.

It is a small distinction, but it is important to note that a KPO does not *own* the program—it is owned by the organization and its leaders. A KPO *facilitates* details of the program on behalf of the organization and for the best interests of all stakeholders. A KPO often reviews ideas after they have been tested and implemented, providing feedback and coaching to the supervisors who were involved in specific Kaizens. A KPO also generally plays a role, as does Franciscan's, in awarding points to staff members that can be redeemed for products.

Franciscan's KPO has helped other hospitals launch Kaizen programs with varying success. A common denominator of those that performed poorly was that they tried to run a program without a KPO because they did not want to allocate a budget. The problem is it is not respectful to the staff to ask already busy people to oversee the Kaizen program on top of everything else they were already doing. It is also likely a waste of time to attempt to implement and run a Kaizen program with a lackadaisical effort. It ultimately leads to frustration and then the incorrect conclusion that Kaizen has failed versus the implementation has failed.

Staffing the KPO

The most costly investment in Kaizen is in human resources—people's time and salaries. A few critical human resource items that will be helpful are creating a KPO, selecting a champion, and dedicating a person or people to facilitate the program's activities.

Since Kaizen involves everyone in an organization, a program should consider how to keep everyone energized over time. The energy required to sustain any type of program is derived from the strength of the purpose of the program and the people who facilitate it. Be sure to ensure that KPO staff members are passionate about empowering all employees to do Kaizen and about creating the kind of culture that is described in Chapter 4. Franciscan's KPO found that a team approach was helpful, as they bounce ideas off each other and consider options from more dimensions.

At Franciscan, the COO is the champion. When the three Franciscan St. Francis Hospitals in Indianapolis launched their Kaizen program, they had 25% of two people's time to facilitate the program for a total of 0.5 FTEs. One of those people was coauthor Joe, and the other was Mischelle Frank, who, as a nurse, helped connect the program with the nursing staff. As the volume of Kaizens has grown, Franciscan increased their staff support. They now have one "regional kaizen coordinator" who dedicates 50% of her time to Kaizen, along with 25% of the manager of business transformation (Mischelle) and 25% of the director of business transformation (Joe), for a total of 1.0 FTEs, focused on running the Kaizen program for their 4,000 employees.

Similarly, Baptist Health Care in Florida has one coordinator for their "Bright Ideas" program who dedicates 50% time for their 6,000 employees.[3] However, their program is mature and well honed. We recommend that resources be front-loaded during the early phases of a Kaizen program. Then, as the program matures and activities are systematized, the central resources can be adjusted accordingly as the Kaizen management practices are embedded in daily management activities.

Activities of the Kaizen Promotion Office

Franciscan's Kaizen Promotion Office does the following to support their program, each of which will be described in more detail below:

1. Facilitates the practice of Kaizen
2. Reports Kaizen metrics
3. Coordinates recognition and rewards
4. Enables Kaizen sharing across the organization
5. Develops Kaizen standardized work
6. Develops and delivers staff education
7. Facilitates the documentation and tracking of Kaizens

Activity 1: Facilitates the Practice of Kaizen

Franciscan's KPO helps the organization facilitate the practice of Kaizen. The KPO periodically interviews staff members and leadership, searching for input that will improve the practice of Kaizen in the organization. A study at Franciscan, in late 2010, showed that the most effective drivers of Kaizens in our top-performing departments are contests, supervisor coaching, and staff meetings. Therefore, the KPO focused their efforts in 2011 on encouraging these drivers in departments that were struggling. The KPO surveyed staff members who had not yet participated in Kaizen and found that over half of them believed, incorrectly, that a Kaizen must be a substantial improvement. Therefore, the KPO improved its communication to remind staff to practice Kaizen by starting really small.

Activity 2: Reports Kaizen Metrics

Franciscan's KPO is responsible for tracking and reporting monthly metrics for departments and the broader organization, including the participation rate and absolute numbers of generated Kaizens. For instance in 2010, 36% of staff and 75% of departments participated in the Kaizen program within Franciscan. There were 3,949 Kaizens completed at the three Franciscan hospitals, which is just under one Kaizen per employee including part-time employees, or 1.6 per FTE. The 2012 goal is 50% staff participation, with an average of 2.0 Kaizens per employee. Franciscan's leaders believe there is still a huge opportunity to continue to expand the use of Kaizen in their organization.

The KPO provides top-level managers with a detailed accounting of the Kaizen programs participation rate and financial impact, which serves to remind them that the benefits far outweigh the costs. Department managers can decide if they would like to print and post their numbers or their performance compared to other departments on their communication boards.

At Franciscan, the completed Kaizens in 2010 resulted in a total documented savings of over $3 million. About $1.7 million of that savings was dollars that flowed directly to the "bottom line," and over $1.4 million of that was "potential" dollar savings through, for example, the saving of someone's time. They try to clearly distinguish how *potential* savings do not immediately flow to the bottom line of the organization's income statement. For example, saving one hour of a nurse's time may not mean one less hour of wages paid. Instead, that time may be used for another purpose such as enhanced patient care, which can be difficult to put a dollar number on.

Franciscan's KPO tallies dollars saved in the Kaizen program because it is important for a successful business concern to have a profit, surplus, or a positive return. Even in a nonprofit or government enterprise, a positive return is required to have money to reinvest in the future of the organization or to repay loans that financed construction. In a Kaizen approach, employees should consider the financial impact of ideas. It is not that finances are the most important thing, but they are one of the many considerations when we carve out time in our day to make improvements.

The participation rate and number of Kaizens are objective numbers that are easy to agree on, but savings can be more subjective. In order to ensure the robustness and accuracy of the financial impact data, Franciscan's KPO assists the Kaizeneer in detailing and verifying the financial documentation for any potential savings identified as being more than $1,000. For those that end up being documented as saving more than $20,000, a member of the financial department reviews them for calculation accuracy and evidence of potential or bottom-line impact.

Like many hospitals, Franciscan leadership holds a monthly or bimonthly management meeting. At one of those meetings each quarter, there are 15 minutes reserved for reporting the status of the Kaizen program to all managers, directors, and VPs. Participation is reported to the organization by regularly publishing the following Pareto charts:

- The top 25 directors by year-to-date Kaizen count
- The top 25 directors by percent staff participation
- The top 25 departments by year-to-date Kaizen count
- The top 25 departments by number of Kaizens per full-time employee
- The top 25 departments by percent staff participation

At Franciscan, leaders are careful to focus on the positive by continually recognizing high performers. They are careful not to harm the dignity of the low performers by publishing anything with their names on it.

Activity 3: Coordinates Rewards and Recognition

Kaizen is an important way we visibly recognize and reward employee initiative.

—Mischelle Frank
Franciscan nurse

At Franciscan, the KPO is responsible to pull the data on a monthly basis about to whom to award VIP points, sending it to the human resources department to ensure employees receive their proper points.

Additionally, the Franciscan KPO conducts an annual awards ceremony in the auditorium where all Kaizeneers who met the annual individual goal are invited, along with representatives from departments that met their departmental goals, as well as the list of the Kaizen high performers.

Franciscan's leaders hand out award plaques to their seven best-performing departments in Kaizen count, also their seven best departments by Kaizens per FTE, along with the top seven money-saving Kaizens, and the seven individuals with the highest Kaizen count. Everyone who met the annual individual goal gets a certificate.

At Franciscan, there are several quarterly contests that reward managers and staff for participation in the Kaizen program. Winners are drawn randomly from a hat, with no analysis of the merit of each Kaizen. For example, they conducted contests that rewarded the three top departments for having the highest staff participation percentage and the highest *increase* in their staff participation percentage with a party. Franciscan also had a contest that rewarded three first-time Kaizen participants, one with an iPod Touch, one with an iPod Shuffle, and one with an iPad. Each contest is different and is tailored to what Franciscan is trying to influence and grow in the Kaizen program at the time. Franciscan budgets $5,000 for Kaizen contests annually.

Activity 4: Facilitates Kaizen Sharing across the Organization

Franciscan's KPO helps ensure Kaizens are posted in prominent places for all to see—cafeterias, departmental bulletin boards, etc. Franciscan also recommends that each campus have a Kaizen bulletin board that is updated periodically. They found that updating the theme of the board to correspond to the season or a holiday makes it obvious the board has been updated.

Activity 5: Develops Kaizen Standardized Work

The Franciscan KPO is responsible for developing and documenting the standardized work associated with the Kaizen program, such as step-by-step process documentation and supporting educational materials. This is done by discovering, documenting, and sharing Kaizen best practices throughout an organization. For example, to facilitate Kaizen reporting, the KPO purchased digital cameras for each campus and created simple instructions for checkout and use. Kaizen educational materials and process documentation are readily available from the Franciscan Intranet, as shown in Figure 10.1.

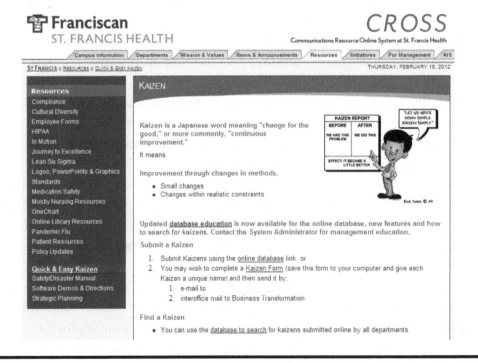

Figure 10.1 The Kaizen intranet site at Franciscan St. Francis.

Activity 6: Develops and Delivers Staff Education

The Franciscan KPO created "how to" training materials for managers to use to train their staff on what Kaizen is and how to create a Kaizen Report. They also offered to conduct training for their staff. About one third of the managers accepted the offer in the first two months of the program. The remainder of the managers either provided the training on their own or did not conduct the training. Brief Kaizen training is provided for five to ten minutes to all new employees during orientation. Kaizen is also included in the annual mandatory training for all staff.

Starting in late 2007, Franciscan offered a series of optional 60-minute sessions to all staff on a number of specific Lean topics. The training was taken to each campus, being offered enough times throughout the day and various days of the week to make it convenient for all shifts and weekend option staff. More on the training is covered in Chapter 11.

In another example, the Utah North Regional of Intermountain Healthcare has developed a 60-minute training session for all managers, directors, and senior leaders that covers topics including employee engagement, the role of leaders in managing improvement, how to promote ideas, and coaching staff members through improvement ideas.[4]

Activity 7: Facilitates the Documentation and Tracking of Kaizens

Franciscan's KPO developed and facilitates the methods for documenting and tracking of Kaizens. More on this KPO activity will be explained in the "Electronic Kaizen Systems" section later in this chapter.

Besides these seven activities, arguably the most important role of a KPO is to continuously infect an organization with the philosophy of Kaizen. Mischelle Frank summarizes their efforts by saying, "Empowerment is just a nice concept unless there is a mechanism and a support system to enable staff to develop their problem solving and continuous improvement skills and abilities." Franciscan has found that an effective KPO provides a support system for staff and for leaders at all levels.

Sustaining a Kaizen Program—Incentives and Rewards

During the second year of their program, Franciscan introduced an incentive system that nominally rewarded people with points for turning in completed Kaizen Reports. All Kaizen Reports are treated equally, as there is no ranking of ideas based on their size. Kaizens with large cost savings are treated the same as a Kaizen about moving the location of a stapler. They have no direct cash payouts for ideas, and they reward for the process of doing a Kaizen.

Franciscan provides staff with a small incentive of 200 "VIP Points" for each Kaizen that is completed and approved. VIP points can be used to purchase merchandise or gift cards. The points are given to each Kaizeneer listed on the Kaizen. The only qualifier for the incentive is that the Kaizen is documented and approved by the supervisor.

At Franciscan, the KPO also gives out rewards when teaching Kaizen or when presenting at a department meeting. They use rewards, like a $5 cafeteria or coffee shop gift card, Post-it note pads, or small writing notebooks, when staff document a Kaizen Report in the training session based on something they have done in the past but had not yet documented. These come after a short training session and are like Kaizen documenting parties.

At the start of their program, the incentive system cost a total of about a $1,000 per year. Four years into the program, the annual Kaizen costs for the incentive system are approaching $4,000. The human resources department picks up the costs for the overall incentive program, as it was implemented for other incentive purposes, such as thank you card incentives, recognition, and birthday wishes.

At Toyota, a supervisor can approve an incentive payment up to $16. In all cases, the minimum payment for an implemented idea is $10. For small improvements (and small rewards), it is not required to "cost justify" or calculate a return on investment (ROI) for an improvement, because many suggestions are of "an intangible nature" where it is "difficult to directly calculate the potential benefit," such as those for safety or quality.[5] Higher payments need to be approved by progressively higher levels of management.

Park Nicollet Health Services gives their employees "Ovation Points" that can be used to purchase items. Jennifer Rudolph, former KEEP administrator & lead specialist, says the points "might pique someone's interest to take initiative and learn about Kaizen, but it's not really a big motivator to participate." Park Nicollet gives small rewards for most ideas, but might reward $150 for a large idea that saved $10,000, says Rudolph. She adds that people aren't using the system just to get points. Rudolph says a points system is "nice to have," but not a critical factor.[6]

Pros and Cons of Financial Incentives

Purely monetary rewards can be a dis-incentive and tend to distort people's motivation for Kaizen.

Table 10.1 Pros and Cons of Incentive Payments

Pro	Con
It is one form of recognition	Focus might turn to earning money rather than fixing the process
Can garner participation from some who would not participate otherwise	Adds another administrative layer to the Kaizen process
Might seem fair to share savings and benefit with staff	Can be hard to gauge the benefits of certain ideas
	Some research shows that financial incentives hamper creativity[8]

Organizations in other industries have sometimes learned that financial incentives for Kaizen can backfire if the focus for people shifts from improvement to the reward itself. In some organizations, employees were known to submit ideas solely for the reward payout. In some of these cases, a reward was given for a mere suggestion, as opposed to something that was actually implemented. To help avoid these dysfunctions, keep these guidelines in mind for a rewards program:

■ Incentives should be relatively small.
■ Incentives should be based on the implementation of an idea.
■ Incentives can be paid for attempts at implementation that were ultimately not accepted as a change (following the PDSA approach).

Ultimately, your organization needs to decide the proper role of incentives and rewards based on your own culture. Some pros and cons of incentive payments are listed in Table 10.1.

The Utah North Region of Intermountain Healthcare does not use official rewards or incentives for their idea program. Some units might give meal tickets or candy bars for ideas, but the primary recognition is given verbally in huddles and staff meetings.[7]

Electronic Kaizen Systems

Our online Kaizen database so improved my ability to do my job well that I would highly recommend starting a Kaizen program with an online database on day one.

—Julia Dearing
Franciscan regional kaizen coordinator

We have found a trend that many organizations have developed electronic online databases to help facilitate their Kaizen program. The evolution of many organizations' path is similar. For example when Franciscan started their program, all Kaizens were handwritten. Shortly after the start of the program, they introduced a PowerPoint template that could be filled out and emailed to the supervisor for approval. Franciscan also had its information services department create a special email box for people to submit Kaizens electronically. Over time, email became the main way Kaizens were turned in. Then, in 2009, a home-grown web-based database was introduced. By the close of 2010, nearly 70% of Kaizens were recorded using the online database, 20% by email, and 10% by paper.

Advantages of an Electronic Online Database

The electronic online database enhanced reporting, tracking, and sharing of ideas. Other key advantages of the online database over paper forms at Franciscan have included the quick entry and automatic routing of ideas, the ability to hold ideas for later, giving electronic approval, and the quick search and retrieval of previous ideas. The next section walks through how the online database is used at Franciscan.

Quick Entry

Online database entry can be quick and efficient. The online entry process has four screens or steps. In the first screen, the basic Kaizen information is collected, such as the title, before condition, after condition, and the effect. Figure 10.2 shows the first screen of the Kaizen entry form used at Franciscan.

At Franciscan, it was useful to add checkbox categories to the online Kaizen Report entry screen, as shown in Figure 10.3. This enables Kaizens to be categorized in the database and helps the Kaizeneer quickly select those categories when there is not a clearly quantifiable benefit. The organization decided to keep the paper Kaizen Report as simple as possible, so check boxes were not added to it.

In the next steps of the online entry process, the Kaizeneer and all contributing Kaizeneers' names are added, and any attachments are submitted, such as supporting pictures or other files.

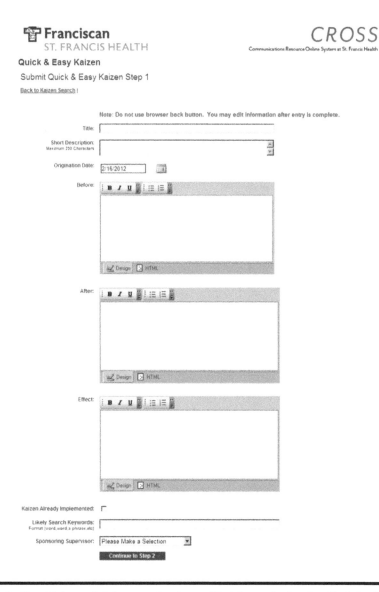

Figure 10.2   Online Kaizen database entry form (Database design by Christopher Carrington, software engineer, Franciscan Alliance).

Franciscan
ST. FRANCIS HEALTH

CROSS
Communications Resource/Online System at St. Francis Health

Quick & Easy Kaizen

Submit Quick & Easy Kaizen Step 2

Enter Kaizen Benefits

Benefit of Kaizen:
Select All That Apply

☐ Time Saved (Indicate Hours Per Year Saved)
(Do Not Include Time Savings Quantified in Dollars Below)   [0]

☐ Money Saved (Indicate Yearly Savings in Text Box) $[0 00]

☐ Paper Saved (Please indicate annual sheet count saved)   [0]

☐ 3 Rs Reduce, Reuse, Recycle

☐ Patient Safety Improved

☐ Patient Satisfaction Improved

☐ Employee Safety Improved

☐ Employee Satisfaction Improved

☐ Quality Improved

☐ Other (Please Explain)   [   ]

The 8 Wastes:

☐ Human Potential Better Utilized

☐ Inventory Saved

☐ Motion Saved

☐ Over Processing Reduced

☐ Over Production Reduced

☐ Rework or Correction Reduced

☐ Transportation Improved

☐ Waiting Reduced

Add Documentation

Related Documents:

Add Related Attachment

Add Attachment: [   ] [Browse...]
*Note: Will not Accept Files Greater Than 2MB in Size

Documentation Stage: [Before ▼]

[Attach Document]

[Continue to Step 3]

Figure 10.3   Form that helps staff members categorize the benefits of Kaizens.

From: Forms@ssfhs.org [mailto:Forms@ssfhs.org]
Sent: Friday, Feb 19, 2010 1:35 PM
To: [Supervisor's Name]
Subject: New Kaizen Submission for Approval
Importance: High

A New Kaizen has been received.

Please Click Here to view the list of submitted
Kaizens and Approve if appropriate.

Figure 10.4   An automatic email that informs a supervisor of a new Kaizen.

Automatic Routing and Electronic Approval

Another advantage of an online database is that completed Kaizen Reports can automatically be routed to the proper supervisor for approval, as in the sample email shown in Figure 10.4.

A link in the email takes the supervisor directly to the database webpage of the Kaizen that has been submitted. On the approval screen, she can either approve the Kaizen or convert the Kaizen to an idea to be implemented later.

Franciscan
ST. FRANCIS HEALTH

CROSS
Communications Resource Online System at St. Francis Health

Quick & Easy Kaizen Supervisor Approval

Idea Listing for Facility

Back to Kaizen Listing for Facility

		Idea Title	Description	Sponsor	Submitted Date	Delete Idea	Restore to Kaizen
288	View/Print Idea	Telephone stabilization	We need some way to stabilize the phones in the patients rooms. They tend to slide off the tables in CCU. Is there some type of bracket--example I-shaped bracket that could be mounted on the table that would hold the phone in place. It wouldn't ha	Wray, Patricia	06/28/2009	Delete Idea	Restore to Kaizen
303	View/Print Idea	Revision of Form Letter for Efficiency	Form letter was revised to assist recipient in determining whether we are responding to a letter went to BG, IN or MV campus.	Jones-Johnson, Pamela	07/21/2009	Delete Idea	Restore to Kaizen
377	View/Print Idea	Multiple IV Attempts	Card/token for multiple IV attempts	Bennett, Marci	10/01/2009	Delete Idea	Restore to Kaizen

Figure 10.5   The "Idea Screen" shows Kaizen opportunities that are on hold.

Once the supervisor views it and any attached files and verifies the Kaizen is complete and meets the criteria for approval, she can print the Kaizen to be posted, and then they can approve the Kaizen. The Kaizen is automatically flagged for the regional Kaizen coordinator to review. Then, once approved, the Kaizen is immediately available for anyone in the organization to search and view. An email notice is sent automatically to the employees who submitted the Kaizen after the online approval process is completed.

Ideas to Hold for Later

Kaizens that are impractical to implement at the moment, for various reasons, can be converted to an idea to be held for later. Ideas held for later are electronically separated and appear on an "Idea Screen," as shown in Figure 10.5, indefinitely until they are reformulated to implement and moved back to the Kaizen portion of the database for approval.

Quick Search and Retrieval

Kaizen Reports can be quickly searched and retrieved. Kaizeneers can quickly search the status of all Kaizens that they have submitted electronically. The search can be done by department, submitter's name, title, or description.

Figure 10.6 shows just a few of the 15 results that came up when searching for Kaizens related to shelves. Users can view or print any of the Kaizens found.

Electronic Kaizen within Intermountain Healthcare

At Intermountain Healthcare's Utah North Region, an electronic "Idea Tracker" system was put in place, as their tactical applications team made modifications to an existing online event reporting system. They use a Visual Idea Board approach, as shown in Chapter 6, and a unit clerk enters ideas that were completed through that process into their electronic tracker.[9] The goal is to make it easier for people

Franciscan
ST. FRANCIS HEALTH

CROSS
Communications Resource Online System at St. Francis Health

Quick & Easy Kaizen

Add a Kaizen | Export Kaizen Listing by Department/Date

Search for Kaizen:

Search Terms: Shelve

Advanced Search

Click Here to Search

		Kaizen Title	Description	Facility	Origination Date
View/Print Kaizen	View/Print Attachments	Compounding Shelves	Cleaned, organized, and ordered shelf labels for each product on the compounding shelves.	St. Francis Hospitals	12/10/2009
View/Print Kaizen	View/Print Attachments	Labeling	Labeling the stock shelves in the cage.	St. Francis Hospitals	01/18/2010
View/Print Kaizen	View/Print Attachments	Leaving meds on shelves	By leaving boxes and bins on the shelves they will stay in their proper areas.	St. Francis Hospitals	01/19/2010
View/Print Kaizen	View/Print Attachments	Organize shelf with supplies on hand	Using supplies we already had we are able to keep the shelves neat and saves time looking for days.	St. Francis Hospitals	01/25/2010
View/Print Kaizen	View/Print Attachments	Shelf size on E.P. cockpit	Lifepak monitor along with a couple other items fitting tightly on the shelves.	St. Francis Hospitals	02/12/2010
View/Print Kaizen	View/Print Attachments	Kenaolg 5ml and 1ml	Medications are packaged the same. Only way to tell them apart is the ml size on the box. Made label to alert that 5ml and 1ml boxes are identical.	St. Francis Hospitals	02/26/2010
View/Print Kaizen	View/Print Attachments	Shelf Stabilization	Had maintenance secure the shelf in the breakroom to prevent injury from shelves tipping and articles falling due to improper installation.	St. Francis Hospitals	03/02/2010

Figure 10.6   Example of Kaizen search results.

across their three sites to search for ideas and share information. Another goal was to be able to roll up statistics about their Kaizen efforts, financial and otherwise, across departments for a more global view of their program and its health.

Electronic Kaizen at Park Nicollet

After starting their KEEP program with paper forms and manual tracking, as mentioned in Chapter 6, Park Nicollet Health Services worked with an outside vendor to customize an electronic tracking system for their Kaizens. Jennifer Rudolph said they wanted an easier way to track, measure, and share improvements that were taking place across service lines. They also wanted to tie the KEEP submission process into their electronic existing system for assigning and tracking staff recognition points.

Small Kaizens of the "just did it" variety are entered directly into the system as a "one-step idea." These ideas are documented after the fact. When ideas are entered, the manager is sent an email asking them to review the idea. The manager has the option of approving, canceling, or putting the KEEP idea on hold. If the idea might impact another department and the submitter did not realize that, the manager might notice this and suggest that they work together to find a more practical solution. In the one-step process, the manager would give this feedback in a face-to-face offline discussion. There is also a more complex four-step KEEP process that is used for bigger projects, where managers can give feedback and track progress electronically. Rudolph said, "We got feedback that face-to-face communication was still happening anyway [with the electronic system in place] and that was more important to the employees."[10]

Electronic Kaizen at Vanderbilt

In 2005, Gregory Jacobson, MD, an emergency medicine and physician and faculty member at Vanderbilt University Medical Center (VUMC), was given a copy of Imai's *KAIZEN* by his department chair, Corey Slovis, MD. Slovis gave him the book because Jacobson was "always the guy asking why things were done one way and not the other," with the intention of improving the processes in the E.D. After reading Imai's book, he decided that the emergency department was a perfect setting to engage the residents and teach them Kaizen principles as a formal method for quality improvement.[11]

Later that year, after educating the residents and faculty physicians on the history and principles of Kaizen, Jacobson and a coworker, Richard Lescallette, built a simple webpage that they called the "Kaizen Portal." This was the place where any emergency medicine physician or employee could submit an improvement idea.[12]

The Vanderbilt E.D. started their program with an electronic idea submission tool, unlike the other hospitals cited in this chapter that added a system after starting with a manual approach. As Jacobson reflected, "I just couldn't have imagined doing this with a paper system because, in the hospital and ED, we were solving many other problems with technology, including the adoption of electronic order entry and the digitization of the radiology department," adding that "you couldn't walk five feet in the department without bumping into a computer." Additionally, there were 300 staff members working in a 75-bed department that was spread across two physical locations and "if we would have had a bulletin board, I wouldn't have known where to put it."[13]

After a resident entered an idea, the Portal would simply send that via email to about a dozen key administrators in the department. Within a few weeks, dozens of ideas poured in, but the Portal was quickly deemed a failure because an "e-mail-only system proved to be disorganized, inefficient, and ultimately non productive."[14] They had to find another way to facilitate the Kaizen ideas that were being generated.

Lescallette and Jacobson went back to the drawing board and built a more fully featured web application that they called the "Kaizen Tracker," which they started using in 2006. The Tracker was configured so that each new idea was sent to one person, the E.D. chair, who then approved or assigned implementation of the idea to others. Now, all comments about a Kaizen were kept in the Tracker, which could be viewed in the web application by anybody, instead of getting lost in people's email inboxes.

As a Kaizen was being discussed and implemented, the author could see and participate in discussion about that idea. When improvements were finalized, a notification was sent to the entire department, to keep people informed about changes. The department was also notified if an idea could not be implemented, creating an important feedback loop to "assure that no concerns are simply dismissed without explanation or discussion."[15] Completed Kaizens were also categorized and kept in the Tracker to be viewed or searched by all E.D. staff.

Some examples of opportunities for improvement that were submitted into the Tracker and led to operational changes include:

■ We need to have thyroid shields in the trauma bays.
■ When one orders foot X-rays, the oblique view does not show up.
■ Often people walk in while a patient is having a pelvic exam. I think this could be solved if we had a sign on the pelvic cart that we could post on the door of a patient's room that states, "Pelvic Exam In Progress."[16]

These ideas, generated by the residents and physicians, are perfect examples of Kaizen improvements. Use of the Tracker also identified cases where communication needed to be improved. In one example, a resident asked for a translation phone system for the E.D., which led to him being told that there had been one in place for over three months. So, the resolution of that idea was to remind and inform staff members about where to find it.

The Tracker was used continuously in the E.D. until 2011, when they converted their system to a newly available commercial version of the web-based application from a startup company called KaiNexus™ that was cofounded by Jacobson after licensing the technology from Vanderbilt. The new software increased the visibility and collaboration beyond a single department, as they expanded its use beyond the emergency department, while adding improved metrics and reporting.

KaiNexus offers an enterprise-level improvement platform designed to help support a Lean and Kaizen program for an entire medical center by supporting staff and supervisors in collecting, routing, tracking, approving, archiving, and communicating thousands of Kaizens. Jacobson says, "KaiNexus isn't intended to replace team huddles and face-to-face interaction," adding, "Using email to manage Kaizen usually fails, but a web-based system is more effective because it's inclusive, transparent, collaborative, and nothing gets lost." Coauthor Mark is the Chief Improvement Officer of KaiNexus. Graban states, "I saw a number of organizations create their own 'home grown' software to support Kaizen programs," adding, "It became apparent to me that these electronic platforms, if utilized correctly, were addressing the communication barriers that hinder the implementation and the sharing of improvements in large, complex organizations."

Jacobson and his coauthors analyzed their Kaizen results for the adult E.D. in a journal article published in 2009. One notable achievement was their success

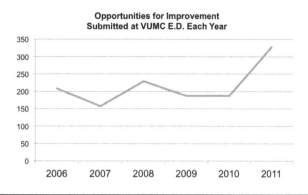

Figure 10.7   The number of ideas implemented each year in the Vanderbilt University Medical Center emergency department.

in engaging residents in Kaizen, as 93 percent of residents submitted at least one improvement idea. Overall, there were 408 opportunities for improvement recorded in the adult E.D. through the Portal and the Tracker systems over a span of 56 months. Of these ideas, 43 percent came from residents, 40 percent from faculty, and 17 percent from other staff. Figure 10.7 shows the published data for the number of ideas generated each year in the adult and pediatrics emergency departments.

> *We no longer have a "complainer" type of culture anymore; if there is a problem, our department's culture now maintains a "don't complain, send a Kaizen" attitude. Our residents and faculty know that feedback occurs in hours to a day or so, and the problem will be fixed, addressed, or an explanation provided on the issue they have raised.*
>
> *It has changed my life. This department is dramatically improved because of it, and our residents and faculty are much more content. It has also increased efficiency as problems are fixed quicker, and finally it allows leaders and managers to be held accountable.*
>
> **—Corey Slovis, MD**
> *Chairman of the Vanderbilt Department of Emergency Medicine*

As of May 2012, the KaiNexus™ software is being used in multiple departments within Vanderbilt University Medical Center and is being implemented at six other major medical centers. The commercial software is the next evolution of Jacobson's work that moves beyond a single department to provide improved functionality for an entire medical center or health system.

Conclusion

If your organization would like to start an organization-wide Kaizen program, it will experience better results if the program is developed well and is committed

Table 10.2 Summary of Potential Costs to Start an Organization-Wide Kaizen Program

Item	Cost
Initial kickoff training	Confidential
Bulletin boards	$4,000 one-time cost
VIP points incentives	$4,000 per year
Contests	$5,000 per year
Electronic Kaizen system	$20,000 initial cost plus ongoing maintentance
Printing forms	$400 per year
Departmental lunch awards	$1,000 per year
Plaques and catering for annual ceremony	$2,000 per year
Staff time and KPO time	Confidential

to by top-level managers. Top-level managers must commit adequate financial resources—a summary of the costs at Franciscan can be found in Table 10.2.

The organization must also put a Kaizen Promotion Office in place that is staffed with dedicated people who are capable of driving such a program with purpose and energy. A timeline will need to be a developed to plan, kickoff, grow, and mature a program. The KPO that is put in place needs to facilitate the practice, report metrics, coordinate recognition and rewards, enable sharing, develop standard work, develop and deliver education, and facilitate documentation and tracking. Systems for electronic management and retrieval of Kaizen ideas should be strongly considered at some point in the development of the program.

Discussion Questions

■ At what point in your organization's Kaizen journey should you consider creating a Kaizen Promotion Office? Can these duties be incorporated into an existing department?

■ What would you like your senior leaders and the organization to do to recognize Kaizen accomplishments? What are some fun ways to do this?

■ What are some of the advantages and disadvantages of having a computer system for collecting and displaying completed Kaizens?

■ Advantages and disadvantages of bulletin boards versus computer systems for managing the entire Kaizen initiation and implementation process?

Endnotes

1. Dague, James, personal interview, July 2011.
2. Dague.

3. Brophy, Andy, and John Bicheno, *Innovative Lean*, (Buckingham, England: PICSIE Books, 2010), 138.

4. Sellers, Bart, personal interview, September 2011.

5. Liker, Jeffrey K., and David Meier, *The Toyota Way Fieldbook* (New York: McGraw-Hill, 2006), 262.

6. Rudolph, Jennifer, personal interview, August 2011.

7. Sellers, Bart, personal interview, September, 2011.

8. Pink, Daniel H., *Drive: The Surprising Truth about What Motivates Us* (New York, Penguin, 2011), 35.

9. Sellers.

10. Rudolph.

11. Jacobson, Gregory, personal interview, September, 2011.

12. Jacobson, Gregory H., Nicole Streiff McCoin, Richard Lescallette, Stephan Russ, and Corey M. Slovis, "Kaizen: A Method of Process Improvement in the Emergency Department," *Academic Emergency Medicine,* Volume 16, Issue 12, December 2009, 1342.

13. Jacobson.

14. Jacobson, et.al., 1346.

15. Jacobson, et al., 1343.

16. Jacobson, et. al., 1344.

Chapter 11

Lean Methods for Kaizen

Kaizen is a mindset. Many lean practitioners put kaizen in their toolbox, but those who strive to live it each day are the people who are making a difference in people's lives.

—Masaaki Imai

At Franciscan, staff are taught basic Lean Healthcare techniques in addition to Kaizen principles. At the end of each training session, participants are asked to immediately apply what they learned in their workplace and to turn in what they did as a Kaizen. This chapter reviews many of those basic Lean techniques that are taught and illustrates them with example Kaizens. For a more complete coverage of Lean principles and methods, you can read *Lean Hospitals: Improving Quality, Patient Safety, and Employee Engagement (2nd edition),* by Mark Graban.

Some of the Lean Healthcare techniques taught at Franciscan are:

1. Adding value
2. Eliminating the eight wastes
3. Visual workplace
4. Workspace organization using 5S
5. Workstation design
6. Problem-solving technique
7. Error proofing

Technique 1: Add Value

Lean goes well beyond a traditional "cost cutting" mindset. Lean healthcare starts by understanding the "value" that an organization currently provides and the value the organization will need to provide in the near future in order to remain competitive and viable. Value is often not well understood, because people can mistake activity and being busy for real value to the customer.

Value is a measure of the benefits received, both real and perceived, from the customer's point of view. Broadly defined, value equals benefits divided by cost. Others, including patient safety expert Robert Wachter, MD, define the value as quality divided by cost.[1] Not all costs are monetary. In healthcare, the patient is often not the primary payer and might not feel costs in a direct way. Costs include all the inconveniences that the customer must put up with in order to receive the benefits, including the time they wait to be served. Reducing cost or increasing the benefit to the patient, including better quality, means better value.

Benefits can include the level of care and service patients receive during their stay at the hospital, the resultant clinical outcomes, or a compassionate moment shared with a staff member. The essence of a Kaizen culture is an organization that constantly and forever looks for ways to produce and deliver value to customers. In our quest to provide value, an organization can lower cost or they can increase the benefits the customer receives.

The Internal Customer's Point of View

> *No problem can be solved from the same level of consciousness that created it.*

> **—Albert Einstein**

In order to identify customer value, you must learn to see the process you work in from the customer's point of view. This can be the ultimate customer, the patient and their loved ones, or it can be an "internal customer," such as another employee or clinician who receives the work that a staff member does. One way to do that is to become a customer and walk in their shoes. Another way to identify value is to ask the patients what they see.

Maggie is the respiratory supply coordinator at Franciscan. She had implemented some changes to her supply room that she was anxious to show coauthor Joe. She had done an amazing job. She had mounted examples of items on the outside of the cabinet doors to make it easier to find what was inside. While Joe was there, he asked Maggie how she had organized her supplies. She had organized them alphabetically, so the respiratory therapists (RT) that came to her supply room would look up each item on the alphabetized list and then go to the location of the item.

During his visit, however, Joe noticed several RTs come in to get supplies. As he observed, they seemed to be assembling systems from parts. Joe then asked a few RTs what they were there to get. They mentioned things like, "I'm setting up a vent for a patient in ICU and a CPAP for a patient in another nursing unit." Joe was noticing a pattern, but that would not mean much unless he could get Maggie, who was the process owner of the supply room, to see it.

So, Joe asked Maggie to ask each RT who came to her supply room over the next week what they were here to get—and to classify each request as to whether it was for a system or for parts. A week later, Maggie reported that 80% of the time RTs wanted to build respiratory systems for patients, rather than just individual parts. So, Joe asked her, "Based on what you just learned, how should your supply room be organized?" She smiled and replied, "by system." She completely reorganized all of her supply rooms by systems. That change cut the average time that an RT takes to retrieve supplies in the supply room in half. Her internal customers, the RTs, were delighted, which meant they could provide better care to the end customers—the patients.

Maggie learned to look at the service she provided from a different point of view—shifting from what made sense to her to what best served her customer's needs. Instead of guessing, she asked and directly observed. Often, people need to look at things from a different point of view to see a different solution. Looking at processes from the customer's perspective is a powerful piece of the Kaizen philosophy, as part of Lean.

Different Forms of Patient Value

Angela, an ultrasound technician, heard a young patient's point of view. "Value" to a patient includes getting an accurate ultrasound scan, but the customer's needs also include being comfortable and happy. Many of the most memorable Kaizens turned in at Franciscan have then those that made a difference for the patients and their families in a way that was not strictly clinical, as shown in Figure 11.1,

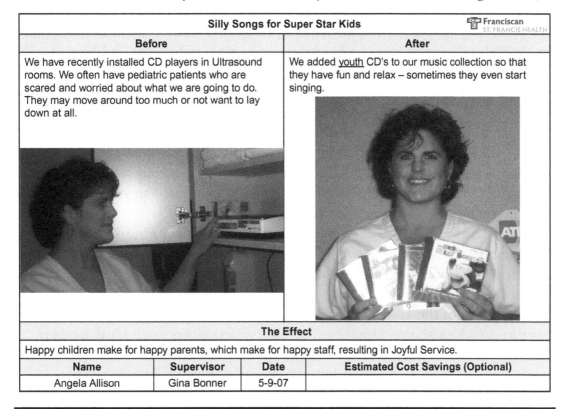

Silly Songs for Super Star Kids		Franciscan ST. FRANCIS HEALTH
Before	**After**	
We have recently installed CD players in Ultrasound rooms. We often have pediatric patients who are scared and worried about what we are going to do. They may move around too much or not want to lay down at all.	We added <u>youth</u> CD's to our music collection so that they have fun and relax – sometimes they even start singing.	
The Effect		
Happy children make for happy parents, which make for happy staff, resulting in Joyful Service.		

Name	Supervisor	Date	Estimated Cost Savings (Optional)
Angela Allison	Gina Bonner	5-9-07	

Figure 11.1 A patient-centered Kaizen example.

Figure 11.2 Young patients value a fun and distracting environment.

At Franciscan, there was large variability in blood draw times for pediatric patients. The average blood draw time for an adult was 5 minutes, but it typically ranged anywhere from 5 minutes to 30 minutes for pediatric patients. They found one of the main sources of the variability was created by the patient's fear of the needle stick. When staff looked at the experience from a kid's eyes, they discovered that the environment was creating some of that fear. Imagine yourself sitting in a chair that has restraint straps hanging off it, in a white walled, sterile room, and in walks a man twice your height, wearing a white lab coat, holding a large needle in his hand and heading straight toward you. It is not surprising a child would be nervous, if not terrified.

The department brought in a pediatric rehab physician who was well known for creating a magical experience for his patients. With his help and a local art teacher, they turned a blood draw room into an undersea adventure, as pictured in Figure 11.2. The room now has a treasure chest filled with toys that are given to the children. It provides the distraction needed to reduce the variability in collection time.

This is a case that illustrates the ability to create value (a fun experience for the patient) at the same time we are reducing the waste of waiting. It is win–win because it also saves time for staff members and improves hospital efficiency and patient flow.

The nurses in the Franciscan Neonatal Intensive Care Unit (NICU) worked together to add a simple innovation to their practice. For each baby in their care, they attach a thank you card to the patient records that is signed by every nurse who cares for each baby. The card is given to the parents at the end of the baby's stay. The card idea was not part of any management initiative or mandate, it was something the NICU nurses wanted to do for

Thank You Kaizen		Franciscan ST. FRANCIS HEALTH
Before	**After**	
The NICU recognized the importance of thanking our patients, but faced challenges in how we would accomplish the task and who would be responsible.	We developed a Thank You card that could be kept in the bedside chart upon admission. Each nurse signs the card when they sign on to the chart. By the time the baby is discharged, every nurse who cared for the baby had signed the card.	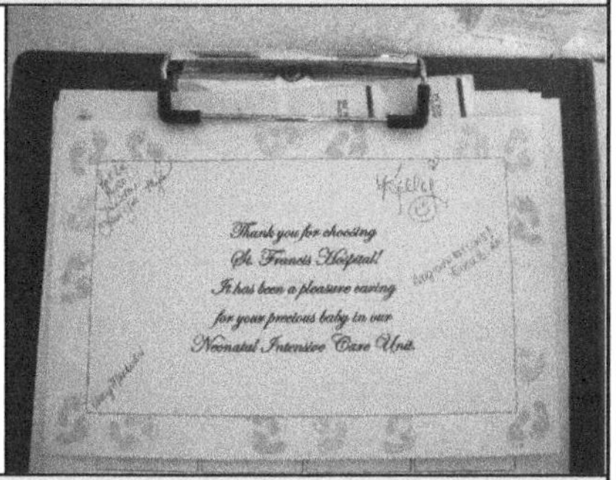
Effect		
Conveys our appreciation to the parents for the privilege of caring for their baby. Ensures all the nurses that cared for the baby are recognized as having contributed to the care. Consistent with our organizational value of compassionate concern. Improves patient and family satisfaction.		

Name	ID #	Dept #	Supervisor	Date
Kelly Butler RN, Juli Stenger RN, & Paula Stanfill RN		Neonatal ICU	Paula Stanfill	10/4/09

Figure 11.3 A Kaizen that shows how small gestures can make a big difference.

the babies' parents, and it helped to recognize each nurse who had a part in caring for the baby. Their Kaizen, documented in Figure 11.3, nicely demonstrates how a simple Kaizen can add meaningful and significant value to the customer experience.

Technique 2: Eliminate Waste

The national numbers for waste in healthcare are between 30% and 40%, but the reality of what we've observed doing minute-by-minute observation over the last three years is closer to 60%.[2]

—Cindy Jimmerson, RN
Author and consultant

Lean is a never-ending focus on reducing waste in the process. Waste can be identified only after one understands what adds value in a process. Waste can be defined as any activity or action that does not add value to the customer or that negatively impacts the value the customer receives. Waste can also be described as any motion, problem, or delay that interferes with the caregiver's ability to provide the safest, most timely, high-quality, caring patient care.

Franciscan taught the eight wastes in training sessions in which they played the "Toast Kaizen" video from GBMP. They then asked participants to identify the wastes they saw during the video and also identify wastes they see in their departments and their work processes. Using the eight types of waste to identify improvement ideas is an effective Kaizen exercise. Read through these types of waste, and then see if you can identify examples of these wastes in the workplace and Kaizens to reduce or eliminate that waste.

Waste 1: Transportation

Transportation includes patient, material, or information movement. It also includes conveying, transferring, picking up or setting down, piling up, and otherwise unnecessary movement, such as:

- Moving patients from location to location (or making them walk)
- Moving equipment to a patient location
- Moving a patient chart from its designated location

Waste 2: Overproduction

Overproduction includes producing more than what is really needed or producing faster (or earlier) than needed, including:

- Preparing labels or packets of documents "just in case"
- Delivering large batches of specimens to the lab faster than can be received
- Making up IV fluids after a patent has been changed to oral medicines
- Reports (lab, radiology, etc.) printed and/or mailed when not needed

Franciscan's CEO let the leadership team know that he would like the organization to move toward a paperless environment. The Kaizen Promotion Office (KPO) communicated the CEO's goal and shared numerous paperless Kaizen examples with all employees, with one being shown in Figure 11.4. In this Kaizen, the value of a paper report that was automatically generated daily

Daily Lab Summary Report Elimination Kaizen		🏛 **Franciscan** ST. FRANCIS HEALTH
Before		**After**
Every night a cumulative lab report for every inpatient would print on two different printers in the Beech Grove lab. An office assistant would assimilate these paper reports and then deliver them to each unit at Beech Grove. A courier would deliver them to the Indianapolis and Mooresville campuses. The unit secretary (or nurse) on every unit would file the reports into each patient's chart. Most of the lab result that were on the cumulative lab report were already available in the computer.		The printing and distribution of the cumulative lab report has ceased, except for those reports that are not available electronic. Those 'special reports' that are not available electronically will continue to be available in a paper version.
The Effect		
Financial – 96,000 pieces of paper a month X 12 month @ .05¢ = $57,600/year.		
Safety – There is a decrease risk that reports will be placed in the wrong chart (decreased risk that patient will be treated based on the incorrect filing of the report)		
Soft savings – Saves time for the lab office assistant. Saves time for the unit secretary on each nursing unit.		

Name	Supervisor	Date	Estimated Cost Savings (Optional)
Debra Orange, Debra Berner, Dr. Alan Gillespie, Lab Nursing Task Force		Effective July 9, 2007	$57,600/year

Figure 11.4   A Kaizen that illustrates how Lean and Green go together.

was questioned, and the report, and the paper consumed, was eliminated. In 2010, an accounting of the Kaizen Reports submitted that year showed that 604,330 fewer pages were being printed because of various Kaizens. The Franciscan KPO then reviewed printer paper supply ordering records across the three St. Francis hospitals and confirmed that number.

Waste 3: Motion

This waste includes any unnecessary movement of people or machines. One should not expect to have stationary workers, by any means, but organizations should improve systems and processes so the walking and motion is minimized. People should also be careful that minimizing walking does not lead to bigger problems, such as bigger batches or waiting times. Generally, time and motion saved can be reapplied into patient care activities, especially in nursing settings. Examples include:

- Searching for things: supplies, equipment, patient charts, records, other care team members, etc.
- Walking to get equipment and medications
- Walking across the room to answer phone
- Walking to get charts

For example, Mischelle Frank, manager of business transformation found a way to cut Kaizen four-part paper forms in half the time, as shown in Figure 11.5.

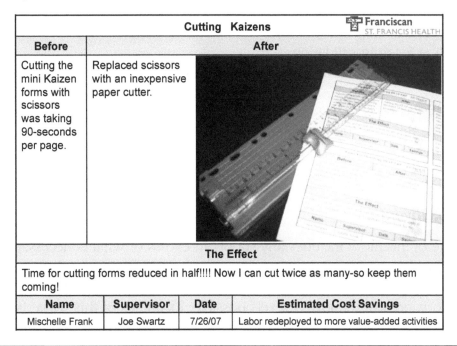

Figure 11.5 A Kaizen that shows a reduction in non-walking motion.

Waste 4: Defects (Errors and Rework)

This waste is related to errors, inspection, and rework, as well as handling and addressing customer complaints. While inspection is considered waste in the Lean framework, we cannot just eliminate inspection if we do not have a better way of error proofing the process to ensure quality. The waste of defects can include things like:

- Relearning due to poor training or lack of knowledge sharing
- Errors and harm to patients
- Missing information, such as orders not being completed before a procedure
- Complaints about service
- Errors or mistakes caused by incorrect information or miscommunication

We have included numerous Kaizen examples that prevent defects and errors later in this chapter.

Waste 5: Waiting

This waste includes idle time caused when people or equipment are waiting for one or the other. Waiting can, of course, affect patients, as well as staff members. Idle time, when it occurs, can be an opportunity to work on Kaizens. When we see waiting, we should improve the system to eliminate the root causes of the problems that cause the delays, such as:

- Waiting to be seen or waiting in hallways to be admitted
- Waiting for missing instruments to start a procedure
- Waiting for callbacks
- Waiting for drug validation
- Waiting for a patient to be properly positioned on a CT scanner table

Some staff waiting is necessary to optimize the overall system. If staff are busy 100% of the time, a clinic or department tends to have long patient waiting times. Sometimes, we need slack in the system to be able to accommodate patient needs, but too much waiting or idle time for staff is not a good thing, either.

Waste 6: Inventory

The waste of inventory includes any supply in excess of what is necessary to provide the right service and patient care. The lack of inventory often creates the waste of motion or the waste of waiting, so the key is to have the right amount of inventory, not just the lowest levels possible. Examples of this waste include:

- Stocks of printed forms
- Hidden and hoarded supplies and equipment

Less Medication Waste		Franciscan ST. FRANCIS HEALTH
Before	**After**	
Low usage meds expiring in pyxis. Sometimes max is #2 and pocket is filled with #10 that will most likely never be used.	Lower max amounts of low usage meds in pyxis to 2 or 3. let techs know not to overfill on meds unless they know it's a high usage med.	

The Effect
Hospital saves money with fewer meds in pyxis. Especially, low usage drugs.

Name	Supervisor	Date	Savings
Sherry Adams	Ronda Freije	5/4/07	

Figure 11.6   A Kaizen that shows a reduction in inventory waste.

- Outdated supplies and expired medicines or specimen collection tubes
- Unnecessary proliferation of different variants of items that cannot be medically justified, like different types of gloves and sutures

Figure 11.6 shows a Kaizen report that addressed medication expiration and waste in a unit.

Waste 7: Overprocessing

This waste can be described as effort that adds no value to the product or service, but is traditionally accepted as necessary, such as:

- Redundant capture of information upon admission
- Giving every patient with back pain a CT instead of first trying physical therapy
- Multiple recording and logging of data
- Producing paper hard copy when a computer file is sufficient
- Making hand copies of computer documents

In the Kaizen report shown in Figure 11.7, a nurse questioned whether pre-op beds needed the same number of linens as longer-stay beds. It turned out that having more than one cover sheet on a bed was unnecessary and wasteful.

Waste 8: Lost Human Potential, Creativity, and Opportunities

Usually referred to as the "eighth type of waste," because it does not appear in some Lean reference books, the waste of lost human potential is considered by many to be the greatest waste of all. Some examples include:

- Employees and staff not being engaged in process or quality improvement
- People consistently working below their education and skill level

Pre-op Bed	Franciscan ST. FRANCIS HEALTH
Before	**After**
Pre-op beds made with top sheet and bed spread. Had to be unmade when bed taken to OR.	Bed made without bed spread and top sheet ready for OR.

The Effect
Time saved making and unmaking the bed for housekeeping, decreased linen waste and cost.

Name	Supervisor	Date	Savings
Laura Sawyer	Jan Rubush	5/20/07	Linen

Figure 11.7 Making and unmaking a bed is a great example of the waste of overprocessing.

An example of working below one's skill level might include nurses cleaning patient rooms after discharge. In cases like this, people are forced to pitch in, or they choose to help as a team player. But not having enough support staff takes nurses away from important patient care duties, which can have an untold impact on patient outcomes and staff morale.

Seeing Waste through Process Observation

> *[Toyota's Taiichi] Ohno urged managers, too, to visit gemba. He would say, "Go to gemba every day. And when you go, don't wear out the soles of your shoes in vain. You should come back with at least one idea for kaizen."[3]*
>
> **—Masaaki Imai**

In order to eliminate waste, you first must see it. In a Lean culture, leaders at all levels spend a significant amount of time at the *gemba*, observing the process and coaching people on their improvements. Gary Kaplan, MD, the CEO of Virginia Mason Medical Center, practices this style of leadership. A national TV news report highlighted how "Kaplan tours the hospital daily, looking for problems and solutions. Everyone is encouraged to look for changes to make work more efficient."[4]

"Go See"

After one understands the value created by a process, one of the best ways to understand and improve the details of process is to go to the *"gemba."* The

Japanese word *gemba* means "actual place,"[5] or the place where work is being done. When there is a problem in a process, leaders need to:

- Go see the "actual site" or the location where the abnormality occurred.
- Go see the "actual thing" in person. Touch it and feel it, if possible.
- Go see the "actual phenomenon" that caused the abnormality.

Ray Seidelman, performance improvement manager at Iowa Health System, tells people he observes in the *gemba*, "I'm not checking to see if YOU are washing your hands, but we're here to honor your work." That builds trust quickly. Leaders build more trust by following those words with a sincere attempt to understand the work being done. When this is done well, people start asking "Hey, when are you going to observe me?" says Gail Nielsen, their director of learning and education.[6]

Spaghetti Diagrams

A "spaghetti diagram" is one method for observing and documenting transportation and motion waste in a process.[7] When tracing the walking pattern of, say a tech cleaning and prepping an operating room between cases, it might look like somebody threw a handful of cooked spaghetti on top of a layout drawing of the room. Studies indicate that nurses spend up to 20% of their time searching for and finding the supplies and equipment they need to perform their work.[8] This takes valuable time away from value-adding activities and patient care.

Christa Smiley, a nursing manager at Franciscan, and Kim Devine, a patient care coordinator, set out to find ways to reduce that time. They followed nurses around and documented their activities. Figure 11.8 contains a hand-drawn layout of the hospital floor that Christa manages. The lines in red trace the path a nurse takes to set up a patient on a patient controlled analgesia (PCA) pump.

You can see that a nurse must get numerous items from different locations. Christa and her team decided to consolidate all supply and equipment items to one location in one nearby storeroom. They cut the time to perform the PCA setup task in half.

Technique 3: Visual Workplace

Visual controls are mechanisms that give workers visual clues about how to perform their work effectively, efficiently, and without errors. They also give visual clues when something is abnormal. A key principle is to make the process visible and obvious to all, including managers and those who do not routinely do the work. Supplies, information, and equipment must be easy to see, easy to use, and easy to return to avoid waste.

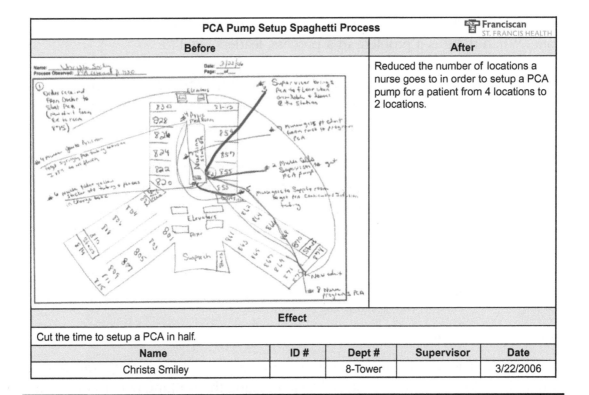

Figure 11.8   A Kaizen that incorporates a "spaghetti diagram."

In a visual workplace, we want to make the following visible and obvious:

■ Flow
■ Performance
■ Problems
■ Opportunities for improvement

In the pathology department at Northampton General Hospital, staff would often waste time by walking around to ask somebody if the track system was available to be loaded. A simple and inexpensive visual control was put in place that made that information available at a glance, as documented in Figure 11.9.

A team at Franciscan discovered that, when the paper chart for a room was opened and in use by a staff member, it was difficult for someone else to find that chart because there was not an indicator of the patient or room number on the chart. This caused the searcher to interrupt people to ask them which chart they were working on. So, the team added a sticker with the room number to the inside cover of the charts. With these two visual signals in place, patient chart search time dropped to less than one minute per chart on average, as pictured in Figure 11.10.

Case Study 1.7

Lean in the Lab: Visual Management

The problem:

The pathology blood science analyser spans a large area in the laboratory, with an automated track that goes around a corner. It requires daily calibration which takes place first thing in the morning and during the calibration the analyser is "off-line" and cannot be used.
It became clear during the lean implementation that staff found it difficult to see whether the analyser was being calibrated or whether it was ready for use. As a result staff spent time walking around the analyser asking people whether it was ready.

The Pathology pre-analytical area with the blood science analyser in the background

Actions taken:

A very cheap and simple visual solution was implemented – two cards were laminated back to back. One side was green with the words "track ready" on, and the other was red, saying "track unavailable." Two sets of cards were made, one for each end of the track, and the person who calibrates the track is responsible for ensuring the correct card is shown.

Results:

Staff can now see from any part of the laboratory whether the analyser is ready for use. This means they can continue with other work whilst the calibration is carried out, and there is no risk of putting blood tubes on the analyser while it is being calibrated. This is a really simple change, that has saved time, improved communication and cost virtually nothing!

Contact us:

If you would like more information on this, or other lean improvements at NGH please contact the lean team on: lean@ngh.nhs.uk.

1.11.2008

Figure 11.9 A Kaizen that illustrates good visual management.

Figure 11.10   Visual management for chart labels.

Figure 11.11   Color coded dots make it easier to assemble charts.

Color Coding

As pictured in Figure 11.11, Susie Thompson redesigned how she puts together information packets for surgeries. She created a color-coded system, where each color dot represents a packet, such as a red dot for endoscopy packets. When Susie makes a packet, she can easily pull the forms that correspond to the color of that type of packet. This change allowed her to create packets for the patient just prior to the patient's visit, rather than preparing packets in batches ahead of time, which cut down on the waste of overproduction.

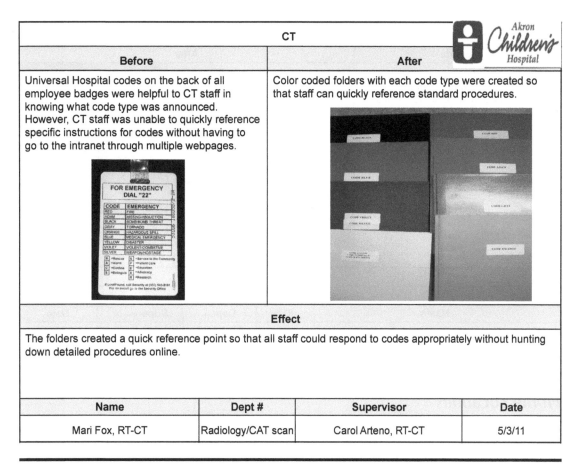

Figure 11.12   Color coding makes it easier to find the right standardized work.

In an example shared by Akron Children's Hospital, color-coded folders were created so CT department staff members could quickly find procedures for responding to different codes that were announced, as documented in Figure 11.12. This is also a perfect example of a Kaizen that can be shared and adopted by other departments.

At Franciscan, nursing supply rooms were not standardized, because each unit organized its supplies differently. They discovered that it was taking four times longer for transient nurses, such as temp nurses, float nurses, and student nurses to find supply items in a nursing unit than it did for nurses who were assigned to a particular unit. Furthermore, at the time of the study, 40% of nurses on the nursing floor being studied were transient nurses.

When the team decided to use color-coding to help nurses find supplies, coauthor Joe turned to Schelee Paddack, a nursing supervisor. Schelee came to classes with colored highlighters that she used to highlight the session workbook. Each color had a special meaning to her. Joe asked her to design with color codes that are so meaningful that a nurse just has to be told once, and they will remember it for life. She came up with the color-coding scheme that is pictured in Figure 11.13. For example, if a visiting nurse needs IV-related supplies, the nurse knows to look in the red section.

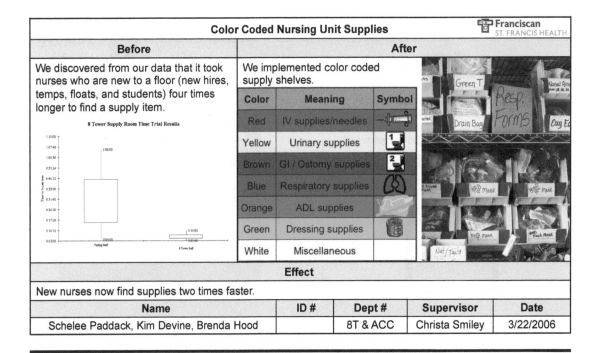

Figure 11.13 Color coded supplies.

Home Locations

Imagine how difficult it would be to have someone send mail or drive to a house if there was no fixed address. In the "Set in Order" phase of the 5S methodology, as described later in this chapter, a team determines where they should place those items that are necessary to the daily work, so they can have optimal efficiency. Then, those movable items are given "homes," where they belong when not being used.

Each item should be labeled with the workstation name or address, so the item will be easy to return if removed from the workstation. Physically mark where the item belongs in the workstation. This can be done by putting borders around the item's home, or putting a name label in its home, so it will be easy to see where it belongs. This is often called a "shadow board," because items look like they have a shadow around them. This has an added benefit in that it becomes easy to see when an item is missing from the workstation with a quick visual glance.

Figure 11.14 shows a Kaizen from Akron Children's Hospital and the establishment of a new, clearly marked home location for a portable suction machine.

Kitchen Example

What is the most organized drawer in a kitchen? For most, it is the silverware drawer, because most people have a silverware tray with compartments for each type of silverware—knives go into one compartment, forks in another, etc. As the expression says, "a place for everything, and everything in its place." What if we had a place for everything in our kitchen? Also, if we could ensure items

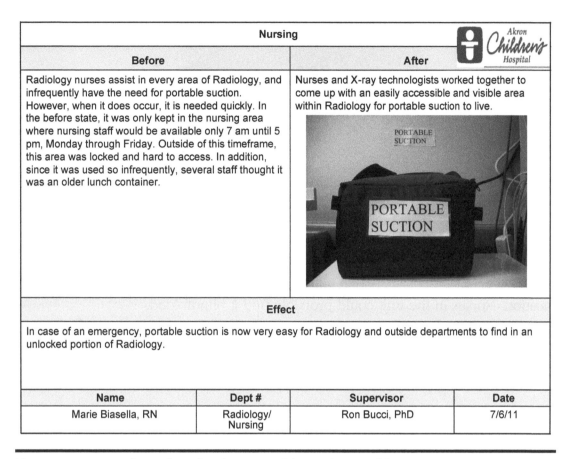

| Nursing | | | | Akron Children's Hospital |

Before	After
Radiology nurses assist in every area of Radiology, and infrequently have the need for portable suction. However, when it does occur, it is needed quickly. In the before state, it was only kept in the nursing area where nursing staff would be available only 7 am until 5 pm, Monday through Friday. Outside of this timeframe, this area was locked and hard to access. In addition, since it was used so infrequently, several staff thought it was an older lunch container.	Nurses and X-ray technologists worked together to come up with an easily accessible and visible area within Radiology for portable suction to live.

Effect
In case of an emergency, portable suction is now very easy for Radiology and outside departments to find in an unlocked portion of Radiology.

Name	Dept #	Supervisor	Date
Marie Biasella, RN	Radiology/ Nursing	Ron Bucci, PhD	7/6/11

Figure 11.14   New home location for a portable suction machine.

were returned to their designated place consistently, then they would be easy to find the next time we needed them.

Borders

Borders act like lines in a parking lot. When there are no lines, such as during a snowstorm, it becomes difficult to decide where to park. Parking becomes chaotic, as people decide to park wherever they please, resulting in less space available for everyone. Lines give people visual clues where they should park, optimizing the use of space, resulting in more available space.

In the adult critical care unit at Franciscan, nurses were searching up and down the hallways for equipment and supply carts. The hallways had become so cluttered that, when a nurse returned a cart, a wheelchair, or other large item, they just placed it in the first open space. The result was that items were moved after each use and were rarely in the same location. Then, when the next nurse needed to find the item, they had to search up and down the hallways, resulting in a considerable amount of wasted time.

They decided to give each item a home with borders, so that each item would be returned to a specified location after each use. Now nurses know where items should be each and every time and can go directly to it. For example, the

Figure 11.15 Home location for the isolation gowns cart.

cart shown in Figure 11.15 containing isolation gowns is now always in its home location. Nurses in the unit could probably find it blindfolded.

When carpeting exists, it is often not practical to use tape outlines. Some options for borders include replacing the area underneath the movable item with carpeting of a different color or pattern underneath an item. Or, you can place borders and labeling along walls so that they are visible when the item is missing.

Technique 4: 5S—Workplace Organization

5S is a method for creating a work environment that is clean, organized, and efficient. As part of the visual management approach, it helps make problems visible. The items you need to use regularly are visible, within easy reach, and always available, reducing frustration and creating a more joyful place to work. 5S can be applied at work or at home to benefit anyone that does any sort of work. For more information, refer to the books *Lean Hospitals*[9] and *Clinical 5S for Healthcare*.[10]

The 5S's

1. **Sort:** Sort through and sort out.
2. **Set in Order:** A place for everything, and everything in its place.
3. **Shine:** Cleanliness is next to godliness.
4. **Standardize:** Simply systematize and standardize
5. **Sustain:** Engage everyone in self-discipline.

S1: Sort

Items that are necessary to the work are separated from the items that are unnecessary, with the unnecessary items being removed from the workspace. The result is a workspace that is less cluttered and contains only those items that are used on a regular basis.

Organized Supplies for Babies			Franciscan ST. FRANCIS HEALTH
Before		**After**	
Before, we had messy countertops, which appeared cluttered and unprofessional.		Now we keep individual items for infants in an isolette. This keeps everything clean and contained.	
The Effect			
This promotes a clean environment. This keeps infant's supplies together in an orderly fashion making time management more efficient.			
Name	**Supervisor**	**Date**	**Benefit**
Anita Stevens, RNC	Paula Stanfill	3-10-08	Saves time.

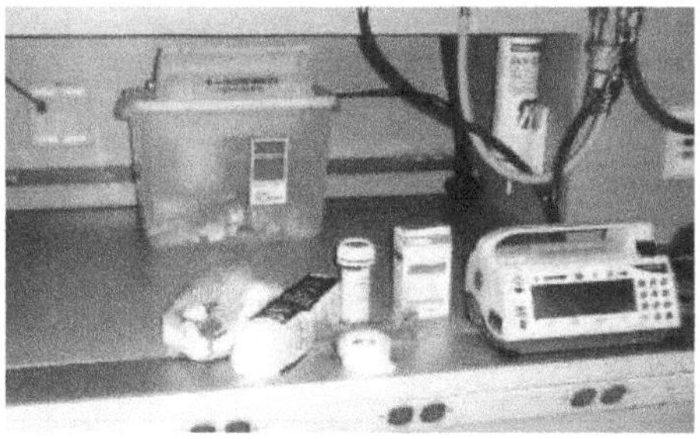

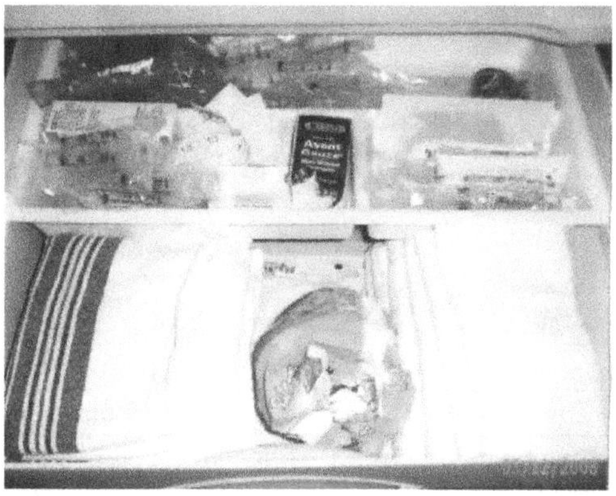

Figure 11.16   Better organization means better cleanliness and more efficient work.

5S reduces clutter in the workplace, reduces waste, and improves effectiveness, as the example in Figure 11.16 illustrates.

S2: Set in Order

Next, a team finds an appropriate place in the workspace for those items that are used frequently. Rather than just straightening things up, staff members help organize things so the most frequently or urgently used items are right at hand. Items that are used less often or less urgently can be stored further away in department or hospital storage areas. Once they have determined the best locations for items, home locations and other visual management practices can be utilized to keep things organized.

Keep frequently used items close to their point of use. For example, if there is a printer that does not automatically staple, then keep a stapler near that printer. This will make it easier to staple items together and cut down on the waste of motion. 5S also can be applied to mobile workstations, as shown in Figure 11.17.

In the laboratory at St. Elisabeth Hospital (Tilburg, The Netherlands), team members organized a drawer to remove unneeded items. They placed the remaining items in spaces cut out of a foam pad, making it more obvious what needed restocking (or what was missing) and keeping items from sliding around, as documented in Figure 11.18.

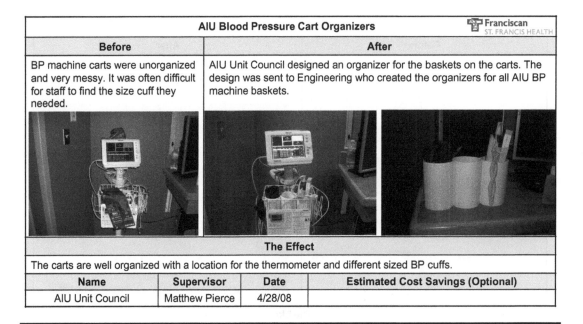

AIU Blood Pressure Cart Organizers			Franciscan ST. FRANCIS HEALTH
Before	**After**		
BP machine carts were unorganized and very messy. It was often difficult for staff to find the size cuff they needed.	AIU Unit Council designed an organizer for the baskets on the carts. The design was sent to Engineering who created the organizers for all AIU BP machine baskets.		
The Effect			
The carts are well organized with a location for the thermometer and different sized BP cuffs.			
Name	**Supervisor**	**Date**	**Estimated Cost Savings (Optional)**
AIU Unit Council	Matthew Pierce	4/28/08	

Figure 11.17   5S practices make it easier to find the right cuff.

S3: Shine

The objective in the Shine phase is to not only clean the workplace, but also to make it easy to keep it clean. After sorting out items that are not needed, an emptied-out room can be given a deep cleaning before items are organized and stored in that space.

Many teams sweep through the process at the end or beginning of work shifts, which means to walk through, put things away, and quickly clean so everything is back in order for the next shift.

Amy Macke, a nurse in Franciscan's NICU, noticed that supplies were not conveniently close by to clean the breast pumps, so she attached baskets to the pumps and filled them with cleaning supplies. Now it is convenient and easy to keep the breast pumps clean, as shown in Figure 11.19

S4: Standardize

Here, the team establishes visual controls and other methods for standardizing the organization of the workplace.

Figure 11.20 is an example of a closet at Franciscan that went from rarely used space to valuable space that was used every day. The closet was across the hall from patient rooms and was an ideal space to make more useful to everyday nursing practice. This example shows how visual borders were used to designate what belongs in the workspace. The wheelchairs now have a home where they belong when not in use.

Figure 11.18   5S applied to a drawer in The Netherlands.

S5: Sustain

Sustaining improvements requires self-discipline from all who work in the space. It typically includes an ongoing audit and feedback system that is conducted by supervisors and more senior managers, along with a system to respond to feedback about practices that are not being sustained. As with any standardized practices, changes made through 5S are improved upon over time, rather than being static.

In summary, having an organized workspace through 5S and visual management can improve patient care and create a less frustrating workplace. It can also save lots of money, as illustrated in Figure 11.21.

Breast Pump Cleaning		Franciscan ST. FRANCIS HEALTH
Before	**After**	
Breast pumps didn't have cleaning supplies close by.	Attached basket to breast pumps and filled with cleaning supplies. Instructions were placed on the front of the pump in a simple laminated form.	

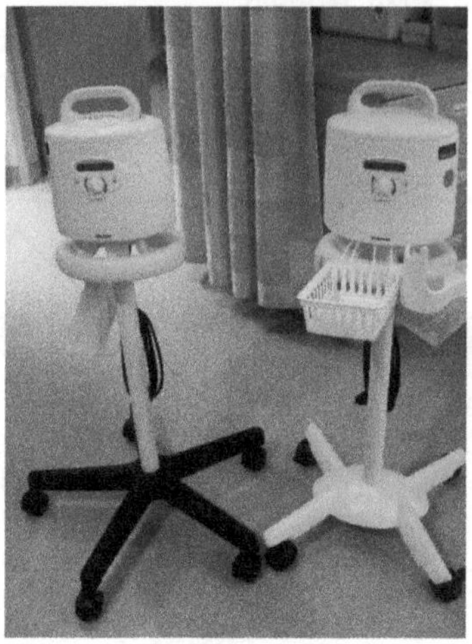

Effect
Infection Control improvement with breast pump cleaning.

Name	ID #	Dept #	Supervisor	Date
Amy Macke RN, IBCLC		NICU	Paula Stanfill	5/27/10

Figure 11.19   Keeping needed supplies close to the pumps makes cleaning easier.

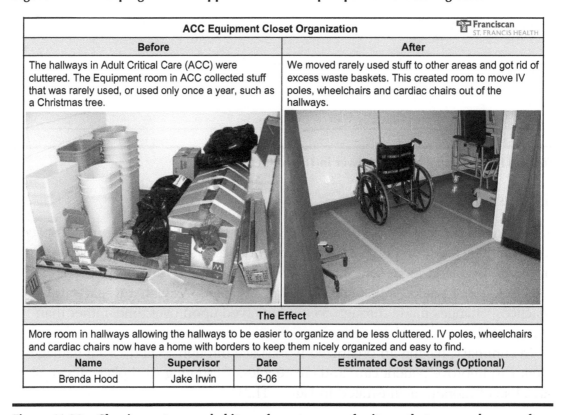

ACC Equipment Closet Organization		Franciscan ST. FRANCIS HEALTH
Before	**After**	
The hallways in Adult Critical Care (ACC) were cluttered. The Equipment room in ACC collected stuff that was rarely used, or used only once a year, such as a Christmas tree.	We moved rarely used stuff to other areas and got rid of excess waste baskets. This created room to move IV poles, wheelchairs and cardiac chairs out of the hallways.	

The Effect
More room in hallways allowing the hallways to be easier to organize and be less cluttered. IV poles, wheelchairs and cardiac chairs now have a home with borders to keep them nicely organized and easy to find.

Name	Supervisor	Date	Estimated Cost Savings (Optional)
Brenda Hood	Jake Irwin	6-06	

Figure 11.20   Clearing out unneeded items frees up space for items that are used more often.

Improved Bed Inventory Management		Franciscan ST. FRANCIS HEALTH
Before	**After**	

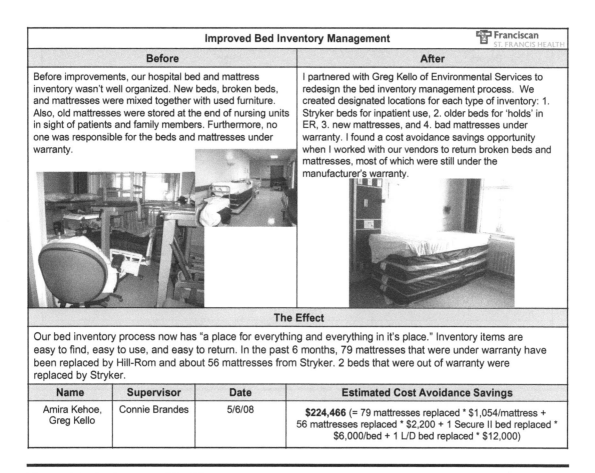

Before improvements, our hospital bed and mattress inventory wasn't well organized. New beds, broken beds, and mattresses were mixed together with used furniture. Also, old mattresses were stored at the end of nursing units in sight of patients and family members. Furthermore, no one was responsible for the beds and mattresses under warranty.

I partnered with Greg Kello of Environmental Services to redesign the bed inventory management process. We created designated locations for each type of inventory: 1. Stryker beds for inpatient use, 2. older beds for 'holds' in ER, 3. new mattresses, and 4. bad mattresses under warranty. I found a cost avoidance savings opportunity when I worked with our vendors to return broken beds and mattresses, most of which were still under the manufacturer's warranty.

The Effect

Our bed inventory process now has "a place for everything and everything in it's place." Inventory items are easy to find, easy to use, and easy to return. In the past 6 months, 79 mattresses that were under warranty have been replaced by Hill-Rom and about 56 mattresses from Stryker. 2 beds that were out of warranty were replaced by Stryker.

Name	Supervisor	Date	Estimated Cost Avoidance Savings
Amira Kehoe, Greg Kello	Connie Brandes	5/6/08	**$224,466** (= 79 mattresses replaced * $1,054/mattress + 56 mattresses replaced * $2,200 + 1 Secure II bed replaced * $6,000/bed + 1 L/D bed replaced * $12,000)

Figure 11.21 Improved bed inventory management.

Technique 5: Workstation Design

Good workstation design is useful for eliminating wasteful motion and preventing ergonomic problems. Years ago, workstation design used to be the exclusive domain of the industrial engineering profession. However, the power of Lean is in teaching everyone basic principles and then empowering them to design their own workspaces. The workstation should be designed with the considerations shown in Figure 11.22.

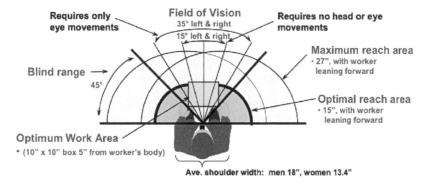

Figure 11.22 Principles of good work station design.

Making The Move Easier			Franciscan ST. FRANCIS HEALTH
Before	**After**		
Moving infectious material to the proper storage area is hard on the back. Pushing the cart while bending is a strain. Environmental Service staff tired at the end of the shift.	Ergonomically correct cart. All materials were scrap. With the help from the maintenance department, Mike was able to have a handle added to the cart. 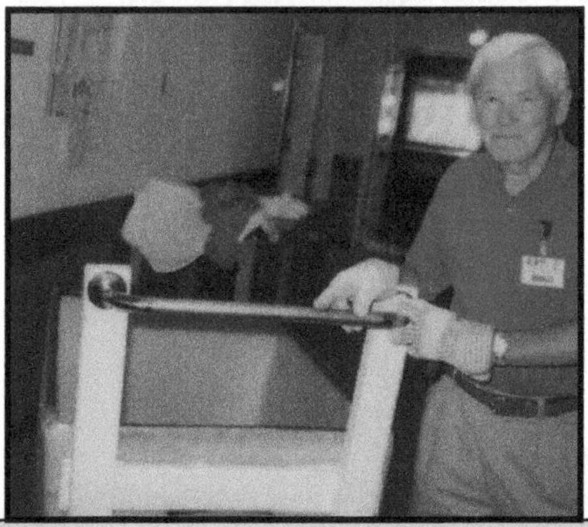		
The Effect			
Staff is less tired at the end of the shift because he can stand upright while pushing the cart.			
Name	**Supervisor**	**Date**	**Estimated Cost Savings (Optional)**
Mike Owens	Leroy Gedek	7-6-07	

Figure 11.23   A Kaizen initiated and implemented by a housekeeping staff member.

Figure 11.23 shows an example of a cart that was modified with help from the maintenance department to place a push handle at an ergonomically correct height so the environmental services personnel could push the cart without bending over, alleviating a strain on their back.

Figure 11.24, shows the use of a reach assist device to overcome a situation where staff had to reach beyond an ideal ergonomic zone. Although it would be better to store the shirts and shorts at a lower height, the unit is making the best use of limited space, and the shirts and shorts are not accessed very often.

Technique 6: Problem Solving

In Kaizen organizations, employees are eager to expose problems since they have supportive leaders who agree these problems represent opportunities to make things better. Problem solving can be like peeling away the layers of an onion. Once you begin investigating a problem, you will learn things that lead you to peel back more layers, until you get to the root cause of the problem.

Problems cannot be solved if they remain hidden. When problems reoccur, they repeatedly consume people's time and effort—and patients can be harmed. As problems reoccur, more time is consumed dealing with problems, which leaves less time for proactively improving the system. It becomes a vicious

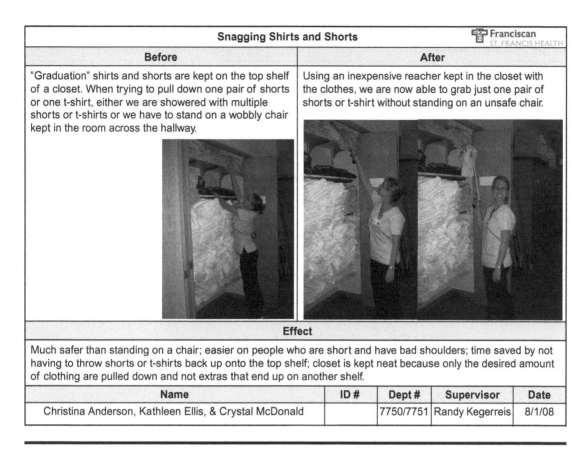

Snagging Shirts and Shorts		Franciscan ST. FRANCIS HEALTH

Before	After
"Graduation" shirts and shorts are kept on the top shelf of a closet. When trying to pull down one pair of shorts or one t-shirt, either we are showered with multiple shorts or t-shirts or we have to stand on a wobbly chair kept in the room across the hallway.	Using an inexpensive reacher kept in the closet with the clothes, we are now able to grab just one pair of shorts or t-shirt without standing on an unsafe chair.

Effect
Much safer than standing on a chair; easier on people who are short and have bad shoulders; time saved by not having to throw shorts or t-shirts back up onto the top shelf; closet is kept neat because only the desired amount of clothing are pulled down and not extras that end up on another shelf.

Name	ID #	Dept #	Supervisor	Date
Christina Anderson, Kathleen Ellis, & Crystal McDonald		7750/7751	Randy Kegerreis	8/1/08

Figure 11.24 Improved 5S can reduce strain and risk of injury.

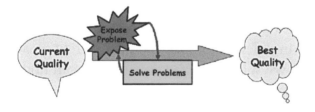

Figure 11.25 Improving quality requires people to expose and solve problems.

reinforcing cycle. As Figure 11.25 illustrates, the way to move from current quality to best quality is to expose problems and solve those problems.

A3 Problem-Solving Technique

One framework that has been adopted by a growing number of healthcare organizations worldwide is the A3. A3s can be used for planning, problem solving, or reporting. The A3 problem-solving technique is named as such because everything is recorded on an A3 size paper (an international size of paper that is very close to 11"×17"). Cindy Jimmerson's book *A3 Problem Solving for Healthcare: A Practical Method for Eliminating Waste* is a good resource on this topic. Also refer back to Figures 7.12a and 7.12b for an example.

Table 11.1   The Relationship between A3 Problem Solving, Kaizen, PDSA, and DMAIC to the Scientific Model

Scientific Method	PDSA	A3 Problem Solving	Kaizen	DMAIC
Make observations	Plan	Define current condition	Find	Define
Gather information		Root cause analysis	Discuss	Measure
Form hypothesis		Develop target condition		Analyze
Perform experiment to test hypothesis	Do	Implement countermeasures	Implement	Improve
Analyze data	Study	Follow-up	Document	Control
Draw conclusions and summarize	Adjust	Future actions and A3 reporting	Share	

A3 problem solving and Kaizen thinking are based on the scientific method, as are Plan-Do-Study-Act (PDSA) and Six Sigma's Define, Measure, Analyze, Improve, Control (DMAIC) model. Table 11.1 shows how the steps are related to the scientific method.

Figure 11.26 is an illustration of a classic Lean problem-solving thought process that is modeled in an A3. Starting with a big vague problem, we then work to grasp the situation and properly define the problem by visiting the *gemba* and seeing the "point of cause" (where the problem occurred). After finding the root cause, countermeasures are employed to improve the situation as part of the PDSA cycle.

A blank A3 problem-solving template that shows the major steps in the process is shown in Figure 11.27 and can be downloaded at www.HCkaizen.com. Additional A3 forms in different formats can also be downloaded from the Lean Enterprise Website at www.lean.org/a3dojo, and you can find a link to their electronic templates at www.HCKaizen.com.

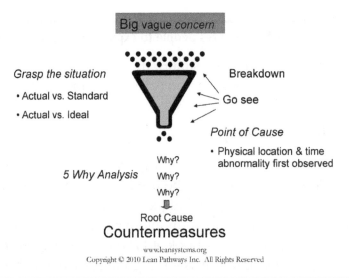

Figure 11.26   A high-level problem solving process (used with permission of Lean Pathways, Inc.).

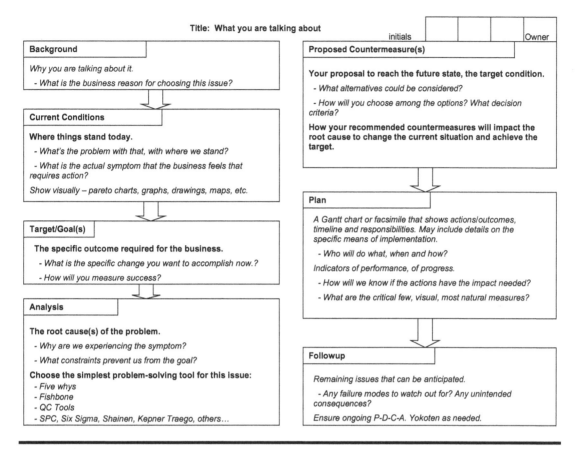

Figure 11.27 A3 problem-solving template (download at www.HCkaizen.com, used with permission of Lean Enterprise Institute).

Problem-Solving Methods Used with A3

There are a number of methods that are useful whether doing an A3 or any Kaizen improvements.

Find the Point of the Cause

During problem investigation, you are looking for clues that paint a picture of what might have happened. The "Point of Cause" is the specific cause of the problem. It answers what specifically happened to cause the error.

> *I keep six honest serving men. They taught me all I knew. Their names are What and Why and When and How and Where and Who.*
>
> **—Rudyard Kipling (1865–1936)**
> *English Nobel Prize–winning writer*

One simple point of cause identification technique is to identify the: who, what, where, when, why and how (5W1H). To use this technique, identify:

■ Who found the problem?
■ What was the problem?

- Where was it discovered?
- When was it discovered?
- Why did it occur?
- How did it occur (list out the sequence of steps that took place)?

Some organizations, including ThedaCare, add the question of "what are the consequences" of the problem to help set context.

For example, at Franciscan, a patient safety problem was discovered when a patient was found in the ER looking for a restroom. An alert employee noticed the patient was wearing a fall risk wristband and an inpatient wristband, as shown in Figure 11.28. The patient was mildly confused and had wandered into the ER.

- Who: ER employee discovered problem.
- What: A patient with a fall risk wristband was walking around without assistance.
- Where: The ER.
- When: 1:00 p.m. on a Friday.
- Why: Patient wandered from the inpatient unit to the ER looking for a bathroom.
- How: The patient was allowed to walk out of the unit, and security allowed the patient into the ER without noticing the fall risk armband.

The consequences, of course, were that the patient could have fallen and gotten injured.

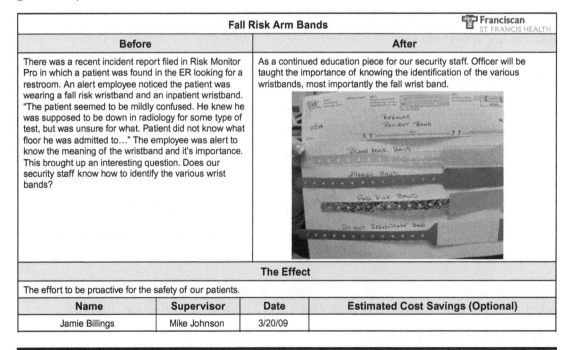

Fall Risk Arm Bands		Franciscan ST. FRANCIS HEALTH
Before	**After**	
There was a recent incident report filed in Risk Monitor Pro in which a patient was found in the ER looking for a restroom. An alert employee noticed the patient was wearing a fall risk wristband and an inpatient wristband. "The patient seemed to be mildly confused. He knew he was supposed to be down in radiology for some type of test, but was unsure for what. Patient did not know what floor he was admitted to…" The employee was alert to know the meaning of the wristband and it's importance. This brought up an interesting question. Does our security staff know how to identify the various wrist bands?	As a continued education piece for our security staff. Officer will be taught the importance of knowing the identification of the various wristbands, most importantly the fall wrist band.	
The Effect		
The effort to be proactive for the safety of our patients.		

Name	Supervisor	Date	Estimated Cost Savings (Optional)
Jamie Billings	Mike Johnson	3/20/09	

Figure 11.28 A Kaizen that incorporated the 5W's and an H.

One contributing cause to this incident was that ER security officers were not previously required to check for wristbands. Because of this, Franciscan ER security officers began checking all people entering the ER for wristbands. Awareness was increased, and an improvement was made to the process, rather than just blaming an individual.

Simple problems can often be resolved fairly quickly, but difficult problems often take considerable discussion, investigation, and problem solving to resolve. Later in this chapter, we will discuss problem-solving techniques for the more difficult problems that ensure we get to the root cause of problems, such as "how and why did the patient get out of their unit?"

Identify the Root Cause

In an effective root cause investigation, you are looking for the cause of the causes. There might be one root cause, or there might be more. For complex problems, you may need to identify each of the multiple contributors and then find the root cause of each of the contributors to the total problem. If a problem is really big, then the contributors may need to be prioritized, with the top priority contributor root causes being found first.

For example, in cases where children are mistakenly given adult doses of heparin, which causes harm or can lead to death, the "point of cause" might be the nurse administering the wrong medication. Punishing the nurse would miss the root causes of such a catastrophe.

Benjamin Franklin's Root Cause Analysis:

For want of a nail a shoe was lost,
for want of a shoe a horse was lost,
for want of a horse a rider was lost,
for want of a rider an army was lost,
for want of an army a battle was lost,
for want of a battle the war was lost,
for want of the war the kingdom was lost,
and all for the want of a little horseshoe nail.

The "five whys" is one Lean method to encourage the identification of root causes. Rather than stopping at the first cause that is identified, the five whys approach challenges people to think deeper.

How is this approach used?

- Ask "why" the problem occurred when and where it occurred. Record the reason.
- Ask "why" the event identified in the above step occurred.

■ Continue until you have identified the root cause of the problem or abnormality. The number five is not a hard rule. Sometimes the root cause is discovered in less than five whys, and other times it may take more than five whys.

In the case of a Heparin overdose, we could ask the following five whys:

■ Why was the child harmed?
  – Because he was given Heparin instead of Hep-lock.
■ Why?
  – Because the nurse took Heparin out of the drawer in the NICU.
■ Why?
  – Because Heparin was mistakenly delivered to the NICU.
■ Why?
  – Neither the pharmacist nor the pharmacy tech noticed during their check, that it was the wrong medication.
■ Why?
  – The system relied on visual inspection at multiple points, and this is not a 100% reliable method.

A five whys analysis helps one see that errors are often more systemic in nature than blaming the person at the point of cause, in this case, the nurse. There are multiple examples of poor processes and systems in the above example.

Where there are multiple contributing factors to a problem, a "fishbone diagram" (also known as an Ishikawa diagram) can be helpful in brainstorming and listing multiple causes, then using the five whys to drill deeper into one of those causes. A fishbone diagram is shown in Figure 11.29. There might be multiple root causes as people investigate questions such as "why are orthopedic implant costs too high?"

Technique 7: Error Proofing

Error proofing, also called mistake proofing, is a Lean mindset and technique that creates devices or processes to detect and prevent errors from occurring in a process, coming from the Japanese term *poka yoke*.[11] Recalling Dr. Deming's teaching that 94% of the problems are due to the system, Lean thinkers are proactive in trying to design systems where it is difficult or impossible for smart, educated, and caring people to have a slip and make an error. Also Lean Thinkers are finding ways to keep errors from becoming defects that harm patients.

An excellent resource on error proofing in healthcare is: *Mistake-Proofing the Design of Health Care Processes*,[12] by John Grout, Ph.D. It was funded by the Agency for Healthcare Research and Quality (AHRQ) and is available for free on the Internet at www.mistakeproofing.com.

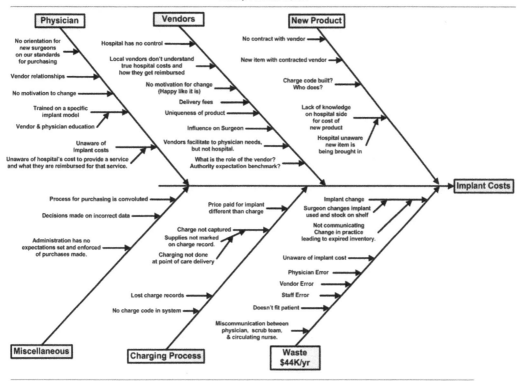

Figure 11.29   Example of a "fishbone diagram."

A simple example of error proofing, combined with 5S and color coding, is Figure 11.30, an example from Akron Children's Hospital. The potential error in the process, before the Kaizen, was that clean items would be unnecessarily thrown away. The color coding does not absolutely prevent an error, but it makes it easier for staff to keep things straight.

> *If you pit a good performer against a bad system, the system will win almost every time. We spend too much time fixing people who are not broken and not enough time fixing organizational systems that are broken. Only leadership has the power and responsibility to change the systems.*

> **—W. Edwards Deming, Ph.D.**

Virginia Mason Medical Center and its "patient safety alert" system is an example of an error proofing process, where clinicians and staff can report any perceived threat to a patient.[13] This approach is modeled after Lean factories, where supervisors scurry to respond to even the smallest of workplace problems when a worker pulls an overhead "andon cord," which signals the need for help. When a problem occurs, the focus is on identifying how to prevent that problem in the future, whether it is a dropped bolt or a medication near miss, instead of blaming individuals.

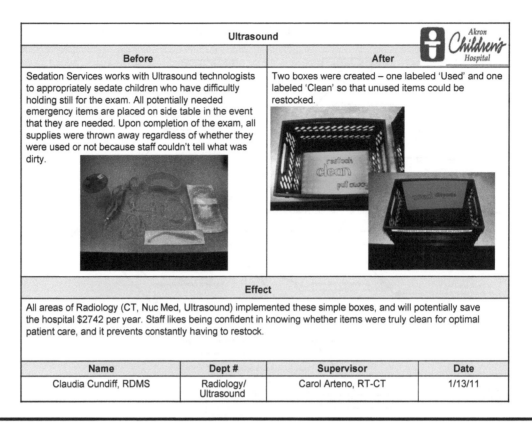

Ultrasound		Akron Children's Hospital
Before	**After**	
Sedation Services works with Ultrasound technologists to appropriately sedate children who have difficultly holding still for the exam. All potentially needed emergency items are placed on side table in the event that they are needed. Upon completion of the exam, all supplies were thrown away regardless of whether they were used or not because staff couldn't tell what was dirty.	Two boxes were created – one labeled 'Used' and one labeled 'Clean' so that unused items could be restocked.	
Effect		
All areas of Radiology (CT, Nuc Med, Ultrasound) implemented these simple boxes, and will potentially save the hospital $2742 per year. Staff likes being confident in knowing whether items were truly clean for optimal patient care, and it prevents constantly having to restock.		

Name	Dept #	Supervisor	Date
Claudia Cundiff, RDMS	Radiology/ Ultrasound	Carol Arteno, RT-CT	1/13/11

Figure 11.30 A simple example of error proofing, combined with 5S and color coding.

Fatal and Preventable Healthcare Errors

In September of 2006, six babies at Methodist Hospital in Indianapolis, Indiana received an overdose of Heparin.[14] They were mistakenly given an adult dosage of Heparin instead of Hep-Lock, receiving 1,000 times the intended dosage. Three of those babies died.

The news made national headlines. The community wanted to know how this could have happened. After an investigation, it was determined that a pharmacy tech with 25 years experience inadvertently placed Heparin in the place where Hep-Lock should have been. At the time, the bottles of each looked almost identical, except for the slightly different shades of blue and the color of the cap, as pictured in Figure 11.31. It was especially easy to make this mistake

Figure 11.31 Two vials that are too easily mistaken in a hospital, leading to patient deaths.

in a darkened room. The two different bottles really looked similar if the grey or green top cap had been removed from the bottles.

Five different nurses each pulled what they thought was Hep-Lock from the shelves, mistakenly administering Heparin to patients. Those nurses had been taught a safeguard check called the "five rights of patient medications," which are:

1. Right patient
2. Right medicine
3. Right dose
4. Right route (i.e., administered through the blood or orally)
5. Right time

During, those times, however, the nurses did not adequately perform the five rights check. For the families of the babies, it was a horrible loss. For the nurses and pharmacy technician, it was their worst nightmare coming true, and they were devastated. Methodist is a neighboring hospital to Franciscan, and some Franciscan nurses knew those nurses at Methodist. Some of the Franciscan staff knew the parents who had lost babies. For the Franciscan staff, it was not just a news story, it was almost as if it had happened to them. Franciscan realized that an error like this could happen to the best, the most careful of us, given the right conditions, as it has happened again at other hospitals.

There were multiple contributing factors to these errors. The fact that five different nurses all made the same error speaks to the systemic nature of the problem. One contributing factor was that the adult dose Heparin was not even supposed to be stocked in the NICU. A series of errors had led to Heparin being delivered from the pharmacy. So, while nurses are always supposed to check medication labels, this case shows how it is difficult to inspect for a problem that is unlikely to occur.

Most incident investigations reveal the same issues. The first major concept is that incidents are the result of a number of multiple small failures that all have to occur together for an accident to occur. James Reason's model[15] of accident causation demonstrated that accidents occur when the errors pass through holes in the organizational defenses. This is also called the "Swiss Cheese Model." Steven H. Woolf added "cascades" or the "chain of events" to the accident model.[16] One condition creates another condition. In the Heparin accident, placing the meds in the wrong stocking location created the condition that the wrong med would be picked up by the nurse.

After the accidents, Methodist put processes in place to double-check labels both in pharmacy and in the nursing unit, and they also eliminated stocking vials with 10,000 units of Heparin.[17] Arguably, eliminating the stock of Heparin vials was a more effective countermeasure than asking nurses to be careful at all times. At Franciscan, the entire organization reexamined every process connected with Heparin and other similar drugs, as well as installing bar coding double check systems throughout the system's hospitals. Now, when medications are administered, staff scan the patient's armband, then the medication, then the nurse's badge, and the computer checks to make sure this medication was prescribed for this patient at this time in this dose with this route, and this nurse is authorized to give this medication to this patient. All of these forms of error proofing help prevent errors.

> *It had dawned on me that the occurrence of a defect was the result of some condition or action, and that it would be possible to eliminate defects entirely by pursuing the cause.*
>
> **—Shigeo Shingo**
> *Japanese industrial engineer and inventor of mistake proofing*

Four Elements of a Zero Defect Quality System

Shigeo Shingo taught that there are four key elements that lead to the elimination of errors and defects.[18]

Element 1: Self-Check and Successive Check

In a system that uses self-check and successive check, each person inspects the quality of their own work and checks the quality of the work of the people in the prior step of the process. A good example of this is surgery timeouts. In surgery timeouts, immediately prior to the start of each procedure the operative team conducts a final verification of the correct patient, correct procedure, correct side and site, correct patient position, correct implants, and other important items.

Element 2: Immediate Feedback and Corrective Action

In a system that uses immediate feedback and corrective action, processes are stopped instantly when an error is detected, and immediate corrective action is initiated, and the process is not restarted until corrected. If an error is found, Lean principles drive us to stop and look for the root cause rather than just fixing the error and moving on.

A Code Blue patient resuscitation procedure is an example of immediate feedback and corrective action. In the Kaizen in Figure 11.32 Franciscan staff error proofed the carts they use for Code Blues.

Element 3: Source Inspection

The proper error-proofing attitude is to recognize that errors are natural for humans. Then, recognize that errors can be eliminated—but by improving the system instead of insisting that people be careful. One of the ways to make the

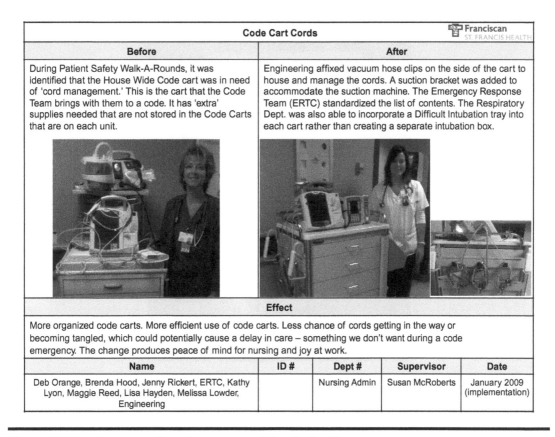

Code Cart Cords		Franciscan ST. FRANCIS HEALTH
Before	**After**	
During Patient Safety Walk-A-Rounds, it was identified that the House Wide Code cart was in need of 'cord management.' This is the cart that the Code Team brings with them to a code. It has 'extra' supplies needed that are not stored in the Code Carts that are on each unit.	Engineering affixed vacuum hose clips on the side of the cart to house and manage the cords. A suction bracket was added to accommodate the suction machine. The Emergency Response Team (ERTC) standardized the list of contents. The Respiratory Dept. was also able to incorporate a Difficult Intubation tray into each cart rather than creating a separate intubation box.	

Effect				
More organized code carts. More efficient use of code carts. Less chance of cords getting in the way or becoming tangled, which could potentially cause a delay in care – something we don't want during a code emergency. The change produces peace of mind for nursing and joy at work.				

Name	ID #	Dept #	Supervisor	Date
Deb Orange, Brenda Hood, Jenny Rickert, ERTC, Kathy Lyon, Maggie Reed, Lisa Hayden, Melissa Lowder, Engineering		Nursing Admin	Susan McRoberts	January 2009 (implementation)

Figure 11.32   Error proofing the carts used for Code Blues.

system better for humans is through source inspection by identifying "red flag" conditions in the process and environment that make errors more likely and eliminating their effects. Shingo recommended that more than half of the error proofing effort be focused on source inspection.

> *Human error is inevitable. We can never eliminate it. We can eliminate problems in the system that make it more likely to happen.*
>
> **—Sir Liam Donaldson**
> *World Health Organization, World Health Alliance for Patient Safety*

Figure 11.33, shows two medications, metoclopramide and methylprednisolone. Would you be able to pick the right one a thousand times in a row? At Franciscan, they taught error proofing techniques to pharmacy personnel. Numerous Kaizens were turned in that error proofed the pharmacy process. In this case, the two medicines with sound alike names were physically separated in order to reduce the potential for errors.

The Broselow/Hinkle™ Pediatric Emergency System is an error-proofing system used at Franciscan and many other hospitals around the world. It is a good example of aiding and guiding humans to reduce red flag error conditions. The system is designed for reviving children and includes all the supplies

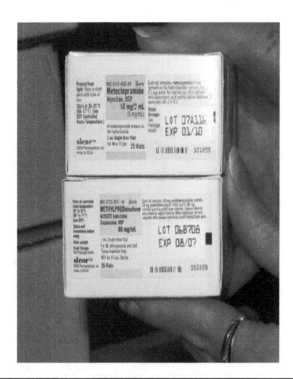

Figure 11.33   Would you be able to always choose the correct medication?

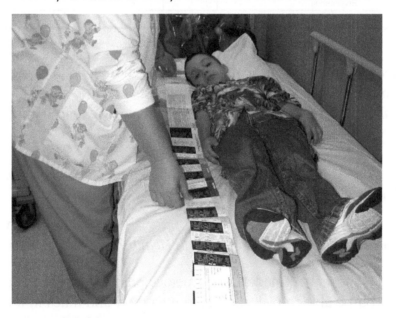

Figure 11.34   A child being measured by the Broselow/Hinkle™ Pediatric Emergency System for error proofing care.

and medicines required to resuscitate a baby or a child from 3 to 36 kilograms. The healthcare provider uses a special color-coded measuring tape to measure the length of a child, as shown in Figure 11.34. There are seven colors, and the color range that is associated with that child's length is used to select a color of drawer, or color of bag, as pictured in Figure 11.35. All the instruments and drugs in that color are right sized for the child based on the child's length.

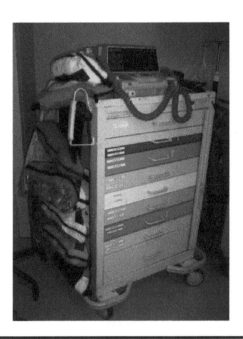

Figure 11.35   A color coded cart used in the Broselow/Hinkle™ Pediatric Emergency System.

This system was an invention of Dr. Jim Broselow, an emergency physician in Hickory, North Carolina. Jim was comfortable treating adult patient, but children 12 years old and younger posed a challenge, because dramatically different tools and medicine dosages were needed for the various child sizes. Treatment can be implemented much faster and more reliably with this system. Studies have shown a 33.88% lower error rate when using the Broselow-Luten setup.[19]

Additional Error Proofing Examples

Franciscan did not have a consistent way of identifying patients who should not have IV sticks, blood draws, or blood pressure checks in a specific arm due to a preexisting condition. Sometimes, it would be written on the chart. The error conditions were that a nurse might not write it on the chart, and a nurse might not see it on the chart. Franciscan needed an error proofed way to ensure a nurse received that information. They found g-sleeves that they now place on patients' arms, as illustrated in Figure 11.36.

Gina Ellis, a pharmacist at Franciscan, worked jointly with Berniece Ashley, a nurse in NICU, to implement a change in the computer system to standardize eye exam administration times, as shown in Figure 11.37. Now the NICU is less likely to administer the medications at incorrect time intervals. This intervention improves the source conditions by making it more likely that medications will be administered at the correct intervals.

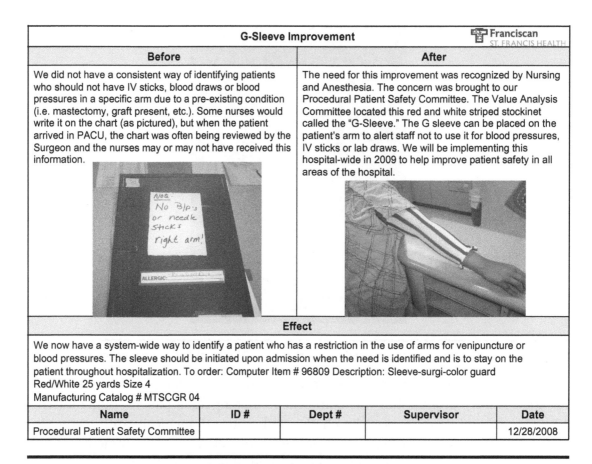

G-Sleeve Improvement		Franciscan ST. FRANCIS HEALTH
Before		**After**
We did not have a consistent way of identifying patients who should not have IV sticks, blood draws or blood pressures in a specific arm due to a pre-existing condition (i.e. mastectomy, graft present, etc.). Some nurses would write it on the chart (as pictured), but when the patient arrived in PACU, the chart was often being reviewed by the Surgeon and the nurses may or may not have received this information.		The need for this improvement was recognized by Nursing and Anesthesia. The concern was brought to our Procedural Patient Safety Committee. The Value Analysis Committee located this red and white striped stockinet called the "G-Sleeve." The G sleeve can be placed on the patient's arm to alert staff not to use it for blood pressures, IV sticks or lab draws. We will be implementing this hospital-wide in 2009 to help improve patient safety in all areas of the hospital.
Effect		
We now have a system-wide way to identify a patient who has a restriction in the use of arms for venipuncture or blood pressures. The sleeve should be initiated upon admission when the need is identified and is to stay on the patient throughout hospitalization. To order: Computer Item # 96809 Description: Sleeve-surgi-color guard Red/White 25 yards Size 4 Manufacturing Catalog # MTSCGR 04		
Name	**ID #**	**Dept #**	**Supervisor**	**Date**
Procedural Patient Safety Committee				12/28/2008

Figure 11.36   Error proofing against drawing from the wrong arm.

Error Proofing Eye Exams Using Cyclomydril		Franciscan ST. FRANCIS HEALTH
Before		**After**
No standardization with order entry of medication used for NICU eye exams (cyclomydril). Resulted in inaccurate administration times showing up for nurses (multiple administration times, wrong duration of administration).		Built a protocol into the computer system to match eye exam protocol of 1 drop in each eye every 5 minutes x3. Dose limit of 3 built into protocol to prevent additional administration times and wrong duration.
Effect		
Decreased time of order entry and improved time from when order written to drug administered. Decreased time for nursing staff because do not have to reconcile additional administration times.		
Name	**ID #**	**Dept #**	**Supervisor**	**Date**
Berniece Ashley, Gina Ellis		Pharmacy	Ronda Freije	11/10/08

Figure 11.37   Error proofing eye exams using cyclomydril.

Element 4: 100% Inspection

True 100% inspection involves using error-proofing devices to automatically inspect for errors and improper environmental conditions. Medical gas connectors on a hospital wall are an example of error proofing that completely prevents an error, because it is not physically possible to connect an air line to an oxygen connector, and vice versa, as pictured in Figure 11.38. An example of error proofing that makes it harder to create an error, although not impossible, would be color coded lines to help prevent a nurse from mistakenly injecting

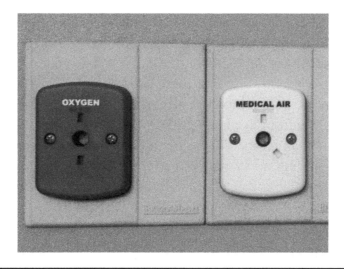

Figure 11.38   Medical gas connectors have good physical error proofing built in.

Azathioprine & Mercaptopurine Duplication Warning			🖨 Franciscan ST. FRANCIS HEALTH

Before	After		
The most recent ISMP Newsletter was published with a warning against duplication of azathioprine and mercaptopurine.	Within 3 hours of receiving this newsletter, our pharmacy team tested our pharmacy computer system to see if the error would be detected and created a work rule to notify the pharmacist in the event that these two drugs had been ordered together. HMM Duplicate Therapy Message: 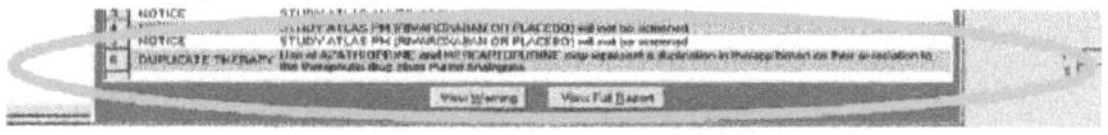 HMM Duplicate Azathiprine and Mercaptopurine Rule: 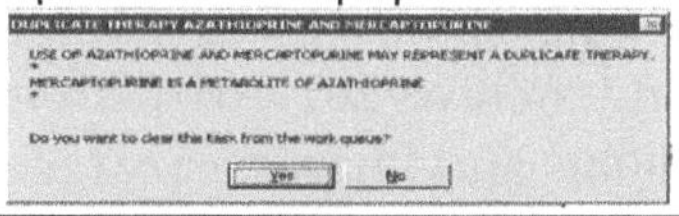		

The Effect			
Pharmacists are now notified when azathioprine and mercaptopurine are ordered together.			

Name	Cost Center	Supervisor	Date	Estimated Cost Savings
Therese Staublin and Berniece Ashley		Susan Brown, Ronda Frieje	8/29/07	Improved Patient Safety – Priceless!

Figure 11.39   A computer system being used to detect medication interaction problems and to notify the pharmacist.

total parenteral nutrition (TPN) food into the wrong line, a mistake that can cause death.

Franciscan uses computer systems to detect medication interaction problems and to notify the pharmacist. This detects errors before they occur, as pictured in Figure 11.39.

Conclusion

In this chapter, we reviewed some of the basic lean concepts Franciscan teaches as part of Kaizen. At Franciscan, these Lean concepts have stimulated thinking and provided a knowledge base to staff practicing and applying Kaizen. There are many other Lean tools and techniques that could be part of a Kaizen training program, yet Franciscan focused on the concepts presented here because they made sense at the start of their program. More recently, two Franciscan Lean leaders, Brian Hudson and Jill Boestler, have taken these concepts and added several other Lean concepts, teaching them broadly at Franciscan St. James Health. In six months, staff completed nearly 450 small Lean projects. Their organization has gone from losing $1 million per month to making a profit, due partly to these Lean efforts. Jill commented, "In true Lean fashion, many small changes are adding up to a large, cultural change."

Discussion Questions

- What Lean concepts should be taught first in your organization to facilitate Kaizen?
- What Lean concepts might be too sophisticated to be part of a Kaizen program?
- How could you start teaching the Lean concepts covered in this chapter in your organization?

Endnotes

1. Wachter, Bob, "A New Year's Potpourri: From Value to Plasma Screens to Knights and Knaves," Wachter's World, January 2, 2011, http://community.the-hospitalist. org/blogs/wachters_world/archive/2011/01/02/a-new-year-s-potpourri-from-value-to-plasma-screens-to-knights-and-knaves.aspx (accessed September 5, 2011).
2. Panchak, Patricia, "Lean Health Care? It Works!" *Industry Week*, November 1, 2003, v. 252(11), http://www.industryweek.com/articles/lean_health_care_it_works_1331. aspx (accessed September 5, 2011).
3. Imai, Masaaki, *Gemba Kaizen: A Commonsense, Low-Cost Approach to Management* (New York: Productivity Press, 1997) , 26.
4. Blackstone, John, "A Carmaker As a Model for a Hospital?" CBS Evening News, June 6, 2009, http://www.cbsnews.com/stories/2009/06/06/eveningnews/ main5068218.shtml (accessed August 14, 2011).
5. Marchwinski, Chet, and John Shook, eds., *Lean Lexicon: A Graphical Glossary for Lean Thinkers* (Brookline, MA: Lean Enterprise Institute: 2003), 23.
6. Seidelman, Ray, and Gail Nielsen, personal interview, August 2011.
7. Graban, Mark, *Lean Hospitals: Improving Quality, Patient Safety, and Employee Engagement: 2nd edition* (New York: Productivity Press, 2011), 58.
8. Ferenc, Jeff, "How Are Your Nurses Spending Their Time?" *Hospitals & Health Networks Magazine*, May 2010, http://www.hhnmag.com/hhnmag_app/jsp/ articledisplay.jsp?dcrpath=HHNMAG/Article/data/05MAY2010/1005HHN_Inbox_ nursing&domain=HHNMAG (accessed August 14, 2011).
9. Graban, 89.
10. Takahara, Akio, and Collin McLoughlin, *Clinical 5S For Healthcare* (Bellingham, WA: Enna, 2010), 1.
11. Van Horn, Carl, E., *Work in America: an Encyclopedia of History, Policy, and Society* (Santa Barbara, CA, ABC-CLIO, 2003), 132.

12. Grout, John, *Mistake-Proofing the Design of Healthcare Care Processes*, AHRQ Publication 07-0020 (Rockville, MD: Agency for Healthcare Research and Quality, 2007), 1.

13. Kenney, Charles, *Transforming Healthcare: Virginia Mason Medical Center's Pursuit of the Perfect Patient Experience* (New York: Productivity Press, 2010), xviii.

14. Kim, Theodore, and Tammy Webber, "Third Baby Dies After Error at Indiana Hospital," *USA Today*, Sep 20, 2006, http://www.usatoday.com/news/nation/2006-09-20-baby-deaths_x.htm (accessed August 9, 2011).

15. Reason, J., *Human Error*, (Cambridge, United Kingdom: Cambridge University Press, 1990), and Reason, J., "A System Approach to Organizational Error? *Ergonomics* 38(8), 1995, 1708–1721.

16. Woolf, Steven H., et al, "A String of Mistakes: The Importance of Cascade Analysis in Describing, Counting, and Preventing Medical Errors," *Annals of Family Medicine,*vol. 2, no. 4 , July/August 2004.

17. WRTV, "Hospital Changes Procedures After Babies' Fatal Overdoses," TheIndyChannel.com, September 18, 2006 http://www.theindychannel.com/news/9879402/detail.html (accessed August 9, 2011).

18. Shigeo Shingo, *Poke-Yoke: Improving Product Quality by Preventing Defects* (Portland, OR: Productivity Press, 1987), p. ix.

19. Frush, Karen, "Study Packet for the Correct Use of the Broselow™ Pediatric Emergency Tape," United States Department of Health and Human Services, http://www.ncdhhs.gov/dhsr/EMS/pdf/kids/DEPS_Broselow_Study.pdf (accessed September 5, 2011).

Chapter 12

Kaizen At Home

You want to be able to find and stash everything easily ... unless you're one of those people who like to live in a mess.[1]

—Julia Child

It is often said that Kaizen becomes a way of thinking and a way of life. This can certainly be true in the workplace, as Kaizen becomes a way of viewing your work different and making improvements on a daily basis. When it really takes root in people's minds, they cannot help but bring this way of thinking home with them. Even after a brief exposure to Kaizen, some people start making improvements in the way they make coffee, organize their closets, and the route they drive to work.

Kaizen at home can be a bit different than Kaizen at work. In some cases, such as deciding what route to take to work, there are some Kaizens you can truly work on independently. At home, we might still have to coordinate with a spouse or partner, which is probably more like coordinating with a coworker than working with your supervisor. You might have a small team, meaning your spouse and children, where it takes all of your "art of Kaizen" leadership practices to get everyone on the same page. Either way, applying Kaizen at home is a great opportunity to practice our Plan-Do-Study-Act (PDSA) improvement mindsets and methods.

Kaizen Tips from an Actress

There are actually a few books that have been written about the application of Kaizen principles in your daily life. One book that might be found by somebody who has not been exposed to Kaizen at work is *The EveryGirl's Guide to Life* by actress and TV personality Maria Menounos. One of the recommendations in her book is to "apply Kaizen, a Japanese philosophy that focuses on continuous improvement in all aspects of life. When something in life is good or works well, remain open and challenge yourself as to how it could be improved."[2]

Menounos adds, "By practicing … Kaizen, I review every part of a production, from how the scenes play to how we transport equipment to what we cater for food. I am always looking for how it could all be done better."[3] One of her costars added that our "minds must remain *in possibility*" and that "we must be open to what is possible, rather than what is impossible."[4] Menounos brings things back from her workplace to everyday life by stating, "before we embark on our journey for better living, we must first have our minds in the same state of possibility."

Some of her other mottos reinforce the Kaizen lessons we have already discussed in our book, including:

- *Learn from other's mistakes.*
- *Maximize every resource, as well as every minute of the day.*
- *Be proactive, not reactive, in life.*
- *Carry a sense of urgency in your day.*
- *Try to act and behave as if you're at the bottom even if you're at the top.*
- *Ask and you shall receive. Why be afraid to ask for things, when all you'll hear is a yes or no?*
- *Do not defend [a] problem by blaming others or sitting back and accepting the consequences of it. Instead, take responsibility for your part in the problem and then attack it until you find a solution.*

Kaizen Tips from a Behavioral Scientist

Robert Maurer, PhD, is the Director of Behavioral Sciences for the Family Practice Residency Program at Santa Monica-UCLA Medical Center and a faculty member with the UCLA School of Medicine. His 2004 book *One Small Step Can Change Your Life: The Kaizen Way* starts with his statement, "Japanese corporations have long used the gentle techniques of Kaizen to achieve their business goals and maintain excellence. Now this elegant strategy can help *you* realize your personal dreams."[5] Maurer explains how Kaizen is used "daily by private citizens across the globe" as a "natural, graceful technique for achieving goals and maintaining excellence."[6]

Maurer writes that people who have a goal, such as losing weight, often look first (as organizations tend to do) at "innovation" strategies—changes that happen in "a very short period of time, yielding a dramatic turnaround" in a way that is fast, big, flashy, and often expensive. Instead, he recommends a Kaizen approach, or "small steps for continual improvement."[7] This comparison between innovation and Kaizen was raised back in Chapter 1.

Advocating for Kaizen, Maurer quotes the Chinese philosopher Lao Tzu as saying, "A journey of a thousand miles must begin with the first step." He also cites the late UCLA basketball coach John Wooden as saying, "Don't look for the big, quick improvement. Seek the small improvements one day at a time. That's the only way it happens—and when it happens, it lasts."[8]

In the personal realm, instead of asking a patient to start exercising 30 minutes a day, a task that might have seemed overwhelming and hopeless for someone in poor health, Maurer asked her, "How about you just march in place in front of the television, each day, for *one minute*?"[9] When the patient came back, she was not getting healthier from that 60 seconds of exercise, but Maurer reports her attitude became much more optimistic. He asked the patient to increase her exercise a minute at a time and eventually she was able to take on a full aerobics routine. Maurer has learned that "low-key change helps the human mind navigate the fear that blocks success and creativity."[10]

Kaizen at Home

Franciscan St. Francis Hospital encourages its employees to apply Kaizen at home because they know that, these days, home life spills over into work life and vice versa. Franciscan has found that what gets practiced successfully at home will be practiced at work. People generally do not write up their Kaizens at home, but some Kaizeneers document and share their improvements with coworkers so a good idea can spread from home to home, as they are put into the online database system.

Kaizen before Work

Kaizen principles can be applied as part of your morning daily routine. For example, coauthor Joe has all morning prep bathroom items in open-top ceramic containers, arranged in order of use and next to the bathroom sink to reduce the time it takes to get ready in the morning.

Kaizen for Breakfast

Rhonda Anders, a director of surgical services at St. Francis, found a way to apply Kaizen at home. Her growing boys consumed a lot of cereal, so she bought their favorite brand in bulk. One day, she noticed that multiple boxes would be opened at one time, resulting in boxes of stale cereal that she would end up throwing away.

She made two quick and easy changes to her pantry to eliminate this unnecessary waste. First, she showed her sons how to roll down the bag inside the box and use a clothespin to clamp it airtight. Second, she started stocking boxes of cereal together in her pantry, with the open box in front and the unopened box behind it. The result was that she wasted less cereal.

Rhonda taught that example to her employees and asked them to notice if they see waste like that at work, such as multiple open boxes of wipes that dry out before being used or extra open boxes of items that have expiration dates. Today Rhonda encourages everyone to try looking at their daily work through their "domestic lenses" to see if new Kaizen ideas come into focus.

Kaizen to Get Ready for Work

How long does it take you to get ready for work in the morning? When this question is asked in a workshop, most people say an hour or more. What if you could get ready everyday in 30 minutes? Would you want to? What would you do with the 30 minutes you save every day? Would you sleep longer, would you invest it in some education, or would you use it to exercise?

Once, a participant said she is ready every day in 20 minutes. When asked how she does it, she first said her husband was a military policeman for 20 years, and he taught her how to be efficient. She said she spends 10 minutes the night before getting her clothes out and ready. So, it really takes her 30 minutes each day. She has everything organized to minimize movement. She cut her shower time down to a minimum. She figured out a fast way to prepare her hair in the morning and uses minimal makeup. She eats yogurt and a breakfast bar, and she is out the door everyday in 20 minutes or less.

So, how would you go about cutting your morning routine time in half? You might go to your personal "gemba" (of sorts) and record how long it takes to do each of your morning tasks. Then, analyze each of the longer tasks for ways to cut the time dramatically.

Shirley Fox, a mission coordinator for Franciscan, competed a Kaizen at home to improve the morning routine for herself and her husband, as shown in Figure 12.1.

Kaizen with Your Coffee

A few years back, coauthor Mark identified and implemented a small Kaizen in his kitchen that saved time and motion by eliminating a step in the process of making coffee. Mark had a coffee maker that was relatively close to the sink. He was somewhat proud that he had minimized walking by placing the coffee maker there, but there were other types of wasted motion besides walking.

As documented in Figure 12.2, the before process involved filling the stainless steel pot with water and then pouring that water into the coffee maker. One day, Mark was reading a cooking magazine and the "reader tips" section had an idea that caught his eye. The reader described how she saved some motion by using the flexible sink faucet to dispense water directly into the coffee maker. As in the workplace, it can be helpful to read about Kaizens done by others so we can use these good ideas for ourselves.

Changes in the Kitchen		Franciscan ST. FRANCIS HEALTH
Before	**After**	
I always had my coffee cups, filters and sweetener above the coffee maker, but had to go to the refrigerator for the coffee grounds and creamer. My husband would forget to take his vitamins. I use to have a ceramic tea pot for my husband to put his change in. His change was always on the counter. Husband's vitamins	I moved my coffee pot to the counter by the refrigerator and rearranged the cabinets to fit the coffee supplies above the coffee maker. Everything we need to start our day out right is all there together. My husbands vitamins are in front of the fruit cups he puts in his lunch. It reminds him to take his vitamins daily. The little jar by the coffee maker says "Green Fees" on it. My husband puts his change in the jar daily. 	

The Effect
Time and energy is saved. Our mornings start out good, my husband is healthier and I do not have to pick up my husband's change daily.

Name	Supervisor	Date	Estimated Cost Savings (Optional)
Shirley Fox	Sherri Walker	6-22-07	

Figure 12.1   Kaizen for the morning coffee.

Coffee Pot Filling Kaizen		Lean Blog
Before	**After**	
Had to bring the coffee pot to the sink, filled water into pot and then dumped it into the coffee machine. 	Using the sink's flexible faucet hose to put water directly into the coffee machine. 	

Effect
Less motion, less time required to fill the coffee machine with water. Does introduce risk, however, if the coffee pot isn't empty from previous pot that things might overfill. Will re-evaluate if that error occurs.

Name	ID #	Dept #	Supervisor	Date
Mark Graban		Kitchen	n/a	12/8/05

Figure 12.2   Kaizen to reduce wasted motion in coffee making.

One thing Mark had to consider was that the direct filling of the coffee maker did introduce some risk of error. If there was coffee remaining from the previous pot, it was hard to detect because the pot was not clear glass. If there was half a pot remaining, and Mark attempted to make a new full pot, he could have a situation where the coffee pot would overfill and spill onto the counter and the floor. As with many workplace scenarios, one has to consider risks and any potential tradeoffs with productivity. After consideration, Mark decided to use the new process while being mindful to check the pot or to not make full pots of coffee. He may be jinxing himself by writing this, but so far he has not had a coffee overflow mishap.

In his kitchen, Joe has all items required to make his morning coffee within arm's reach when standing in front of the coffee machine.

Kaizen to Get Dressed

Beyond her kitchen, Shirley also applied a series of Kaizens to improve her home organization and her life. To reduce frustration in finding clothes, she grouped like items together. She also placed her shoes just above her clothes to make it easier to choose the right pair, as shown in Figure 12.3.

Then, to save time each day, she decides on Sunday evening what she plans to wear for the week. She checks the weather forecast and pulls out her clothes

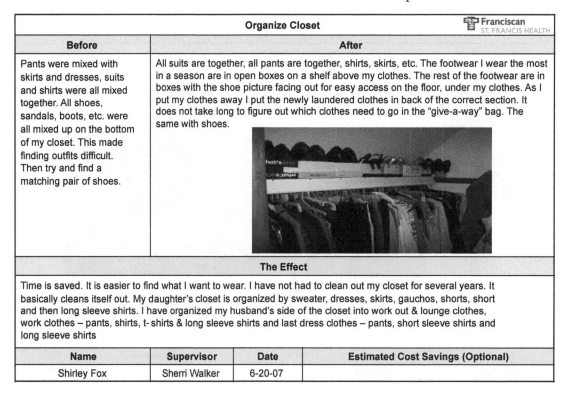

Organize Closet		Franciscan ST. FRANCIS HEALTH

Before	After
Pants were mixed with skirts and dresses, suits and shirts were all mixed together. All shoes, sandals, boots, etc. were all mixed up on the bottom of my closet. This made finding outfits difficult. Then try and find a matching pair of shoes.	All suits are together, all pants are together, shirts, skirts, etc. The footwear I wear the most in a season are in open boxes on a shelf above my clothes. The rest of the footwear are in boxes with the shoe picture facing out for easy access on the floor, under my clothes. As I put my clothes away I put the newly laundered clothes in back of the correct section. It does not take long to figure out which clothes need to go in the "give-a-way" bag. The same with shoes.

The Effect
Time is saved. It is easier to find what I want to wear. I have not had to clean out my closet for several years. It basically cleans itself out. My daughter's closet is organized by sweater, dresses, skirts, gauchos, shorts, short and then long sleeve shirts. I have organized my husband's side of the closet into work out & lounge clothes, work clothes – pants, shirts, t-shirts & long sleeve shirts and last dress clothes – pants, short sleeve shirts and long sleeve shirts

Name	Supervisor	Date	Estimated Cost Savings (Optional)
Shirley Fox	Sherri Walker	6-20-07	

Figure 12.3 Kaizen for getting dressed in the morning.

Clothes for the Week			Franciscan ST. FRANCIS HEALTH
Before	**After**		
Every morning I would stand in my closet looking at my clothes thinking, "What do I want to wear today?" I would think about the day's activities to dress accordingly. Then I would have to iron it if needed (usually needed). Set up the iron board and wait for the iron to warm up.	On the weekends I look at my work schedule and the weather, then pick out my clothes for the week. I iron the clothes all at once. I hung a rack on the outside of the closet and hang the clothes in the order I want to wear them. I have been asked, "What if on Friday you don't want to wear the last outfit?" My reply, "It is clean and ironed, why wouldn't I want to wear it?" 		
The Effect			
Time saved! Lower electricity bill.			
Name	**Supervisor**	**Date**	**Estimated Cost Savings (Optional)**
Shirley Fox	Sherri Walker	6-21-07	

Figure 12.4 Organizing the week's wardrobe saves time and frustration in the mornings.

for each day. Then, she irons all her clothes that night, which means she only has to setup the ironing board and heat up the iron once a week, rather than each day. Her Kaizen is shown in Figure 12.4

Shirley found that her necklaces would get tangled and take a long time to untangle. She organized her necklaces for ease of access and eliminated their tangling, as shown in Figure 12.5.

Then, she organized her makeup in the order she uses it and keeps it next to the sink, which saved an estimated 5 minutes per day, as documented in Figure 12.6.

Shirley organized her sock drawer and her sweaters, as shown in Figure 12.7 and 12.8.

Not satisfied with just organizing her sweaters, Shirley placed a sweater shaver and duct tape next to her sweaters, so she could quickly and easily clean burrs off her sweaters before putting them on, as documented in Figure 12.9.

She organized her laundry and uses a yardstick on the island counter as a visual indicator that signals when to start the dryer, as written up in Figure 12.10.

Through these Kaizens, Shirley was able to cut the time it takes to get ready in the morning by 35%. Now she has an extra 20 minutes to use in ways that are more fulfilling, constructive, or fun. When asked about all of her household improvements, Shirley says she "was doing Kaizens before she knew what Kaizens were." She says, "Growing up as the only girl and doing all the 'girl' chores, I had to come up with faster and better ways to get things done so I would have more time to do homework and study."

Jewelry		Franciscan ST. FRANCIS HEALTH
Before	**After**	
My necklaces would get tangled in the jewelry box. I would make several trip from the jewelry box to find the right necklace to wear with my outfit. I would waste time trying to pair earrings or just trying to find the one I want.	I hang my necklaces on a coffee mug rack. They do not get tangled. The rack is by the rack where I hang my clothes for the week. I can easily pick out necklaces to match my outfits. I also put my pierced earrings pair together on a ribbon if they can not hang with the necklaces. 	
The Effect		
Time and energy saved. And I accessorize better.		

Name	Supervisor	Date	Estimated Cost Savings (Optional)
Shirley Fox	Sheri Walker	6-22-07	

Figure 12.5 Kaizen for jewelry.

Makeup		Franciscan ST. FRANCIS HEALTH
Before	**After**	
I kept my makeup along with other odds and ends in my makeup bag. I wasted time looking for what I needed.	I put my makeup on a tray in the order I use it. I no longer search for what I need to put on next. It is right there! I have small sizes of odds and ends to take on a trip in my makeup bag. When I pack, my bag is ready, I just add my makeup. 	

The Effect			
My time of putting on my makeup was cut in half. I can sleep 5 more minutes!			
Name	**Supervisor**	**Date**	**Savings**
Shirley Fox	Sherri Walker	6-22-07	

Figure 12.6 Kaizen for makeup.

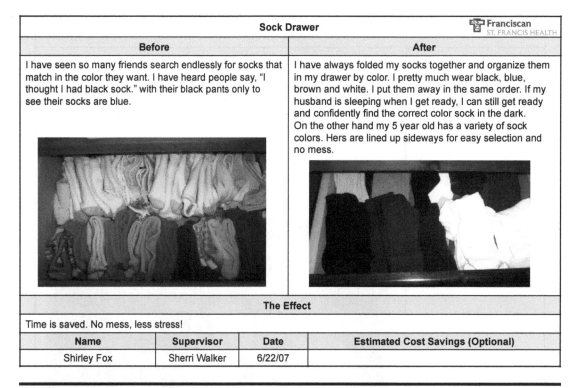

Sock Drawer			Franciscan ST. FRANCIS HEALTH
Before		**After**	
I have seen so many friends search endlessly for socks that match in the color they want. I have heard people say, "I thought I had black sock." with their black pants only to see their socks are blue.		I have always folded my socks together and organize them in my drawer by color. I pretty much wear black, blue, brown and white. I put them away in the same order. If my husband is sleeping when I get ready, I can still get ready and confidently find the correct color sock in the dark. On the other hand my 5 year old has a variety of sock colors. Hers are lined up sideways for easy selection and no mess.	
The Effect			
Time is saved. No mess, less stress!			
Name	**Supervisor**	**Date**	**Estimated Cost Savings (Optional)**
Shirley Fox	Sherri Walker	6/22/07	

Figure 12.7   Kaizen for the sock drawer.

Sweaters		Franciscan ST. FRANCIS HEALTH
Before	**After**	
My sweaters took up several dresser drawers. I would have to search for the right drawer and look under each sweater unless by chance the one I wanted was on top. Sometimes this created a big mess, especially when I really did not know what I wanted to wear.	Instead of smashing sweaters in a drawer or having hanger ends molded into my sweaters, I stack my sweaters on a shelf in my closet. All sweater are nicely folded and arranged by color. I can look at all my sweaters at one time making selection easier. I pull out the sweater I need and lower down any on top. If a sweater is not worn (usually on the bottom) for a season it goes in the "give-a-way" bag.	
The Effect		
Time and energy saved. Better organized.		
Name	**Supervisor**	**Date**	**Estimated Cost Savings (Optional)**
Shirley fox	Sherri Walker	6-19-07	

Figure 12.8   Kaizen for sweaters.

Sweater Shaver and Lint Brush		Franciscan ST. FRANCIS HEALTH
Before	**After**	
I used to keep a sweater shaver and a disposable lint brush in the laundry area. I would never use them as I pulled clothes out of the dryer. I would bring my clothes downstairs to shave or get the lint off my clothes prior to wearing.	I keep the sweater shaver and duct tape (much cheaper and lasts longer) in my clothes closet. When I get my clothes ready for the week, I use the shaver and duct tape at that time. I also keep a roll of duct tape in my desk drawer at work for touch ups. 	

The Effect			
Time is saved by not running downstairs and by doing a weeks worth of clothes at one time.			
Name	**Supervisor**	**Date**	**Savings**
Shirley Fox	Sherri Walker	6-19-07	

Figure 12.9   Sweater shaver and lint brush.

Laundry	Franciscan ST. FRANCIS HEALTH
Before	**After**
#1 We used to put all our laundry in one basket. I would waster time sorting laundry only to find out there was not enough laundry for a load of either darks or whites/lights. #2 I seemed to be the only person who could start the dryer. (We never let the dryer run when we are not at home)	#1 I keep a white laundry basket for whites and light colored clothes and a beige laundry basket for dark colored clothes in the bottom of our bathroom closet.. When the basket is full enough for a load I take it downstairs and start a load, #2 I set the dryer up so all my husband has to do is push the start button when he gets home from work. I leave a yard stick on the counter to remind him. If he still does not get it, my 5 year old sees the yard stick on the counter when she gets off the school bus and uses the yard stick to reach the start button on the dryer. 

The Effect			
Time and energy is saved. My five year old is empowered to help out. And believe it or not my husband puts his clothes in the correct basket. ....Now if the clothes could come out of the dryer folded... hmm....			
Name	**Supervisor**	**Date**	**Estimated Cost Savings (Optional)**
Shirley Fox	Sherri Walker	6-20-07	

Figure 12.10   Kaizen in the laundry room.

Figure 12.11 Kaizening cup clutter.

Kaizen to Reduce Cup Clutter

Dan Lafever, a manager at Franciscan, has a family of six and noticed they were using, on average, 21 cups and glasses per day for drinking water and other beverages. Dan made a cup holder out of a shoebox, as shown in Figure 12.11, to reduce usage to one cup per person per day. In the morning everyone gets a clean cup, placed upside down in the cup holder. The cup is flipped over when it is first used and remains upright as it is reused all day. Each hole has the initial of the persons name next to it to mark each person's home position. The rubber band has the person's name on it and he can put it on so, if the cup is taken away, it will not get mixed up with the others.

Kaizen on the Way to Work

A few years back, Mark was working with a new client in a primary care clinic. In their first week, the team was learning basic Lean concepts, and they were starting to practice Kaizen. The very next week, one of the team members walked in and proudly reported, "I've driven the exact same way to work every day for the last 17 years! Today, I tried a different road!"

She was performing her own improvement experiment in a PDSA approach. She said, "Before Kaizen, I would have never considered thinking if there was a better way to drive to work. I was stuck in a rut." Her hypothesis was that a new route would be faster or maybe more interesting. Mark asked her if it was faster and she said, "No, I don't think so. I'll try it again tomorrow, but I might go back to that old way."

In keeping with the PDSA mindset, she left open the idea that the change might not really be an improvement. By trying a new way, she confirmed that the old way was actually pretty good, which happens sometimes in the midst of Kaizen work.

Kaizen in the Home Office

Coauthor Mark has applied many Kaizen lessons in his home life, although his home and life are far from waste free. As a budding Kaizeneer (without having been given that distinction formally by Franciscan), Mark continues to look for opportunities for improvement at home, seizing upon them in small, easy, inexpensive ways when possible.

Kaizen on the Computer

Even as a person who generally embraces change, maybe more than most, Mark was reminded that change can be awkward and uncomfortable, to the point of making one want to go back to an old way of doing things. As an avid Mac user, Mark upgraded when Apple released a new operating system, OSX 10.7 "Lion."

In this update, Apple changed how the mouse wheel or trackpad scrolling worked. Previously, to move to a point lower in a document, you would scroll downward with your fingers. Scrolling down moved text up so you could read further in a document, just as it has worked on Macs and Windows computers for a long time. With OSX 10.7, Apple changed things so that scrolling on a Mac works more like an iPhone or iPad. Now, to read lower in a document, one needs to push the page up. So what used to be a downward motion is now an upward motion to accomplish the same result.

This change was very disorienting at first for Mac users. People complained about it online, and Mark shared his trepidation in a blog post.[11] While Apple called this new approach "natural scrolling," they anticipated that people might think the old way was more natural to them, so the software had a setting that allowed you to switch the scrolling back to the old, familiar direction.

With the change in OSX, it would be hard to measure if the new scrolling method were really better. Does the new approach save time or reduce errors for the user? It would be hard to gauge—in Mark's workplace, his computer, it was just different, not necessarily better.

After a frustrating first day of this so-called "natural scrolling" feeling decidedly unnatural, it was tempting for Mark to switch back to the old way. This probably happens in any workplace changes. Assuming that the change is really an improvement, it might feel awkward at first when during a period of a "learning curve," the new method is actually slower until it becomes more comfortable. It can be a tough choice to give up or to persevere to see if the new way is really better. The idea of "seven days' grace" as taught at Franciscan is a powerful idea in the workplace and with Mark's Mac. Mark decided to stick it out and keep working with the new scrolling direction. After about 48 hours, he was no longer making errors by trying to scroll in the wrong direction. Instead of seven days grace, it required just two before the change stuck.

Kaizen on the Physical Desktop

In 2011, Mark bought a new desk for his home office, something that does not really qualify as a Kaizen, since it was not like Amazon CEO Jeff Bezos and his famous "ramshackle desk" made out of an old door as an example of frugality.[12] Mark's new desk has a laminate surface that proved to be somewhat slippery compared to his old desk.

The Bluetooth® keyboard and track pad for his computer are relatively lightweight. So, Mark found that, when he was typing or using the track pad, they would tend to slide away from him a bit on the desk, causing a bit of annoyance. The little rubber feet and pads on the bottom of the devices were not quite tacky enough to grab onto the desk securely.

Mark was trying to think about how to solve this situation, and he ordered a small desk pad that he could place under the keyboard and track pad. This pad would provide a good writing surface, and it would protect the desk surface from damage. But again, buying something for $30 is not the best form of Kaizen. Mark would have been accused of being a "catalog engineer" by the originators of the Toyota Production System. There had to be a better way that could have been implemented cheaply and immediately.

He found some tacky putty that is used to hang signs or posters on a wall. The putty molded to the bottom of the keyboard and track pad perfectly. Neither device slid when used and the improvement cost only a few minutes of brainstorming. The Kaizen Report is shown in Figure 12.12.

As often happens with Kaizen, Mark's first improvement created a minor side effect. With the putty being placed only on the back of the keyboard, the front edge now rattled a bit when Mark typed, leading to this second Kaizen, shown in Figure 12.13.

Keyboard & TrackPad Slide No More		Lean Blog
Before	**After**	
Keyboard and trackpad slid on desk a bit when using them. Annoying and maybe bad ergonomically.	Put putty on the bottom of keyboard and trackpad to prevent sliding.	
Effect		
Keyboard and trackpad no longer slide on desk. Can still be repositioned as needed.		

Name	ID #	Dept #	Supervisor	Date
Mark Graban		Home Office – Constancy, Inc.	n/a	6/24/11

Figure 12.12   Kaizen on the physical desktop.

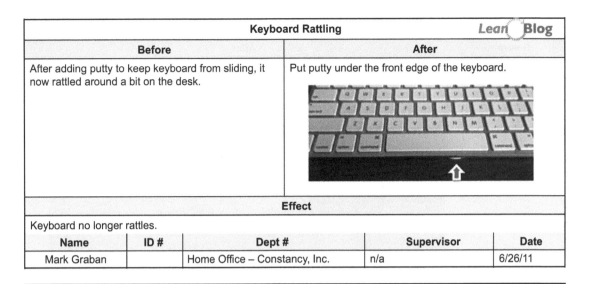

Keyboard Rattling		*Lean* Blog
Before	**After**	
After adding putty to keep keyboard from sliding, it now rattled around a bit on the desk.	Put putty under the front edge of the keyboard.	
Effect		
Keyboard no longer rattles.				

Name	ID #	Dept #	Supervisor	Date
Mark Graban		Home Office – Constancy, Inc.	n/a	6/26/11

Figure 12.13   Addressing a problem caused by the previous Kaizen.

Kaizen after Work

Kaizen can also be applied after work and on weekends, making life easier and freeing up time.

Kaizen for Dinner

Shirley has two related Kaizens for planning and shopping for dinners. After getting frustrated with cooking the same meals over and over, she created a running list that she updates as she discovers new dinner ideas, as shown in Figure 12.14.

Shirley's approach for grocery shopping planning saves her time in the store, as well as money, by having a more deliberate approach, as pictured in Figure 12.15.

When Mark and his wife moved into their home in Texas in 2005, it was like many moves where you are just tired and want to get everything just put away somewhere so you can say you are done. The way things got put away in the kitchen created a situation where waste that occurred daily went unnoticed until a random spark of Kaizen hit.

In prepping for a meal, Mark chops and cuts while working at a center kitchen island. The cutting boards were conveniently stored in that island. However, in the rush to get the house settled, a hasty decision was made to store knives in a drawer that was not as conveniently located. To get a knife, Mark would have to turn around and walk back and over about eight feet to the knife drawer.

Embarrassingly for a Kaizen thinker, Mark had this wasted motion built into his cooking process each and every time. It was a good example of a workplace that just sort of evolved rather than being consciously designed. The same thing often happens in hospitals in the rush to design and move into a new space, especially when there is a large team and no clear ownership over the space and layout.

Menu Idea List		Franciscan ST. FRANCIS HEALTH
Before	**After**	
I was fixing the same old, same old for dinner, or so it seemed.	I made out a list of all the things I like to cook. I separated the list into anytime meals and seasonal meals. When planning meals for two weeks, I look at my Menu Idea List as a reference. As I come across new recipes I like, I add them to the list. My recipe basket has the recipes in the order they are on the list. If the recipe is in a cook book the book name and recipe page number are next to the Menu Idea. 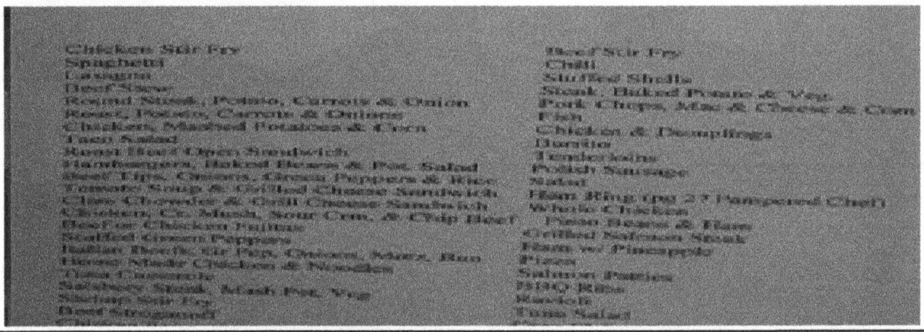	

The Effect			
Time is saved. Cooking is fun. Meals are not boring. We eat a good variety.			
Name	**Supervisor**	**Date**	**Estimated Cost Savings (Optional)**
Shirley Fox	Sherri Walker	6-22-07	

Figure 12.14 Kaizening the dinner menu.

2 Week Menu & Grocery List		Franciscan ST. FRANCIS HEALTH
Before	**After**	
I use to go to the grocery store without a list and without any idea of what I was going to fix for meals or anything else we needed. I spent time roaming the grocery store, buying things I did not need, or items that did not complete a meal and spent more money.	Now I make out a two week menu on or around pay day. I first look through the cabinets and freezer to see what I have for meals. I start my menus with those meals. I look to see what is on sale at the store. As I make out the menus I make out the grocery list. I can also look to see what I already have for those meals. I keep a magnetic paper pad on the refrigerator to use for my grocery list. As I see something is running low, I add it the list. I keep a envelope with coupons in a kitchen drawer. I go through them after my grocery list is completed. 	

The Effect			
Saves money – I don't buy things we don't need. We don't waste food. I get store discount and double coupon discount with my grocery card. I also save money on gas since I don't have to make several trips to grocery store. I also get 10 cents off every gallon of gas for every $100 I spend at the grocery store. Suggestions: 1.Use a dry erase menu board. 2. You do not have to go in same order as the menu plan. 3. Always fixing the same old same old....see Quick & Easy Menu Idea List.			
Name	**Supervisor**	**Date**	**Estimated Cost Savings (Optional)**
Shirley Fox	Sherri Walker	6-22-07	

Figure 12.15 Two week menu and grocery list.

Finally, about a year after moving in, Mark's wife saw him cooking and asked why he was doing it that why. Why didn't he store the knives in a drawer in the center island, right above where the cutting boards were kept? It was such an obvious improvement, but it was a great example of being unable to see waste in your own work. Because Mark does all of the cooking (and enjoys it), it took outside eyes to point out the waste and to make a suggestion. They quickly worked together to swap out the items in those two drawers. One has to be able to see the waste to be able to eliminate it through Kaizen.

Kaizen in the Backyard

Dan Lafever took Kaizen home with him. He had a truckload of mulch delivered to the driveway of his house and enlisted his oldest son to move it to the back-yard. After 15 minutes of frustration, they stopped. They took a break and spent some time thinking though how to make it quicker and easier. Dan got a pad of paper and began a list.

Improvements

- Scooping and pushing mulch directly into a wheelbarrow instead of shoveling it in (saved 30 seconds)
- Pull the wheelbarrow backwards
- Clear pathways for the wheelbarrow
- Prepare spots in advance
- Pitch fork from our neighbor
- Bigger wheelbarrow

They then implemented the improvements and began moving mulch again. He estimates that they cut the remaining move time in half because of the improvements. It was a valuable lesson for Dan and his kids. His son said, "Dad if you ever want to do something like this again, I'll help, because this made a boring chore into a fun game."

Joe's backyard Kaizens include a dedicated tool closet with all tools and home improvement supplies grouped and organized to save time spent looking for things.

Kaizen for Home Repair

In 2010, Joe bought a house through an auction at a great price. It was in disrepair and needed a major and systematic overhaul of just about every major system in the house. He has been applying Kaizen by dedicating about four hours each week to fixing up the house. He has found, over the course of a year, that four hours of work each week adds up significantly to over a month of full-time work. What was an unlivable place a year ago has now become a pleasant place to come home to after a long day at work.

Kaizen for the Earth

One day, Dan's son came home from school asking how he could save the world from an energy crisis in his generation. Dan asked him to remember the lesson of the mulch. They began brainstorming a list of things they could do to reduce energy consumption in their home. Over the next year, they reduced their energy costs by 40%. It taught his son a valuable lesson, that he really can make a difference, and that it can be accomplished through Kaizen.

Kaizen in the Bathroom

One of Mark's household jobs is making sure bathrooms never run out of toilet paper and, as part of that, making sure that there is always a ready supply in the garage as a source for restocking the bathrooms. After a few mishaps of almost running out, Mark applied Kaizen and Lean lessons from work at home.

Since toilet paper is relatively inexpensive, and they had storage space in the garage, Mark decided to set up a "two-bin kanban system"[13] to ensure that there was always a supply of toilet paper at the house. Like a workplace two-bin system, it was a simple, visual approach to inventory management. Each "bin," in this case, is a large warehouse club pack of 36 rolls. When one "bin" is completely empty, the outer plastic packaging becomes a signal that it is time to buy more. Because there is still a second full "bin" of toilet paper when that first one is empty, Mark and his wife do not have to drop everything immediately to drive to the store. They can wait until the next weekend, using the empty wrapper as a reminder of what they need to buy.

"Kanban" is a Lean method for materials replenishment and supply chain management. With kanban, inventory levels are set based on expected usage, and the reorder points (when you order more) and the reorder quantities (how much you order) are standardized for frequent replenishment of supplies from a stockroom or a vendor. The reorder point is normally made very visual, using a laminated kanban card (often with a barcode) or an empty bin as the signal that more supply is needed. You can read more about kanban in *Lean Hospitals*.

With this system, the Grabans have not run out of toilet paper. The same approach is now used in their home for paper towels and other inexpensive supplies and toiletries, like deodorant, shaving cream, and toothpaste. Now, because there is always a second shaving cream can on hand, Mark no longer runs out of shaving cream at inopportune times (which is especially problematic because it is very hard to gauge how much remains in a can). So when he does run out, he just goes to the pantry instead of running to the store.

Joe has a similar system in his home, because he organized items that need purchased for the bathroom in labeled clear bins in a closet, with two of each item in each bin—a simple *kanban* system. Joe updates his shopping list when one item is pulled from a bin.

Kaizen and Your Kids

A natural extension of Shirley's closet Kaizens was to help her young daughter stay organized and ready to leave the house from head (Figure 12.16) to toe (Figure 12.17).

Hair Bow Drawer		Franciscan ST. FRANCIS HEALTH
Before	**After**	
My five-year-old's hair bow drawer was a mess. We used to dig for matching colors and shades.	A couple of years ago, I received three small containers as part of a gift. I decided to use them for my daughter's hair bows. I then put the other colors in zip lock baggies. I also have a tin for other hair pieces. Now if she messes them up, she cleans them up. As you can see, she has many hair bows now. I keep two of each color on her hair brush for when we are taking a trip or in a hurry and have to fix her hair away from home. The color we need is always there.	
The Effect		
Time is saved in the mornings, especially now that she is in school.		
Name	**Supervisor**	**Date**	**Savings**
Shirley Fox	Sherri Walker	6-20-07	

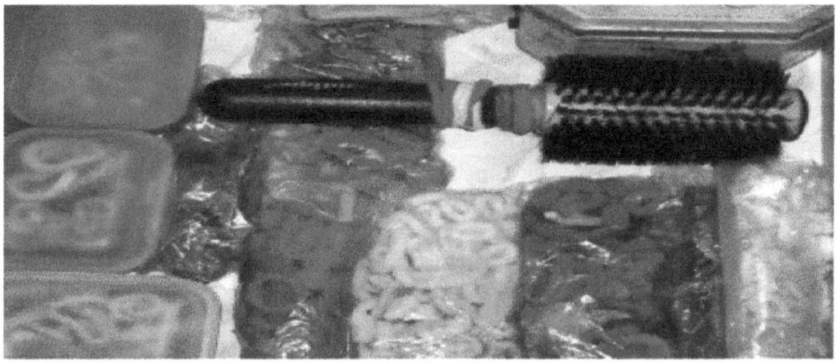

Figure 12.16 Kaizen for the kids – the hair bow drawer.

Daughter's Shoes		Franciscan ST. FRANCIS HEALTH
Before	**After**	
Whenever we were going somewhere, my daughter would try to find her shoes that were mixed in with her toys in her upstairs bedroom.	All three doors to go out are on the first floor. The laundry closet is in the center of all three doors. I do not use the top of the dryer, so we put her shoes there. Now she is responsible for putting her shoes away. When she is getting ready to leave the house, her shoes are ready to go 	

The Effect			
Saves time, gives my daughter responsibility and decreases stress.			
Name	**Supervisor**	**Date**	**Estimated Cost Savings (Optional)**
Shirley Fox	Sherri Walker	6-22-07	

Figure 12.17   Kaizening the shoe closet.

Vacation List		Franciscan ST. FRANCIS HEALTH
Before	**After**	
Whether it was an overnight trip or a week trip, I would make a list of what my family and I needed. Every time it was the same old same old….a list of clothes, necessities, just in case medications, camera, etc., only to realize I forgot to put something on my list.	I took my last list and put it on the computer, adding the things I forgot. Each of us in the family, including our dog, has a list. There is also another list of items such as camera, sunscreen, bottled water, magazines, coloring book and crayons, etc. As items need change or need to be added, I just open the file and make the changes. When we getting ready for a trip I print out the list and check off as item (s) is packed.	
The Effect		
Time is saved. No list to make out and think over and over again. Leaving on a trip more relax knowing we have everything we need. Money saved! Not having to buy something that was forgotten.		
Name	**Supervisor**	**Date**	**Estimated Cost Savings (Optional)**
Shirley Fox	Sherri Walker	6-19-07	

Figure 12.18   The vacation list.

A Vacation from Kaizen?

Shirley's Kaizen for vacation packing (Figure 12.18) saves preparation time and helps ensure that she and her family do not forget anything on their way out the door.

Kaizen for Repetitive Tasks

Like Shirley, Joe created a checklist, but this checklist was to ensure his periodic repeating tasks were not being missed. There was a daily checklist with items including reviewing of appointments, reviewing his "urgent file," and doing calisthenics. Joe also had a weekly checklist that included planning, writing thank you notes, and carving out time for Kaizen. He found that he was missing tasks, especially when he got really busy. He created a daily and weekly checklist he carries in his planner and refers to daily. He has also added longer-term repeating tasks to his electronic calendar with reminders.

Another way to deal with repetitive tasks is to automate them. Joe automated his monthly bill payments by signing up for automatic bank deductions. He eliminated writing and mailing checks and the cost of stamps for each monthly bill.

Automating bill payment, for things like a monthly cable TV bill, would have helped Mark avoid a time-consuming situation a few years ago. When he first started using online bill pay through his bank, he had to manually enter the amount to pay for each bill. One time, he missed a decimal point and he entered a payment to the cable company for something like $8450 instead of $84.50. Mark's bank hit him with an overdraft fee and put his account into negative territory, causing problems for other pending bills, instead of just bouncing or refusing that one erroneous payment. It took many phone calls and a lot of stress to get a somewhat quick refund from the cable company. From that point forward, Mark has either automated bill payments, as Joe has, or he error proofs against missing a decimal point. He does this by always rounding up bills to the nearest dollar. That cable bill would have been paid as $85, rather than attempting to enter $84.50. This overpayment leaves a small credit balance that gets applied toward the next bill, which works fine for bills that are paid monthly.

Kaizen for the Kaizen Process

Shirley, for all of her home Kaizen progress, felt like she was not making the best use of the free time that suddenly appeared. Not surprisingly, she wrote up a Kaizen, pictured in Figure 12.19, about how to make sure she had "to do" items always teed up for those times, much like the Visual Idea Board from Chapter 6, where ideas are ready to work on or discuss when time becomes available.

Conclusion

As the examples in this chapter show, the Kaizen thought process is pretty much the same, whether it is used at work, at home, or in the home office. In our daily lives, we can identify problems or opportunities that lead to small, low-cost, low-risk improvements that make our lives easier, freeing up time for what is truly important, meaningful, or fun. The practice of Kaizen bleeds over from work to home, and our continued practice at home allows us to be more effective in the workplace.

To Do List	Franciscan ST. FRANCIS HEALTH
Before	**After**
I would have all the things I need to do in my head, which created stress from feeling overwhelmed. When I would have 15 to 30 minutes to do something, I could not think of anything that could be completed in that amount of time. I would just sit down and watch a little TV, only to think I could have done this or that.	I keep an ongoing list of all the things I need "to do" that are not done regularly. Ex: patch and paint a nick in the wall, take down wall border, trim a tree, pull weeds, caulk a window, etc. Now when I have a moment, I go to my list and find something to do. As I see something that needs to be done and don't have time at that moment I add it to the "to do" list. To Do List clean garage clean carpets patch and paint nicks take down wall border trim tree pull weeds Honey Do List edge lawn caulk window wash vehicles organize sporting equipment

The Effect
Time is managed better. I feel a sense of accomplishment and am not dragged down by depressing TV. The house and yard look better. This also works great for "Honey Do" lists!

Name	**Supervisor**	**Date**	**Estimated Cost Savings (Optional)**
Shirley Fox	Sherri Walker	6-19-07	

Figure 12.19 The to-do list.

Discussion Questions

- What is the first Kaizen you would do at home?
- How would you apply lessons from this book to encourage others at home to do Kaizen?
- Does the idea of people "resisting" change apply at home as much as the workplace?

Endnotes

1. Smithsonian National Museum of American History, Museum Display, 2006.
2. Menounos, Maria, *The EveryGirl's Guide to Life* (New York: Harper Collins, 2011), xiv.
3. Menounos, xv.
4. Menounos, xvii.
5. Maurer, Robert, *One Small Step Can Change Your Life: The Kaizen Way* (New York: Workman Publishing, 2004), 1.
6. Maurer, 2.
7. Maurer, 8.
8. Maurer, 11.
9. Maurer, 15.
10. Maurer, 17.

11. Graban, Mark, "Changes in Mac OS X "Lion" and Parallels to Workplace Changes," *LeanBlog*.org, July 22, 2011, http://www.leanblog.org/2011/07/changes-in-mac-osx-lion-and-parallels-to-workplace-changes/ (accessed August 31, 2011).

12. D'Souza, Dinesh, "The Billionaire Next Door," *Forbes.com,* October 11, 1999, http://www.forbes.com/forbes/1999/1011/6409050a.html (accessed August 31, 2011).

13. Graban, Mark, *Lean Hospitals: Improving Quality, Patient Satisfaction, and Employee Engagement: 2nd edition* (New York: Productivity Press, 2011), 101.

Conclusion

Coming together is a beginning. Keeping together is progress. Working together is success.

—Henry Ford

Have you seen the original 1984 version of *The Karate Kid*? In the film, Daniel, a teenager who was beaten up by classmates in his new city, started training under Mr. Miyagi, a karate master. Daniel's first assignment was to wash Miyagi's cars. Miyagi showed him how to wax the cars with a particular arm motion—"wax on, wax off." Daniel also had to sand Miyagi's backyard deck with a "big circle" motion. Finally, Daniel had to paint Miyagi's wooden fence and house with specific "up, down" and "side, side" motions. At this point, Daniel thought he was being was taking advantage for selfish home improvement needs. How could these chores be helping him train for karate? Daniel was ready to give up, but Miyagi stopped him and said, "Show me wax on, wax off." As Daniel showed him the technique, Miyagi threw a punch toward him and the waxing motion blocked the punch. Daniel's eyes opened wide. He realized that the motions from the chores were really basic karate skills.

Initially, Daniel wanted to learn karate so he could defend himself or exact revenge on the bullies who tormented him. Daniel was facing a short-term crisis, which meant he was not very interested in exploring the philosophies of the martial arts. Leaders facing a crisis, in any industry, sometimes want to quickly learn tools, tips, and tricks to solve today's crisis. In doing so, they sometimes miss the opportunity to study, understand, and practice the deeper mindsets of Kaizen that might serve them better over the long run.

Daniel could not become a karate black belt overnight, nor can an organization create a Kaizen culture that quickly. Kaizen is about developing and growing basic improvement skills in everyone, every day. Kaizeneers and leaders need to practice the PDSA mindset continually, over many years, to create a Kaizen culture. This culture will contribute greatly to meeting patient needs, creating a more enriching workplace, and having an organization that is financially secure for the long term.

If you want one year of prosperity, grow seeds. If you want ten years of prosperity, grow trees. If you want 100 years of prosperity, grow people.[1]

—Chinese Proverb

A Minute to Learn, a Lifetime to Master

The basic concepts of Kaizen might seem simple at first. Ask your employees for ideas. Say yes to most of them. Let people implement their own ideas, but help them as a servant leader, if needed. Document the improvements simply. Recognize and thank people for their improvements. Share the ideas with others.

The term "Quick and Easy Kaizen" refers to employees identifying and implementing easy improvements that can be done quickly. Creating, growing, nurturing, and sustaining a Kaizen program is neither quick nor easy in a department or a healthcare system. Leaders need to help initiate and support Kaizen, while working tirelessly to create the conditions that encourage people to openly identify problems and work together with their colleagues on improvement. Kaizen requires leaders at all levels to actively make time to inspire, coach, mentor, and recognize people.

It's not what you do once in a while, It's what you do day in and day out that makes the difference.

—Jenny Craig

It will take time to create a Kaizen culture. Through this process, leaders and front-line staff will challenge themselves to grow, personally and professionally. It is inevitable that there will be missteps and lessons learned along the way. It is important not to let small setbacks discourage your continued learning and progress, individually or as an organization.

Your Next Steps

In this book, we have shared core Kaizen mindsets, as well as different methods and approaches for managing local improvements and broader programs. While we have shared some recommendations and lessons, we believe strongly there is no single right way to do Kaizen. We hope you will feel free to adapt and improve upon what we have presented in the spirit of PDSA. Some of the principles are nonnegotiable if you want to call your approach "Kaizen," but there is room for variation and creativity in some of the specific techniques and methods.

Now that you have read the book, it is time to take action (if you have not already done so). Regardless of your role or level, one of the first things you can do is to find a problem or opportunity within the scope of your own work.

Develop an idea, and talk with your coworkers and your supervisor. Ask for their input, and work to find a something to implement, measure or gauge the impact, and consider whether the change is really an improvement. Remember to follow the scientific method and the PDSA process. Document your improvement, and share it with others. You may set off a wave of Kaizen throughout your organization, leading to broader program and a thriving Kaizen culture.

Building a Kaizen Community

We wrote about sharing within your organization—your department, your clinic, your hospital, or your health system. We hope that you will consider being a part of a broader Kaizen community. Does your state, province, or country have venues for sharing and collaboration? If not, can you help create them?

Please participate in the Kaizen community we are building at our website, www.HCkaizen.com. We hope you will share your methods, your lessons learned, and even your Kaizens. Would our broader healthcare system improve more quickly if we did more to share Kaizens across organizational boundaries? Asking that question is part of our own personal PDSA cycle, as authors. We hope that you will join us.

Best wishes to you and your organization in using Kaizen to further your important mission.

Endnotes

1. Liker, Jeffrey, K., and David P. Meier, *Toyota Talent* (New York: McGraw-Hill, 2007), 3.

Index